Gary Cooper

Jeffrey Meyers is a well-known biographer whose subjects include Humphrey Bogart, Robert Frost, F. Scott Fitzgerald, Joseph Conrad and D.H. Lawrence. Meyers has taught literature at many universities and was for two years a visiting scholar at the University of California, Berkeley. He lives in Berkeley.

Other biographies by Jeffrey Meyers

A Fever at the Core: The Idealist in Politics
Married to Genius
Katherine Mansfield
The Enemy: A Biography of Wyndham Lewis
Hemingway
Manic Power: Robert Lowell and His Circle
D.H. Lawrence
Joseph Conrad
Edgar Allan Poe: His Life and Legacy
Scott Fitzgerald
Edmund Wilson
Robert Frost
Bogart: A Life in Hollywood

Gary Cooper

AMERICAN HERO

Jeffrey Meyers

ROBERT HALE · LONDON

ISBN 0 7090 6823 9 (hardback)
ISBN 0 7090 7332 1 (paperback)

Robert Hale Limited
Clerkenwell House
Clerkenwell Green
London EC1R 0HT

Typeset by
Derek Doyle & Associates, Liverpool.
Printed by St Edmundsbury Press Limited, and
bound by Woolnough Bookbinding Limited

Contents

Illustrations

19. Filming *The Plainsman*, with Jean Arthur, 1936 (Estate of Gary Cooper)
20. Cooper, with Harry Carey, Frances Dee, George Raft and Olympe Bradna, 1937 (Frances Dee McCrea)
21. Cooper, with Edward Arnold, in *Meet John Doe*, 1941
22. Ernest Hemingway, with Cooper, Sun Valley, 1939 (Photo by Lloyd Arnold)
23. Ingrid Bergman, 1940 (Kobal Collection)
24. Cooper on USO tour in New Guinea, 1943 (Montana Historical Society)
25. Patricia Neal, with Cooper, 1948 (Patricia Neal)
26. Cooper in *High Noon*, 1952 (Estate of Gary Cooper)
27. Roberta Haynes, with Cooper and Barry Jones, making *Return to Paradise* in Samoa, 1952 (Roberta Haynes)
28. Lorraine Chanel, with Cooper, on the set of *Vera Cruz*, 1954 (Lorraine Chanel)
29. Cooper, in front of a stone bridge, Acapulco, early 1950s (Lorraine Chanel)
30. Cooper, sitting on a rock, Acapulco, early 1950s (Lorraine Chanel)
31. Cooper, with Richard Widmark and Susan Hayward, 1954 (Richard Widmark)
32. Rocky and Maria, c. 1950 (Photo by Jean Howard, Estate of Gary Cooper)

Acknowledgements

I am pleased to acknowledge the generous help I received while writing this book. Gary Cooper's only child, Maria Janis, became an enthusiastic participant in my research. She helped me in many ways, investigating Cooper's years at Grinnell, showing me her files and scrapbooks, sending videotapes and photographs, introducing me to his family and friends, answering fully and frankly many hours of questions during our meetings in New York and weekend retreat to a convent in Connecticut. Though she will not agree with everything in this work, I hope it proves worthy of her trust.

Many friends provided books and videotapes, photocopies and clippings, addresses and phone numbers, references and leads, encouragement and advice: Alfredo Bonadeo, Jackson Bryer, Marguerite Frank, Valerie Hemingway, Richard Hertz, Evelyn Keyes, Phillip Knightley (who drove me to Dunstable), Camille Laurent, Peter Lieberson, Ellen Nims and Helen Scholz.

For personal interviews I would like to thank: Slim Aarons, Paul Adams, Michael Anderson, Harry Balfe, Colin Bourne, John Buckledee, Georgia Cooper Burton, Lorraine Chanel (for conversations, letters and photos), Barnaby Conrad, Veronica Cooper Converse, Howard Cooper, Jeff Corey, Warren Cowan, Arlene Dahl, Thelma Dahl, Frances Dee, André De Toth, Amanda Dunne, Richard and Margaret Durrance, Richard Eyer, Douglas Fairbanks, Jr., Alice Fleming, Father Harold Ford, Stephan and Lillian Groueff, Mother Dolores Hart, Roberta Haynes, Patrick Hemingway, Joe Hyams, Donald Hyatt, Deane Johnson, Dorris Johnson, Evie Johnson, Dr. Rexford Kennamer, Ring Lardner, Jr., Joan Leslie, Mae Walton Lessley, C. Locke, Jody McCrea, Walter Mirisch, Ivan Moffat, Richard Moore, Patricia Neal (for an especially long and rewarding talk), Marvin Page, Suzy Parker, Annabella Power, Bud and Ruth Purdy, Luise Rainer, Meir Ribelow, Jeffrey Robinson (of London), Dr. Rex Ross, Moe Rothman, Richard Seeland, Walter Seltzer, Virgil and Betty Sherrill, John Springer, Robert Stack, Joseph Stefano, Warren Stevens, Ray Stricklyn, Shirley Temple, Connie Wald, Watson Webb, Richard Widmark, Billy Wilder, Mignon Winans, Sidney Wood, Fay Wray, Teresa Wright, Jane Wyatt, Mary Taylor Zimbalist and Fred Zinnemann.

For letters and phone calls about Cooper I am grateful to Steven Bach, Fred Crawford, Ronald Davis, Dominick Dunne, Wayne Grover, Charlton Heston, Delbert Mann, Nell McDonald, Virginia McKenna, Dan Moss, Rod Steiger, Peter Viertel, Malvin Wald and Robert Wise; and to various institutions: the alumni records office of Dunstable School, Bozeman Senior High School, Montana State University, Grinnell College, Archdiocese of Los Angeles, *Christian Science Monitor* (Virginia Hooke), *Classic Images*, Directors Guild, Friars Club, Gallatin County Historical Society, Screen Actors Guild and Spotlight Casting and Directory (London).

The main sources of unpublished material, clippings, scrapbooks, oral histories, photographs and rare films on Cooper are at the Doheny Library, at the University of Southern California, which has the Warner Bros. Archive: research and legal files, contracts, memos, correspondence, scripts, daily production logs and publicity material (with the extraordinarily helpful curator, Ned Comstock); and the Margaret Herrick Library of the Academy of Motion Picture Arts and Sciences, which has the Paramount Archive as well as the Gladys Hall, Hedda Hopper, Fred Zinnemann and Motion Picture Association of America papers (curator: Scott Curtis).

I also did research at the American Film Institute, British Film Institute, Berkeley Public Library, University of California, Berkeley, Boalt Law Library, Berkeley, Montana Historical Society (curator: Brian Shovers), Museum of Modern Art (curator: Charles Silvers), New York Public Library of the Performing Arts, Pacific Film Archive, Stanford University and University of California, Los Angeles. I received additional information from the University of Arkansas (USIA papers), Boston University, Columbia University (Oral History Research Office), George Meany Library (AFL papers), Hemingway Collection, John F. Kennedy Library, Library of Congress, National Archives (USO tour), Southern Methodist University, State Historical Society of Wisconsin, Wesleyan

University, Whittier College (Jessamyn West papers) and University of Wyoming.

As always, my wife, Valerie Meyers, helped with the research, read each chapter, improved the book and compiled the index.

Preface

The film critic André Bazin, distinguishing between the classically heroic persona of Cooper and the more modern, ambiguous and morally contradictory persona of Bogart, wrote: "Bogart differs from those prewar heroes for whom Gary Cooper might be the prototype: handsome, strong, noble, expressing much more the optimism and efficiency of a civilization than its anxiety." Gentle and appealing, the son of a Judge, Cooper had been a Montana ranchhand and was linked through upbringing, experience and film work with the history of the "real west." After dropping out of college and with no training as an actor, he started as a stuntman in silent films and, almost accidentally, became a successful leading man.

Cooper excelled in romantic comedies, where his youthful charm and hesitant manner contrasted with the intriguing sexuality of Marlene Dietrich and Claudette Colbert. But he became an American icon in cowboy roles, and took care to make a Western every few years to reinforce his aura of integrity and heroism. Beautiful as well as handsome, as glamorous as any fashion model and one of the most photogenic subjects in Hollywood, he was never narcissistic. In real life he was a quiet loner who had, apart from Ernest Hemingway, few intimate friends.

Cooper had an authentic and utterly convincing style of acting, and appealed powerfully to both men and women. While stars like Bogart and Cagney radiated edgy abrasiveness, he represented a different kind of charismatic yet restrained masculinity, a powerful sweetness, an almost feminine sensitivity. Bogart was an interior actor, viewed through a haze of cigarette smoke, surrounded by a circle of drinkers; the diffident Cooper seemed to bring an outdoor freshness to the screen.

Frank Capra's *Mr. Deeds Goes to Town* and *Meet John Doe* capitalized on Cooper's portrayals of awkward, honest men, and gave the country the forceful image of an ideal hero. Cooper's acting was so natural and effective that he seemed as simple as the Everyman who defeated the forces of evil. But his inner life was torn by moral conflict. A well-known ladies' man, he married the young, beautiful, well-connected Veronica Balfe. Her strong, shrewd character helped direct his career, their alliance gave him access to New York and European society, and they were a famous couple at home and abroad. Though Cooper was careful not to disrupt his domestic life or hurt his public image, he eventually resumed his affairs with co-stars and other women.

In the late 1940s the middle-aged Cooper fell in love with the young Patricia Neal, who precipitated a personal crisis. After this experience his film roles tended to reflect a more complex personality. In pictures like *High Noon* and *The Naked Edge* he played weary, tense characters, tainted romantics struggling with agonizing decisions. His own life reflected the growth of the nation as he developed from innocent provincial to cosmopolitan sophisticate. Critics complained that in *Love in the Afternoon* he was out of character as the older man who gradually falls in love with the charming young Audrey Hepburn. But he really was, with his many mistresses, a worldly and slightly dissipated roué.

Just as Cooper managed to weather his personal crises, so he survived the political convulsion of the House Un-American Activities Committee. A well-known conservative, he was persuaded to be a "friendly" witness. But he did not name names, and later supported Carl Foreman, the blacklisted screenwriter of *High Noon*. In a business where talent bloomed early and soon withered in the glare of envious publicity, Cooper's acting became increasingly skilled and impressive, and his career flourished as he grew older. To the public he was an inspiring figure whose performances touched their deepest emotions. In Hollywood he remained universally liked, admired and trusted. He was an elegant philanderer, and his life recalls a happier, more spirited time than our own.

The influential historian Frederick Jackson Turner believed that the frontier—so often portrayed in Cooper's Westerns—had shaped American identity. While the east imitated the Old World, the west converted Europeans into Americans by founding new traditions, fostering patriotism and encouraging a connection to primitive modes of existence:

The frontier is the line of most rapid and effective Americanization. The wilderness masters the colonist. It finds him a European in dress, industries, tools, modes of travel, and thought. . . . It strips off the garments of civilization. . . . It puts him in the log cabin . . . and runs an Indian palisade around him. . . . Little by little he transforms the wilderness, but the outcome is not the old Europe. . . . Here is a new product that is American. . . . The advance of the frontier has meant a steady movement away from the influence of Europe, a steady growth of independence on American lines.

Cooper's extraordinary mixture of English parentage and schooling with western birth and background combined two major elements in our culture. Shaped by his experience in Montana, playing men of both action and principle, he helped create a powerful version of the history of the west. In movies—which came into being just as the life portrayed in Westerns was coming to an end—he also became the icon of our longing for lost purity and innocence. His visual and spiritual force defined the classic American hero.

Actors like Gary Cooper are in themselves, as material objects, "realistic," seeming to bear in their bodies and their faces mortality, limitation, the knowledge of good and evil.

Robert Warshow, *The Immediate Experience*

Gary Cooper

1

Montana

1901–1909

I

Gary Cooper, the quintessentially American film hero, was a distinctive blend of English gentleman and Montana pioneer. Wholly English by origin, he had the tall, fair, blue-eyed look of a country squire. His strict Victorian parents influenced his manners and beliefs, and their strength of character had a powerful impact on their son. The Coopers had been farmers in England for centuries. John Cooper, Gary's grandfather, came from Tingrith, near Dunstable, in Bedfordshire. He owned several farms, raised stock, had a milling firm in town and a dairy business, thirty-five miles southeast, in London. Charles Henry Cooper, Gary's father, was one of nine children. He was born on September 15, 1865 at the White House, the family home for four generations, in Houghton Regis, outside Dunstable.

After finishing secondary school, the eighteen-year-old Charles couldn't count on much of an inheritance and had to emigrate to make his fortune. In 1883 he sailed from Liverpool to Boston in the wake of his brother Arthur, a locomotive driver in America. After working for two years in Wisconsin, the adventurous Charles arrived in Helena, in the Montana Territory. When Charles reached Montana, Gary later wrote— in a sentence that suggested his own lifelong interest in animals, Indians and solitude— "buffalo were still running, Indians roamed the plains, [and] the distances between ranches averaged a hundred miles."

As recently as 1876 General George Custer had been killed by the Sioux Indians in the massacre at the Little Bighorn. Arthur and Charles both got jobs with the Northern Pacific Railroad, which ran through

Indian territory and linked the upper midwest to the Pacific coast. It reached Helena in 1883, and the last stagecoach left town that year. Started by James J. Hill, the Northern Pacific was eventually taken over by J. P. Morgan. In nearby Butte the Rockefellers took control of Anaconda Copper. By 1885, said Gary, who was knowledgeable about western history, "cattle were crowding the last of the buffalo off the prairie. The United States Cavalry was keeping the Indians from going on the warpath. Large-scale silver mining was replacing the every-man-for-himself gold boom, and range wars [between cattlemen and homesteaders] were killing nearly as many men as saloon brawls."

In Montana, a major mining state, lucrative deposits of gold, then silver and finally copper had been discovered. Charles and Arthur may have been drawn to the rich territory by reading about the skilled Cornish miners, who played an important role in the silver boom, and the British corporations that invested in Montana mines. In 1899 Montana produced 61 percent of American and 25 percent of world copper; ten years later the mines turned out $46 million of raw wealth, unevenly distributed among the inhabitants of the mining towns.

The small towns were surrounded by high forests and mountains, separated by great distances and vast emptiness. The state population climbed from 38,000 in 1880 to 132,000 a decade later to 243,000 at the turn of the century (1.7 persons per square mile), but was still only 376,000 in 1910. Yet Montana was surprisingly cosmopolitan. In 1910 a quarter of the population was foreign-born and spoke more than twenty languages.

In 1885 Charles settled in Helena, which became the state capital in 1894. Important surface deposits had been discovered in Last Chance Gulch in 1864, and Helena, "well-situated on major transportation routes, well-supplied with foodstuffs from the nearby Prickly Pear Valley, and located close to other mining towns," grew from a rough camp into a prosperous trading center. Though the surface gold was soon exhausted, it was replaced by silver, lead, zinc and quartz lodes, and by ranching and farming. Stone buildings, including a bank and United States Land Office, were built in 1867. By 1870, despite its remote location on the mining frontier, Main Street "was lined with impressive commercial buildings, illuminated by electric lights, and traversed by electric streetcars."[1] Helena, as if to remind its respectable citizens of its rough past, had a lively red-light district (women also worked as rooming house managers, laundresses and servants) as well as a Hanging Tree. As late as 1895 the town issued printed invitations—with photos of those about to be killed—to witness the public execution. This was the gritty world that was later glamorized in so many Western movies.

The copper dome on top of the capitol in Helena symbolized the decade when copper was king. During the 1890s' boom Helena had fifty millionaires—more per capita than any other city in America. This sudden access of wealth led to an orgy of ostentation among the town's parvenus:

> They lived in pretentious mansions . . . and rode about town, first in coaches driven by top-hatted and swallow-tailed coachmen, and later in electric coupes that moved at a dog-trot on the level and stalled on the hills. A small army of maids, butlers, and other servants waited on them, and served them foods and wines as different as possible from the sour-dough, beans, and raw firewater of their prospecting days. The houses they built were ornate affairs in a variety of designs, with exteriors featuring turrets, cupolas, and porte-cochères; interiors decorated with hand-carved mahogany, oak, and maple, with a fireplace in nearly every room; spacious grounds within stone walls or iron fences, with iron deer on the lawns and stone lions or other figures at the entrances. Some lawns were further adorned with fountains, lead statuary, granite mounting blocks, and carved stone hitching posts.

When the price of silver fell in 1893, this florid period suddenly came to an end.

II

In 1889 the territory became a state and the "local citizens could elect their own executive and judicial officers, thus ending the long procession of federally appointed 'carpetbaggers' whom Washington had sent to govern them." In this promising context Charles Cooper began his legal and political career. After studying stenography and law at a local business college, the industrious young man worked as a court stenographer and apprentice in the law office of John Shelton, and was admitted to the Montana bar in 1892. For many years he served as district court reporter.

Charles also attached himself to a couple of powerful political buccaneers. In 1895, thirty years old and recently married, he left John Shelton and became assistant to Preston Leslie. Twice elected governor of Kentucky, Leslie had been appointed territorial governor and then U.S. district attorney. "He could make his maximum of fees by constant travel on trains," Charles later told Hedda Hopper, "and so I had all the work to do in the office."[2] The following year Charles joined the law firm of Colonel Wilbur Fisk Sanders, who had commanded a company of infantry in the Civil War and whose clients included the Northern Pacific Railroad. Prosecutor, vigilante leader (who made good use of the Hanging Tree) and head of the anti-South, pro-Negro Radical Republicans, Sanders—known for his caustic wit—served in the Montana legislature and became a U.S. senator in 1890. While working for Sanders, Charles—who always sympathized with the underdog—defended several Chinese immigrants who were threatened with expulsion from America.

Gary described his father's early career as "studying law, a little court reporting, the preparation of legal briefs for lawyers, some clerical work for the Supreme Court, a little campaigning for the Republican Party, and an unofficial law practice of his own." But Charles became a respected trial lawyer, and in 1904 campaigned with Theodore Roosevelt, "introducing him to leaders and bosses in the various precincts of his itinerary." Charles remained active in politics, voted—like Robert Jordan's father in For Whom the Bell Tolls—"the Republican ticket all his life" and was rewarded in 1908 when Roosevelt appointed him U.S. attorney for Montana.[3] A writer and an intellectual who later corresponded with Carl Sandburg about Lincoln, the impractical, unmechanical Charles never learned to drive a car. He was a 32nd degree Mason, and at the family dinner table would recite poems by Robert Burns and speeches by Shakespeare. Charles taught his sons and grandson to quote poetry and use an adult vocabulary. Classmates considered Charles' grandson, Howard Cooper, who learned his lesson all too well, a strange little boy.

Charles met Alice Louise Brazier, who had also come from England to Montana to visit her brother, in 1893. In the panic that followed the collapse of the silver market, nearly every bank in Montana had crashed. Alice consulted Charles about how to retrieve the money she had saved to pay her passage home. Her Huguenot family had emigrated to England in the seventeenth century, and her father was a shipwright on the Isle of Sheppey in Kent. Born in Sheerness in 1873, she grew up in Gillingham, on the Kentish coast, and came to Montana as a teenager in 1891.

Alice retained a hint of her native accent, and had an impressive vocabulary and refined speech. A formidable woman, she believed there was only one way to do things—her way. Not unkind, but more austere than affectionate, she was the dominant one in the family—a "stand up, chin in the air, straight back sort of person." In later years she looked and tried to act like Queen Mary, the consort of George V. But she was not a grande dame and once, when she'd had too much port, revealed that her early life in a working-class household had been hard. Charles and Alice, who shared the same background, adventurous spirit and love of the outdoors, married in 1894. Their grandchildren described them as very English, Victorian and proper. Compared to the rough types who dominated Montana, they were sophisticated and socially refined. They gave their children a principled, loving and literate upbringing. The actress Colleen Moore, who met them in Hollywood in 1928, said: "Naturally, I expected the typical midwestern type who owned a ranch and all. On the contrary. They were very, very British."[4]

III

The Coopers gave their children solid English names. Gary's brother, Arthur Leroy (named for his uncle), was born in 1895. On May 7, 1901, Gary—christened Frank James Cooper—appeared. In 1901 Queen Victoria died and Edward VII became king, William McKinley was assassinated and was succeeded by Teddy Roosevelt. As the mechanical age reached the western frontier, the first motorbike was manufactured, and the first message sent by telegraph. Marlene Dietrich, Clark Gable and Walt Disney were also born that year.

At the turn of the century Helena, still on the frontier, had a population of 10,770 as well as wolves and coyotes, rattlesnakes and grizzly bears which often came right into town. Cowboys and Indians walked the streets, and Gary both heard about and actually saw wolf hunters and desperadoes, cattle rustlers and horse thieves, whorehouses and bar-room shootouts—the very stuff of Western movies. The recent history of the west—the mining booms and busts, range wars and extinction of the buffalo, vigilante committees and battles with the Indians (which did not end until the early 1880s)—was a living memory to the older generation. Later on, speaking from personal experience, he said of the real west: "it actually started from the gold rush in 1849 [and lasted] until about 1880 when the railroads were spanning the continent and transportation became more rapid than the covered waggon and the pony express, and that was the end of the west really, although the cattlemen and the big ranchers and the miners and all the colourful characters of the west continued on in rather the old style, until about the turn of the century. . . . [Montana] was a state in which the last of the wild buffalo were found. I knew as a boy some of the real old characters."

Gary was born during an electrical storm, on the second floor of a modest two-story, red-brick house, surrounded by high cottonwood trees, at 730 Eleventh Avenue.[5] Alice, always punctilious about words, recorded his first expressions in her baby book. At three months he had his first scolding and cried for two hours but didn't "remember feeling particularly crushed about it." He spoke his first recorded sentence, "I gonna have my picture taken with a flower I pooked," while posing for his mother's photographs. He appears in one of them, at the age of three, wearing an elaborately beribboned white bonnet and long furry coat.

Gary went to Central grade school and Johnson grammar school, where the girls considered him a prize catch. The boys thought he was a regular guy. Dressed like Huckleberry Finn, he wore a denim shirt, overalls and high shoes. In those days, after the spring flood in Last Chance Gulch, he could still find enough gold flakes to buy a week's supply of licorice and candy. He played cowboys and Indians; hunted for arrowheads, wolf dens and jackrabbits; and filled his room with Indian artifacts and animal trophies. "My mother knew a woman who wanted two birds for her hat," Cooper wrote, remembering his first job. "So I went out and shot them and stuffed them. . . . I really did it, the first time I tried. I got a dollar for the work."[6]

Like most small towns, Helena offered its reputable citizens some wholesome family entertainment: "Fourth of July picnics, where someone always recited the Declaration of Independence; church services on the second floor of the school building . . .; exclusive dancing parties, with armed chaperones at the door to remove roughnecks with guns under their belt or liquor on their breath. Even in a three-saloon mining town, amenities could be observed." The actress Myrna Loy, four years younger than Gary, later recalled her childhood near the Coopers in Helena: "We lived high off the hog on Fifth Avenue. . . . It was just a nice middle-class neighborhood. Most of the richer families were building on the opposite mountainside. Helena is a spacious city, climbing up Mount Ascension and Mount Helena from Last Chance Gulch, so we had wonderful, steep streets. When it snowed you could slide past Judge Cooper's house all the way to the railroad station in the valley part of town. The Coopers lived just below us in a fairly elegant house with an iron fence around it."

Gary's most striking childhood memories focused on the exotic, the urban and the perverse, and marked his transition from innocence to experience. The Northern Pacific Railroad had brought in a gang of Turks, as strange as the natives in films like *Morocco*, to repair a section of track. Curious and eager to learn about their life, Gary said he was drawn to "these colorful people [who] wore fantastic costumes with red fezzes and carved daggers or knives. None of them spoke English, but in spite of that, when they sat around on their haunches telling stories after sunset, I sat by and watched." As a teenager Gary, who would spend most of his adult life in Los Angeles, helped a rancher take a "carload of cattle to St. Paul. Bunking in the cattle car and awaking in the morning to the excitement of a large city—this was adventure. I came home feeling that at last I had become a man." Many years later, while watching handsome young Mexican boys dive from a cliff in Acapulco, he turned away, looked up at the sky and suddenly said: "When I was a little boy in Helena and walking across a bridge, a bearded man came up to me and kissed me on the mouth."[7] Later in life the handsome Cooper would attract a few men as well as many women.

Most of Gary's childhood adventures occurred on the ranch, the 7 Bar 9, which Charles bought—when Gary was five and Arthur eleven—in 1906. Charles' father, who owned four acres in Bedfordshire, liked to call himself "the squire." Charles, who also wanted to be an English squire and have the peasants bow down to him, realized his ambitions in Montana. Beginning in 1900 the Northern Pacific sold most of its land grants for up to $8.50 an acre. Charles rented two thousand acres from the government and bought six hundred from the railroad. On moving day Charles and Arthur rode to the ranch with the family goods in a wagon, through steep canyons and along the curving banks of the Missouri River, to one of the most spectacular landscapes in the American west.[8] Alice and Gary traveled by train, which went from Helena to Great Falls and stopped especially to let them off.

A local newspaper said the ranch—thirty-five hundred feet high and fifty miles north of Helena, near Craig—"is in the heart of the Rocky Mountains, in the Missouri river canyon, north side of the river, and consists of [six hundred] acres, mostly scenery in the shape of granite mountains, great cliffs, pine trees, open places here and there, and a cluster of [buildings] scattered about a small mountain stream." Gary recalled that when they first arrived, Alice was received by the ranch-hands "as a queen, and I was probably treated like a little prince. We were taken inside a mostly empty house, and had to wait several hours for my father to arrive with the furniture, bedding, and just about everything we had. That would have been in the summertime when the days were long, but it was after dark when the wagon and horses finally pulled in. By then I'd probably decided that I liked living out in the country." The property, on a bend in the river, had a ranch house, a cottage for the foreman, barns, corrals, haying equipment and four hundred head of cattle, with two hundred more running wild around the timberline.

Alice later said that Arthur and Gary were not hard to raise. Though Charles was sometimes cross and short-tempered, his sons adored him. Gary was very blond till the age of nine and spent every summer on the ranch. He learned to ride there, and for him "one of the most beautiful sights in the world is a running horse, with a man that sits on it real pretty."[9] He played with the five other children, white and Flathead Indian, who had their own one-room schoolhouse. He sketched the eagles and deer, the cowboys and Indians, who taught him how to track animals and understand nature. Like most Montanans, Arthur looked down on the Indians, but Gary respected their culture, and learned how to make moccasins, shawls, beaded vests and elaborate war bonnets. (As an adult he also meditated with an Indian shaman, took part in fasting and purification during a "sweat lodge" ceremony and was made an honorary chief of the Blackfoot tribe.) Indians brought out the more spiritual side of his nature, which, even within his own family, was rarely revealed.

But the ranch was not entirely idyllic. Speaking of her early years of marriage, Alice remarked that "we had nothing for a long, long time." No delicate lily, she used to pitch hay, shear sheep and brand cattle. Gary once saw her, during the war years, "swinging an ax at twenty below zero to break open bales of frozen hay." The bursting of the Hauser Dam, when he was almost seven years old, was the most traumatic moment of his childhood. "On April 14, 1908, water began seeping between the plates and the bedrock, and in less than ten minutes, water had destroyed five company houses, an office building, and a stable. Thirty men employed at the dam escaped with their lives, but frantic calls were made to residents of Craig to evacuate." In Cooper's recollection of this dangerous episode he was an infant, and his dramatic rescue resembles an adventurous scene from one of his films: "I was little more than a baby, and I remember that my father and mother and I were almost drowned in the flood that followed. We were sleeping in a tent when it happened. I do not know what would have happened if the dogs hadn't begun to bark. They made an awful racket and we woke up. The water had overflowed the banks of the Missouri River and was washing up on the tent flaps. My mother leaped up, lifted me to a horse—and the three of us galloped away to safety."[10]

2

Dunstable and Grinnell

1910–1924

I

The ranch was paradise for the Cooper boys, but their genteel mother never really liked Montana. Alice heard them swearing, was shocked by their coarse manners and thought they were turning into little savages— one step removed from the Indians. She wanted to polish their rough edges and broaden their culture, to make her sons like "those dear little lads in England, all so neat and polite." In the summer of 1909, when Gary was eight and had just finished the second grade, she took them "home" to visit her mother in Kent and enroll them in Dunstable School. Britannia, filled with righteousness and glory at the height of its imperial power, ruled the world as well as the waves. Gary saw English ceremonial pomp in the funeral procession of Edward VII in the spring of 1910 and the coronation of George V in the summer of 1911.

After Charles and Alice returned to America, the boys lived with their father's cousins, William and Emily Barton, in the ancestral farmhouse adjacent to the village green and to the vast estate of the Duke of Bedford. Though the cousins were kind, they were complete strangers and the young Gary desperately missed his parents. A notice advertising the sale of the rambling country place in 1928 described it as "The White House, Houghton Regis, Beds., comprising a delightful, old-fashioned, detached residence, with pretty lawn, kitchen garden, greenhouse, stabling, barns, outbuildings, excellent enclosure of rich old meadow land, in all extending to 4 acres." After Arthur entered the school as a day boy on September 23, 1909 and Gary—giving his father's occupation as

"Farmer (owns land)"—on January 22, 1910, they lived across from the school, with another Barton cousin, at 157 High Street North (now a grocery store).

Dunstable School was housed in a large red-brick Victorian building with high turrets and a mock-Tudor façade, an asphalt playground and a primitive outdoor lavatory. It was founded with the charitable bequests of an eighteenth-century benefactor, who left £14,500 for a grammar school to educate, at moderate expense, the sons of middle-class professional men and tradesmen. But the cornerstone was not laid until June 1887—four years after Charles had left for America.

L.C.R. Thring, an alumnus and headmaster during Gary's time, rigorously enforced "the real Public School system of strict discipline, hard work, compulsory games [especially soccer and cricket], and the punishment to fit the crime." With the help of plentiful whacking, the school turned out conventional gentlemen, "young men of character and general all round ability . . . directly in the tradition of Dr. Arnold," the founder of Rugby School. There was a Drama Society, ice skating and snowball fights during the winter frost and public readings from the headmaster's favorite books: Tennyson's *Idylls of the King* and Dickens' *Pickwick Papers*. Under the house system, with master, prefects and fags (junior boys who had to serve the older ones), a prefect "would stand bawling for a fag, then all the little boys would go scuttling down passages and stairs to answer the call, and the last one to arrive would be given some task to do." The 140 boys, many of them foreign or with parents overseas in the service of the Crown, wore the school uniform: an Eton-style wide stiff collar, short black coat and short trousers, long socks and either the school cap or the locally manufactured straw boater. Patriotism was deeply embedded in the spirit of the school, and 62 old boys would sacrifice their lives in the Great War.

Dunstable was like a college prep school—much more rigorous and advanced than an American grade school. "The great event of the academic year," wrote the school historian, "was the periodical examination by the London School of Examiners, in the course of which every boy in the school submitted written papers and was afterwards orally examined in every subject." Forty-five years later Cooper recalled his interview at the beginning of term with the formidable headmaster. Dressed in black gown and mortarboard, he intimidated the cocky American by asking him about subjects—Latin and algebra—that he couldn't possibly have studied when he was only eight years old:

My first day there was miserable.

"No Latin, Mr. Cooper?" asked the headmaster.

I'd never heard of it.

"No French, Mr. Cooper?"

I'd heard of French, but that wasn't enough.

"No English history, algebra, Shakespeare?"

I "didn't know nothing."

Looking back now I can appreciate all that was done for me—special classes, sympathetic tutors and an earnest effort to make me feel at home.[1]

He was also ticked off by the headmaster for engaging in fisticuffs with a local newsboy, who belonged to the despicable lower classes.

His English classmates, who hated anything that deviated from the norm and tended to bully new boys, were first curious, then hostile. Firmly convinced that white men were still engaged in bloody battles with the redskins, "they asked me [Cooper wrote], in hushed voices, if I had ever shot an Indian, what a cowboy was like, and did I have a gun?" Unable to resist some boastful embellishments, he "enjoyed telling them quite a number of surprising if not exactly accurate things." But they also put him in his place by mimicking his accent, poking fun at his clothes and making his life miserable for a long time. When Cooper revisited the school with his wife and daughter in the 1950s, he pointed out the place where he'd had a memorable fight with another boy.

Eventually Gary became accustomed to English ways and began to enjoy going to school, playing with hoops and tops, taking bike rides to see his paternal grandfather and car trips to visit his mother's relatives during the holidays. Letters from home were especially welcome. On May 13, 1909, soon after he arrived in England, his father sent him a charming letter from Montana, addressed "My Dear Frank," about the things that would interest a little boy:

I was very glad indeed to get your nice card. I suppose the next time you write you will tell me all about the bicycle you are going to have. Have you been down to see Grandfather yet? And did you tell him all about the ranch? Miss Lakin says to tell you she was very happy, to receive your card; that she hopes you are having a good time, and she says she will write you a letter. Be sure when you write again to tell me all the news. I think I told you that the Kitty had a nice black kitten, and is getting along nicely. She sits on Mrs. Argerbright's lap at meal times just as she used to sit on your mama's lap. We have quite a lot of little pigs, and they are looking fine. The grass is getting a little green, but it will be much better later on. Write soon.

Your loving papa.

At Dunstable—as in high school and college later on—Gary did not distinguish himself in scholarship, sports or dramatics, though school plays were regularly performed. Arthur, much older and more interested in athletics, made more of an impact. But he also had to be put down. The school newspaper superciliously exclaimed that the misguided Arthur "should not constitute himself a conductor of touring parties to Cathedral Cities until he is thoroughly acquainted with the route." Gary's one moment of success came in the spring of 1912, when the school magazine reported that he ran 220 yards in 34 seconds and took second place in the race for under eleven-year-olds. Unlike A.E. Housman's young athlete—chaired through the marketplace, "the time you won your town the race"—Gary had to be content with his brother's reflected glory. His childhood playmate and cousin Dorothy Barton remembered him as "a happy-go-lucky kid and I'm sure he thoroughly enjoyed himself at our house in the High Street. They say he was sickly. He was not terribly robust, but he had only the usual childish ailments and his main trouble was biliousness. Still, that didn't rob him of his appetite," which became formidable as he grew older.

During their three years away from home Arthur and Gary, who had quite different personalities and interests, became close for the first and last time. On December 3, 1911 the Cooper boys, now more conscious of status and giving their father's profession as "lawyer," took confirmation classes and were baptized in the Anglican parish church of Houghton Regis.[2] Their English education had fulfilled Alice's expectations and transformed her sons into well-behaved little English gentlemen. One school friend recalled that "Gary was a quiet boy, very much so. He was gentle more than anything. I should imagine that neither he nor Arthur would dare say anything out of place, otherwise his mother would tick them off. She kept them in order—no one could fault them."

Alluding to his original interview with the headmaster, Gary summarized his intellectual acquisitions by stating: "after my three years at Dunstable I could speak French, recognize Latin, wear a top hat, bow from the waist, solve an equation, and say 'Thank you, sir' in an English accent." But used to denim clothes and open spaces, he also expressed his dislike of the formal uniforms and constricted landscape: "I didn't like England, particularly, although I did admire the extraordinary heroics of English history. I didn't like the Eton collars and the long trousers and short jacks and high hats we were made to wear on Sundays. I didn't like the close compactness of the tiny gardens, tended for centuries, and the ultra-formal parks. It weighed down on me."

Dunstable School had a profound influence on Gary. Like all English public schools in the tradition of Dr. Arnold, it taught the boys to "play the game" and show school spirit. But such schools could also engender homosexuality, snobbery, racism, sadism and cruel wit. Dunstable had a rigid hierarchy and a subordination of younger boys that encouraged compliance, bullying and flogging. It frowned on the expression of personal feelings and, in its official distrust of solitude, made sure that the boys had no opportunity to do anything in private. Its emphasis on sports and philistine disdain for art and intellect taught, as Harold Nicolson wrote of Wellington School, that "intellectual prowess was in some way effeminate, and that it was only by physical prowess" that one could show manliness.[3] Its conformity and social stratification were, like the class-conscious clothing, antithetical to Gary's individualistic and demo-cratic ideals. But he readily accepted the school's—and his parents'—conservative political beliefs and code of dutiful self-sacrifice as well as its admirable emphasis on discipline, loyalty, patriotism, honor and pluck—qualities he would later embody in adventure films like *Lives of a Bengal Lancer* and *Beau Geste*. He liked the school well enough to return for visits in 1932, in 1936 and again in the 1950s.

II

In April 1913, nine months after the boys had left Dunstable, the school magazine reported that Arthur and Gary had seen Niagara Falls on their journey home and had arrived safely in "Montana, U.S.A." In July Arthur aroused the English boys' envy by telling them that he and a friend had caught a staggering 156 trout in one day. But not everything went well for the boys in Helena. The school officials, unimpressed by the superior standard of English education and strict interrogation of the London Examiners, put Gary back a grade. Just as his American accent and clothes had aroused hostility in England, so his English manners and dress provoked ridicule and outrage in America. Gary, who had to change himself back into a Montanan, later recalled that "I talked like a genuine Britisher, and my clothes were a riot. I must confess, the girls and the teacher rather liked my short trousers, my Eton collar and my straw hat. But the boys went mad. I had to run for my life down the alleys to get away from them. They said I was a 'cissy,' and got socked for saying it."

Gary also had to readjust, after an absence of three years, to living at home with his parents. "Mother became an expert photographer," he wrote. "She had an elaborate darkroom in the cellar. If I am any good at posing for cameramen, it is because I can still hear mother saying, 'For goodness' sake, will you please stop wriggling? This is a time exposure.' " The little pigs that Charles had mentioned in his letter of 1909 had now grown into fat hogs. One reckless night (after running out of money) he lost them all in a poker game. "The next day Gary and his brother Arthur came up the road . . . afoot, driving the herd of pork to pay off the debt. . . . One of those hogs lit into the brush and Coop tackled him like a football player."[4] Gary also got to know Charles' great friend Wellington Rankin, a wealthy, powerful and spellbinding young Republican. In 1946 he wrote Rankin: "I shall never forget the boxing lessons you used to give me in your office at the most unorthodox hours and I also hold you partially responsible for my good fortune in Hollywood because you were the first to put the bee in my head about becoming an actor." Alice later told Rankin: "Gary just worshipped you as a boy, and I know he would as long as he lived."

After his return to Helena Gary, a talented amateur, hoped to become a commercial artist. He admired the western artists Frederic Remington and Charles M. Russell, a friend of Charles Cooper. Russell first came to Helena as a cowboy in 1880 and lived there till the 1890s. A self-taught, rather sentimental painter who portrayed the real west that was heading for extinction, Russell "found himself exactly at the right place and time to explore the full expression of the western cult, the cult of masculinity and the brotherhood of cowboys." Gary admired and often studied Russell's *Lewis and Clark Meeting Indians at Ross' Hole* (1911) in the state capitol building in Helena. The vast colorful mural depicts an 1805 encounter of the explorers, trying to find a path through the mountains, and the Flathead Indians in southwestern Montana. Later on, while criticizing clichés about the Old West, Cooper portrayed the artist as an ideal figure, and stressed the need to "recapture the characterizations of C.M. Russell, Will Rogers, Mark Twain and some old-timers I have personally known, whose grand and kind humor springs mainly from the 'great outdoors'." He passionately loved the spectacular scenery and teeming wildlife of Montana that Russell had captured in his art and described in words: "Shut off from the outside world, it was a hunter's paradise, bounded by walls of mountains and containing miles of grassy open spaces, more green and beautiful than any man-made parks. These parks and the mountains behind them swarmed with deer, elk, mountain sheep, and bear, besides beaver and other small fur-bearing animals. The creeks were alive with trout. Nature had surely done her best, and no king of the old times could have claimed a more beautiful and bountiful domain."[5]

Cooper continued to draw and paint (sometimes on the film set) throughout his life. His high school notebook contains an ink sketch of an eagle on a rock, and his daughter owns two drawings, signed "Frank Cooper," of an Indian head and a mountain lion. One of his political cartoons was published in the Helena *Independent* on November 2, 1924. In later life, when he became a serious collector of modern art, he did paintings of the family house in Southampton, New York, and of his daughter completing her own work of art.

In about 1916 Gary was seriously injured in a car accident. Previous accounts state that his school friend Harvey Markham, who had been crippled by polio and had special controls for his Model T Ford, lost control of the car on a steep hill. But in Cooper's three accounts of the accident, *he* was the driver and crashed into an unknown object:

> I was driving a touring car, whizzing along contentedly, when there was a sudden impact. The car began to roll over and then came to a full stop, upside down. . . . I rolled on the ground while the car stood on its nose, and then the car rolled on me. . . . I got up and walked to the curb, not dizzy, nor weak, my senses sharpened to a superhuman degree. And then my left side failed me. It hung like a heavy dead thing. And everything went blue. I guess that is the way you feel when you faint. I awakened in a hospital. They said I had a broken leg, and other complications too numerous to mention.

The local doctor did not take X-rays, despite Gary's grave injuries, or realize that he had also broken his hip. Instead, he recommended vigorous horseback riding to cure his aches and pains. With several fractures, Gary must have been very tough indeed to follow his instructions.

This misguided therapy caused lifelong problems. Cooper developed a characteristically stiff, off-balance walk. In the saddle, he rode at a slight angle and minimized the bounce with a closer seat.[6]

In 1917, a year after the accident, America entered the Great War. Arthur enlisted, and the rise in farm prices made ranching more profitable. "Over the past eight years," wrote one historian, "ample rainfall and high food prices had nurtured a persistent farm prosperity; and since 1915, lucrative new markets for American foodstuffs had opened in war-torn Europe. . . . Entry into the Great War had an immediate, decisive effect on agriculture, as the demand for food and the prices of commodities soared." To help meet this demand, Gary dropped out of school for two years. While his father continued to practice law in Helena, he and his mother grew alfalfa and raised five hundred head of cattle up at the ranch. He dug irrigation ditches, cut hay, drove a four-horse team and herded the steers. In the summers he rounded up the wild ones and ran them down to the rich pastures in the bottomland. In winters, when it was forty degrees below zero, he'd get up at five o'clock to feed the cattle and shovel frozen manure. The outdoor life suited him so well that he grew an inch a month for thirteen months and reached his full height of six feet, three inches before he was seventeen. His extreme thinness, stilt-like legs and towering height made him awkward and shy.

Charles prospered at first, but did not do too well financially after the war. He poured his cash and heart into the land, Gary said, but had no business sense and "lost his shirt ranching. The old bonanza of soaring land values were over." At the same time, Charles did not have the right temperament to make much money as a lawyer. He "was a little too honest . . . not enough of an extrovert, not the forward-pushing, hard-swinging type of fellow who made a colorful [and successful] lawyer."[7]

III

When the war ended, the radical and progressive Democrats in Montana were soundly defeated in the elections and Charles Cooper's party, the conservative Republicans, took control. He allied himself with Wellington Rankin, who had a law degree from Harvard and had studied at Oxford, owned more than a million acres of land, advocated women's suffrage (granted by the Nineteenth Amendment in 1920) and was elected attorney general of Montana that year. Charles had tried cases in state, federal and appellate courts, and ran unopposed for the state supreme court in the Republican primary. He was elected for a six-year term on November 5, 1918, a week before the war ended, and served as associate justice on the three-man (later five-man) court from January 6, 1919.

During his tenure Justice Cooper wrote 133 decisions (his fellow judges issued only seven dissents), published in seventeen volumes. Gary proudly called them "masterpieces of brevity." The most striking aspect of his opinions was his consistent support of workers' claims against employers, frequently overturning decisions of the lower courts. The plaintiffs in these cases, sometimes foreign and usually without resources, either sought compensation for injuries or were related to men who had been killed while employed by the powerful mining and railroad companies. In *Hassan v. Northern Pacific Railway* (1921) Charles held the company negligent when loose railroad ties fell on an employee. He wrote that the foreman "might have delayed his order until the danger was past or have given the plaintiff timely warning of the fallen tie. . . . It was the foreman's duty to observe immediate conditions and not to regularly send plaintiff into a place of danger." In *Matson v. Hines* (1922), another case against the Northern Pacific, he cited precedents from English law and emphasized his reluctance to overrule the decisions of a jury. He again concluded, after a worker was ordered to help lift a 750-pound railroad rail, that "the employee never assumes risks growing out of the master's negligence."

The violent events that took place on Miners' Union Day, in Butte on June 13, 1914 provided the background for Charles' next case. During the traditional parade union rebels attacked the marchers and roughed up the leaders, sacked the meeting hall and threw office records into the street. The rioting continued and reached a climax during a union meeting on June 23, when a crowd gathered, shots were fired and two men were killed. After another week of anarchy, the governor called in the National Guard, which restored order and defeated organized labor in Butte. In *Butte Miners' Union v. City of Butte* (1920) the miners injured in the parade sued the city for damages. After discussing the origins of the Anglo-Saxon police system and the English principles of community responsibility from the Middle Ages to the present, Charles concluded that Butte was obligated to protect a peaceful assembly and that "the defendant city was liable for injuries to the property of the plaintiff, done or caused by mobs or riots."

The *State v. Newman* was a sensitive rape case in which the sixteen-year-old victim was forced to testify in court. Charles was as interested in protecting the girl as he was in punishing the criminal. With a Shakespearean phrase, he delivered a humane and progressive decision. The victim, "from the moment of her induction into the foul atmosphere of the scene of her undoing to the end of the trial, was 'more sinned against than sinning' . . . Had the prosecuting officer been more intent upon shielding the innocent than he was in punishing the guilty, he would not only have avoided the degradation so fatal to her moral fiber, but healed, to some extent, at least, the wound that is now festering on the body politic."[8]

On August 30, 1924, four months before his term was due to end, Charles resigned from the supreme court. That same day Wellington Rankin resigned as attorney general and, to enhance his prestige and strengthen his chances of election that fall, was appointed to serve out the rest of Charles' unexpired term. Alice had become weary of Montana, the ranch had lost money and Charles, who had made some unfortunate investments, wanted to earn a higher income. In the *Montana Record-Herald* of September 2, 1924 he wrote: "I tendered my resignation as a member of the Montana Supreme Court because of the fact that I was recently appointed executor of the estate of a near relative. The estate consists of property situated in three states widely separated. I resigned because I felt that I could not give the time necessary to properly fulfill my duties as Associate Justice without jeopardizing the interest of the property committed to my care." Twenty-one years later, in a letter to Hedda Hopper, Charles clarified the situation by explaining that "some cousins who owned the townsite of Lincoln, Nebraska, sold out and went out to Wyoming. When they sold out they had gathered an estate of several hundred thousand dollars and moved to California. Wanting my help, I drew their wills and when they died I moved [to Hollywood]." Charles' grandson added that when he left Montana, he was broke and had the big companies "gunning for him." Many people had been killed in Montana for opposing, as he had, the Northern Pacific Railroad and Anaconda Copper.

In his six years on the bench Charles was involved in more than a thousand cases. Alice was sometimes critical of his disastrous business ventures, but she was always very proud of his legal career. The liberal strain in Charles' conservative politics and his consistent defense of the weak had a profound influence not only on his son's political activities but also on the kind of heroes he played in his films. As Gary said of his role in *High Noon*: "I knew it was a natural for me. My dad used to . . . tell me stories about the sheriffs he dealt with in his days on the Montana Supreme Court Bench."[9]

IV

After losing a year on his return from England and two years while working on the ranch, Gary was now three years behind his age group in school. In the spring of 1919, while attending high school in Helena, he took art courses at Montana Wesleyan College, which had been founded by the Methodists in 1890 and had moved from the Prickly Pear Valley to Helena in 1898. In the Spring 1919 issue of the student magazine, the *Prickly Pear*, under the heading "Too late to classify," a photo of Frank Cooper appeared with the caption "An artist of no small ability."

In Helena High School, where he had trouble readjusting to the classroom and little interest in academic subjects, he was older than most students but became notorious for pulling childish pranks and getting into mischief. He greased the car tracks on steep hills so vehicles slid backwards and set off blasts in town with dynamite filched from the mines. He put limburger cheese on the study hall radiators, forcing the students to evacuate the school, and was promptly expelled. Judge Cooper exploded and sent his son out of town. The principal regretfully recalled that Gary "didn't seem to apply himself very hard. He was a bright boy and should have done better. I don't think he really had a purpose till he went over to Bozeman" in 1919 to complete his last three years of high school.

Cooper said that Bozeman, a hundred miles southeast, "was a smaller town than Helena, and more intimate, without the pretense of a capital city. Everyone in town knew everyone else. Maybe every little town in the country became hysterical after the Armistice, and maybe that helped bring on Prohibition. Well, Bozeman was no exception." He shared an apartment with some older boys and spent weekends with horses on a nearby ranch. He majored in English history at Gallatin County High School, and took notes, which still exist, on the Elizabethan stage, Shakespeare's plays and Montana politics. When bored, a classmate remembered, he'd amuse himself by leaning forward and widening the holes in her hairnet with his pencil.

Encouraged by his favorite teacher, Ida Davis, Gary took courses in Debate and Public Speaking, and developed a liking for dramatics. "Being shy," he said, "too tall for my age and self-conscious about it, even then, she made me go in for Declamation as a means of acquiring some poise and bearing." He read Scottish poetry with a convincing accent to the school assembly and in the spring of 1922 recited David Starr Jordan's "College Spirit" in a declamation contest. His team lost the debate on Japanese immigration, but had the decision reversed when the opposing team was caught plagiarizing. He showed no interest in the three movie theaters in town and, though not especially talented, appeared in school plays.[10] The night before graduation, he starred in *The Gibson Upright*, a three-act comedy by Booth Tarkington and Harry Leon Wilson, directed by Miss Davis. He found it difficult to propose to the leading lady, who stood all the way across the stage, and could scarcely bring himself to kiss her when she agreed to marry him.

In the spring of 1920, while still a high school student, Gary also took three art courses—Freehand Drawing, Perspective in Art and Design in Art—at Montana Agricultural College (now Montana State University) in Bozeman. "He received a grade in one, the other two were not completed. The transcript bears a note written in red ink [that suggests a family crisis]: 'Canceled May 31, 1920. Necessary to return home.' " But he finally cobbled together enough credits from art courses at Montana Wesleyan and Montana Agricultural to enable him to graduate, with seventy-five other boys and girls, on May 19, 1922.

He decorated Mae Walton's scrapbook (now in the Pioneer Museum, Bozeman) with sketches of a sailboat on a lake, an angel singing with a harp and a long-mustached cowboy in the style of Charles Russell, and gave as his motto: "Smoking never stunted my growth." He also wrote a modest, good-natured inscription in her high school Graduation Book: "If I were to write of my true self upon this page I'm sure the book would be misused. However I hope you remember me as you know me now and overlook my many blunders, social and otherwise. My last year in Gallatin will sure stay in my memory and mainly because of all those events in which I was lucky enough to participate in your presence."

Cooper had matured since his expulsion from Helena. Ida Davis, who also saw him outside of class and was a kind of substitute parent, called him "one of the finest, most straightforward boys I have ever known. Tractable, too, but not to be led by the nose." Inspired like so many youths by a sympathetic teacher, he became very fond of her and gave her credit for rescuing him from a lifetime of idleness: "Miss Davis saw to it that I learned English and mathematics, put me on the debating team and into dramatics and made me go to college. She was a great and good influence on every boy who ever studied under her. She kept me from being a bum!"[11]

V

Most of the high school graduates who continued their education attended the local state college. But Gary, guided by a Montana friend, Mark Entorf, a war veteran and Junior at Grinnell, went to that far-away college to study art. Josiah Grinnell thought he had discovered the west in Iowa when he founded the town and brought in the coed college, originally endowed by the protemperance and antislavery Congregationalists in 1846. Gary thought he'd discovered the east when he arrived in Iowa in 1922. The town then had five thousand people, the college seven hundred students. Each freshman had to wear a red and black beanie or risk being paddled by an upperclassman. Under the strict college rules, public dancing and smoking were forbidden. There were no fraternities and, during Prohibition, very little drinking. In a decade of short-skirted Charleston dancers and red-hot jazz, cigarette-smoking flappers and coonskin-coated devotees of bootleg whiskey, Grinnell's Roaring Twenties were distinctly muted and muffled. It offered, instead, "cultured companionship in the midst of idyllic surroundings."

Grinnell prided itself on being a poor man's college where plain living merged with high feeling. Working your way through college to pay the annual $625 for tuition fees, room and board was considered a "social asset because it upheld a Grinnell tradition." The energetic Gary mowed grass, trimmed shrubbery, chopped down trees, cleaned yards and shoveled snow. He lived in the Langan Hall dormitory, above the main dining room, and at Professor Matlack's home "did chores in return for meals. He helped in the family garden, washed windows, waxed floors, and even operated a cider press." Cooper and some friends once stole a five-gallon jug of Matlack's cider, tried to make it hard, then lost patience and drank it before it fermented. To destroy the evidence, they put a firecracker in the neck of the jug and blew it up like a bomb.

A rarity from Montana, he was called "Cowboy Cooper," sang a mournful version of "Bury Me Not in the Lone Prairie" and recited

Robert Service's "The Shooting of Dan McGrew" in one of his unsuccessful tryouts for the dramatic club. During his first year at Grinnell, wearing handmade buckskin and beads, and a knife wrapped in eagle feathers, he did an Indian dance at the local high school. At the end of the dance he shocked the audience by plunging the knife under his armpit and falling straight backwards—without breaking his fall—as if he had stabbed himself. Cooper became art editor of the college year-book, and did cartoons and drawings for the *Scarlet and Black*. He had a "gorilla-like reach" as a boxer and "could store away pancakes and fried eggs beyond human belief."[12]

Gary took a tough schedule of courses and was always having academic difficulties.[13] Placed in a nine o'clock Spanish class and ten o'clock Greek class, he remained hopelessly confused in both languages. Though he later spent a good deal of time in Mexico and France, he never learned to speak a foreign tongue. While in Paris, he wrote the bilingual Lorraine Chanel: "It is stupid not to know the language and I think I'm particularly dumb about it—just like my Spanish! . . . So many of my American friends are here that I've learned all of six words of French."

Three years older than most of his classmates, Gary was rather a loner. Though he formed no close friendships at Grinnell, he fell in love, for the first time, with the curly-haired, oval-faced Doris Virden (who bore a striking resemblance to his mother) and went steady with her for more than a year. The daughter of the manager of a local corn-canning factory and of a socialite patron of the arts, Doris had attended college in Florida. She completed her last year and a half at Grinnell and graduated with a B.A. in English in 1923. Extensively trained in speech and elocution, she was a talented poet, violinist, singer and leading actress in the dramatic club. When Cooper became a star, Doris followed him out to California and taught drama at Hollywood High School. In the late 1920s, after he had appeared in several silent films with Fay Wray, Doris sent Fay a long letter, saying she felt awful about losing Gary and desperately wanted him back. Always in frail health, Doris died of throat cancer in 1934.

During the summers of 1922 and 1923 Gary drove a stiff-springed, open-air, ten-passenger yellow bus in Yellowstone National Park in Montana. He earned $90 a month plus room, board and tips. Most of the passengers, who were from the east, expected savage Indians and wild buffalo to come charging down from every gully. In order to increase his tips, one of his old companions explained, Gary would try to dramatize the journey: "Frank Cooper and I were gear-jammers together in the park. We drove busses and spieled for the tourists. Frank worked there during the summer while he was at Grinnell and we called him 'The Sheik.' Frank was a fine driver, but not much of a spieler. One fellow claimed that his Yellowstone experience was his first real acting for pay. To get tips out of the tourists, he would make the treacherous drive through the park seem even more treacherous by grimaces and exaggerated pulls at the wheel."[14]

Classmates remembered Gary as a pleasant, gentlemanly but quite ordinary young man who "took an active part in half-time high jinks at football games, worked as a dishwasher in a campus dining hall and at a local café, and drew cover art for the playbills of productions that he couldn't participate in as an actor." But he had no interest in sports, and his academic record was discouragingly poor. Eager to start his commercial art career, he felt it would be a waste of time to finish the last two years of college. He didn't tell friends he was leaving, and simply failed to turn up the following term.

Stressing its rather bland qualities, a notable graduate wrote that "Grinnell is not the place in which to look for eagerness of enquiry, youthful audacity of thought or action, really stirring intellectual currents. But it has always had and does still have a personal and intimate charm." The young Gary Cooper was remarkably similar to the typical Grinnell man: "a sort of youthful, highly idealized portrait of a Rotarian." The Grinnell spirit—"a vague radiance, confident of an undefined mission, utterly untested, utterly innocent, tragically absurd"—along with Gary's idealism and personal charm, characterized his film persona of the 1930s: the provincial common man, Mr. Deeds and John Doe.

Though Gary never graduated from Grinnell, he remained fond of the place. As one of its most illustrious alumni, he returned for a triumphant visit in October 1929. Arriving by plane, he was greeted by the state governor, met old friends, attended the air races, had dinner with the president and settled into his student rooms in Langan Hall. At the homecoming football game and Saturday night dance, he "caused co-ed hearts to flutter" and said: "I just want to be one of the folks at Grinnell for a few days." He liked to reminisce about his college days when, he honestly remarked, "I spent my dimes and nickels and got a little education on the side."

Montana had a greater impact on his personality. Surrounded by wilderness for much of his childhood, he valued solitude. He turned inward, kept his own counsel, spoke little, and liked to take long hikes by himself. "I discovered taking a walk always helped me dope out my problems. I used to do a lot of walking when I was up on the ranch recovering from my injury in the auto accident. It enabled me to think clearly. It became a sort of habit the rest of my life."[15] He learned laconic speech from both the Indians and the English, and had a unique mixture of Montana geniality and British restraint. Just as he could have two distinct identities, American and English—and change from one into the other and back again—so he would also, as an actor, both play a role and manage to be himself.

3

Stuntman to Star

1924–1927

I

Cooper entered movies by accident and soon became a star. He had originally wanted to be a landscape painter, with a style combining the precise detail of John James Audubon and the epic scope of Charles Russell. More realistically, he thought he might work as a political cartoonist on a newspaper or as a commercial artist in an advertising agency. In the fall of 1924, just after Charles had retired from the supreme court and moved to Hollywood, he wrote affectionately to Gary: "It appears I may be here on this case for a long time. Mother and I both miss you. I think it would be a good thing if you ambled down this way and let mother see how her growing boy is doing. Besides, don't you miss her fine home cooking?" Heeding his father's summons, Gary arrived in Hollywood, two months after his parents, on November 27, 1924—just in time for Thanksgiving dinner.

"Unlike most actors," Cooper noted, "I can't say that I dreamed of the stage or the movies ever since childhood. And I can't say I was attracted to Hollywood by its glamour, or money, or beautiful women. When I went to Hollywood in the fall of 1924, I was just drifting in to see the folks. . . . You might say I was in the movies because dad had mixed up some ranching with his lawyering"–and had to leave the bench when he lost money on the ranch. Gary's plan was to work just long enough in films to pay for a professional art course in Chicago. He later explained that "I liked drawing and had a flair for it, so I was told, but the tedium of sitting for hours, sketching, to get one little thing flawless was too great a demand on a restless spirit."

   He was immediately struck by the great contrast between the spectacular scenery and rugged frontier towns of Montana and the orange
blossoms, swaying palm trees, tile-roofed Spanish houses, tacky commercial architecture and wide, empty streets of Los Angeles. He moved in
with his parents, who were renting a house at 7511 Franklin. It was two-
storied and shingled, with shuttered windows and a brick front porch, set
high off the street at the corner of Gardner. Hating the sedentary routine
of office work (he later said he'd rather be a hobo than a clock puncher)
and eager to support himself, he got a series of unpromising jobs that
lasted for only a few weeks. He sold classified advertisements, helped
paint ads on theater curtains and (recalling his mother's hobby) was a
door-to-door salesman for a baby photographer. After extracting a dollar
deposit from his clients, he'd book appointments for portrait sittings in
the studio on Vermont Avenue. But he quickly realized these jobs were all
boring dead ends.
   In December, striding down Poverty Row on Gower Street, which
turned out cheap silent Westerns, Cooper ran into some cowboys from
Montana. They were earning good off-season money by working as
extras and stuntmen in the movies. Their leader was the six-foot, four
inch, 170-pound Jay "Slim" Talbot, who had been born a few years
before Cooper on a ranch in Basin, Montana, twenty-five miles south of
Helena. He had been winning rodeo contests since he was sixteen, and
was one of the best riders, ropers and bulldoggers in the west. He'd been
a pilot during the war and done barnstorming exhibitions in the early
1920s. When Cooper became a star, Slim—his friend and hunting
companion—worked for the next thirty-five years as his stuntman and
stand-in, the tedious job of taking the actor's place while the lights are
being set up. An outdoorsman, he was as shy as Gary when he had to
embrace the heroine. Slim eventually earned as much as $600 a week
working for Cooper and closely identified with his alter ego: "Yeah, I
guess I've become Gary Cooper pretty much, even to myself. . . . I've
copied his mannerisms and habits so long, in order to be Cooper auto-
matically in front of a camera, that they're ingrained now."
   Gary had no acting experience, but possessed two valuable qualities:
good looks and riding skill. As he remarked a few years later: "I've had
lines on my face since I was twenty. Wind and sun put them there. . . .
The years I rode herd gave me knowledge of the west which is now a
great help in my western pictures."[1] The pay, much better than he'd been
earning, was five dollars a day for an extra and double that for the

dangerous work of stuntman. As a bonus on location the riders got a free lunch, usually a plate of stew and a cup of coffee, in the commissary tent.

The mob of extras stood outside the studios, like Mediterranean peasants or workers on the docks, and waited to be called. Gary appeared as an extra in three Zane Grey Westerns—one of them with Tom Mix, who was making $10,000 a week—and would sometimes play a cowboy in the morning and an Indian after lunch. In *The Johnstown Flood* (1926) he was both a victim and a survivor. In *The Eagle* (1925), about the Russian empress Catherine the Great, he was part of a Cossack troop. With other cowboy riders in a Boer War movie, he was driven on a big bus from the Fox lot to the mountains above Hollywood. Wearing a fake beard and colorful uniform, he did his bit for dear old England by taking a few falls during a gunfight on horseback.

Cooper later recalled the blunt instructions for his stunt in this film: "The director told us what the scene was all about. Then he ordered us to get on our mounts and wait for his signal, which was a blank gun that he would fire when ready. Each of us was given a rifle. The director came up to me and said, 'You, there. When this charge gets under way, I want you to ride along with the bunch halfway down this field. Then you throw your rifle in the air and fall off your horse. Got it?' " There were two ways, one slightly less cruel and menacing than the other, to make the horse fall. "The horses," he explained, "would be run into a nest of ankle-deep wires strung from pole to pole: this tripped them and hurled their riders with great realism—too great, for riders often were injured and horses frequently had to be destroyed. Later the riders themselves controlled a wire-and-strap lashup [that ran from the saddle to the horse's front ankles] so they could trip the horses themselves and at least know when the fall would come." The rider's trick was to break the impact of the fall and avoid landing on his face by thrusting out his arm and rolling over on his shoulder.

Hoping to break out of the risky ranks of stuntmen, Cooper invested $64 (including the rental of a horse) in his own twenty-second screen test. Galloping toward the camera, he reined in and jumped off the horse, leaped over a fence and, in a close-up, flashed a "ghastly grin." He also hired Nan Collins, a studio casting director and small-time agent. She told him that two other Frank Coopers—one a stuntman and the other a character actor—were already in the movies, and a third one, on the east coast, had just murdered his wife and run away with a tart. So she changed his forthright first name to the slightly more unusual Gary, after her grim hometown in Indiana. Through the magic of Hollywood, the name became synonymous with elegance and romance.

In these early days in Hollywood both parents did all they could to advance his career. His mother—who called him "son" rather than "Frank"—"steered him clear of some of the sharks." Devoted to but extremely possessive about her handsome young boy, she said: "I was his valet, his chauffeur and his only feminine companion. I'd get up early in the morning, get his clothes ready for his day's work, and then after breakfast I'd drive him to whatever lot he was called."[2]

Cooper, without really knowing what he was doing, got his first break in 1925 through Marilyn Mills, queen of the two-reel Westerns, who helped him at the request of her father, a client of Judge Cooper's. Emphasizing Gary's naiveté and innocence, Mills said he was so skinny that he had to wear five extra shirts when he appeared in *Tricks* and *Three Pals*:

> He said the closest he'd ever been to a studio was waiting outside a casting director's office. He had never been interviewed. He had some photographs of himself and showed them to me. They were very sophisticated and George Raftish-hair sleeked down and most of them had cigarette smoke curling up. Or else a pipe in his hand.
>
> I was sorry for the kid because even though he was as old as I was, he seemed bewildered by the whole business. I told him I'd try to give him a break in my next picture, a little opus called *Tricks*. When Cooper arrived on location, Bruce Mitchell, the director, said he looked like a human string bean and refused to put him in the picture.
>
> I finally insisted the kid get a break, but we never put him in a scene with our leading man, the late J. Frank Glendon, unless one of them was on a horse because he made Glendon look like a shrimp.

Cooper channeled his artistic talents into acting instead of painting, and his easygoing temperament and boyish manner helped him get started.

In the age of silent movies, with their flickering images and jerky movements, the actors could talk and directors could bark out commands while the scenes were actually being shot. Fay Wray, one of Cooper's co-stars, explained how scenes were lit, fights were staged and make-up was applied in those comparatively primitive days:

> In the Westerns, there were very few close-ups. We had to be in the studio early because the pictures were almost always shot outside and

work began as soon as the sun was up. . . . Reflectors (large boards covered with tinfoil and angled to turn the sun's light onto a scene) could make it a struggle just to keep your eyes open. . . . For fight scenes, glass windows were really made of sheets of candy; furniture flung about or used to bash a cowboy over the head couldn't hurt him very much because they were made of yucca. . . . The wood part is porous and almost hollow, yet strong enough to be shaped into chairs or whatever is needed to "furnish" a fight scene. . . .

   We put on our own greasepaint, making our faces very light, our mouths very dark. This was the recommended contrast suitable for the film of the time. It also helped our faces to register in the long shots.

Cooper, now a featured player, also wore heavy make-up, especially around his eyes. Speaking of *Tricks*, in which he played a villain, he used uncharacteristic irony to mock the effeminate, operatic and absurd aspects of acting: "I would apply lipstick, powder and mascara. I would know what the story was all about, and I would emote. Instead of seeing the stars from a distance, I would poke one right in his mascaraed eye, and ride off to my den of iniquity, holding the other in my foul clutches. My name would appear on the screen with the Cast of Characters. I would be an actor."[3]

II

Cooper's career—impelled by luck, good looks and useful love affairs—was meteoric. His first important role came in 1926; he was a star two years later and was earning $6,000 a week by 1933. His screen test, name change and tyro's experience had paid off. On June 1, 1926 he signed a contract with Samuel Goldwyn for $50 a week and went to the barren Black Rock Desert, six thousand feet high and a hundred miles north of Reno, Nevada, to make *The Winning of Barbara Worth* (1926). Goldwyn was born in Warsaw, began as a glove salesman and had left his name in MGM when he departed to build his own film company. He paid $125,000 for the movie rights to the best-selling novel by Harold Bell Wright, and constructed a new town on a dry lake near the Oregon border for this massive production. He dug wells, put in showers, mess hall, bake shop and special refrigerators, and added a special spur of the Western Nevada Railroad. The studio's publicity pamphlet boasted that "the town was complete in itself, with drug stores, hotels, radios, electric lights, and even a newspaper and a motion-picture theater." Twelve hundred people, most of whom lived in tents and constructed the town, spent ten weeks under extremely difficult conditions. The heat reached 130 degrees during the day, fell below freezing at night and was accompanied by fierce sandstorms that did $10,000 worth of damage.

Cooper went out as an extra, and got a featured part when another actor failed to finish a picture on time and didn't turn up in the desert. During a screen test, when Cooper was supposed to lean over a water hole and take a drink, he revealed the natural advantage he had over someone trained on the stage. Instead of making a theatrical gesture, he blew the dust off the top of the water and cupped it into his mouth with his hands. He knew what a cowboy would do and brought instinctive authenticity to his screen roles.

In the movie he plays Abe Lee, a young engineer who discovers a fault in the new dam. When it bursts, he makes an exhausting ride and alerts Ronald Colman and Vilma Banky just in time. After saving their lives, he dies a hero's death. The flood scene at the climax of the film must have reminded Cooper of the bursting of the Hauser Dam in his childhood. The director, Henry King, told Cooper how to play his crucial scene:

"If I wanted you to come up to this door," I said, "and fall flat on your face—flat, even if it smashes you to pieces, could you do it?"

"Yes, sir."

"I don't mean you to break your fall with your hands. I mean you to fall flat. Like a corpse."

"Yes, sir."

"When you knock on that door, I want you to knock like a tired man. How tired would a man be if he'd ridden twenty-four hours on a horse?"

"Mighty tired."

"Well, I want you to *be* that tired."

King remembered the sight of Cooper "standing full length in that door, looking across the room and saying, 'Mr. W-W-Worth . . .' and falling flat on his face. As he went down, Ronnie Colman and Paul McAllister grabbed him, and Cooper's face missed the floor by two inches."

In *The Winning of Barbara Worth*, unlike his later films, Cooper didn't get the girl and had to be buried in the sagebrush. But he "found that dying on the screen was a lot easier than falling off a horse and a lot more comfortable. I just lay in Colman's arms and pretended I was taking a nap." Colman, an established star, gave the newcomer some good advice about the kind of natural, minimal acting that would become Cooper's trademark: "Easy does it, old boy. Good scenes make good actors. Actors don't make a scene. My own feeling is that all you have to do is take a nap, and every woman who sees the picture is going to cry her eyes out."

The actors in early movies, which had no dialogue, used hyperactive movement and exaggerated expressions to convey meaning. Cooper, by contrast, was tentative, shy and restrained, and seemed honorable and courageous when confronted with death. After the critics had raved about the "dynamic new personality," Cooper was offered $65 a week and held out for $75. The head of casting, the film director and Goldwyn himself all thought one of the others had signed him up. During the confusion Cooper, who still had serious doubts about his ability as an actor, had to be forcibly persuaded to accept a long-term agreement with Paramount. The producer Jesse Lasky recalled that when he asked Cooper, " 'How'd you like to become a regular actor?' . . . he fiddled with his hat and was silent. 'Well, I don't know if I could.' He hemmed and hawed and seemed anxious to escape. We almost had to bulldog him to get his name on a five-year contract."[4] He began at $175 a week, and the studio soon turned him into a superstar. When Goldwyn wanted him later on, he had to pay $6,000 a week.

As Cooper achieved success in Hollywood, he bought his parents a modest, single-story, tile-roofed house, with a pillared entrance and large living room window, at 529 North Cahuenga, in a quiet residential enclave just north of the Wilshire Country Club. For a while he continued to live at home. The reserved, rather austere Charles—about five feet, nine inches tall—then had a craggy face and shock of white hair. The strong-willed Alice—a tall woman with a distinct English accent—was gracious, lively and high-spirited. Gary looked more like his mother, but had his father's temperament.

In 1929 a Hollywood reporter who visited the Coopers seemed disappointed by the home and found the family solid, unpretentious and hospitable. Gary's tiny room reflected his two great loves—the Indians and his mother.

[The Coopers] live in a rambling, old-fashioned house. The living-room contains furniture of no especial distinction; a piano, Gary's steel guitar, the radio-phonograph that was Gary's Easter present to his mother, and one picture of Gary from *Lilac Time* [1928]. In the dining room is a long, wide table and enough chairs to fill a banquet hall.

No matter what time of day, the table is always set, for the Cooper door is ever open to friends. Friends are always urged to "have a bite of supper." The latter consists of a plentiful meal prepared by mother.

Upstairs there are three bedrooms and two baths. The elaborate tiled bathrooms are the household's one concession to modernity. Gary's adjoins his room and is a rose-and-black tiled hole-in-the-wall, with barely enough room for a shower. Gary's room is rather bare except for some Indian beadwork hung around the walls and chairs, and a picture of his mother on the dresser.

Soon afterward, when Gary became romantically entangled with his leading ladies, he escaped from his spartan room and his parents' surveillance, and moved into the Castle-Argyle Arms, a large seven-story apartment building at 1919 North Argyle, just north of Franklin.

Myrna Loy, who'd known the Coopers in Helena, felt that Alice "transplanted the poor judge from Montana to Hollywood, where he always seemed lost and lonely." But Arthur's children, who lived with the older Coopers in the twenties and thirties, recalled that the judge had a law office at the corner of Cahuenga and Hollywood boulevards, went to the Los Angeles Courthouse every workday and "knew everyone downtown." Charles would ride down Wilshire Boulevard with Howard, reading the newspaper and taking in the California air. When he wanted the boy to amuse himself, he'd grandly peel off a five-dollar bill and say, "Here, kid."

Alice could, on occasion, "go off like a rocket." She once threatened to shoot her husband and said she wanted to divorce him. Forbidding her to mention the subject, Gary told her she was crazy. In about 1930 Charles told a reporter that Gary was much shrewder than he seemed to be and that he always relied on his son's good advice: "Some people think Gary hasn't much sense. You think he's not paying any attention, but you'll find that he's taken in everything that was said, and digested it. He doesn't say much, but when he does, he just seems to have reached the nubbin of the situation, in a few words. He has a sound business head, and I'm inclined to listen to him carefully."[5]

In April 1928 Charles went back to Helena to repurchase the old Cooper homestead near Craig. Acting as agent for Gary, who originally planned to use it as a location for films, he bought it for $4,000. In the summer of 1930, boasting a string of ponies and a polo field, Sunnyside opened as a dude ranch for easterners. But the ranch was mismanaged, and as clients dwindled throughout the Depression, it lost money and had to be sold. His grandson noted that Charles had a "speculative side" and "got swindled." The family blamed him for the financial disaster, which provoked many quarrels, angry recriminations and bitter feelings. But Gary remained devoted to his father and in 1939, shortly after the ranch was sold, helped Charles realize a lifetime ambition by sending him on a round-the-world trip on the *Empress of Russia*. Charles spent most of his time ashore urging foreign theater managers to show more movies with Gary Cooper.

III

When Cooper went into films in the mid-1920s, he was six feet, three inches tall and weighed 185 pounds. He had a thin face, narrow shoulders, long arms and large hands, and would habitually hook and pull his fingers. He looked like a Remington cowboy, slouched a bit and moved slowly. His face was at once handsome, rugged and kind. With hollow cheeks, a delicate, sensuous month, light brown hair and striking blue eyes, he radiated integrity and personal warmth and "was more beautiful than any woman except Garbo." "Unique in that his beauty never made anyone think less of him as a man," he accepted the adoration of women, friends and fans with engaging modesty. The fashion photographer Cecil Beaton, who, like Charles Laughton, had a crush on Cooper, called him an "erudite, charming, spectacularly constituted man."[6]

Cooper had grown up in a male world, was rather innocent about women when he first came to Hollywood and remained shy throughout his life. Speaking of his limited experience, he recalled that "girls were not unknown to me. I had gone to some employee dances when I was a bus driver in Yellowstone Park, and once at Grinnell College I had practically become engaged" to Doris Virden. In Hollywood, however, his personal charm and astonishing beauty had a devastating effect. He had only to put his hand on a woman's arm, and she would succumb. The sophisticated German actress Luise Rainer was inspired to come to Hollywood by Cooper's performance in *A Farewell to Arms*. When she saw him in the lobby of the Beverly Wilshire Hotel, she felt weak at the knees and was ready to surrender. Recalling the early years at Paramount, Budd Schulberg, whose father ran the studio, wrote: "Cooper was the secret dream and in many cases the literal love of the entire studio secretarial pool. All typing stopped, all eyes turned to devour what Father's head secretary described as 'the most beautiful hunk of man who ever walked down this hall!' Uncle Sam Jaffe's secretary, the pleasingly plump, happy-dispositioned Jean Bair, carried on a semi-secret . . . affair with Gary for years." A Paramount script girl agreed that Cooper's gentleness and physical stamina meant he "could have had any girl he wanted. . . . The word got around what a good lover he was . . . so warm and kind. And satisfying . . . I overheard Mae West and Clara Bow talking to their hairdressers about the men in their lives. Even a script girl learns fast in Hollywood."[7]

Richard Widmark said Cooper "was catnip to the ladies." In life, as in films, he always got the girl. The worldly Howard Hawks, who directed two of Cooper's best pictures, explained that the "aw shucks," down-home cowboy persona in his films was, in reality, an effective mode of seduction: "If I ever saw him with a good-looking girl and he was kind of dragging his feet over the ground and being very shy and looking down, I'd say 'Oh-oh, the snake's gonna strike again.' He found that the little bashful boy approach was very successful."

The director Stuart Heisler put it more bluntly: "Coop was probably the greatest cocksman that ever lived. They fell over themselves to get him to take them to bed. He couldn't stop screwing around. The women wouldn't let him. They'd go lay down for him in his portable dressing room by the soundstage. I guess he had the reputation for being a wonderful lay." Arlene Dahl, more thoughtfully, believed women fell in love with Cooper's combination of unusual traits. He never talked about himself, always questioned women and was a great listener. He was shy, sensitive and vulnerable; sophisticated, mysterious and romantic. His boyish nature made them want to cuddle, nurture—and seduce him. He had a hypnotic quality, a "spiritual essence." When women looked into his dreamy blue eyes, "the Red Sea parted."[8]

Clara Bow was the first in a long series of leading ladies who became Cooper's mistresses. Born in 1905, she came from a desperately impoverished background. Her father was alcoholic, her mother insane. Sexy, feverishly animated and intensely emotional, with an atrocious Brooklyn accent, she won a beauty contest in her teens, got bit parts in New York studios and came to Hollywood. She made fourteen silent pictures in

1925, was billed as "The Hottest Jazz Baby in Films" and was soon receiving forty thousand fan letters a week. She lived quietly in her Beverly Hills and Malibu houses, playing poker with her servants. But she was flamboyant in public, driving a bright red car filled with seven chow dogs whose coats were dyed to match her flaming red hair.

Bow's fusion of boundless energy and electric personality, of bobbed hair, sparkling eyes and sensuous figure, made her dynamite on the screen. Scott Fitzgerald, whose stories portrayed the glamorous youth of the 1920s, cited Clara Bow as "the quintessence of what the term 'flapper' signifies as a definite description. Pretty, impudent, superbly assured, as worldly-wise, briefly clad and 'hard-berled' as possible. There were hundreds of them—her prototypes. Now, completing the circle, there are thousands more—patterning themselves after her." In his story "A Patriotic Short" (1940), Fitzgerald defined her as the sexual symbol who propelled the flaming youth of America toward reckless behavior: "She was the girl of the year, the It girl . . . the girl for whose services every studio was in violent competition . . . This girl was the real thing, someone to stir every pulse in the nation."[9]

The fan magazines and gossip columnists soon made the Cooper-Bow affair a public event, and the two glamorous stars became romantic idols. The lovers began to feed the flames of gossip, commenting in print on each other's personal characteristics and cinematic roles. Emphasizing, like Fitzgerald, her insouciance, sexual freedom and professional expertise, Cooper said, after appearing in three films with her: "She was a new type of girl, glamorous, full of fun, devoid of jealousy. I was grateful to her and admired her. . . . You couldn't steal scenes from Clara Bow. Nobody could. She doesn't 'mug' the camera. Never that. She just naturally walks away with every scene she's in. She's marvelous. She has everything." The uncharacteristically florid and romantic inscription on the photograph he presented to Clara seemed copied out of a popular novel: "To Clarita, whom I love, whose beauty and life by day are as real as the sun at noon, and by night have all the mysteries and allure of the northern lights, with the softness of the summer moon. You are that. I love you. Garyito."

Bow, in her own self-promoting and suggestive way, reciprocated his feelings. Stressing his childlike, unpretentious charm, she opened with a double entendre and exclaimed: "Gary's such a *big* boy, so strong, so manly, and so bashful. I always wanna rumple his hair an' listen t'all his troubles. . . . He's so sweet t'me. He always lets me take my dog in the tub when he gives me a bath every mornin'!" She also announced, to the shocked but riveted public, that Cooper had "the biggest cock in Hollywood an' no ass t'push it with. . . . He's hung like a horse and he can go all night. . . . His appetite for sex was the same as mine, but it's tough to find a man who's not only a terrific lay, but a gentleman, too."[10] Clara couldn't have children and said Cooper didn't have to worry about "knocking her up."

Cooper had a tiny part in Bow's most famous film, *It* (1927). It was based on the short novel by the English writer Elinor Glyn, which had been serialized in Cosmopolitan in 1926 and published the following year. The studio persuaded Glyn to change the emphasis from the man to the woman who has "It," and apart from the suggestive title, the film bore no resemblance to the story. "It," or sex appeal, is defined in the first title card in the movie as "that quality possessed by some which draws all others by its magnetic force." Glyn—large, fat and ugly, without the slightest trace of "It"—rather incongruously appears in the film to explain the concept. Bow, "positively top heavy with It," pouts her lips and raises her eyebrows when flirting with the men. She throws out saucy lines like "I'll take the snap out of your garters" and eventually snags the wealthy boss.

The budget was $180,000, of which Glyn was paid $14,000 for the story, Bow carried $10,400 for the starring role and Cooper, not mentioned in the cast list, got $10. He appears halfway through the silent movie as a bronzed, lean, lantern-jawed reporter, on the street and outside the door of an apartment, chewing gum and taking notes. Though briefly on-screen, he looks magnificent and makes a striking impression. His appearance in a movie that was a great success and grossed more than a million dollars (then a prodigious figure) helped Cooper's career.

IV

Wings, about fliers in World War I, was shot on an airfield in San Antonio with an astronomical budget of $2 million. In 1927 it won the first Academy Award for Best Picture. As Kevin Brownlow wrote: "This is primarily an action picture, and death and destruction have seldom been more lyrically and sweepingly portrayed. The camera is in an aircraft for the more memorable scenes; the audience is given the vicarious thrill of shooting down balloons, engaging the enemy in a dogfight, bombing a village, machine-gunning columns of troops, and chasing and destroying a general's staff car." The banal title cards, broad comedy and operatic acting—Bow plays the pert and sassy girl who becomes a Red Cross driver at the front—provide a ludicrous contrast to the realistic battle scenes, daring stunt flying and exciting plane crashes.

Cooper—in the midst of his affair with Bow—appears in only one brief scene. Wearing a pilot's cap and goggles, a long leather coat and high polished boots, he plays an experienced flier. He shares a training camp tent with two new cadets, Buddy Rogers and Richard Arlen, the stars of the film. Combining boyish charm with manly swagger (he doesn't carry a good luck charm), and looping his fingers in his belt as he speaks, Cooper says: "Guess we'll be seeing a lot of each other." He's a hero to the two recruits, who give him a candy bar in a childish gesture of admiration. Taking a quick bite of the chocolate, he throws it aside and says he has to "do a flock of figure eights before chow." In a striking close-up, he stares at the two cadets with intense beacon-like eyes and nonchalantly utters his last words: "Luck or no luck, when your time comes, you're going to get it." As he takes off on a routine test flight, his plane throws a shadow on the ground. After his unseen crash and the rush of the ambulance, the camera focuses on the half-eaten chocolate and on the faces that reflect the drama of his death. It's astonishing that Cooper—without speaking a word and in less than two minutes—could, by his mere physical presence, his charm, charisma and devil-may-care attitude, make such a powerful impact. At that crucial moment a major film star was born.

The director William Wellman, like the scriptwriter John Monk Saunders and the actor Richard Arlen, had been a flier during the war. After rehearsing Cooper in his hotel suite the night before shooting, he printed the first take and thanked him for his impressive performance. Cooper, unaware of the effect he had achieved, and more concerned about controlling his every gesture, asked if he could play the scene again. Wellman said: " 'You don't know what you're doing. I do. I see it. I know it was good. It was great, or I wouldn't have printed it. But just because I'm interested, I'm curious, because of you.' He was getting a little scared. 'Tell me why you didn't like it.' He said, 'Well, in the middle of the scene, I picked [i.e., touched] my nose.' I said, 'Listen, you son of a bitch, you keep right on picking your nose and you'll pick your nose right into a fortune.'

During the filming of *Wings* Cooper stayed in San Antonio to be with Bow and formed close friendships with Rogers and Arlen. Rogers, soon to be surpassed by Cooper, emphasized that he was "super quiet" and later said: "We didn't consider him a great actor, but his strong personality made him a star." He also recalled that the three companions, anxious about the nerve-racking transition to talkies, "made a pact to protect the one of us that we figured would turn out not to have a voice; the other two would give him a certain segment of our salaries until he could find something else to do." Errol Flynn, another companion, gave a lively account of their boyish adventures at sea: "Dick Arlen took Gary Cooper and Jack Oakie for a fishing trip on the *Joby R.* and Oakie arrived in what might be the Esquire's idea of a Patagonian Rear Admiral's Coronation uniform. . . . The two enraged, dungareed players dumped him overside and towed him around the harbor. . . . Jack Moss, Gary's three-hundred-pound manager, fell in after a yellow-tail and, despite his indignant denials, had to be hauled back aboard with the power winch."[11]

In the late 1920s Cooper also became quite friendly with the more cultured but less successful stage and film actor Anderson Lawler. A well-born Virginian, "tall, thin, freckled, with a choirboy's face and plentiful red hair," he had an obscene tongue and mocking laugh. A capable archer, swimmer, mountaineer, sailor and hunter, he shared Cooper's keen interest in outdoor life and sports. Also knowledgeable about art, music and literature, he took Cooper to plays and concerts, and moved into the family house for a time when Charles and Alice were away in Montana. Later on, Lawler became Tallulah Bankhead's disciple and protégé, produced plays by Tennessee Williams and came out of the closet. Notorious for cruising nearly every night, he pimped for and passed on his tricks to the director George Cukor, and was arrested several times on morals charges.

Clara Bow helped Cooper get a leading role in *Children of Divorce* (1927), which she felt would give him a more romantic aura and enhance their public image. "We'll go places and do things together," she told him. "We'll become an 'item.' " But the still-inexperienced Cooper, who had played tiny parts as a cowboy and war hero, was not ready to abandon his own character and become a New York smoothie—a witty and spoiled society boy, serious about love but reluctant to marry. Horribly miscast and insecure about his ability, he worked on this picture in self-conscious, agonizing shyness. Unlike most creative people, who work in solitude and silence, actors have to perform in front of a crowd. "I couldn't make love to a girl with a camera snooping at me," he rather naively said. "It just didn't seem decent, especially with a girl I hardly knew."

Hedda Hopper, who was then an actress and appeared in the film, remembered the first day of shooting as the most painful performance she had ever witnessed: "the set was my swank Park Avenue apartment. The characters were super-sophisticated Manhattan youths merrily going to hell. The scene was a cocktail party and Gary's job, of all things, was to breeze into the room and make the rounds from one flapper to another, sipping champagne out of their glasses, cadging a nonchalant puff from their cigarettes, and tossing sophisticated wisecracks as he strolled along. . . . He was a New York man about town, the script read, yet only a few months before he'd been riding the range in Montana. Completely unnerved, Cooper spilled champagne on Clara for twenty-three straight takes. He turned the sophisticated drama into a slapstick debacle and almost finished his film career.

Esther Ralston, the other leading lady, spent an entire day filming her love scenes with Cooper and had to reshoot them because he seemed so amateur. As he lost confidence, became nervous, hesitated and forgot his lines, the director, Frank Lloyd, said he couldn't work with him any longer. Cooper was taken off the picture and replaced with a new leading man. Deeply distressed by his own ineptitude, by the trouble he was causing on the set and by the hostility of the director, Cooper suddenly disappeared on a "solitary walk" in the wilds. Three days later he was found, unshaven and exhausted, in a Hollywood restaurant.

When the replacement didn't work out, B.P. Schulberg rehired Cooper—who'd been ready to leave Hollywood but was willing to finish the picture—and asked Ralston to give him as much help as possible. " 'I know he can't act now,' said Mr. Schulberg. 'But I am sure he's got a face—something unusual. He just needs experience. If you'd just work with him, Esther, be nice to him, make a friend of him.' Conscious of my newlywed status, I said hesitatingly, 'Just what did you have in mind?' Miss Loring [the scenarist] spoke up. 'You see, dear, Gary is so stiff in the love scenes, as though he was afraid to touch you for fear you'd break. Take him to lunch, Esther, talk to him. I'm sure you can make him feel more at ease.' "

His confidence restored by his rehiring, Cooper made significant improvement. This time round the director was replaced by the eminent Josef von Sternberg. He remade Lloyd's version at night, in order to accommodate the actors who had moved on to their next picture, and

Lloyd got screen credit for the work von Sternberg had done. Cooper was saved not only by the superior artistry of von Sternberg, but also by the perception of Schulberg, who recognized his talent and saw a way to use it. Sam Jaffe, then working at Paramount, remembered that Schulberg said: "You know, this'll work. This'll work well, his hesitancy. Let him *do* just that. The public won't know that he's fishing for lines."[12]

After completing the traumatic *Children of Divorce*, during the next three years at Paramount Cooper made twelve mostly forgettable Western, aviation, adventure and romantic movies. *Arizona Bound* (1927), for example, his first starring role, was a routine cowboy picture. It was shot in only fifteen days in Bryce Canyon, Utah, on a low budget of $73,000. Cooper worked with the "Wonder Horse," Flash, and did his own stunt by jumping from the horse to a runaway stagecoach. *Nevada* (also 1927), based on a Zane Grey story, was shot in three weeks on a budget of $165,000, from which Cooper was paid $1,200. A fan magazine revealed one of the dangers in making these movies by reporting that a cowboy was really "shot to death by another of his kind during an actual scene in the film." He fell off his horse, as planned, and was found, when the director called "cut," to have been murdered: "It was a local feud. All the local cowboys knew who had done the murder; none of them could prove it."

Children of Divorce was Cooper's last film with Clara Bow. By the time it was completed, their intensely emotional but short-lived affair was all but over. The Hollywood writer Adela Rogers St. Johns emphasized the dangers of Bow's unfocused and rather meaningless existence, which depressed Cooper and eventually drove him away: "There seems to be no pattern, no purpose to her life. She swings from one emotion to another, but she gains nothing, stores up nothing against the future. She lives entirely in the present, not even for today, but just for the moment. And you go on loving her, feeling sorry for her, and praying that she won't get into any real trouble."

Cooper was also jealous of her numerous lovers, especially the tall and physically powerful Victor Fleming—a ladies' man, sportsman, car racer, aviator and tough guy. When someone asked Cooper why he didn't marry Bow, he turned scarlet, mumbled, "Too late," and mentioned "a fellow she's flipped for." "Gary was big and strong," Bow egoistically explained, "but Vickie was older and understood me. I needed someone t'soothe me. Vickie was like that. I mothered Gary, but Vickie mothered me." Another problem—which recurred with other girlfriends—was that the possessive and proper Alice Cooper inevitably disliked Clara. And, as Clara said, "his mother ran his life."

After retiring from films in 1931, Bow suffered from mental problems, poor health and ballooning weight. As early as February 1927, while making *Arizona Bound*, Cooper sent a telegram expressing his concern: "Darling Clarita. Very unhappy to hear you are ill. I miss you. I love you. Please inform me of your condition. Have someone wire me at Arizona Hotel. Take care of yourself. Love, Gary."[13] After their "final" quarrel they continued to enjoy secret sexual relations for the next two years. Clara's extreme emotions released many of Cooper's inhibitions, alleviated his self-consciousness and made him more poised as a man and actor. She prepared the way for the Mexican spitfire Lupe Velez.

4

Lupe Velez and *The Virginian*

1928–1929

I

In the late 1920s Cooper made nine unmemorable silent films (eight of them for Paramount), playing a French Saharan soldier, doomed war pilot, English farmer, shipwrecked captain, RAF flier, Chesapeake Bay fisherman, American soldier, fur trapper and Viennese artist who is killed in a toboggan crash. *Beau Sabreur* (1928), the first of these films, was a sequel to Ronald Colman's *Beau Geste* and used desert footage left over from the earlier film. It was shot in thirty days on a budget of $396,000. Cooper's leading lady, Evelyn Brent, earned $8,000, he about $2,000. Though he was no Douglas Fairbanks, his athletic ability, "gorilla-like reach" and a French fencing coach made him an effective swordsman, and he rescued Brent from an evil Arab sheik.

Once again Cooper became the lover of an experienced and worldly actress, who gave him both guidance and status. Two years older than Cooper and (like Clara Bow) brought up in Brooklyn, Brent had been an extra in movies made in Fort Lee, New Jersey, played leads by 1916 and, while still in her teens, co-starred with John Barrymore. She often acted gun molls, and at the premiere of *Underworld* (1927), her film with von Sternberg, was asked to come onstage and greet the audience. She took Cooper along for reassurance, but found he was just as frightened as she was: "I made Gary Cooper go with me because I was scared to go alone. And Gary went down . . . and he was so embarrassed. He didn't know what he was gonna do, and we didn't have to do anything! Went out and took a bow and then talked to a lot of people backstage, and that was it."

The actress Louise Brooks didn't think Brent had much talent: "Evelyn's idea of acting was to march into a scene, spread her legs and stand flat-footed and read her lines with masculine defiance." She thought Brent's manner was warm and friendly, but later found "she was like Baked Alaska—very cold inside." Brent made a decorative appearance in silent pictures, graduated to sound and then disappeared into a swamp of mediocre movies.

A Hollywood photographer called Brent a snazzy but stupid woman. Cooper more gallantly told a reporter: "In Evelyn Brent I found the companionship of a woman who was wise and brilliant." Alice Cooper, delighted to have disentangled Gary from the vulgar Clara Bow, made a valedictory statement that sounded like a letter of recommendation. She politely praised Evelyn's thoughtfulness and refinement, and felt she had had a positive effect on her son: "Evelyn Brent has been good to Gary; she has given him poise, she has taught him to think, her influence has been excellent, and I will always regard her with affection and gratitude."[1]

Cooper's friend, the actor Joel McCrea, thought Brent was eager for marriage, but that Cooper had doubts and held back. She was more successful, wealthy and sophisticated than he was and (unlike Bow) made him feel like a hayseed, unable to deal with a lady of the world. Brent was fascinated by his hesitant and awkward shyness, which brought out her maternal instinct, but she couldn't penetrate his reserve and arouse his deepest feelings. She said: "I liked Gary very much. . . . He was a doll, he really was, a very nice guy. . . . The women were so crazy about him. More than any other man I knew. I think what attracted people was he had a great shyness, he kept pulling back, and it intrigued people. He really was a very quiet, quiet guy."

Cooper made four movies with Fay Wray (the heroine of *King Kong*), including *The Legion of the Condemned* and *The First Kiss*, both 1928. A well-established star who earned four times as much as Cooper, Wray thought him rugged and impressive, with lovely long eyelashes, smoky in color. He was attractive in all camera angles, mysteriously conveyed both gentleness and strength, and was personally refined and trustworthy. Dazzling together on screen, they were publicized by the studio as "Paramount's glorious young lovers." In their first scene together in *The Legion of the Condemned* she played a French spy and sat on his lap. Still in love with Evelyn Brent, he was stiff and impersonal when he kissed her, and there were no romantic sparks. In all the years she knew him,

Wray never had a real conversation with Cooper.

The First Kiss, their next picture, was filmed on location in Chesapeake Bay. The cast had an entire Pullman car to themselves and the director gave the porter a whole dollar to look after them, but Wray did not get to know Cooper any better during that long journey. His old Montana buddy Lane Chandler had a small part in the picture. When they stopped in Kansas City, the two men went to look at the town, missed the train and had to fly to the next stop to catch up with the group.

In St. Michaels, Maryland, they all lived in an old hotel, with a telephone booth out on the broad lawn. Cooper took possession of the phone and made a great many impassioned long-distance calls to Brent. Wray remembered an incident that illustrated Cooper's extraordinary remoteness. In one scene of the movie, Wray had to be rowed out on a dinghy to board Gary's fishing boat. As she stood up in the dinghy, she lost her balance, pushed against the boat and, fully made up and wearing an elegant gray silk suit, fell into the water. Her string of pearls disappeared into the sea and was retrieved by the oystermen. Throughout this dramatic incident Cooper—too shy to express concern and ask how she was—remained aloof and absolutely silent. "He didn't talk much," said Colleen Moore, his co-star in *Lilac Time* (also 1928). "He didn't have to. The small bit of talking he did do was about himself and Evelyn Brent. I found him bright, but no intellectual and not a great reader. He didn't have to be. Gary Cooper was a natural"—but still socially awkward and tongue-tied.[2]

Cooper attended Wray's small Maryland wedding after *The First Kiss* was completed. Finally, while making *One Sunday Afternoon* (1933), after five years of almost total silence, he suddenly exclaimed: "I imagine it would be wonderful to go to bed with you." Thoroughly shocked by this direct remark, Wray pretended she hadn't heard it. Until that time she had no idea what he was thinking or feeling, and thought of him as a brother. "Now that I knew," she said, "I didn't want to know."

II

Cooper's intense affair with Lupe Velez, begun while they were making *Wolf Song* in 1929, was the most important romance of his early life. Much more like Clara Bow than the elegant Evelyn Brent, she was born

María Guadalupe Velez de Villalobos in San Luis Potosí in 1908, the daughter of an opera singer and an army colonel who was killed in action. Only five feet tall and 110 pounds, she had a knockout 37"-26"-35" figure. Educated in a San Antonio convent, the wild, exuberant Mexican loved chihuahuas, boxing matches and stock car races. Nonconformist, vegetarian and a collector of perfumes, she spoke and gestured rapidly with her mouth, eyes, hands and shoulders, and could not remain still for more than a minute. Though her knowledge of English was limited, she had a quick wit. She said that her mother, greedy for Lupe's money, had carried her for nine months and now "wanted her to pay rent." During her movie career Lupe played all kinds of exotic women, from Chinese and Hindus to Eskimos and Indians, and "her cinematic blend of passionate nature, bustling activity, and mercurial reversals of mood established her as the foremost example of the generously endowed and correspondingly fickle female of her race."

Though Cooper was renting an apartment on Argyle Avenue, he spent most of his time in Lupe's Spanish-style house at 1826 Laurel Canyon Road, where he built a large cage for his pair of golden eagles. A contemporary observer described her chaotic household, with Gary sitting around "strumming a guitar and singing mournful cowboy songs while Lupe was welcoming eight accordion players, a couple of organ-grinder monkeys and an English butler, all of whom were playing or chattering or bowing at once without Gary's paying the least attention to them." When Lupe tripped over his long legs, she angrily turned around and bit them. Unable to open a window to kiss him good-bye, she tried to break the glass. Her boudoir—"theez eez where Lupe make loff"—had a vast low bed, was painted black, gold and silver, and looked like a set from an epic film.

Lupe, who liked to refer to herself in the third person, had an uninhibited, temperamental and explosive personality that was just the opposite of Cooper's silent reserve. "I theenk I keel my Garee," she exclaimed, "because he does not get angry when Lupe eez angry weeth heem." Boxing fans often saw "the tempestuous Lupe in the front row at the Hollywood Legion Stadium, pounding on the blood-stained canvas of the ring and screaming profane Mexican incantations at brownskinned countrymen who were failing to live up to her high standards of combat. . . . 'Hijo! Get up, you son-of-a-bitch.' " Lupe also had a crude but vivid sense of fun. One day she shocked the director William Wyler by asking, " 'Did you know Gary was an artist? . . . He can draw good pictures. Look.' And she pulls out one of her tits and there was a nose with two eyes and a mouth. He had drawn a face with lipstick around her nipple."[3]

When Cooper took his nephew, Howard, to visit Lupe, she was lavishly affectionate. She'd gush—"You're such a darling little boy. Look at those big blue eyes"—and would grab him, smother him with hugs and kisses, bring him milk and cookies, and make her dog do tricks for him. Delighted by Lupe's Latin love of children and by the contrast between the Coopers' English restraint and Lupe's overwhelming emotions, Howard saw "a new dimension in life" and thought: "I like this very much and don't want to leave." Ignoring the proprieties, after a few drinks she would climb onto Charles' lap, tug his ear and whisper: "You do loff me, jodge, don' you? You loff Lupe make whoopee!" As the judge, not used to such intimacy, purred with pleasure, Alice would do a slow burn.

If Lupe behaved this way with Howard and Charles, she must have gone wild with Cooper. Madly in love with him, she'd tell everyone: "Is he not beautiful? I have never seen anyone so beautiful as my Gary." They were a stunning couple as they toured the nightclubs, despite the fifteen-inch difference in height, and at the Trocadero, Scott Fitzgerald "smiled wryly when the cameramen pushed him aside because Lupe Velez had just come in with Gary Cooper."[4]

Equally adoring, Cooper praised Lupe's self-confidence, ability and talent as he had once praised Clara Bow: "The kid can act. She can step out and get a few thousand a week. I'm just a type." They shared a passion for primitive, elemental things, like the golden eagles, and he was powerfully attracted to the woman who "flashed, stormed and sparkled." "I'm in love," he remarked to the ecstatic fan magazines, as he announced their formal engagement. "I'll never be any more in love as long as I live." Retrospectively he qualified this by stating: "I was in love with Miss Velez, or as much in love as one could get with a creature as elusive as quicksilver."[5]

Wolf Song, in which Lupe earned $14,000 and Cooper $2,750, was directed by Victor Fleming, who had replaced Cooper as Clara Bow's lover and had also had an affair with Lupe. Cooper, a fur trapper dressed in buckskin, falls in love with, kidnaps and marries Lola Salazar, a fiery Mexican girl (Lupe), despite the opposition of her tyrannical father. When he hears the wolf song, or call of the wild, he deserts his broken-hearted bride. But he finally returns, after being ambushed by some treacherous Indians, to her eager embrace.

In the course of their torrid screen romance Cooper (in a part-talkie version) sings "My Honey, Fare Thee Well." When Lupe's father threatens to shoot him if he approaches his daughter, Cooper's shy smile suggests he's going to seduce her. Fleming was ridiculed by one critic for prolonging a violent kiss until it became more absurd than passionate, but he was more discreet about Cooper's nude swimming scene, which was shot from very far away above the waist. This rare film shows Cooper, tanned and muscular, in profile and with tousled hair, sitting on a grassy bank with his back turned to the camera. Their real-life love affair received a huge publicity campaign, and their personal appearance in dozens of cities coincided with the opening of *Wolf Song* and helped make it a commercial success. Cooper told one journalist that their life together made the film seem more real: "The Depression hit pretty hard and people needed romance. Seeing us in love on the screen and then in person was proof that movies are not all make-believe."

The director Delmer Daves stressed the physical and emotional intensity of their all-consuming and ultimately hopeless love: "Lupe excited him. She was like a wild cat and he'd never met anybody like that before. She would scratch him and bite him and do strange things but he'd laugh. She'd hit him and he'd laugh. He'd think this was the funniest thing that ever happened to a man. It's like, well you know how you get a pet dog that leaps all over you, well, Lupe would leap all over him. She was a little wild one. But when he got over that affair I don't think he ever had another one of that kind. I think you have one Lupe in your life and then you move on to calmer seas."[6] Before Lupe, Cooper had always been embarrassed by love scenes, but his real-life lover released his inhibitions. As he began to let go, their sexual dynamism and passionate excitement exploded on the screen.

III

In *The Shopworn Angel* (1928) Cooper plays a boyish, idealistic soldier who falls in love with a showgirl before being shipped overseas to war. He had only seven lines in the wedding scene at the end of the mostly silent movie, but it was released for commercial reasons as a talkie. At the beginning of 1929, only about fifteen hundred theaters out of the twenty thousand in America were wired for sound, but the wildly popular talkies soon replaced the silent films. The studios were seriously concerned about which actors would succeed or fail in this revolutionary upheaval. Since everyone thought those who'd performed on stage had a much better chance, some stars, like Jean Arthur, went back east to take voice lessons from a coach. During this crisis studio executives took the opportunity to break contracts, slash salaries and tame their arrogant stars. Suddenly, the advent of sound forced many screen idols like Clara Bow and John Gilbert into obscurity—and paved the way for the rise of young stars like Gary Cooper. The new stars gradually bought the expensive estates of the old ones, and life went on almost as usual.

There was always a great deal of noise during the shooting of silent films. But after the shift from melodramatic action to explicit dialogue, the director called for quiet. As stillness settled over the set, everyone focused on the trembling actors, who had to speak with conviction. The slapstick, used to cue the soundtrack, was held in front of their noses, and its violent clack often blew the lines right out of their heads. The makers of silent pictures had wanted as much action and as little talk as possible. Then, quite suddenly, since they couldn't move the cumbersome camera or primitive microphone—which had to be close to the actors but out of camera range—they had to have as much talk and as little action as possible. George Cukor recalled his difficulties with the whirring gears of the early equipment: "The actors weren't trained, the places not equipped and the sound technicians had been radio operators on boats. So it was rather clumsy. And it was not flexible. . . . There was no camera movement at that time because the cameras were not silent. And they had these booths that were soundproofed. And then these cameras would go inside, so that the pictures lost a good deal of the flexibility that they had before."

When talking pictures came in, Cooper's naturally deep and clear, well-modulated and pleasantly drawling voice seemed perfectly consistent with the characters he played on screen: "His voice sounded tentative and unequivocal at the same time . . . [and he had] a paradoxical presence, heroic and uncertain, able to hold his own in the most awesome confrontations"—yet always vulnerable. As other actors struggled to survive, he effortlessly made the transition from silents to sound. Combining "the *soft* masculinity of the 'pretty boy' and the *hard* masculinity, of the 'he-man' " he was seen as the heir of both the romantic Rudolph Valentino and the rugged cowboy William S. Hart.[7] The two aspects of Cooper's screen image were popularized by Irving Berlin and by Norman Rockwell. In his song "Puttin' on the Ritz" (1930),

Berlin wrote of being attired like a million-dollar trooper and attempting to resemble Gary Cooper. On a *Saturday Evening Post* cover of May 24, 1930 Rockwell depicted Cooper in profile, wearing an elaborate cowboy rig—decorated vest, wide chaps, boots and spurs, huge gun and outsize hat—sitting on a saddle and having his face made up.

The Virginian, based on the 1902 novel by Owen Wister that had sold a phenomenal 1.6 million copies, was the first major sound film ever shot outdoors. The actors, moving to Sonora in the High Sierras of California, were followed by a snaky caravan of trucks, tractors, cranes, sound equipment and electrical generators for the lights. The movie was shot in only twenty-four days in May and June 1929 on a budget of $415,000. The director Victor Fleming got $75,000, the villain Walter Huston $20,000, Richard Arlen and Cooper (who had caught up to his old buddy since *Wings*) about $3,400 each. Cooper liked to make Westerns, which allowed him to wear comfortable clothes, ride horseback and get plenty of outdoor exercise, and called this his favorite film. Playing a rugged man of the west finally freed him from the jazz-era label (associated with Clara Bow) of "the It boy."

At the start of the film, Arlen remembered, Cooper had difficulty concentrating on his part, and the sudden appearance of Lupe Velez intensified the problem: "We began shooting and at the end of three days we only had about forty seconds of Coop on film. He just couldn't remember his lines, and he spoiled take after take. He was going with Lupe Velez at the time, and Lupe showed up on location and distracted Coop even more. But the worst part of it was that Lupe [like Clara Bow] had been the girlfriend of Vic Fleming, who was the director." Nevertheless Arlen considered the dramatic scene, in which Cooper has to hang him for stealing cattle, a triumph: "Trying to react as his best friend gets a rope around his neck and remembering lines wasn't easy for him. He kept flubbing dialogue. I came up with the idea of jotting his lines on my chaps because my back was to the camera. It worked. There was some concern, too, that Walter Huston might steal the picture, but, as usual, Coop underplayed. He never tried to shout, snarl, or rush. He didn't have to."

The Virginian was one of the first sound pictures to define the western hero's code of honor. In the old west, where life was cheap and death came suddenly, the hero never shoots anyone in the back. And—though in reality most unmarried women in frontier towns made their living as barmaids or prostitutes—he never makes improper approaches to the heroine. The classic themes of the film were the conflict of good and evil, the struggle for law and order on the wild frontier, the clash between the westerner's and the easterner's code of behavior, and the test of skill and courage in the final confrontation.

The leisurely pace of *The Virginian*, which slowly builds to a crisis, provides a social context for the code. Cooper's opening fight with Walter Huston (Trampas) over a Mexican girl in a bar establishes his character with two of the most famous lines in cowboy movies. Huston first exclaims: "This town ain't big enough for both of us!" And when he calls Cooper "you long-legged son of a . . .," his rival coolly responds: "If you wanna call me that, *smile!*" "With a gun against my belly," Huston says, "I always smile"—and flashes his unusually large white teeth.

After Cooper rescues the new schoolmarm from a tame steer, we see the first emergence of his classic screen image: "the elegant, lean, amusingly silent romantic loner of his early Western and aviation films." Beanpole-thin, narrow-waisted and with a loose-limbed walk, he stoops over the girl, speaks slowly and seems thoughtful. Shy but self-assured, he radiates boyish charm. He looks down at his nails when formally introduced to the girl, then clasps his hands and licks his lips before he talks to her.

Richard Arlen, by contrast, joins Huston's gang, helps steal two hundred cattle and takes them across a river. Surprising the rustlers at night, Cooper captures Arlen as Huston escapes from the posse and agonizes about the inevitable execution of his friend. When the devoted schoolmarm learns that Arlen has been hanged, she's shocked by the rough frontier justice, but an old lady tells her she must face reality in the west.

In a dramatic climax that foreshadows *High Noon*, Cooper plans to marry the girl just before his showdown with Huston, who gives him "till sundown to get out of town." Trying to save him, she begs him not to fight and urges him to run away. But he insists: "It's somethin' nobody else can do for me. . . . I've just got to stay." He says that if he doesn't face the enemy now, "there will be no tomorrow for you and me"—and watches what may well be his last sunset. As the townspeople rush away and leave the streets empty, Cooper walks slowly down the wooden sidewalk. Prowling through the saloon and using Arlen's gun to restore order to a violent world, he draws fast and kills Huston.

The Virginian helped establish the conventions of the Western movie that have lasted from the 1920s to the present time. The hero is always tall, handsome and shy; the villain ugly, rough and dressed in black; the schoolmarm and wife-to-be sexually pure and morally innocent. The rustlers play poker, drink whiskey and flirt with the Mexican girls in the bar. Virtue always triumphs in the final shootout. The cattle drive, the comic christening, the tragic friendship with Arlen, the violent "walk-down" with Huston, the theme of rough justice, the insoluble conflict between the wife's values and the husband's code—all these elements still make *The Virginian*, after seventy years, a very good film. As Robert Warshow wrote in his famous essay on the Western: "Having chosen to sacrifice his friend to the higher demands of the 'code'—the only choice worthy of him as even the friend understands—he is none the less stained by the killing, but what is needed now to set accounts straight is not his death but the death of the villain Trampas, the leader of the cattle thieves, who had escaped the posse and abandoned the Virginian's friend to his fate."[8] The romantic image of the cowboy as the embodiment of male freedom, courage and honor was created by men who had lived a rugged life in the west: in words by Teddy Roosevelt and Owen Wister, in art by Frederic Remington and Charles Russell, and in film, preeminently, by Gary Cooper.

5

The Man in Morocco

1930–1931

I

As Cooper's career accelerated, his life became exhausting and complicated. Nothing in his background had prepared him for the emotional and physical demands now made upon him. Kept constantly at work by the studio, he had several years of intensive on-the-job training. He had no formal tuition, in school or on stage, but learned acting under the most competitive circumstances from some of the best people in the business. He was also in demand socially and had a series of entangling affairs. Naturally reserved, introspective and self-contained, he loved physical activity, the outdoors and solitude, and eventually reconciled this essentially private character with the peculiarly public life of a famous Hollywood actor. He became a sophisticated man of the world who managed to preserve his fundamental simplicity and integrity. Describing the kind of man he was, his character and interests, helps explain his attitude toward his work and his fame.

Cooper's long silences, meager utterance and slow speech, his innate modesty, and lack of egoism—all in the western manner—gave the talkative, self-promoting Hollywood types the misleading impression that he was beautiful but dumb. The gossip columnist Sheilah Graham repeated a perhaps apocryphal anecdote that contributed to Cooper's taciturn image: "Randy Scott tells the story of when he called on Gary with his new car and said, 'Let's go for a drive.' They drove around for an hour without speaking a word. On the way back a bird flew overhead. Coop put his arms and hands into the shape of a rifle, said, 'bang,' and that was it." Cooper defended himself against this sort of story by asserting: "If others have more interesting things to say than I have, I keep quiet."

The actress Patricia Neal, who knew him well, agreed with Colleen Moore that though he was not talkative and intellectual, he was intelligent. Fred Zinnemann, an extremely cultured director, said Cooper was more interested in action than in words. But, he added, Cooper was no rough diamond; he had great charm and beautiful manners, and would soon be courted by the highest ranks of international society. Walter Brennan, a personal friend who often played his crony in films, rejected the conventional image and insisted that Cooper talked enthusiastically about topics that appealed to him: "Mention any subject that might interest any adult, well-educated he-man, and you can have a conversation with Cooper. Mention horses or cattle or guns, and he'll out-talk *you*."[1] Later on a New York *Post* journalist and Barnaby Conrad, the American bullfighter and author, both found him articulate and well informed. To them he talked freely about finance, the stock market, film production, sports cars and modern art.

An effective comedian in his Lubitsch films of the 1930s, Cooper also had a lively sense of humor off screen. While fixing a Bloody Mary for his mother, he put tomato juice in a huge hypodermic syringe and terrified her by slowly drawing the "blood" from his arm. When his friend the tennis champion Sidney Wood went into the laundry business, Cooper once joined him in the company truck. Loving jokes and game for anything, he enjoyed being an ordinary guy for an afternoon and delivered the laundry in person to astonished customers.

Though once close to his brother, Arthur, Cooper grew apart from him after their boyhood years in England were over. A conventional banker, who was not "rooted in the earth" and did not share his passion for outdoor life, Arthur found his modest achievements were quickly eclipsed by his brother's universal fame. Though Gary was both liked and respected by a wide circle of acquaintances, he didn't confide in anyone. He was a hard man to get close to, worked out his own problems and liked to be alone. Just as he preferred to keep his own counsel and remain independent, so—as he became quite wealthy—he was always careful about money and not overgenerous when it came to helping others. As Slim Talbot remarked, with a tinge of bitterness and envy, "Cooper wasn't a person to go out of his way to do anything for anybody out of pure love for his fellow man."[2]

Cooper had an English sense of propriety in matters of work and refused to be pushy about his career. After he'd become a superstar and reached an exalted position in the studio, he never (except for Josef von Sternberg) "refused to work with a director, a leading lady or a cameraman, never complained about billing and never asked for special favors"–for himself or anyone else. Joel McCrea agreed that Cooper got along well with everyone, including the director whose love life had been so entangled with his own, but who shared his interest in hunting and fast cars: "Coop never fought, he never got mad, he never told anybody off that I know of; everybody that worked with him liked him, particularly a guy like Vic Fleming; Coop loved him. He did *The Virginian* with him and he was excellent. He liked Henry Hathaway; he liked Lubitsch."

Cooper's even temper made him an agreeable companion. He refused to fight with Lupe and was amused when she attacked him. He rarely cursed but would say, when really angry, "goddamn bastard." Pompous and boring people he quaintly called "Lord and Lady fuzzy nuts." The director Stuart Heisler, in a self-serving anecdote, recalls witnessing an eruption of anger: "Coop had a temper that no one likes to discuss. I saw him rip into everyone on the movie set once and he tried it on me. I told him where he could shove it and he apologized." But such lapses were rare indeed. He was sufficiently relaxed while making a film to stretch out on the floor or under a tree, often with his head on a saddle, and nap between takes. When summoned from sleep to camera, he'd effortlessly resume his role.

In the early years of his career Cooper felt the strain of his ever-increasing fame. As acquaintances and fans, for whom he became a vicarious lover, made greater and greater demands on him, his privacy disappeared under the glare of publicity. He became reserved, guarded and tired, but never short-tempered and reclusive. He usually enjoyed being a famous figure, though it made his love life public knowledge, and got a kick out of all the attention, flattery, applause and recognition. He also responded warmly to individual fans. When some San Diego sailors bought a map of the stars' houses, parked in his driveway and drifted into the garden, he served them beer around the pool and talked to them for hours. The novelist Jessamyn West, a Hollywood outsider, observed his inner resources and natural behavior, amid rapturous and fawning devotion, during a dinner party given by the director William Wyler: "He was aware of course, of this focusing of attention. But his very lack of innocence permitted him to be himself. And he had a self to be. That was the important and comfortable thing about Mr. Cooper. Somehow the years of adulation, the cameras, the women's voices scarcely able to convey the weight of admiration they felt without breaking, had not engulfed him."[3] As Tyrone Power's wife Annabella noted, Cooper was a charming and modest person who behaved like an ordinary man. He never revealed the egoism one would expect from a handsome and world-famous film star.

Cooper's humility was genuine, yet with the press and in social gatherings he cultivated an aura of modesty to protect himself from the pervasive envy of Hollywood. Like all stars, he knew that his position was always precarious—subject to age, health, luck and fashion, to the power of the studio and whims of the public. One of his favorite homespun expressions reflected the uncertainty of his professional life: "There ain't never a horse that couldn't be rode, there ain't never a rider that couldn't be throwed."

In one outspoken interview he condemned the self-importance and narcissism of movie stars who forgot their humble origins and were ungrateful to those who had helped their careers: "I don't like to see exaggerated airs and exploding egos in people who are already established. . . . No player ever rises to prominence solely on his or her extraordinary talent. Players are moulded by forces other than themselves. They should remember this . . . and at least twice a week drop down on their knees and thank Providence for elevating them from cow ranches, dimestore ribbon counters and bookkeeping desks." Robert Taylor, his hunting companion, said everyone liked Cooper because he had no phoniness or pose, was honest and absolutely straight. He had a presence: graceful, calm, undisturbed, even wise. The European director Otto Preminger—seeing through the screen persona of naive hick and wooden hero—called him "a charming, witty, intelligent and entertaining companion, appreciated by men and adored by women."[4]

II

In the days when actors constantly smoked on screen to emphasize their toughness or sophistication, Cooper was thoroughly addicted. He would try to stop smoking and quit for a month or two, but could never completely give it up. He'd have a Scotch when he came home from the studio and, though he had a wine cellar, rarely drank wine with dinner. But he knew about wine, and when he lunched with Hedda Hopper at the studio's expense, he ordered Chambertin-Clos de Bèze, the aristocrat of French Burgundies. Since Cooper was a sober fellow, everyone tried to get him loaded. Slim Talbot had been to several all-night parties with him, but had never seen him really drunk.

Cooper's appetite was prodigious, but no matter how much he ate, he always remained thin. During his early days in Hollywood, working at odd jobs and living with his parents, he said, with some comic exaggeration, that his "starvation diet at the time ran to no less than a dozen eggs a day, a couple of loaves of bread, a platter of bacon, and just enough pork chops between meals to keep me going until I got home for supper." His specialty on hunting trips was gargantuan: wild duck covered with bacon strips, enhanced by four eggs and steak. He could, like a growing boy, eat a whole cherry pie and drink a quart of milk for lunch. But when he met the journalist Gladys Hall at a fashionable Hollywood restaurant, he dined more delicately on pork sausages and green salad. Asked his favorite recipe for a book about what actors eat, he gave one of Lupe's hot Mexican dishes. After his first adult trip to Europe in 1931, he developed a taste for French cooking and impressed one reporter by telling him about the finest little restaurants in Paris, how to prepare his favorite Continental dishes and the best way to eat baby lobsters.

Cooper had natural good taste, always wore elegant clothes and was one of the best-dressed actors in Hollywood. He inspired fashion stories in *Flair*, *Women's Wear Daily*, *Esquire* and *Movietime*, and if he hadn't been a movie star, he could have had a great career as a model. In 1932 he went to Aintree, near Liverpool, for the Grand National Steeplechase wearing a stylishly cut overcoat, dashing scarf and derby hat. In London he bought handmade clothes at the finest shops: shoes at John Lobb's, shirts at Turnbull and Asser, hats at James Lock's, suits on Savile Row. When he told an aristocratic friend about his tailor and she said, "What do you know about it?" he confidently replied: "I went to this tailor when I was a schoolboy in England."

The English fashion photographer Cecil Beaton, who had a session with him at the Paramount studio in December 1929, carefully noted his popularity with the technicians, the boyish Montanan beneath the elegant outfit (Cooper suggested they go off and take some shots at tin cans) and his desire to escape the overwhelming pressure of work:

He was absolutely charming, very good looking with black eyelashes as thick on the lower lid as on the upper. Very tall, a good figure and such a good sort that he made one feel such a swine. He was on such good terms with everyone. The electrician offered him a cigar. "Are they all right?"—"Well they should be. The three cost 25 cents": and so Gary lit up and the cigar did not explode. He was extremely smartly dressed with a brown hat to match his suit and gloves, very elaborate gloves with green spots in the lining. He is just a very charming cowboy and it was amusing to see him so smartly turned out. His success is stupendous. He is about the most popular actor on the screen and is paid fabulous sums. It is an extraordinary phenomenon this sudden leaping to fame. He has only been in the business three years and now it saps him entirely. He longs to get away, but can't—he can't spend his money even.[5]

In a hostile interview of 1931 Cooper is supposed to have said, "I haven't read half a dozen books in my life," a remark that was often repeated. But he had gone to a strict English school, been taught in Montana by the demanding Ida Davis and had (unlike most movie stars) studied Greek and completed two years of college. He preferred to walk, ride, play sports or do "something vital" than sit motionless for hours and read. But when the press portrayed him, along with Richard Arlen and Buddy Rogers, as one of the Three Musketeers, he listed his favorite author as Alexander Dumas. He read widely on American Indians and the history of the old West. Inspired by Charles Russell's painting in Helena and intrigued by the fact that the northwest explorers had passed near his ranch, he was particularly interested in the journals of Lewis and Clark. Always on the lookout for books that would make good films, he sent Fred Zinnemann Kathryn Hulme's *A Nun's Story*, which was made with Audrey Hepburn in 1959.

Cooper blew the harmonica and strummed the guitar; played backgammon and bridge; grew corn and avocados on the Encino ranch he bought in the early 1930s and loved to work with his tractor in the garden. Fond of dogs, at various times he owned boxers, Dobermans and Great Danes. He and his wife also raised Sealyhams, showed dogs on the circuit and bred a champion that appeared with him in 1936 on the cover of *Western Kennel World*. He worked out regularly with a punching bag and weights, sparred with a boxing coach and went to the fights with Lupe and, later on, with his family and his friend Paul Shields. Despite problems with his stiff hip, he was keenly interested in sports and (with the enthusiastic participation of his wife) kept in shape with hiking and riding, tennis and golf, archery and skiing, trout fishing and spear fishing, swimming and scuba diving.

His greatest passions were cars, guns and hunting, and the male camaraderie that went with them. He liked driving fast cars and talking about
them. Though he was never reckless, his lust for speed sometimes made
his girlfriends nervous and his family was "not too thrilled by his wild
side." His favorites were the cars that didn't go into high gear until they
reached a hundred miles an hour. He also knew how cars worked and
how to repair them, and liked to tinker in the electrical shop at the
studio. He set up a mechanic's bench in his garage, where he souped up
a beat-up brown Plymouth. After installing bucket seats, police brakes
and a Chrysler engine, he'd accept challenges to drag race and suddenly
speed away from astonished rivals.

In college he had a Harley-Davidson motorcycle and was always
roaring around at high speeds. In 1927 he bought a jazzy red Chrysler
roadster which, racing by, looked like a streak of blood. When he first
arrived from Montana, he wanted to look like a cowboy. But when he
became a leading man, he "went the whole route and bought the most
expensive automobile made, a [1930] Duesenberg, with a wardrobe to
match." The gleaming, high-grilled "Yellow Peril," primrose yellow
trimmed with parkway green, was as long, lean and elegant as Cooper
himself. His proudest possession had two and a half times more horse-
power than the most expensive Packard and a hundred more horses than
the rival Cadillac V-16. "The instrument panel provided a complete
range of information, some of which was previously encountered only
in aircraft. Besides the 150 mph speedometer and 5,000 rpm
tachometer there were, among other niceties, a split second chrono-
graph, an altimeter, brake pressure gauge and service warning lights."
The Duesenberg was also owned by such luminaries as Greta Garbo,
Tyrone Power, Mayor Jimmy Walker of New York, William Randolph
Hearst, the Nizam of Hyderabad, Prince Nicholas of Romania and King
Alfonso of Spain. Clark Gable, who had a sexual and professional rivalry
with Cooper, insisted that his custom-built Duesenberg be one foot
longer than Gary's. Cooper road-tested the car in the sand flats of the
Mojave Desert and took Arthur on a 125-mile-per-hour drive on
Olympic Boulevard to show him "how fast this baby will go." In Clifford
Odets' play, *Golden Boy* (1937), a character sees an expensive sports car
speed by. Expressing both admiration and envy, he remarks: "Gary
Cooper's got the kind I want. I saw it in the paper, but it costs too
much—fourteen thousand."[6] Later on he owned a Bentley and had a
Mercedes built to his own specifications. When he picked it up at the

factory in Stuttgart, paying with marks from a blocked account, he crawled under the car and talked about its fine points with the mechanics.

A year after the war broke out in Europe, Cooper rejected his expensive existence, felt he had to live a simpler life and criticized his own motives for buying luxurious cars: "When I first came to Hollywood I used to dream, Boy, if I had money I'd have the hell-firedest automobile ever assembled! I had one, I had two. I flashed around. In a lot of ways. For a time. Then I got to wondering why I wanted those sensational cars. . . . It gave me a feeling of superiority to pull up beside some other fellow's car in my de luxe job."

The mechanical side of Cooper's life was balanced by a love of nature and the outdoors. In July 1930, just after his dude ranch opened, he told a fan that "I spent part of my boyhood on a ranch and take every opportunity now to go back for a visit. I am fond of outdoor life and I usually turn to sports for diversion. My hobbies are riding, fishing, and hunting." On location, Slim Talbot would bring along a hand trap and clay targets, and Cooper would blast away at them during the long waits between takes. He was an expert taxidermist, and shot Canadian geese, pheasant, deer, elk and bear. His favorite sport was hunting bobcats in the Malibu hills with a .22 pistol.

He belonged to the Pin Tail Duck Club in Bakersfield, which owned a big section of flooded marshland. To get an early start, he'd drive up the night before and stay in a seedy motel (the only one in town). Before dawn the next morning, he'd put on high rubber boots and row out with his dogs to the blind, a little box big enough for two or three men. Sitting on a stool next to his lunch, decoys, shells and guns, he'd shoot wild birds as they whirred in formation right over the wetlands. When a man from the Howard Hughes Company invited him to fly to Texas in a converted B-25 for a turkey shoot, he jumped at the offer. He spent many hours cleaning and repairing his pistols, rifles and shotguns in the room where he kept the weapons. One day, in his Brentwood house, he got out a big Civil War rifle to show Van Johnson's wife. Despite her fearful warning, he pointed it at her. The gun suddenly went off, narrowly missing her and chipping the stone fireplace. Having broken the cardinal rule by forgetting to check and empty the rifle, the experienced gunman, absolutely stunned, turned white and muttered a feeble apology. Cooper had many interests and sometimes, after a long workday, would think about retiring and say, "If I were a rich man I would do nothing but play golf and hunt for the rest of my life." Then, on reflection, he'd realize that without work he'd "go nuts."[7]

III

Just as *High Noon* is the greatest film of Cooper's later career, so *Morocco* is the pinnacle of his early work. Based on a popular French novel named after the heroine, Amy Jolly, it was rapidly shot in twenty-seven days during July and August 1930. Marlene Dietrich was paid $5,625 and Cooper got a thousand more; Jules Furthman earned $10,000 for the script and Josef von Sternberg $33,000 for directing. Ideal for the part, Cooper had played a legionnaire in *Beau Sabreur* and had worked with von Sternberg when he'd redirected several scenes in *Children of Divorce*. Languid and romantic, Cooper was lit and photographed as if he were a beautiful woman. His graceful and prominent legs, draped over a chair in the cabaret, are almost as impressive as Dietrich's.

She had just made the sensational *Blue Angel* in Berlin with von Sternberg, her discoverer, creator and lover, who had brought her to America and to Paramount. "She was lonely and sad," Cooper told the press; "she felt friendless, and was painfully conscious of the thousands of miles that divided her from her country, and the daughter to whom she is so deeply devoted." Cooper did everything he could to comfort her, and Dietrich, in her obsessive way, baked cakes for him and tidied up his dressing room. In a reassuring letter to her husband, she said that Lupe, who guarded Cooper jealously, came close to fornicating with him on the set: "Gary Cooper is pleasant and good-looking. The newspapers have said that Lupe Velez (his girlfriend) has threatened to scratch my eyes out if I come near him. How can I? She sits on his lap between scenes. I don't go close enough, God knows, to see what they're doing, but it looks like they are doing something that is usually done in private." Lupe also teased Cooper at parties by doing a maliciously amusing impersonation of Dietrich.

As soon as Lupe relaxed her vigilance, Cooper started doing things in private with Dietrich, who (like Lupe) had a strong sexual appetite and was notorious for sleeping around. Steven Bach wrote in his perceptive biography that the casting of Gary Cooper "had chemistry. It was the first pitting of Marlene's exoticism against the rough-hewn, down-to-earth maleness of an American type who cut her down to size and kept her ambiguity in line. Sexual tension leaped from Dietrich to Cooper with their first glances at each other and then right off the screen." With Dietrich as with Bow, their real life affair ignited their on screen performance. John Wayne, who had an affair with Dietrich in the early 1940s, found her a "torrid lover": eager, responsive, voracious and willing to try anything. After her passion for Cooper had subsided and both had moved on to other lovers, she rather sourly dismissed him as a beautiful hunk who couldn't act: "Cooper was neither intelligent nor cultured. Just like the other actors, he was chosen for his physique which, after all, was more important than an active brain. . . . Those long drinks of water, like Cooper and Wayne, they are all alike. All they do is clink their spurs, mumble 'Howdy, Ma'am,' and fuck their horses."[8] They also fucked Dietrich and left her, which provoked her caustic comments.

Cooper's affair with Dietrich exacerbated his conflict with the tyrannical director. Born plain Jonas Sternberg in Vienna in 1894 (he invented the "von" to enhance his status in Hollywood), he was short, unattractive, obsessed with Dietrich and jealous of Cooper—then at the peak of his physical beauty. In *Morocco* von Sternberg saw and portrayed himself as the wealthy and elegant expatriate La Bessière (Adolphe Menjou), who becomes engaged to Amy (Dietrich) but loses her to Tom (Cooper). Dietrich said von Sternberg "couldn't stand it if I looked up at any man in a movie—he always staged it so that they were looking up at me. It would infuriate him—and Cooper was very tall. And you know, Jo was not. I was stupid—I didn't understand it then—that kind of jealousy."

Dietrich adored and trusted von Sternberg, who gave the actors only a few pages of dialogue at a time instead of the entire script. He was rough, even cruel to her, but she was willing to tolerate methods that produced such brilliant results. In the scene when Tom plans to desert the Foreign Legion and Amy impulsively agrees to run off with him on a freighter bound for Europe, a buzzer announces that it's time for her act to go on. She walks to her dressing room door, turns, looks back at Tom and says: "I'll be back. Wait for me." Dietrich recalled that "von Sternberg said, 'Walk to the door, turn, count to ten, say your line and leave.' So I did and he got very angry. 'If you're so stupid that you can't count slowly, then count to twenty-five.' And we did it again. I think we did it forty times, until finally I was counting probably to fifty. And I didn't know why. I was annoyed. But at the premiere of *Morocco* . . . when the moment came and I paused and then said, 'Wait for me,' the audience burst into applause. Von Sternberg knew they were waiting for this—and he made them wait and they loved it."

Cooper also recognized von Sternberg's genius. But more confident of his status at Paramount, he was not willing to put up with arrogance, rudeness and bullying. In his misleadingly favorable "Foreword" to von Sternberg's autobiography, *Fun in a Chinese Laundry* (1965), cobbled together from fan magazines after Cooper's death, he noted that after *The Virginian he* was the major star. Since *The Blue Angel* was not released in America till after *Morocco*, Cooper believed that he made Dietrich "popular by association."

William Powell, who appeared in *The Last Command* (1928), had warned him that von Sternberg was callous, disdainful and unable to motivate an actor. The director thought the actors were puppets and he was the puller of strings, but he did allow them to diverge from the script and was more interested in the sense and the feeling than the literal words. "I got along with von Sternberg reasonably well," Cooper politely wrote, "as all his direction and his instructions were given to Marlene, and the rest of us were left more or less to do as well as we could. I cannot remember that he ever told me how to play a scene."

The truth was much more dramatic—and violent. Jules Furthman recalled that Cooper, in a rare outburst, became infuriated, nearly throttled the director and then treated him to a patriotic speech:

He must have thought Joe barking in German was the height of arrogance. . . . Coop gets up and takes a few steps over towards Joe. I think Joe may have told him to sit back down, and said it in English, but Coop went right toward him and then picked him up, just grabbed him around the neck by the coat and lifted him. Joe's no more than about five-four. Coop is strangling him. Then he puts him down on his feet but keeps the hold on his shoulders and starts to shake Joe back and forth, really jostling him. All the color has gone from Joe's face—he's in shock, the only time I ever saw him that way. Coop is still holding him when he says, "You god-damned kraut, if you expect to work in this country you'd better get on to the language we use here."

Later von Sternberg graciously told Cooper that he was one of the best actors he had ever worked with because he "could stand still and look interesting." But when Cooper refused to work with him on another Dietrich picture, the director retaliated by claiming in his book that his

assistants had to clown and make comic grimaces to help Cooper overcome his shyness. He added, rather absurdly, that the studio executives
thought Cooper was "harmless enough not to injure the film."

In *Morocco* the sets, costumes, lighting, music and dance, even the call
to prayer from the minaret, all create an evocative oriental atmosphere.
It opens with a map of the country and with an Arab struggling with a
donkey as a troop of legionnaires march through the dusty streets. When
Cooper signals to an Arab woman, who drops her veil, his sergeant asks,
"what are you doing with those fingers?" and he suggestively replies:
"Nothing—yet." In the original, uncut script, Dietrich flirtatiously sings,
"I love a man who takes things / Into his hands."

A small steamer then approaches Mogador on the Atlantic coast.
"Leaning on the rail," von Sternberg wrote, "peering into the foggy night
that shrouds her destination, is a mysterious woman, her forlorn counte-
nance made luminous by a beam of light."[9] Menjou introduces himself by
assisting Dietrich (who also wears a veil) when she accidentally spills the
contents of her suitcase. Asking the ship's captain about her, he's told:
"We call them 'suicide passengers'—one-way tickets. They never
return"—and she never does.

Dressed in men's formal clothes, with white tie and top hat, Dietrich
sings with a mixture of intimacy and disdain to a louche audience in a
Moorish café. Cooper—wearing a soft white képi and white trousers,
high boots and dark belted tunic adorned with a campaign medal—
languidly blows smoke from his nose and mouth. But he perks up when
she appears on stage. The cross-dressed Dietrich (who in real life had love
affairs with both men and women) arouses Cooper's interest by boldly
kissing the lips of a woman, who then hides her face behind a fan. She
takes the woman's flower and offers it to Cooper. He slaps the hand of a
Spanish lady who tries to snatch it and places it, like a girl, behind his ear.
The sexual ambiguity of their roles as the camera lingers deliciously on
their faces, Dietrich's bold pursuit and Cooper's sly response, is both
shocking and exciting.

For her next song the bare-legged Dietrich, as if blown in from the
beach, wears a more revealing camisole, trimmed with a feather boa.
Watching her intently, Cooper shifts in his seat and smells the flower she's
given him. As she approaches with the apples she's selling at outrageous
prices (two weeks' pay), he shifts his képi to a jaunty angle to match the
on stage tilt of her top hat. In a similar way, she later imitates his abbre-
viated two-finger, two-stroke salute. Cooper, before a fascinated

audience, then takes part in her performance. Munching his apple, he pulls her down to him, and she slips him the key to her dressing room. The censorship office found the key episode "objectionable not only in itself but also because among men who accept keys are husbands whose wives are present in the Café," but the studio managed to retain this scene.

Both actors move and talk slowly to suggest the intense heat. There's a great deal of curling smoke, swishing fans, sidelong glances, drugged stares and reflecting mirrors. Stopping to enter her room, he says, "you can smell the desert tonight." He can also smell her, and establishes the crucial conflict between freedom and love, cynical sophistication and romantic longing. Once in the room, he plays with her dolls and also uses a fan to shield their first kiss from the camera. When she poignantly remarks, "There's a Foreign Legion of women, too. But we have no uniforms—no flags—and no medals when we are brave. . . . No wound stripes—when we are hurt," she reveals that she too has been wounded by love. Their dreamy, vulnerable and melancholy eyes belie their world-weary expressions and restrained amusement when they speak their lines. She doesn't believe he can restore her faith in men and tells him to leave because she's beginning to like him.

Meanwhile, Dietrich's being courted by Menjou, who gives her an expensive bracelet. She instinctively questions his motives by calling him (with a charming accent) "a stwange man" and by stating that "every time a man has helped me, there has been a price. What's yours?"[10] But he loves her and will do anything to make her happy: "He is the ideal victim, always indulgent, always passionate, always dignified, always manly enough to be hurt afresh each time." Cooper asks her to join him when he deserts, and she agrees. But when he sees her luxurious bracelet, he changes his mind, writes his farewell with lipstick on her mirror and gives her up to Menjou.

His commander, whose wife is Cooper's lover, sends him away on a suicidal mission. Cooper nonchalantly dismisses the Moorish enemy by asserting: "Those walking bed sheets can't shoot straight." The departure of the soldiers, as in an opera, reprises their entrance at the beginning. As Cooper goes off to the desert, Dietrich goes off to Menjou. But during the formal engagement dinner in his palatial residence, she hears the drums of the returning soldiers and spills the pearls of her necklace as she had once spilled the contents of her suitcase. Believing that Cooper's wounded, she frantically searches for him with the aid of the self-sacrificing Menjou.

Cooper could easily have deserted as planned, but doubt and delay intensify their passion and desire for freedom. Cooper is more constrained, Dietrich more impulsive. He hesitates, commits himself, then changes his mind. But she immediately agrees to rush off with him when he deserts. She abandons her engagement dinner to search for him in the wilds, and gives up her country, career and the promise of fabulous wealth. Appearing out of the fog, she finally vanishes into the sand.

As Cooper marches off without her, Dietrich, dressed for a wedding journey rather than desert expedition, carries her flame into the wasteland. Like a fevered animal in a Saharan love dance, she follows some goats up a sand dune and disappears over the horizon to join the "Foreign Legion of women." "Jo *made* me walk after the camp followers," she wrote, "—into the desert, in my *high-heeled shoes!* We had such a fight about that. Finally, he let me take those stupid shoes off, halfway through the shot. Of course, the burning sand scorched the soles of my feet, but in the film, *first* with the shoes on looks right. He knew. He saw that in his mind's eye, and now everyone loves it."

Furthman's brilliant script (with its fog, fans, smoke, veils, shadows and pearls), von Sternberg's erotic direction, Dietrich's European charm and the absurd but magnificently romantic finale made *Morocco* Cooper's most decadent and sophisticated film. The Foreign Legion evoked the exotic ambience of *Beau Geste*, and the escape to the isolation of the desert was intensely romantic. *Morocco* was conceived by von Sternberg as a vehicle for Dietrich, and the sexually charged songs showed off her talent as a cabaret singer. The film swirls with an hypnotic sexual undercurrent as the arrogant and adored Dietrich is humbled by love. Cooper's greatest leading lady brought out an aspect of his character that had never been seen before. He's utterly convincing as the remote but sensual man for whom this adventuress would willingly give up her newfound luxuries. *Morocco* changed his screen image from the one dimensional ideal hero of *The Virginian* into a more complex, introspective character who carelessly dallies with Arab, Spanish and French women until he too is finally overcome by love. As Richard Watts wrote in the New York *Herald Tribune*, "The understandably popular Gary Cooper, who underacts more completely than any other player within memory, never has been as effective and certainly never as expert an actor as he is in the role of the hero."[11]

IV

No actor on a long-term studio contract could hope to sustain the level of an extraordinary film like *Morocco*. Cooper's next project for Paramount was a lively but run-of-the-range Zane Grey Western, *Fighting Caravans* (1931). He earned $8,000, and the strongly accented French actress Lili Damita, who would marry Errol Flynn in 1935, got four times as much. As in *Wolf Song*, the main conflict is between the freedom of the wilderness and the bondage of love. Persuaded that she's saving his life, Damita agrees to pose as his wife and then discovers she's been duped. When Cooper says, "Seein' we're 'married,' we ought to get better acquainted," she becomes indignant. Meanwhile, the lively action balances the sentimental romance. As their wagon train moves, during the Civil War, through the snow and mountains of the unprotected west, the simple-minded Indians want to buy a fire engine to make firewater. Frustrated and angry, they attack the wagons at a river crossing, but a powder explosion enables the whites to escape. When they reach California to keep the hard-won foothold of civilization, the tamed and domesticated Cooper agrees to "eat with a napkin around my neck for the rest of my life." The movie ends as he breaks down and asks: "Will you marry me, yes or no?" "*Oui, monsieur.*" "Oh, yes!"

The infinitely more interesting *City Streets* (1931), Cooper's only gangster picture, had an original screenplay by Dashiell Hammett. Cooper said his work schedule was so intense that "one day I was up in the mountains saving Lily Damita from the Indians. . . . Then I jumped into my car and made it to Hollywood, a hundred miles away, for my scenes with Sylvia Sidney in *City Streets*." A lanky westerner, Cooper (The Kid) works in the shooting gallery of a carnival and courts Sidney (Nan), whose stepfather runs a bootlegging racket. At first, she takes him for a circus sap and tries to recruit him:

Nan:	You sure pick jobs with no dough. Why don't you let me talk to Pop? He could put you in right.
The Kid:	I wish you weren't in that racket. You'd have different ideas about things.
Nan:	What have your ideas got you? . . . Racketeers are smart, not dumb like some people I know.

When she takes the rap for her Pop, Cooper, wearing a nouveau-riche fur-collar coat and black derby, visits her in prison. They kiss through a screen, and she's now horrified to learn that he's joined the gang. Instead of having her smile conventionally when he arrives, and cry when he leaves, the innovative director, Rouben Mamoulian, suggested she try something more original: "Reverse the procedure! When you see him, cry with joy; and when at the end he tells you he's a gangster, don't cry at all but rather smile with the kind of smile that transcends sorrow."[12] In this film Mamoulian also introduced a new cinematic device, the voice-over. When Sidney is taken back to her cell, she relives her memories of the past, during a silent close-up, with Cooper's voice and her own thoughts echoing on the soundtrack. Though the studio executives thought the audience would not accept or understand an audible inner monologue, the innovation worked remarkably well and became a standard technique.

The film has several distinct Hammett touches. Cooper picks Sidney up in a big car outside the prison gates for her jailbird's equivalent of a debutante's "coming-out party." Echoing his famous line in *The Virginian*, Cooper tells one of the cigar-smoking mobsters: "When you talk to me, take that toothbrush out of your mouth." And after disarming instead of shooting the killers who've been hired to get him, he cracks: "Go home and tell your mama you've been born again tonight." Despite his gangster garb and tough talk, Cooper, a decent guy gone wrong, looks too nice to be a villain. Unconvincing as a criminal, he never again tried to play that role.

Cooper had an affair with the blond, brassy and uninhibited Carole Lombard (who later married Clark Gable), during the making of their otherwise unmemorable *I Take This Woman* (1931). Though she said, "I like you lots, Studs," the liaison seems to have ended badly. It provoked, as with Dietrich, some hostile comments about the laconic and somewhat mysterious Cooper. "In a conversation," Lombard said, "by the time he opens his mouth it's tomorrow." And her biographer wrote that "Gary Cooper was the one man she worked with whose personality remained impenetrable to her. Off screen he was the quiet presence suggested by his performances, but the similarity ended there. Carole regarded him as a dilettante—markedly effeminate, especially in his mannerisms, and not at all the stalwart he impersonated so effectively on film."[13] Though *Morocco* was a tremendous success and his career was thriving, by 1931 his overwhelming work schedule became more than he could bear. The difference between his screen image and his real character, noted by Lombard as well as by Cooper himself, soon led to a physical and mental crisis.

6

Breakdown and the Countess di Frasso

1931–1932

I

During his casual affairs with Dietrich and Lombard, Cooper remained emotionally entangled with Lupe Velez. He always needed and always had strong women in his life, and the strongest of all was his domineering mother. Hedda Hopper described her as "a rather snobbish English Episcopalian," and Alice had called herself "his only feminine companion." But Cooper was drawn to Lupe, as he had been to Clara Bow, because her reckless exuberance was a complete contrast to his mother's conventional behavior. Lupe was lively, enthusiastic, sexy and deeply in love with him. Though educated in a convent, she looked and behaved—especially to Alice Cooper—like a loose, immoral woman. Before meeting Gary, she'd had melodramatic love affairs with Douglas Fairbanks, Sr., Tom Mix, Clark Gable, Charlie Chaplin and Victor Fleming. She was also Catholic, indelibly alien, hyperemotional and wildly out of control.

When Cooper strummed his guitar and sang their favorite song, "*Viejo Amor*," all was well. But when he provoked her jealousy and rage and she screamed, "You laugh at your Lupe's love?," their arguments would escalate and she'd become violent and dangerous. Lupe was also epileptic. He was afraid that if she had a fit at night, the doctors would find him in her house. This could harm or even ruin his career, for the morals clause in all actors' contracts gave the studio the legal right to dismiss players who got involved in alcoholic, sexual or criminal scandals. She frightened him one night by chasing him with a knife and even stabbing him. His wound, she boasted, marked him as her prey: "Real problem that Cooper has. He runs for women who are not like his mama! . . . He gets excited when we fight, and I tell you one thing. Lupe was the only one who scarred him for life. I got him with a knife once . . . in the arm, and he sweat and bled. Boy, he sweat. We were cooking dinner and Gary could not duck this time. He has the scars."

The original antagonism between Alice and Lupe—fueled by her disapproval of Lupe's race, religion, temperament, jealousy, violence and scandals—soon grew into open animosity. Cooper later played down the conflict and made it all seem like harmless fun: "My folks didn't know what to make of her. Her exuberant Latin spirits baffled mother, but Dad was charmed into helpless laughter. If she started tearing our house apart with one of her extravagant dances, Dad would put on one of his Judge-of-the-Supreme Court looks, but that would only inspire her to more outrageous goings-on."[1]

In various interviews that made headlines in the fan magazines, Lupe blamed Alice's undisguised hatred for the end of the affair. But Lupe herself hastened the breakup by her own fierce jealousy. This even extended to his eagles, which she described as "vultures": "Garree always ask Lupe for favors. He'd come to my house and say 'Hello' to birds first. Sometimes he played with them for too long and I have to drag him in the house. I told him, 'Garree, you clean and feed them!' So he did, and was at my house all the time. People tell his mother we're [going to be] married and she hates me. I said, 'Garee, all your fault that your mama spit when she sees me. I tell her about those vultures and she say that they were my idea to get you.' " Lupe also accused Alice of lying to control and possess her son: "Every time Gary didn't do as his mother wanted him to do, she became ill. 'She is just trying to hold him by sickness,' Lupe sobbed. 'I can easily imagine his mother saying, "These women are trying to take my boy from me with their appeal." ' Lupe explained that Paramount thought she was hurting Gary's career and joined Alice in opposing their marriage. In a moving outburst, she affirmed her love and said Alice had destroyed her: "I'm not good enough for him. I know that. But I tried to make him happy. I *did* make him happy. I would have done anything in the world for him. His mother! I hope she never cries the tears that I have cried. I hope she never knows the suffering I have known. I didn't hate her . . . that much. She said I wasn't good enough for Gary. She told him that when I was in New York I was seeing other men. She told him that I wasn't faithful to him. He believed what she told him."[2]

In 1931, after the final rupture, Alice spoke out in her own defense. Emphasizing Lupe's malice and taking a high tone, Alice minimized her own disapproval but found Lupe sadly wanting in both morality and decency:

> During these agonizing years [Alice] has been pictured as flinty-hearted, cruel, conniving. A mother devoid of any but the most selfish motives, conspiring against her son's happiness by tearing him from the one he loved, breaking his sweetheart's heart, undermining his health to the point of nervous prostration.
>
> "It shocks me, of course, to read in headlines that I have invaded Lupe's home to get various personal knicknacks that belong to Gary . . . that she demands of Gary that I be kept from bothering her . . . that I threatened to kill myself if Gary married Lupe. . . . Perhaps I have not entirely approved of any of the women with whom Gary has been romantically associated. . . . The most important [qualities in a wife] are respectability and fair-mindedness."

After breaking with Cooper, Lupe, like Clara, went into a steep decline and ended tragically. With all her faults, she remained a poignant and sympathetic figure. Passed around from celebrity to celebrity, she had unhappy affairs with Jack Dempsey, John Gilbert and Randolph Scott. She married Johnny "Tarzan" Weissmuller and, calling him "a furniture-breaking cave-man," divorced him in 1938. Six years later Lupe, who had always wanted children, became pregnant by Harald Ramond, a minor French actor twelve years her junior, and publicly announced their engagement. When he refused to marry her, she told a friend that as a Catholic she could never have an abortion but (rather illogically) might commit suicide: "I don't know what to do. It's my baby. I couldn't commit murder and still live with myself. I would rather kill myself." On December 11, 1944, when she was only thirty-six, she had her hair and nails done, filled her room with flowers and spent the evening at the Trocadero nightclub. She returned home after midnight, lit a ring of candles, put on blue satin pajamas and swallowed seventy-five Seconal pills. In a suicide note to the man who had jilted her, Lupe, naive and passionate as an operatic heroine, said she had chosen death to dishonor: "May God forgive you and forgive me, too, but I prefer to take my life away, and our baby's before I bring him shame or kill him. How could you, Harald, fake such a great love for me and our baby when all the time you didn't want us? I see no other way out for me, so goodbye and good luck to you. Love, Lupe."[3]

II

Outwardly, Cooper seemed normal and well adjusted, but he was really quite vulnerable and insecure. In May 1931, after he finished *I Take This Woman*, the combination of exhaustion, physical illness and the conflict between his possessive mother and jealous mistress led to a nervous breakdown. This crisis eventually made him question the whole basis of his life in Hollywood. He withdrew and fled the scene, wondering if he'd ever return.

Remembering his arduous labor on the ranch during the war, Cooper once said, half-humorously: "Having to work hard never had any real appeal for me, and that may have some connection with me being in the movies." But his breakdown was brought on by sheer overwork. As the studio tried to capitalize on the tremendous success of *The Virginian*, he regularly toiled fourteen to sixteen hours a day, and sometimes as long as twenty-three straight hours, making one movie in the daytime and another at night. Though strong and in excellent physical condition, even Cooper couldn't endure the strain of this schedule. He became completely exhausted, suffered from anemia and jaundice and, as his weight dropped dangerously to only 148, lost more than 30 pounds. "Now I was approaching thirty," Cooper said, "not really old—but what energy I had was gone. I felt like an old man. Hollywood had burned me out, and I hadn't even begun to act. I felt like tossing in the towel. I was very depressed."

Brief rest cures in a hospital and in Arizona failed to remedy his exhaustion and depression. The doctors told his mother: "You'd better get your son out of here for a long time or he won't make it through the year." Eager to save him, Alice announced that he might abandon his acting career and devote all his time to business ventures: "He will not spend his entire life in Hollywood. In a few years the public will have forgotten him and Gary will move on. He will probably return to the ranch where he spent a large part of his boyhood. Sunnyside has been converted into a dude ranch and with other real estate holdings in the

Coachella Valley [near Palm Springs], Gary will have plenty to do to manage his properties."[4]

Though highly successful and well rewarded, Cooper was bitterly angry about the way the studio had enslaved him. In Montana he had witnessed the violent labor wars between the miners and copper bosses. But he thought the movie business was even worse and warned his nephew, Howard: "Kid, stay out of Hollywood. It's a dirty place." Filled with self-doubt and bitter about the studio that had first nurtured and then exploited him, he could no longer tolerate its artificial atmosphere, its lies, malice and duplicity. "This is a terrible place to spend your life in," he said. "Nobody in Hollywood is normal. Absolutely nobody. And they have such a vicious attitude toward each other. . . . They say much worse things about each other than outsiders say about them, and nobody has any real friends."

In an uncharacteristically candid and revealing statement, Cooper said that he too had been deeply hurt by his break with Lupe. And, in an unmistakable allusion, he criticized his mother (as Lupe had done) for destructively meddling in his personal affairs:

You mustn't give everything in any human relationship. Especially in love. The person who falls in love—all the way—is bound to lose. He loses control of himself and the whole situation. . . .

I shall never be dominated by other people again as I had allowed myself to be until that time. I had drifted, taken advice, let people get at me through my emotions, my sympathy, my affections. Perhaps through a sort of apathy, too, because I was not well. You don't realize the hold you are letting people get on you until you find yourself enmeshed and entangled and helpless.

Sudden fame, substantial wealth, importunate strangers, false friends and family conflicts had forced Cooper—always a rather silent and solitary figure—to withdraw from intrusive publicity, and protect his private life: "Six years in Hollywood make a person 'shell up'—crawl into a hole. . . . The reason you do is because somebody is always staring at you, talking to you, or trying to sell you something you don't want. . . . [Fame] does cut down the circle of [an actor's] confidants and it literally isolates him in a crowd of his fellow mortals outside the industry. It makes him a public figure, and at the same time separates him from a good part of humanity with whom he cannot mingle comfortably."⁵ He felt lonely, and isolated by his fame, and a part of him still yearned for a small-town society to which he could belong.

Cooper's meteoric rise to stardom—with men clamoring to latch on to his money and women constantly trying to take him to bed—also caused psychological pain: it made him feel guilty and doubt his inner worth. He became depressed, wondered if he was nothing more than a composite of celluloid characters patched together by a series of directors, and raised some disturbing questions about the very roots of his own identity: "What did this composite look like? Who was he? And how could I be responsible for him? . . . Was I a star simply because I happened to screen well? Was I a figment of a director's imagination or did I have some stuff of my own?"

After his nervous breakdown, Cooper realized he would not be able to recover his health and stability unless he escaped from Hollywood and Paramount, from Alice and Lupe. He instinctively wanted to retreat to the simpler things of life, to some wild, natural place that would provide a restorative antidote to the falsity of film life. "Right now I'm all shot," he confessed. "I'm going to South America or down to Mexico. . . . I'm going to get a pack horse and a guide and go up into the mountains . . . I'm going to get so far away that I won't see any moving pictures and I won't hear about them."⁶ Seeking to rediscover his real self before it was buried beneath the screen image, he took another "solitary walk," as he had during his crisis with *Children of Divorce*. Instead of retreating to the wilderness, he fled to Europe, where another transformation awaited him.

III

During his year abroad (May 1931 to April 1932) Cooper seemed like an innocent American out of a novel by Henry James—dazzled, seduced and transformed by an aristocratic and sophisticated European society. After bidding farewell to his family, friends and Duesenberg, he boarded the boat for Algiers. When he got off, he realized that his film persona had followed him. He was besieged by a mob of street urchins who made pistols with their fingers, pointed them at the actor and, in tribute to his prowess on screen, yelled, "Boom! Boom!" He then crossed the Mediterranean to Italy, where Mussolini had been in power for nine years. He was sunning himself on the Lido in Venice when he received a telegram from Walter Wanger, a producer at Paramount, suggesting he look up the Countess di Frasso in Rome. "She runs a sort of open house for celebrities, dignitaries, royalty on the go, and other congenial characters," he wrote. "She'll welcome you with open arms." Once more Cooper would be guided through a new society by a woman who adored and dominated him.

The countess knew all the powers in Hollywood and everyone in international society, but remains an obscure and elusive figure. Thirteen years older than Cooper, she was born Dorothy Taylor in Watertown, upstate New York, in 1888. Her grandfather was a governor of New York and her father, Bertrand Taylor, a leather goods tycoon who made $50 million on Wall Street and left $12 million to Dorothy. She married the British aviator Claude White in 1912, divorced him four years later and in 1923 married the charming but penniless Roman, Count Carlo Dentice di Frasso, thirty years older than herself. Though neither good-looking nor elegant, the blue-eyed, black-haired, buxom countess dressed tastefully and had an attractive personality. Douglas Fairbanks, Jr. described her as charming, interesting, unpredictable and amusing. Her niece said she had a lively sense of humor and a keen enjoyment of life, told witty stories and was a vivid "character"—a dominant personality who drew people like a magnet and was always the center of attention. She had a talent for friendship and cultivated influential people all over the world. A brilliant horsewoman, she rode sidesaddle with Italian cavalry officers. She also arranged for the former stuntman to exhibit his horsemanship and compete against the leading riders of Italy in the grueling and dangerous Tour di Quinto steeplechase. Cooper pleased the countess by completing the course that vanquished most of the competitors.[7]

Count Carlo owned the majestic Villa Madama—across the Tiber, on the slopes of Monte Mario, at the northwest edge of the city—and Dorothy owned the count. The villa had been built by Pope Clement VII, nephew of Lorenzo de' Medici, in the early 1520s. Designed by Raphael, who filled its gardens and woods with fountains, it had a superb loggia, an open gallery with paintings and stucco decorations by his pupils Giulio Romano and Giovanni da Udine. The magnificent villa had slowly deteriorated for four centuries. Dorothy spent more than $1 million to restore the damp floors, stained walls and faded murals to their former splendor. She installed elevators so that guests would not have to climb the tall marble staircases, and covered the interior with silk curtains and Renaissance paintings. Writing in 1928, three years before Cooper arrived, an architectural historian praised the count (rather than Dorothy), who, "having taken over the Villa in its semi-ruined and sadly decayed state, has converted it with loving care, patience and no inconsiderable expense, into the relatively beautiful condition in which it exists today."

The social life at the Villa Madama, sustained by an army of servants, was worthy of the setting. Dorothy once hired some prizefighters to entertain her guests. Barbara Hutton, the million-heiress and one of Dorothy's regular clients, said "it was hard to tell whether the Countess threw one party that lasted all summer or a series of weekend parties that lasted all week. Guests just came and went as if the Villa Madama were a Grand Hotel." When Cooper returned to New York for a month in August 1931 to make *His Woman* with Claudette Colbert at Paramount's studio in Astoria, Long Island, Dorothy arranged a lavish going-away party. The distinguished guests, in the days when there was still a monarchy in Greece and Italy, included Prince Christopher of Greece, Prince Umberto of Italy, the Earl and Countess of Portarlington and the Duke of York, who became King George VI when his brother Edward abdicated to marry an American divorcée. Impressed by his romantic good looks and international fame, the titled rich courted the glamorous movie star. The well-bred son of English parents, Cooper got along very well with these grandees.

During his months at the Villa Madama the countess taught the cowboy about good food and vintage wines, and enough French and Italian to read the menus in the finest restaurants. She deepened his understanding of art by guiding him through the museums and galleries of Italy, and also let him drive her collection of racing cars. With his mother safely across the ocean, Cooper put himself in Dorothy's hands and surrendered to her dynamic, authoritative and sometimes smothering will. She loved to show off the gorgeous young man who was, after the palazzo, her proudest possession. Cooper had come a long way from the ranch in Craig, Montana. He adjusted to the uneasy role of gigolo and cuckolded the complaisant husband in his own home. He reveled in Dorothy's adoration and developed a taste for the luxurious life she offered, met a number of powerful people and quickly learned the ways of their world.

IV

While Cooper was in New York, the countess, desolated by his absence, found a way to prolong their liaison by gratifying his taste for wild places. She arranged an introduction to James Preston, who bred horses on a ranch overlooking Lake Nyasa in southwest Tanganyika. Preston invited Cooper (and of course Dorothy) to stay at the ranch and to accompany him on a safari in East Africa. As soon as Cooper completed the inconsequential movie, he sailed back to Italy. He and Dorothy then took a boat from Naples to Alexandria, a short train ride to Cairo and a three-day chartered plane flight down the Nile, stopping in primitive villages from Egypt and the Sudan to Nairobi.

After swimming in the lake and getting water in his ear, which increased the pressure, Cooper fired an elephant gun whose powerful explosion made him partly deaf. Preston organized enough cars, trucks, camping gear and luxurious supplies, as well as native trackers, gunbearers and servants, to supply a regiment. Wearing pith helmet, puttees and boots, interested in the landscape as well as the animals, Cooper joined the convoy that moved slowly north along the dusty red dirt roads for big-game hunting on the slopes of Mount Kenya. "The Prestons turned out to be fine sportsmen," Cooper remarked. "They really hunted, they didn't slaughter; and they always gave the game a chance. With them I learned to wait for the charge before firing."[8]

Big-game hunting, a rich man's sport, had been made famous and fashionable in 1910 by Teddy Roosevelt's *African Game Trails*. In *Green Hills of Africa* (1935), Hemingway described his own safari, which took place only two years after Cooper's. "We were entering a country," he wrote, with a keen eye, "the loveliest I had seen in Africa. The grass was green and smooth, short as a meadow that has been mown and is newly grown, and the trees were big, high-trunked and old with no undergrowth but only the smooth green of the turf like a deer park and we drove on through shade and patches of sunlight."

Though the hunters used guns and killed the animals at a distance, hunting the big five—lion, leopard, buffalo, rhino and elephant—required considerable skill and courage. Hemingway described the excitement that Cooper must have felt when a lion charged him in the open and he killed it with a "lucky shot": "There was the short-barrelled explosion of the Mannlicher and the lion was going to the left on a run, a strange, heavy-shouldered, foot-swinging, cat run. I hit him with the Springfield and he went down and spun over and I shot again, too quickly, and threw a cloud of dirt over him. But there he was, stretched out, on his belly, with the sun just over the top of the trees, and the grass very green."

While on safari Dorothy shot thirty-five thousand feet of home movies, the length of three feature films, which she tried to sell to the studios and which have now disappeared. In February 1932, when the rains ended the hunting season and their five-month sojourn in East Africa, Cooper and Dorothy took a ship from Mombasa on the Indian Ocean to Aden, Djibouti and Port Said, and through the Suez Canal to the Mediterranean. In a contemporary photograph the healthy, tanned and muscular Cooper stands on the deck of the *Saturnia* in a striped singlet and white striped trousers, looking like a pagan god.

After bagging two lions and sixty head of game in darkest Africa, Cooper returned to Europe with a changed outlook that intensified his love of the wilderness, yet made him appreciate what status and money could buy. He now thought, like a modern Jean-Jacques Rousseau, that "it's education, culture and civilization that breed and foster unhappiness." He felt Africa was a more extreme version of Montana (which he had once contrasted to the cramped English landscape) and admired the savagery he associated with Lupe Velez: "The biggest thrill in the world to me was the time I was in Africa shooting big game. I love Africa. I love its bigness, its toughness, the savagery you can feel all around you at any place in the continent."[9]

In addition to his stuffed trophies, Cooper brought back a live chimpanzee he named Toluca, after the lake in North Hollywood. Always at ease with animals, he was photographed like a proud papa, standing on the deck of a ship and holding his pet snugly wrapped in a blanket. Back at home, he mocked the social pretensions of Hollywood—and the company one had to keep in the business. Served by his butler, Cooper was photographed dining al fresco with the chimp. Compared to Rome, Los Angeles now seemed a provincial backwater. He had gained maturity and confidence by mingling with rich and aristocratic foreigners, and in their society had learned to value himself for the person he really was instead of for his image on screen.

V

Dorothy di Frasso has been credited with getting rid of the old-fashioned watch chain that dangled from Cooper's waistcoat button, with buying his complete wardrobe and teaching him how to dress. But he had known good English tailors from his schooldays and had already become, when photographed by Cecil Beaton in 1929, a stylish, even elegant dandy. He confessed, however, that in Europe he had "bought everything the Continental gentleman was supposed to wear, balking only at a monocle, spats and cane," but including white gloves and a high round derby hat. "Outwardly I was playing my new role," he wrote, "a poised man of the world. Inwardly, I was a scared young man. Paramount had shown no signs of wanting me back."

For the past year he had put pleasure before career and ignored several urgent calls to return to duty at the studio. Paramount had retaliated by hiring a dashing rival, Cary Grant, whose stage name reversed Cooper's initials and first name was unnervingly like his own. According to Suzy Parker, the generally good-natured Gary "had a hate" for Cary Grant, who had threatened to replace him at the studio and had onscreen mannerisms that always "got on his nerves."[10] When Cooper announced he was leaving Italy, the countess tried to assuage his fears by offering to *buy* the studio. Cooper gave one friend "the impression that it was a 'cute' gesture on her part—and *that's* how much she wanted to hang on to him." When they returned to Los Angeles, local wits called her "a mature connoisseur of Hollywood juveniles" and said that Cooper had left Hollywood broke and returned, as if she were an ocean liner, "on the Countess di Frasso." Even as their tepid affair waned and he became more interested in other women, Dorothy loyally tried to advance his career, helped him negotiate contracts and introduced him to the real power brokers in the studios.

Cooper's relations with di Frasso were satirized in Clare Boothe's popular play *The Women* (1937). In this comedy the much-married Countess de Lage—"a silly, amiable, middle-aged woman, with careful, waved, bleached hair"—takes Buck Winton, a dumb cowboy, to Hollywood, turns him into a film star and then loses him to a rival. The love-smitten matron quotes Buck's song: "Oh, a man can ride a horse to the range above, But a woman's got to ride on the wings of love," and absolutely swoons over his beautiful physique: "Buck Winton is nice. So young. So strong. Have you noticed the play of his muscles?"

Abandoning high society in Rome, Dorothy lingered in Hollywood. After Cooper's marriage in 1933, she took up with the gangster Bugsy

Siegel, whom she met at the Santa Anita racetrack, and sailed with him to search for buried treasure off Costa Rica. She also persuaded some of the most illustrious figures in Hollywood to invite the hoodlum to their homes. In a caustic article, the well-born Humphrey Bogart, alluding to di Frasso and Siegel, condemned the gangsters, fakes and nouveaux riches in Hollywood as "the clique of ex-bootleggers and phony baronesses that get all dressed up in chinchillas and tailcoats to see the world premiere of a movie" that had already opened in the provinces. Helen Hayes, who appeared in a film with Cooper soon after he returned from Europe and had a Broadway actress' disdain for the tawdry aspects of Hollywood, was also severely critical of the countess. She was "a very possessive and terrifying woman. A rough sort of woman. As for the idea that she gave him polish, I seriously resent that. He could have given her a lot of style if she'd been recep-tive. After the romance with Gary broke up she had a fling with a gangster in Palm Springs, Bugsy Siegel. That doesn't reflect much style and taste, does it?" On January 4, 1954 the countess—adorned with furs and $500,000 worth of jewels, accompanied by the actor Clifton Webb and traveling on a train from Las Vegas to Los Angeles—suddenly died of a heart attack.

Joel McCrea, who had first met Cooper at the Douglas Fairbanks' house in the 1920s, took a long walk with him in the Hollywood Hills after his return from Europe. He was struck by the "unexpectedness and canniness" of Cooper, who now spoke quite eloquently. He had listened carefully to the discussions at the Villa Madama and, a year before Hitler took power, came away with an acute understanding of Continental politics. Beginning with " 'that European situation is a hell of a mess' . . . he launched into as intelligent a discussion of interna-tional affairs as I have ever heard. He knew everything that had happened—names, places, dates and facts. He also had figured out what was going to happen in the future and he was right, too, as subse-quent events have proved."[11]

After a year in Europe and Africa, Cooper came back to Hollywood healthy, energetic and ready to resume his career. Whatever her faults, Dorothy di Frasso had given him encouragement, support and a good time. He had gained a clearer perspective on the film industry and the wider world in which he was a public figure. With Dorothy he had also learned to be at ease in high society and developed a taste for the kind of life he would soon share with his wife. Just as England had changed him in 1910 and Hollywood in 1926, so Italy had also transformed his character in 1931. His two long trips to Europe, as a boy and as a young man, helped define him as an American.

7

Paramount Star

1932–1933

I

When Cooper returned to Paramount in April 1932 and drove under the delicate wrought-iron grilles and huge arches at 5451 Marathon Street, he found the most powerful studio of the 1920s in deep trouble. The president Adolph Zukor, general manager B.P. Schulberg and head of production Walter Wanger had built a movie company that owned studios in Los Angeles, New York and Paris, an international distribution network and the largest theater chain in the world. It had turned out as many as 104 pictures a year and had a huge backlog in case of strikes or disasters. Its leading directors (who would all work with Cooper) were von Sternberg, Lubitsch and Mamoulian. Its top stars were Mae West, Marlene Dietrich, Carole Lombard, Sylvia Sidney, Claudette Colbert and Miriam Hopkins; W.C. Fields, Charles Laughton, Fredric March, George Raft, Bing Crosby and the Marx Brothers.

Talkies had kept Paramount prosperous after the Wall Street crash of October 1929, and it continued to expand. Between September 1929 and May 1930 the studio acquired five hundred theaters. Its thirty-two-acre lot contained an architect's office, censorship department, children's school, hospital, library and arsenal, and thousands of employees. There were writers, actors, directors, producers, cameramen, electricians, grips, musicians, photographers, schedule estimators, drapers, firemen, gardeners, janitors, restaurant workers—and "a great many people who seemed to do little except drift from set to set to chat around the coffee percolators." But when the Depression brought the good times to an end, the management's failure to control its payroll and expenses plunged the business into bankruptcy. Sam Jaffe said that in 1929 Schulberg, his brother-in-law, had been making an astronomical $6,500 a week, which had an adverse effect on his character and behavior: "Ben couldn't take that kind of success. He went crazy. He gambled, he screwed, and he drank. He was screwing every girl that came along. He was handsome, he was intelligent, but the business was going down, and he was fired finally [in 1932]. He ruined himself." Schulberg became an independent producer, but his career soon evaporated.

By 1932 Paramount found it impossible to meet its enormous mortgage payments on the recently acquired theaters. Budgets and most salaries were cut by a third, and many executives were fired. It went bankrupt in 1933, went into receivership in 1934 and was reorganized out of bankruptcy in 1935—with debts of $95 million. Finances began to improve in 1936, when the corporation earned a profit of $6 million. During the war, when the public craved distracting entertainment, all the studios did well. Paramount had a $10 million profit in 1941, $16 million in 1944, $44 million in 1946 and was finally free of debt the following year. But in 1932, when people were being fired all over town, Cooper was greeted at Paramount with open arms. His star status was not affected by his absence, and in the years to come he helped revive the studio's fortunes and shared in its prosperity.

Moviemaking was and still is a collaborative as well as a highly expensive undertaking. Paramount mobilized its army of artists and technicians—most of whom were under contract with the studio—for the scores of movies it made each year. The accounting department drew up a detailed budget, the screenwriters wrote and rewrote the script, the legal section checked it for libel and copyright, the censorship office for moral infractions. Profits depended on speedy production schedules, and as the studios juggled actors, technicians and sound stages to maximize their enormous output, a typical picture was made in a matter of weeks.

Readers and writers, who worked in hive-like offices on the lot, raided history and literature for plots and characters to supply the studio's constant demand for new material. Backed by the research department, the studio devoted enormous effort to create realistic settings, costumes and make-up, but in its haste to turn out salable pictures tended to ignore the most blatant absurdities in the scripts: ludicrous conventions, farfetched coincidences, cardboard characters, fatuous plots, contrived conclusions, and lack of logic, structure and meaning. Morality was black and white. Villains were always dark and fat, ate greedily and smoked cigars, while heroes were young, slim and handsome. Intellectuals wore glasses and carried pipes. Cooper more than earned his keep in many poor Paramount movies. He looked the part of romantic hero and could make the tawdriest script seem fresh and convincing.

While the movie was being made, the unit manager, who tried to keep the picture on schedule and on budget, sent a daily progress report to the studio executives. He carefully noted the number of completed scenes, setups and takes, the total amount of footage shot and minutes of finished film each day. As soon as the film was developed in the lab and brought to the projection room, the producer and director would see the daily rushes in order to select the best takes and judge the quality of each picture in production. A rough cut was made day by day, and after the movie was shot, the film editor cut and spliced the footage into a ninety-minute dramatic sequence. Music was composed and conducted; sound and sound effects were recorded. During the filming hundreds of technicians, from electricians to firemen, were at work. When the picture was finished, the publicity, advertising, sales and distribution departments took over.

Shooting on location—where permission, food and lodging had to be arranged, and equipment and crew transported to a distant site—was much more complicated and expensive. On Cooper's *Peter Ibbetson* (1935), for example, the unit manager reported to the studio heads that filming was repeatedly delayed. Time was lost in changing setups, lighting and rehearsing a boom shot, and lining up a special-effects shot; waiting for the latest version of the script, trying out new lines, rewriting the dialogue and story; applying old-age make-up and remodeling Cooper's ill-fitting costume. Other delays were caused by the lateness of actors and actresses, performances that failed to satisfy the director and the illness of the director, who had to go home; by bad weather, cloudy skies, high fog, failing light and a faulty valve in the Pasadena water supply that stopped the artificial rain. There were always airplane noises, and local pilots often had to be bribed not to fly overhead. Nestor Almendros, a leading cameraman, has described the technical advantages of shooting in the studio: if actors "are disturbed by traffic in a shot or a helicopter passing over and you have to call 'cut' every minute because the take is no good for sound, the performers get in a bad mood; all the stopping and starting disturb them. When you are in the studio, you control your work; you are comfortable and the actors perform perfectly."[1]

But working in the studios in the 1930s was far from comfortable. They looked like prisons, with uniformed guards checking credentials at the front gate and high walls surrounding the vast space. The sound stages, which resembled airplane hangars, were sealed with huge steel doors and enclosed within the studio lot. There was no air conditioning, and the sets got very hot during the Los Angeles summer.

The director, having planned the shooting schedule and thought out the camera positions and moves, chose the first scene to be shot and summoned the actors to the set. Except for the action scenes, he used only one camera. The master shot, at the beginning of the film, established the setting and characters and made them clear to the audience. Practicing emphasis, revising or discarding lines that did not work, the actors ran through their speeches over and over again till the scene came photographically and dramatically alive. The director—who could be a domineering martinet, like von Sternberg—told the actors precisely where to stand, where they had come from and were going to. Striving for pace and tempo, fluidity and energy—for there must always be movement in a movie—he would stage the scene. The director and cameraman aimed for dramatic angles and precise images, and used light and shadow to suggest mood and character. They tried to make the scenes and sequences flow together in one natural continuous movement, to create the illusion of reality.

The powerful images that supplied this illusion depended largely on actors, and rewards were great for those, like Cooper, who could convey ease and naturalness in the midst of the mechanics of filming. Glaring lights and reflectors, supported by miles of thick serpentine wires, blazed in the actors' eyes, and the heavy camera and crane-like sound booms loomed close to their faces. They had to repeat the same scene over and over again until the director was satisfied with the take. To increase efficiency and reduce costs, pictures were shot according to setting and out of sequence. Because actors often appeared in only part of the film, they lacked the camaraderie that developed in the theater. They briefly rehearsed, tried several variations of a short take, played their scenes and left the set. Actors in the same movie sometimes never got to know, or even see, each other. They put in long hours, and spent most of them waiting to go on camera.

When he first came to Hollywood in the mid-1920s, Cooper said, "I was bowled over by studio life. I was drunk on what, at first glimpse, appeared to be its utter freedom and lack of restraint, and what I learned later is the most delusive thing about it. There is no real freedom in Hollywood." In return for the financial security of an actor's long-term contract, the studios extracted their due. Players were virtually owned by the studio and were required to act in all the films assigned to them. If they refused a role, they risked indefinite suspension without pay. Cooper balked a bit about poor roles but, especially after his prolonged absence, was generally compliant. Actors could be "rented" to other studios for a higher salary, while the studio that owned them kept the substantial difference between the original salary and the rental fee.

Though top actors were well paid, their apparently glamorous life was in many ways dangerous and degrading. Cooper's frequent injuries did not end with his career as a stuntman. He explained that in the course of making movies he was choked, punched, bloodied, submerged and drenched: "Part of a bridge fell on me one time during a demolition scene, nearly tearing off my arm, and I've been scorched while dueling with blank cartridges, but the fires were easily put out. I've been slammed, and banged, and ruptured four times, dived on by drone planes falling out of control, kicked by mules, hooked by steers and bitten by dog stars." His trick of napping helped him avoid some of the boredom of waiting. But, he lamented, in a twelve-hour day, with allowance for rehearsals, retakes, make-up repairs and changes of costume the actor still has to hang around about eight hours between takes."[2]

Like all actors, Cooper tried to animate himself by combining intense physical projection and deep emotional realism. He attempted, in the words of the actor-writer Simon Callow, "to give fresh and original life to something existing only in the author's imagination and on a piece of paper." Unlike stage performers, movie actors had to wait months to get an audience reaction—and perhaps discover their best work had been altered or completely cut by the editor. Early in his career Cooper's shyness and embarrassment made it torture for him to display feeling with bright lights, huge camera and mob of technicians only a few feet from his face. His habitual underplaying led many to believe he was hardly acting at all. But he proved to be the master of the close-up, of acting to the camera's lens rather than to an audience. Cooper's eloquent eyes and gestures could register the very slightest change of expression on his sexy and likable face. In the most difficult circumstances he could summon up his intuitive ability, guided by an inner discipline.

When working, Cooper woke up at about 6:30, arrived at the studio at eight, and went first to the make-up and wardrobe departments. The studios provided historical costumes, but male actors usually supplied their own clothing for contemporary roles. He then went to the set on the sound stage (the back lot was used for exterior scenes), which often had a clammy, closed-in smell. He checked with the assistant director, who had a list of actors appearing in the film. While waiting to be called, he reread the script, touched up his make-up or sat around chatting with Slim Talbot and friends in the cast. He might also return to his dressing room (elaborately graded according to his current status) to see studio press agents or Hollywood journalists. He might drink a Coke or a beer, whittle wood, play cards and scan the newspapers. He would also read hunting, fishing, rod, gun, taxidermy and sports car catalogues. The manly decor of his dressing room reflected his Montana background and passion for hunting. He brought in four red leather club chairs, covered the sofa with a handwoven Indian blanket, and decorated the walls with Mexican serapes, Indian artifacts, feathered headdresses, lariats, rifles and stuffed animal heads.

Completely exhausted after filming, Cooper usually came home for dinner at 6:30, studied his lines for the next day and went to sleep early. But the workday was often extended to deal with unexpected problems, finish a setup or shoot at night, and a six-day week was standard. If a director kept him late, he had his own way of protesting. He'd ignore the 9 o'clock call the next day, turn up casually at 10:30 and keep the cast and crew waiting. As Walter Brennan remarked: "He never said anything, but when they kept him after, he made it up someplace else."[3] In his professional life, as in private, Cooper was easy to like and maintained good relationships with everyone. Though he inevitably acted in many poor films, Paramount also gave him some excellent roles with some of the finest directors and co-stars. The studio nurtured him, and he was never out of work or out of favor.

II

Cooper returned from Italy to Hollywood with a butler and maid, Ugo and his wife, Maria. He rented Garbo's old house, built in the Spanish style with a beamed living room ceiling and large oval fireplace, on Chevy Chase in Beverly Hills, and moved in with the servants. The intensely cluttered bachelor decor combined cowboy spurs, Navajo rugs, Indian war bonnets and stuffed eagles (did Lupe kill them in retaliation?) with the sixty mounted trophies he'd shot on safari. The Masai spears and shields, hunting rifles and elephant tusks, zebra skins and lion heads, and the chimp, Toluca, who ran freely through the house, turned it into a combination of western saloon and African jungle.[4] Garbo would not have been pleased.

After settling into these bizarre surroundings, Cooper began work on May 11 on *The Devil and the Deep* (1932). Most of the film was completed in five weeks in the studio, but the desert scenes—the locale was a submarine base in North Africa—were shot in Yuma, Arizona. Charles Laughton, who played the insanely jealous husband, earned $1,750 a week; Cooper (his wife's lover in the film) got $2,500; and Tallulah Bankhead, the sensual, unfaithful wife, received $4,000. Bankhead had been a great success on the London stage. Notorious for her tempestuous personality, uninhibited behavior, sultry voice and raucous laughter, she was also bisexual, a heavy drinker and a cocaine addict. Like Carole Lombard, she was foul-mouthed, wise-cracking and quick-witted. She called the countess "nothing but an old whore" and said she'd "worn Cooper to a frasso." Asked why she'd come to Hollywood, Tallulah confessed she was determined "to fuck that divine Gary Cooper," and he did not disappoint her.

Cooper liked to prepare for his role by immersing himself in research that would help him understand and portray his character. For *The Devil and the Deep* he read technical books, histories and novels, like Jules Verne's *Twenty Thousand Leagues Under the Sea*, about submarines. Sparked less by books than by Bankhead, his restrained delivery and sensual, even voluptuous masculinity, were spellbinding. As Simon Callow observed: "Cooper, with his ravishing androgyny, full of lip, luxuriant of eyelash, gentle of manner, had—at least in his performing personality—found [as in *Morocco*] the perfect balance between his masculine and his feminine elements." "Bankhead's doomed, chain-smoking beauty," Callow added, "burnt out by the emotional violence which has been done to her, snatching an anonymous night in the desert with Cooper . . . is startlingly real."

Cooper's cool elegance is the perfect foil for Laughton's crazed captain, who dominates the film. Laughton admired Cooper's physical beauty, and his real-life attraction gave extra power to the jealously ironical remarks he makes in the film. With his own ugly face in a close-up, Laughton sneers enviously at Cooper: "It must be a happy thing to look as you do. I suppose women love you." Laughton also admired the natural performance of Cooper—who held his own with two accomplished stage actors—and always cited him as a paragon of film acting. "Gary had something I should never have," he said. "It is something pure and he doesn't know it's there. In truth, that boy hasn't the least idea how well he acts. . . . He gets at it from the inside, from his own clear way of looking at life." John Barrymore, another great theater performer, agreed with Laughton about Cooper's intuitive talent: "This fellow is the world's greatest actor. He does without effort what the rest of us spend our lives trying to learn—namely, to be natural."[5]

The movie opens as Cooper's irritating rival, Cary Grant, playing a young officer under Laughton's command, is sent in disgrace off the ship (and off the film) for dallying with the captain's wife. When Bankhead pleads, "I wish you'd believe in and trust me," Laughton bitterly replies: "Does it amuse you to torture me?" Separated from Grant and spurned by Laughton, whose jealousy is a disease, Bankhead rushes into the casbah to watch the whirling dervishes. She is rescued by Cooper—Grant's replacement on the ship. He asks her, "What do you want?" and (alluding to Job's "Let the day perish wherein I was born") she unhappily replies, "Never to have been born." Sceptically sucking in his cheeks and pursing his lips, he is commanding with Bankhead, but deferential with Laughton. Laughton discovers her adultery, sets sail with his wife on board and plots revenge.

The climactic scene was shot on a model sub in the studio tank. Laughton, now quite mad, cuts the radio wires, gives suicidal orders and makes Cooper responsible for the impending shipwreck. Laughing wildly, he axes Bankhead's portrait and drowns himself in the rising waters. Cooper takes command and saves the crew. Bankhead—escaping from "the sunken sub by floating up thirty feet of water in a black chiffon gown—is 'camp' elevated to surrealism." His love affair with the captain's wife has made Cooper guilty of conduct unbecoming an officer, but the captain's death clears the way for the lovers to come together. Throughout the picture—and this is one of its delights—Laughton and Bankhead express intense, operatic, over-the-top emotions that highlight Cooper's slow, deliberate speech and laid-back portrayal.

A Farewell to Arms (1932), based on Hemingway's novel, was a more ambitious and commercially successful movie. Cooper (Frederic Henry) and Adolphe Menjou (Major Rinaldi) got $15,000 each and the tiny Helen Hayes (Catherine Barkley), a leading star of the New York theater, earned $38,000. Once more Cooper had a powerful effect on his co-star. Hayes, a rather proper lady married to the writer Charles MacArthur, confessed that "if Gary had crooked a finger I would have left Charlie and my child and the whole thing." Despite her physical attraction, their on-screen lovemaking was compared to two "icebergs crossing off the Greenland Coast."[6] Like Esther Ralston, Hayes was encouraged, while making publicity stills, to thaw Cooper out. But his restrained acting is much more effective on film than Hayes' theatrical, mannered and sometimes mincing performance.

The picture opens with a shot of a dead soldier as an ambulance, with Cooper asleep in the passenger seat, descends from the mountains to deliver the wounded to a military hospital in Milan. During an aerial bombardment Cooper meets Hayes, a nurse in the hospital, whose fiancé has been killed in the war. She's now being courted by Cooper's friend Menjou, an Italian surgeon, and by Cooper himself. As they sit beneath a huge equestrian statue, Cooper boldly kisses her, she slaps him, and he sensitively touches his jaw and then his lips. He then argues that they must seize the chance of love:

> *Frederic:* Back home I'd have courted you and sent you flowers.
> *Catherine:* Out here you crowd it all into one hour.
> *Frederic:* Isn't that the way it's got to be out here? Look, tomorrow morning I've got to go up to the front again. And if a shell got me and you never saw me again, then we'd both be sorry we'd been so formal and waited. Besides, what's there so fine in putting it off, dragging it out, giving me your lips tonight. . . .
> *Catherine:* No.
> *Frederic:* . . . your throat tomorrow?
> *Catherine:* No! No, wait! Please! No.

Melting, she rather stiffly says, "I'd be glad to have you kiss me now, if you don't mind," and they instantly become lovers.

Badly wounded by an explosion at the front, Cooper is taken down to the hospital and operated on by Menjou. As Cooper's wheeled in, the dark and shadowy lighting suggests that his life hangs in the balance, that their love, connected by wounds and death, is doomed. An unusually subjective sequence of three shots conveys the viewpoint of the wounded and disoriented man:

> The first is a long travelling shot looking up at the [painted] ceiling from the trolley on which Frederic is lying. The second, in Frederic's

hospital room, ends with Catherine coming up to the camera to kiss Frederic. . . . There is then a second two-shot of the couple with the camera looking at them side-on. . . . Although the whole scene is not particularly long, it is sufficiently striking to stand out clearly in the film.

In a scene completely contrary to the spirit of the novel, they murmur marriage vows in a do-it-yourself pseudo ceremony at Cooper's hospital bedside. Recovering, he quotes Andrew Marvell's ominous "But at my back I always hear / Time's wingèd chariot hurrying near," and she foreshadows their tragedy by telling him, "I see myself dead in the rain." He returns to the front; she realizes she's pregnant and flees to Switzerland. The jealous Menjou intercepts their letters, and Cooper, during a confusing montage of war, jumps into a river to escape the guards and rows up Lake Garda to find her. As Cooper chokes out a desperate prayer, "I'll do anything for You if You don't let her die," Hayes delivers a stillborn child.

Hedging his bets, the director Frank Borzage shot two different endings, printed both versions and made both available for distribution. Theater managers were allowed to select the version they wished to screen, and most of them chose the happy ending. In the conventional deathbed scene Cooper tries to comfort her as the *Liebestod* from Wagner's *Tristan und Isolde* surges in the background:

> *Frederic:* Whatever happens you'll not be afraid?
> *Catherine:* I'll not be afraid.
> *Frederic:* We've never been apart, really; not since we met.
> *Catherine:* Not since we met.
> *Frederic:* And never can be.
> *Catherine:* Never parted.
> *Frederic:* In life and in death. Say it, Cat.
> *Catherine:* In life and in death. We'll never be parted.
> *Frederic:* You do believe that, don't you, Cat?
> *Catherine:* I believe it, and I'm not afraid.[7]

Then—as Italy wins the war, bells ring and doves fly upward—she makes a miraculous recovery. When the picture was re-released in 1948, Hayes, more appropriately, dies in Cooper's arms.

Menjou has an authentic accent and touches and hugs Cooper in the

Italian way. Their male camaraderie and rivalry are more subtle and dramatically effective than Cooper's sentimental liaison with Helen Hayes. *A Farewell to Arms* distorts Hemingway's novel and quite deliberately ignores its political and moral meaning and tragic themes. But it's an entertaining film that capitalized on Cooper's matinée idol status, a touching 1930s love story, a doomed romance and nothing more.

III

In 1933 Cooper made three mediocre films, and his career went into a brief decline. *Today We Live*, like so many Hollywood movies, was a misconceived project that wasted a good deal of talent. It was based on "Turnabout," a *Saturday Evening Post* story by William Faulkner, who came back to Hollywood to work on this script for the director Howard Hawks. Though Faulkner got screen credit for the story and dialogue, the "adaptation" was credited to two other writers.

Hawks would later direct Cooper in *Sergeant York* and *Ball of Fire*. Like Victor Fleming and Henry Hathaway, he was a man's man. He shared Cooper's interests in weapons, hunting, fast cars and elegant dress, and became a good friend. Born in Goshen, Indiana, in 1896, the son of a wealthy paper manufacturer, Hawks went to Exeter and graduated from Cornell in 1917 with a degree in mechanical engineering. He was a lieutenant in the Army Air Corps in World War I, and after the war built airplanes and a racing car that won the Indianapolis 500 in 1936. Physically impressive, Hawks was "six-feet-three, broad shouldered, slim-hipped, soft-spoken, confident in manner, conservative in dress, and utterly distinguished overall. . . . For years it was said that only Gary Cooper rivaled Hawks as a marksman. When [an acquaintance] put the question to him, he said, 'Coop was better with a rifle, but I could beat him with pistol or shotgun.' " The screenwriter Niven Busch found Hawks formidably distant and frigid, with a "reptilian glare . . . ice-cold blue eyes and the coldest of manners. He was like that with everyone—women, men, whatever. He was remote; he came from outer space. He wore beautiful clothes. He spoke slowly in a deep voice. He looked at you with those frozen eyes."

Hawks emphasized spontaneity and improvisation, rehearsed very little and shot off the cuff. Using a rough script to try out his scenes, he kept rewriting them on the set and handing out new pages to the actors as the film was shot. He later recalled how the MGM executives, who had "borrowed" Cooper from Paramount, distorted and weakened the story by forcing a female star into a war movie. " 'Who have you got?' [they asked]. I said, 'I've got Gary Cooper and two young fellas, Bob Young and Franchot Tone.' They said, 'Well, you've got Joan Crawford too.' I said, 'No, there's no girl in the picture.' They said, 'There is one now. We'll lose a million dollars if we don't have something for Joan Crawford. So you're stuck.' I called Faulkner and told him, 'Bill, we gotta put a girl in this story.' " Franchot Tone, who made his debut in this film, preempted Cooper by having an affair with Crawford during the shooting.

The title, *Today We Live*, suggested the intensity as well as the brevity ("for tomorrow we die") of life in combat. Faulkner's original typescript is very different from the final film. But in both works the telegraphic dialogue, more shorn than clipped, ludicrously attempts to imitate British military speech: "They reported you dead." "Not dead though. Glad." When one of them is blinded, the script reads: "Eyes. Left him there. Came for you."

Oddly, three years before Humphrey Bogart became a star in *The Petrified Forest*, Cooper is named Bogard and called Bogie in the film. Like Bogart in *Casablanca*, he wears an old trench coat with a tied, not buckled, belt and moves from neutrality to commitment in war. An American in England in 1916, he rents Crawford's country house and courts her as her brother (Tone) and fiancé (Young) go off to fight the war in a torpedo boat. After Cooper and Crawford declare their love, she joins an ambulance unit at the front and he becomes a pilot in the RFC. In a macho mode Cooper takes Young up in his bomber, which allows Hawks to use real footage of aerial combat, and they make an extremely dangerous landing with an unreleased bomb hanging down from the plane. Young, still engaged to Crawford, remains ignorant of her affair with Cooper, the source of much guilt and handwringing on her part. After Young is blinded, he and Tone are killed on a suicidal mission— ramming a German cruiser in Kiel harbor. Cooper flies back to Crawford and, in a bitter thematic speech at the end of Faulkner's script, wishes that the leaders who'd started the war had also been destroyed: "If they had only all been there: generals, the admirals, the presidents, and the kings—theirs, ours, all of them!"

Faulkner intended his story to portray "the old universal truths of love and honor and pride and pity and compassion and sacrifice," but these themes are not convincingly dramatized in his script or in the picture. The romantic and military scenes are not well connected, and the adventurous story of male comradeship becomes, as Crawford tries hard to be one of the boys, a cliché-ridden, tear-jerking soap opera. Crawford is much too strong a personality for the sugary sweetheart role, and there is little for Cooper to do but be noble and patriotic. In a devastating review *Variety* said that "the film was 20 minutes too long, Crawford was unconvincing, Hawks used too much footage from *Hell's Angels* [1930], the 'Gowns by Adrian' were extreme and annoying, and the story was superficial."[8]

Operator 13, an amateur and truly absurd movie, was great fun to make. It also gave Cooper, through his co-star, Marion Davies, entrée to an American version of the Villa Madama—the magnificent hilltop castle at San Simeon, two hundred miles up the coast from Los Angeles, that was owned by her lover, the newspaper tycoon William Randolph Hearst. Since Hearst was a great power at MGM (he even directed a few scenes himself after a disagreement with the nominal director, Richard Boleslawski), shooting proceeded at a leisurely pace.

Davies noted that Cooper, as usual, ate enormous spicy meals, never gained an ounce and took regular naps: "We'd have luncheon in a big tent. Beans and potato salad and hot tamales and beer. I'd be watching Gary, and he would eat more than anybody in the whole cast. He'd have the beans, and God knows, he loved hot peppers, and then after luncheon he'd just throw himself down on the grass and rest until he was called. Then he'd get right up and go, and he'd look skinnier than anybody else." Cooper recalled that the delightful prima donna, whose liaison with Hearst later inspired Orson Welles' *Citizen Kane*, would "show up about ten, do two or three setups, and then retire to her dressing room for lunch, pretty wet and pretty long. After a nap, we'd do two or three more shots, then high tea, which was martinis, then Marion was off home. Helluva way to make a movie."

In the film Davies is recruited as a Union spy during the Civil War and disguised first as a black laundress and then as a southern belle. Cooper seems to have difficulty keeping a straight face during these farcical proceedings. He plays a Confederate scout who unmasks her, falls in love with her and is rescued by her. Even Hearst's fabulous wealth and limitless influence couldn't save this lavish production, wavering between low comedy and high romance, from well-earned disaster.

Design for Living, a more promising project, was based on Noël

Coward's successful Broadway play, in which Coward starred with Alfred Lunt and Lynn Fontanne. Paramount paid $50,000 each to Coward for the rights and Ben Hecht for the screenplay. Hecht used only one of Coward's lines, a toast "To the good of our immortal souls" during Cooper's drunken scene, and came up with his own equally sparkling dialogue:

> Cooper: I haven't a clean shirt to my name.
> March: A clean shirt? What's up? A romance?
> Cooper: I'm not talking pyjamas. Just a clean shirt.[9]

The film was directed by the German-born Ernst Lubitsch, known for his delicate touch and Continental charm. His gift for suggesting a poignant sadness beneath the gaiety was a perfect match for Coward's bittersweet comedy.

In *Design for Living* Cooper (in Coward's stage role) abandoned the war, action and adventure roles he'd played in recent years and returned, this time with greater maturity and confidence, to the witty sophisticate of *Children of Divorce*. He now plays an American painter in Paris who forms a lighthearted *ménage à trois* with his best friend and the girl they're both in love with. Unlike *Morocco*, where von Sternberg had concentrated on Dietrich and left Cooper to find his own way, Lubitsch supervised his performance closely and taught him a great deal. A fellow director said that he used to show the actors "how to do everything right down to the minutest detail. He would take a cape, and show the star how to put it on. He supplied all the little movements. He was magnificent because he knew his art better than anybody." Just as Ronald Colman had once advised the young Cooper to slow down and be natural, so Lubitsch gave him the same sort of valuable advice: "Look, Gary. Stop trying to save film. I have lots of film. You don't have to charge through a scene in one second, like a bull. Take two seconds. Do like Freddie [March]. He pauses. His pauses are valuable to me. They use up film, but they make a subtle point, and that's what film is for—to make a point. Now, you are just as big a star as Freddie. Your pauses are just as valuable to me."

The film begins amusingly as Miriam Hopkins sketches Cooper and March while they sleep in a train en route to Paris. They first speak to her in French, but when she exclaims "Oh, nuts!" they realize she is American. Both young men immediately fall for the same girl. She later recalled that in the train scene she "wore one of those hats that clung to the head and came down over one eye" and thought: "Oh, goodie, now I'll look like Dietrich."[10] In the film she compares Cooper to "a rugged straw hat with a very soft lining—a little bit out of shape—very dashing to look at and very comfortable to wear."

Cooper hangs his drawings and March displays copies of his plays when Hopkins, with newly marcelled hair, visits their bohemian garret and decides she wants both men. She moves in with them, and they agree to live together platonically. When March gets a play accepted and leaves for London, Hopkins, unable to resist Cooper, remarks: "It's true we have a gentleman's agreement. But unfortunately I'm no gentleman." She also sleeps with March when he returns, is discovered by Cooper and solves her dilemma by leaving them both. She then marries her boss, who forgives her past, and returns to America. They follow her, break up a stuffy party at her house and take her back to their completely amoral life in Paris. The brittle, somewhat static film, which takes a comic approach to the potentially tragic triangle, has theatrical entrances and exits and long, stagy speeches. But Cooper shows real versatility in this frothy part. Deft, lively and quick-witted, he moves gracefully between jolly friendship and angry rivalry—and makes fun of himself along the way.

Design for Living, wrote Molly Haskell, demolished a staggering number of sacred cows: "premarital virginity, fidelity, monogamy, marriage, and, finally, the one article of even bohemian faith, the exclusive, one-to-one love relationship." It was not surprising, therefore, that when Paramount wanted to re-release it in 1940, six years after the Production Code came into effect, the Breen Office, which censored films called it "a story of gross sexual irregularity, that is treated as comedy, and in which there is no 'compensating moral value' of any kind." They ruled that it was not acceptable under the current code. Interviewed by *Photoplay* while making the film, Cooper took a surprisingly dark view of the amorous relations and said that "two men could love the same woman, but not for a very long time. . . . Life is too drab a proposition to continue the gay, light manner such a situation would require."

Lubitsch, delighted by the performance that had extended Gary's range as an actor, said that "Noël Coward means nothing to most of [the audience]. Gary Cooper means something to them, and they will be happy to see that he is an accomplished light comedian." Cooper, March and Hopkins gave Depression audiences the image of carefree, charming youth, striving for success. Cooper's fans, as enthusiastic as Lubitsch, tore his suit to shreds at the Hollywood premiere. His acquaintance with Noël Coward was enduring. Cooper courted his future wife while making the movie and married her soon after it was completed. She still has a copy of Coward's autobiography, *Present Indicative* (1938), with the inscription "To Rocky, to celebrate an old friendship."[11]

8

Marriage to Rocky

1933–1934

I

Cooper's year with the Countess di Frasso introduced him to the fashionable world beyond Hollywood, gave him a taste for travel and luxury, and aroused his social ambitions. His future wife, Veronica "Rocky" Balfe, would accelerate his transformation from Montana cowboy to international sophisticate. Connected to Hollywood through her uncle, the art director Cedric Gibbons, she was a shy but polished and worldly New York debutante. Cooper already had wealth and status in Hollywood, but his marriage gave him access to other privileges and pleasures.

Rocky's grandfather Harry Balfe, an immigrant from County Meath in Ireland, settled in Newburgh on the Hudson. His brothers started a bank in Newburgh, left the Catholic Church and, abandoning their Irish heritage, became Presbyterians. Balfe began in business by manufacturing sparkling water, and eventually made millions as an industrialist and financier. He later raised thoroughbred horses on a ranch near Fresno, California, which Rocky and Gary sometimes visited.

Rocky's mother, Veronica Gibbons, had a desperately unhappy marriage to the ne'er-do-well Harry Balfe, Jr. She fled to Paris with her daughter and obtained a divorce, when Rocky was nine, in 1922. Bitter about his terrible temper and cruel treatment of her mother, Rocky did not see her father for many years. Veronica wiped out her first marriage as if it had never existed, and Rocky always looked down on the Balfes. One day, while shopping with her mother in Bergdorf's on Fifth Avenue,

Rocky walked around the counter to talk to a strange man. When the slightly puzzled Veronica asked, "Who was that?" Rocky replied: "Mother, that was father!"

In 1926 Veronica married the Wall Street tycoon Paul Shields. Veronica's relations with Harry Balfe, Jr. had taught Rocky about the humiliation and pain that marriage could bring, but her mother's second marriage was harmonious and lasting. Shields, a devoted stepfather, became Cooper's father-in-law and close friend. Born in St. Paul in 1889, he "grew up in Canada where his father was president of Dominion Iron and Steel Co. He graduated from Loyola, flunked out of Cornell Law, sold real estate, took a crack at investment banking and in 1923 went into the brokerage business for himself."[1] By 1938 Shields and Co. was one of the largest houses in Wall Street and had twenty offices in America and overseas. A "tough, cold operator," who made a lot of smart deals, Shields was a friend and adviser to Roosevelt's secretary of the navy James Forrestal, and provided a useful "link between Wall Street and the New Deal." Despite his poor eyesight (from cataracts), he was an accomplished golfer and yachtsman (his brother Cornelius won the *America's* Cup). Unlike the devout Veronica, he was an ex-Catholic and refused to come back into the Church even when, late in life, he was dying of cancer.

Though Shields was a staunch family man, he apparently did his share of philandering. Truman Capote, impressed by Shields' reputation and athletic ability, translated his financial skill into sexual power. In one of Capote's fictional "profiles," Marilyn Monroe exclaims that Shields was her greatest lover. When Marilyn says: "I met a man, he's related to Gary Cooper somehow. A stockbroker, and nothing much to look at—sixty-five, and he wears those very thick glasses. Thick as jellyfish," Capote identifies Shields as "that old swordsman" who "really scoots around. . . . He's supposed to be sensational."

Rocky's nickname, short for Veronica, was a tribute to her athletic prowess. She had always been a tomboy, and the fashion editor Diana Vreeland called her "the lifeguard." It was ironic and amusing that the classy socialite had the same nickname as her famous contemporaries the Italian-American prizefighters Rocky Marciano and Rocky Graziano. She grew up on Park Avenue and went to a posh finishing school that emphasized the social graces. Educated to become the wife of a wealthy man, she had physical beauty, a debutante's background and social connections, elegance and good taste, sporting ability and skill as a hostess, shrewdness and common sense. She did not finish high school and went into the world to find a desirable husband. One of her girlfriends, Anne McConnell, married Henry Ford II. Rocky's friends, like Tom and Daisy Buchanan's in *The Great Gatsby*, "drifted here and there unrestfully wherever people played polo and were rich together."[2]

In 1933 Rocky traveled to Hollywood to visit her distinguished uncle Cedric Gibbons, and see if style and good looks could lead to a career as an actress. He was the supervising art director at MGM from 1925 until 1956, and his stunning stark white film sets influenced the interior decor of wealthy American homes. Born in Brooklyn in 1890, the son of an Irish architect, he was six feet tall, handsome, charming and wealthy. Impeccably dressed in dark blue suits, gray homburgs and matching gloves, he drove a gleaming white Duesenberg. Gibbons had designed the original Oscar, and the light-filled house he built in Santa Monica Canyon embodied "his impeccable taste and commitment to modern design, his fondness for luxury and innovation, and his mastery of theatrical effects." Fay Wray, a frequent guest, wrote that his own house was like a film set: "a wide staircase rose from the entrance to turn at a right angle before long windows and reach, on the second level, a large living room. . . . There were built-in lounges and a sense of great space." To complete the perfect picture, Rocky's uncle was married to the actress Dolores del Rio, whose portrait by Diego Rivera hung above the fireplace. Born into a wealthy Mexican family, she played elegant, ladylike roles and was a sharp contrast, both on and off screen, to the tempestuous Lupe Velez.

Rocky, accompanied by her old nanny, suddenly turned up in this stage-like setting to grace the scene at his dinners and parties. The stylish eastern debutante—a slim, fine-boned, titian-haired beauty, five feet five inches tall and 120 pounds—made a striking appearance. She stood out, even among the gorgeous actresses, and impressed the Hollywood crowd. Encouraged by her uncle and using the professional name of Sandra Shaw, she dabbled briefly in films. She had a bit part that was later deleted from Cooper's *Today We Live*, landed a featured role in *Blood Money* (1933) with George Bancroft and Frances Dee, and was thrown to her death by the gorilla in *King Kong* (1933), in a gory scene that was subsequently cut. Instead, Rocky can still be seen silhouetted in a high window, screaming in horror as the huge ape climbs up the skyscraper. When she asked Fay Wray, the star of the film, the best way to scream, Fay told her: "Imagine yourself in a dangerous situation."

Suitably modest about her brief moment as a starlet, Rocky later told reporters: "Could we just not go into my film career? I had no talent whatsoever. . . . Don't remind me of those days. I was the most awful actress in the world and I never had a chance."[3] Rocky, was a strong-willed young woman, and if she'd been seriously interested in a film career, she would have made more of an effort and used her connections to achieve greater success. She merely tried movies for a lark, and her heart was not in it.

Rocky was often criticized by Cooper's friends and acquaintances. Considered a cold, distant, pretentious and arrogant easterner, very old money and Park Avenue, she despised most people in Hollywood and used her sharp, critical tongue to cut the "ill-bred savages" down to size. Lonely at first in the unfamiliar Hollywood world, Rocky held back and did not go in for the meaningless glad-handing and air-kissing. The naturally friendly Cooper defended her by explaining that "Rocky was afraid. She was . . . living in a strange place. She wanted to be liked, but gave the impression she was stuck up."

Evie Johnson, her friend and neighbor, said that Rocky was quite the opposite of the person she was commonly supposed to be. She was shy not stand-offish, unassuming rather than assertive. Her daughter, Maria, agreed that she was shy and hated to be stared at when she entered a room. The more insecure she was, the worse her behavior seemed, and her overcompensation sometimes appeared as arrogance. Cooper's nephew called her reserved, polished, savvy and sophisticated. Connie Wald, another close friend, said Rocky had great curiosity, kept up with everything and was always well informed. When you got to know her, she was capable of great personal warmth. The screen writer Ivan Moffat, noting Rocky's reputation as a strong, tough character, found her sharp-witted. He liked her direct manner and admired her "glittering eye."[4]

Cooper met Rocky at a boating party and then at Cedric Gibbons' house in 1933. They seemed like complete opposites, and nobody thought they were right for each other. She was the wealthy urban debu-tante of Park Avenue, Southampton and Palm Beach—social, outgoing, talkative and domineering. Cooper, for all his glamour and European sophistication, was still very much the small-town westerner and outdoorsman—solitary, reserved, laconic and unassertive. But both had physical beauty, style and elegance as well as a keen interest in sports and complemented each other perfectly. As Jack Hemingway, who knew them in Sun Valley, observed, Rocky "flaunted a veneer of tough aggressiveness from which she derived her nickname. It made a startling contrast with Cooper's very shy and gentle manner and natural westerner's way."

After he'd been away from Hollywood for a year and recovered (with Dorothy's help) his emotional equilibrium, Cooper was ready to settle down. But he needed a regulated existence to provide stability. Rocky was not the sort of girl you had an affair with. Very young and very religious, with no sexual or occupational experience, she had unusual strength of character and no desire to become a competitive actress. Though out of her native element, she ignored all the gossip that swirled around her and—flawlessly dressed and groomed—entered the public eye. Their visual image as a couple—Mr. and Mrs. Gary Cooper—was important to both of them and would help keep them together in times of trouble.

Rocky's family was not well pleased with her choice of a notorious philanderer who had slept with almost all his leading ladies. Though he had freely enjoyed the favors of many young women in the past, Cooper unashamedly upheld the sexual double standard and insisted: "The girl I ask to be my wife must come into marriage unsoiled. In true male style, I shall expect the girl who marries me not to be 'damaged goods.' "[5] In a similarly old-fashioned manner, he amazed everyone by formally asking Cedric Gibbons for permission to marry his niece. Just as traditional Westerns always contrast the hero's Mexican mistress with the Anglo girl he finally marries, so in real life when Cooper became involved with an innocent easterner, he abandoned all the Lupes and dubious dark ladies of his past.

II

Rocky had always been extremely close to her mother. After her marriage she continued to see her, write to her or speak to her on the phone—in the days when long-distance calls were difficult and expensive—nearly every day of her life. Dispensing with a church wedding (since Cooper was not Catholic) as well as best man, ushers and reception, he and Rocky were quietly married at the Shields' residence, 778 Park Avenue, on December 15, 1933, when he was thirty-two and she was twenty. Their marriage and honeymoon in Phoenix, where they met Cooper's parents, inspired a flood of "eligible bachelor caught by deb" articles in the film magazines and popular press. The actor Robert Stack remembered Rocky, her reddish hair flying in the wind, looking dazzling as she raced by in Cooper's Duesenberg. After marriage, she made him put the top up and remarked: "I hooked him. Do you think I'm now going to ruin my hair?"

One friend noted that Cooper was transformed by his marriage: "All of a sudden, he just seemed to have control of himself and his life"—or Rocky did. Joan Crawford added: "He was trying to live down his past indiscretions. He was a homebody then. He told me his wife got up early to make him breakfast and every evening he left the studio in time to have dinner with her. According to him, Rocky read all his scripts and he valued her opinion because she could be objective." In fact, Rocky hated cooking and let the servants make breakfast. She was not domestic, but did create the design, decor and social style of their home. She did not cue other parts for him when he was learning his lines, but looked over his scripts and took part in his decisions and his career.

In the mid-1930s it became fashionable to buy a "ranch" over the Hollywood Hills in the San Fernando Valley, where Gable and Lombard, Robert Taylor and Barbara Stanwyck, Spencer Tracy and the producer Hal Wallis all played gentleman farmer. Rocky refused to live in his "African zoo" on Chevy Chase and thought they should own a house with some land around it.[6] Shortly before his marriage he bought a six-acre ranch in Encino, with chickens, walnut trees, and groves of oranges and lemons.

After living for two years in what was then the countryside, Rocky tired of the joys of rural life and wanted to be closer to the social scene in Hollywood. In 1936, planning to have a family, they bought land and built a large white Bermuda-Georgian house, with stucco walls, white roof and gleaming red doors, at 11940 Chaparal, just above Sunset Boulevard in Brentwood. The rather stark, ultramodern interior, which looked like one of Gibbons' sets, had "marble floors with inlays in dusty pink, black, and Paris green. The window shades were of uncut chenille. Zebra skins were used for stair covering. Baguette glass tables and innumerable mirrors lent sparkle to the soft grey walls. . . . The walls were an avocado shade, the floors a deeper green. A [baby] grand piano dominated, and there was a huge fireplace. The wood-paneled library had gilded leather volumes"—decorative objects chosen for their rich colors.

The beautiful three-and-a-half-acre estate included a swimming pool, tennis courts, ducks, chickens, dogs and lush landscaping as well as a vegetable garden, citrus grove and avocado orchard that Cooper cultivated with a small tractor. A live-in Scandinavian couple, successors to

Ugo and Maria, looked after the house, and a gardener cared for the grounds. Rocky had covered the staircase with zebra pelts, but Cooper's arsenal of pistols and rifles, sufficient to outfit a small task force, and his hunting trophies, many of which he himself had stuffed, as well as his saddles, bows and arrows, javelins, model boats and planes were relegated to a separate "gun room" or exiled to his Paramount dressing room. The pampered chimpanzee was declared persona non grata and banished to a distant animal sanctuary, to which Cooper retained visiting privileges. But there were no more intimate dinners with his pet. Despite the attempt to simplify their lives, they wound up, as Cooper said, "in Brentwood, with a bigger house and three acres of agricultural problems."[7]

Cooper was not particularly athletic in his teens and twenties (he didn't even know how to play baseball), but became keenly interested in sports after he married Rocky. Proud that she could ride, shoot and do all the things he liked to do, he told a reporter about their athletic way of life: "Rocky and I usually play a few sets of tennis before dinner, that gives me a workout. We keep a couple of saddle horses on a ranch a half hour's drive from our house. We go up there and ride in the hills. Once in a while we go to a night club. I like to dance." Their sporting activities were also competitive. Rocky was an expert swimmer and tennis player but had never handled a gun before they met. To share a sport her husband loved, she learned to skeet-shoot and became the women's champion in California. She later surpassed Cooper (still bothered by his old hip injury) in skiing.

Cooper's celebrity forced him to protect his privacy and inevitably cut him off from ordinary people. Servants did the household tasks, and his manager handled his money. Most at ease with his fellow actors, he tended (like most stars) to see the same movie people in the same hermetic round of parties. The Coopers' social life revolved around sports, games and dinners with old and new neighbors who were also in the business: the directors William Wellman and Frank Capra, and the actors Tyrone and Annabella Power, Robert Taylor and Barbara Stanwyck, the Fred MacMurrays, Van Johnsons, Cesar Romeros. Joel McCrea and his wife, Frances Dee, replaced Cooper's bachelor friends Richard Arlen and Buddy Rogers. Born in Pasadena, four years after Cooper, McCrea graduated from Hollywood High School and Pomona College, and acted in the Pasadena Playhouse. The grandson of a western stagecoach driver who had fought against the Apaches, he raised his own horses. A passionate outdoorsman and large-scale rancher, he invested wisely in livestock and real estate, was a staunch Republican and frugal millionaire. The tall, rangy cowboy looked a bit like Cooper and often played the same sort of roles. Like Cooper, he was a good listener and a modest, gentle, sweet-natured man.

On special occasions Marion Davies invited the Coopers to join her guests for a weekend at Hearst's castle in San Simeon. The screenwriter Frances Marion described the lavish ambience, in which precious works of art had been thrown together in a tasteless way: "Some of the guests gazed in admiration at art treasures such as one rarely finds outside a museum; twelfth-century tapestries, silver, and furniture from raided palaces of Europe, paintings by old masters, and Grecian sculpture. The moguls from Hollywood, more interested in high finance than in art treasure, discussed 'big deals' while they drank magnums of champagne, ate shellfish flown by planes from New Orleans, and dined off service which had once belonged to Marie Antoinette." After dinner the latest movies were shown in a palatial theater.

Rocky, an efficient and well-organized woman, ran her own domain with style and panache. She soon became, with Mrs. Henry Hathaway, one of the leading hostesses in Hollywood "high society." She would erect huge tents, give two or three large parties a year, with hierarchical A and B lists. Invitations to her smaller, more select gatherings were prized and sought after. According to the director Otto Preminger, mere "producers were never invited, nor writers, except those with international reputations. The group was restricted to actors, studio heads, and directors."[8]

In a revealing statement, Rocky described the difficulties of being the wife of a world-famous actor: "As a big star, he had to be number one, as any wife married to one can tell you. A woman married to a star has to get used to the fact that everyone looks at him first, especially women. . . . Coop told me fights always upset him and we just weren't going to have any. He laid down the law and I listened. You have to, if you don't want to lose your husband." In fact, most friends felt *she* was more strong-willed and dominant than the gentle Gary. Cesar Romero, for example, was embarrassed when Rocky was rude to Cooper in public. As her husband told a long, familiar story, she'd become impatient and sharply interrupt him by asking: "Why don't you get to the point?"

Cooper shared Rocky's close relationship with her mother and stepfather. But Rocky did not get on with his comparatively humble family, and among her friends talk of Gary's Montana boyhood was strictly *verboten*. The Coopers lacked the wealth and sophistication of the Shields and couldn't possibly fit into their glittering social circle. Rocky, more than a match for the once-powerful and still-possessive Alice, gradually drew Cooper away from his parents. Arthur had remarried after the death of his first wife, and his children, Georgia and Howard, spent a good deal of the time with their grandparents in Hollywood. Arthur eventually became a savings bank executive near Palm Springs, and saw Gary only at Christmas and Easter.

In 1934 Judge Cooper suffered back and knee injuries when he was hit by a car at a pedestrian crossing in Hollywood, and retired from law practice the following year. He now walked with a cane and became silent, gruff and stern. His granddaughter Maria found him quite scary. Alice, who would ham it up to attract attention, was much more outgoing and gregarious. When she waved her lovely hands around as she talked, Gary would tell her: "Mother, stop windmilling!" Like her son, Alice had a healthy appetite. She'd make toast in the oven and smear a soft avocado on it, and when Gary cooked a Sunday barbecue she'd eat three grilled franks on buns with all the trimmings: onion, pickle, relish and mustard.[9]

Alice wanted to be invited to his home more often, but Rocky, though she was always extraordinarily polite to her mother-in-law, would roll her eyes at the prospect of Alice coming to dinner. Howard recalled that at Rocky's dinners the family always dressed up properly and felt "under great tension." They'd discuss safe topics like the old days at the ranch or the current price of gold. But Charles' debacle over the sale of the dude ranch still rankled in the family, and the country club façade barely disguised the palpable strain between Rocky and Alice.

Rocky's wealth and social connections, like those of Dorothy di Frasso (their families had both made millions on Wall Street), enabled Cooper to bridge the gap between the glitter of Hollywood and the society of Park Avenue. As Elsa Maxwell remarked, Rocky encouraged him to get "out of Hollywood as soon as he finishes a film. She never got accustomed to the movie crowd." The Coopers visited Sun Valley for hunting and skiing, and took frequent trips to Europe. They would spend most summers at the Shields' luxurious country house on Ox Pasture Road in Southampton, Long Island. The rambling, two-story, gray shingled house had shuttered bay windows, four tall chimneys and a long, graveled driveway dominated by a weeping beech. The wide, tree-filled grounds had a tennis court and a chipping-and-putting green. The atmosphere was formal, with luncheon at precisely one o'clock, and jacket and tie required at dinner, but the conversation was lively and stimulating. Cooper loved swimming and lying on the beach, searching for osprey nests, sailing on the Shields' ample yacht, or flying around in their private plane.

III

Wanting to spend more time with Rocky during their first year of marriage, Cooper made only one movie in 1934. *Now and Forever*, a comedy with serious implications, was directed by Henry Hathaway, who would make six more films with Cooper during the next twenty years. Though Cooper got on well with him, Hathaway, a consummate professional specializing in action pictures, was a rough director—hard on both cast and crew. A worldly, hospitable, cigar-smoking man with a wry sense of humor (he called Françoise Sagan's novel *Bonjour, Trieste*), Hathaway—according to Richard Widmark—was "a tough customer who kicked the hell out of us." If performers missed a line he'd ridicule them publicly, and once referred to a hopeless actress as "a dumb cunt." But he had a very high opinion of Cooper, rated him above Cagney and James Stewart, and called him "the best actor of all of them."

Cooper also impressed the five-year-old Shirley Temple, who plays his self-possessed, precocious and wise little daughter in the film. When they first met, he instantly won her devotion by kneeling down to her level, drawling, "Hi, Wiggle-Britches!" and asking for her autograph. He knew how to please a child who had everything and bought her some beautiful toys. During setups he taught her how to draw with a box of colored pencils.[10] Though Cooper found it irritating to be corrected by a small child who knew everybody else's lines as well as her own, he was impressed by Shirley's intelligence and charm.

Cooper acts exceptionally well with Shirley Temple, and their tender relationship is the most absorbing part of the picture. He plays a smooth confidence man who's been living in Paris while his late wife's family has been caring for his little daughter. He returns home prepared to let them adopt her—for $75,000. He admits that it's "not a nice way to make money," and his second wife, played by Carole Lombard, disapproves of his behavior and leaves him. He's insulted by his in-laws and rolls his eyes in anguish when asked to sign away his rights, but quickly establishes rapport with Temple (as he had in real life). Brought up in a joyless, stultifying atmosphere, she's instantly charmed by her rascally father. When they return from a short ride on a sailboat, she exclaims: "It's been a wonderful adventure." After this delightful episode, he changes his mind and decides to keep her. Defying the oppressive family, the doting father takes his little girl on a spree in New York. When they overdo it and he has to give her a dose of castor oil, he makes a compassionate face.

Cooper and Temple rejoin Lombard in France. But she knows that he still plans to live by fraud and theft, and threatens to leave again if he doesn't reform. Despite his obvious love for the child, she thinks he's a bad influence and says, "he hasn't any business with that kid." Sure enough, he gambles away her school fees in a casino, steals a necklace and hides it in her teddy bear. Meanwhile, he overhears her deceiving another child and realizes she's now imitating his crooked ways. When she discovers the missing necklace and learns that her father's a thief, her grief wrings his heart. Bending down for a close-up with Temple, Cooper imitates her scowl but understands that he can no longer charm his way out of the pain he's caused her. He returns the stolen jewels, but is shot in the struggle to get them back from a crooked accomplice. Though partially redeemed by the child's love, he knows that he's an unworthy father. In a surprising twist of plot, he makes a poignant sacrifice and gives her up to a rich lady who adopts her and will be a much better parent.

Now and Forever, usually ignored by film critics, is full of charm and interest. The child expresses the values of the film. At the party where Cooper steals the necklace, Temple tap-dances and sings a delightfully moralistic song about how she "owes the world a living" in the relentlessly cute style that made her so famous. Cooper's fine acting makes this movie worth watching. His volatile relations with Lombard provide a contrast with his steadfast love for his daughter, and he moves from the shady deception of a con man to the outraged indignation of a frustrated father. He displays dubious behavior in his criminal activities, fine anger with his relatives and tender sympathy for his daughter, moving effortlessly from worthless thief to devoted parent. His phrasing makes the dialogue sound natural, and his slightest gesture seems spontaneous.

IV

In 1934, after Cooper had married and bought a house, worked less and spent more, he had to put his financial affairs in order. In Fitzgerald's

Last Tycoon (1941), Monroe Stahr takes the Communist agitator Brimmer to lunch in a Hollywood restaurant and sees Cooper with a group of prosperous parasites: "Gary Cooper came in and sat down in a corner with a bunch of men who breathed whenever he did and looked as if they lived off him and weren't budging." Fitzgerald was probably referring to Cooper's three-hundred-pound agent, Jack Moss, who had been lifted from the water by a winch when he fell off Richard Arlen's boat, and to his lawyer, I.H. Prinzmetal. According to the hyperbolic estimate of the screenwriter Philip Dunne, "Jack was Coop's manager, business manager, and general factotum, an amazing fellow, great, one of the really brilliant minds of the picture business." Slim Talbot, in a more precise account, said that in 1933 "an assistant director named Jack Moss, who was working for Paramount in [Astoria,] Long Island, heard about Cooper and signed him for the Marion Davies movie, *Operator 13.* . . . Jack Moss took over Cooper's management and wangled a $5,000-a-week contract with Paramount to make *Lives of a Bengal Lancer*" in 1935.[11] Moss remained his agent until Cooper formed his own production company in 1944, and was later succeeded by Charles Feldman.

Izzy Prinzmetal, whose brother Myron was a leading Hollywood doctor, was born in Buffalo in 1906, earned his undergraduate and law degrees at Berkeley, and was resident attorney at MGM before starting his own practice. The heavyset Prinzmetal was a talented amateur painter and father of six children. Alice Fleming, who later bceame Cooper's adoring secretary, found the lawyer arrogant and difficult to work for. The producer Walter Seltzer said he was a "fierce tiger" who was hard to negotiate with but always got good deals for his clients. Prinzmetal lasted longer than Moss, but he and Cooper had a falling-out in the 1950s, when Cooper suspected him of dishonesty and replaced film with Deane Johnson.

After Cooper married Rocky, Paul Shields rather than Prinzmetal handled their investments. In 1935–36 Cooper gave his father $5,000 and lent Arthur $8,000 to start a coal business. He had a share of the vast Gang ranch in British Columbia, where he went hunting and ate tall stacks of pancakes. He leased, with his parents, two thousand acres of land east of Palm Springs and planned to sink fifty-two oil wells. He later sold the leases, and the precious real estate became the site of the Palm Springs airport. In his will of February 1936, which named Rocky and Jack Moss executors, Cooper left the desert land to his parents, $10,000 to Arthur, a gold cigarette case to Moss and all the rest to Rocky. Disputing his high income tax bill of 1936, Cooper explained the expenses that were necessary to maintain his status as a star. He'd paid Moss $38,300 in commissions and claimed deductions for a trip to New York, wardrobe and automobile depreciation, telephone, still photos and donations to charity.[12]

As the effects of the Depression diminished, Cooper shared Paramount's increasing prosperity, and made huge leaps in salary every year. He earned $85,000 in 1932, $133,000 in 1933, $258,000 in 1934, $328,000 in 1935 and $370,000 (or more than $7,000 a week) in 1937. In 1939, when two-thirds of all American families made between $1,000 and $2,000 a year, Cooper surpassed the heads of IBM, Lever Brothers and General Motors, and earned $482,826, the highest salary in the United States.

After his return from Europe and break with Dorothy di Frasso, Cooper had reestablished himself at Paramount and married a beautiful, well-born and wealthy woman. He became good friends with her stepfather and uncle, lived in an elegant house, summered in Southampton and moved from the fringe to the center of Hollywood society. He would soon become a father. Already an accomplished light comedian and an authentic western actor, he would transform his screen image as the heroic common man in Frank Capra's *Mr. Deeds Goes to Town*.

9

American Apollo

1935–1937

I

After his wedding in 1933, Cooper took off most of the following year to settle into his new house and enjoy married life. In 1935 he made two noteworthy films: *The Wedding Night* for Sam Goldwyn and *The Lives of a Bengal Lancer* for Paramount. Though *The Wedding Night* was a failure at the box office, it is an interesting story of cultural conflict. Cooper plays a character based on Scott Fitzgerald, a burnt-out alcoholic writer with a southern wife, who retreats from the world to his family home in Connecticut to recover his health and his talent. But first his wife and then his Japanese servant find the place too cold and remote, and abandon him. He sells some land to neighboring Polish immigrants and meets their young daughter (Anna Sten), who's being forced into marriage with a brutish farmer (Ralph Bellamy). Cooper tells her, "It's lonely as the deuce here; my wife deserted me," and the girl brings him milk from the farm, lights the stove and makes his breakfast. Inspired by Sten, Cooper overcomes his writer's block and tells her story in his novel, and the two fall in love.

When Sten struggles home in a snowstorm and Cooper rescues her, she's forced to spend an (innocent) night in his house. Convinced she's been compromised, both father and fiancé are furious. The conflict is not only between traditional culture and the New World, but also between rural and urban, peasant and sophisticate. To complicate matters, the writer's wife suddenly returns, reads his novel and discovers why her

1 Alice and Charles Cooper, 1930s. Gary said that his father "was a little too honest, not enough of an extrovert, not the forward-pushing, hard-swinging type of fellow who made a colorful lawyer."

2 Gary with Alice Cooper, 1927. "A stand up, chin in the air, straight back sort of person," Alice looked and tried to act like Queen Mary.

3

Cooper, in an elaborately beribboned white bonnet and long furry coat, with Arthur, outside their house in Helena, c. 1904
Estate of Gary Cooper

4

Cooper, with Arthur and English relatives, Dunstable, c. 1910. "Gary was a very quiet boy, very much so. He was gentle more than anything."
Montana Historical Society

Cooper at Montana
Wesleyan College,
Helena, 1919.
"An artist of no small
ability"
Montana Historical Society

5

6

Cooper at Grinnell
College, 1922. He had a
"gorilla-like reach" as a
boxer and "could store
away pancakes and fried
eggs beyond human belief."
Estate of Gary Cooper

7

Cooper in *The Winning of Barbara Worth*, 1926. He knew what a cowboy would do and brought instinctive authenticity to his screen roles.

Estate of Gary Cooper

8

Clara Bow, with Cooper, 1927. She said: "He's hung like a horse and he can go all night."

Evelyn Brent, c. 1936. A
snazzy but stupid woman,
"she was like Baked Alaska —
very cold inside."
Kobal Collection

9

10
Lupe Velez, with Cooper, 1929. Lupe said she "was the only one who scarred him for life."

11

Fay Wray with Cooper, 1933. After five years of almost total silence, he suddenly exclaimed: "I imagine it would be wonderful to go to bed with you."
Fay Wray

12

Cooper with his new Duesenberg, 1930. The gleaming, high-grilled "Yellow Peril" was as long, lean and elegant as Cooper himself.
Auburn Cord Duesenberg Museum

13

Cooper, with a Masai mother and child, Tanganyika, 1931. "I love Africa. I love its bigness, its toughness, the savagery you can feel all around you."
Estate of Gary Cooper

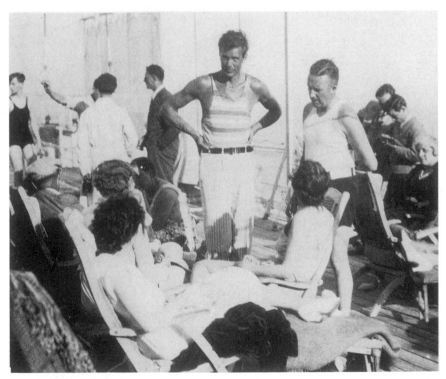

14

Cooper, on a ship returning from East Africa, 1932. Wearing a striped singlet and striped white trousers, he looks like a pagan god.
Estate of Gary Cooper

Tallulah Bankhead, 1931. She was notorious for her tempestuous personality, uninhibited behavior, sultry voice and raucous laughter.
Kobal Collection

15

16

Rocky, with Cooper, on their wedding day, December 15, 1933. She was reserved, polished, savvy and sophisticated. Estate of Gary Cooper

husband is now ill at ease and cold toward her. She tries to end the affair by telling the girl: "With you he's got nothing more than he had with me before it wore off, but what he and I have now, after these five years, is . . . well, after all, five years." He declares his love for the girl and insists on a divorce. Instead of exploring this tension in a realistic way, the script simply builds to an operatic climax. Incongruously dressed in a business suit in a throng of brightly costumed peasants, Cooper dances with the bride after the elaborate wedding procession. Bellamy, drunk and jealous, tries to kill him. Sten, attempting to save him, falls down a flight of stairs and dies. The film ends as Cooper recalls their lost love.

Though Cooper is not wholly convincing as an alcoholic, he does suggest the isolation of a writer's life, and registers frustration and misery on his mobile face. When he's shocked by the rejection of his latest book, his expression becomes defeated and angry. At the crude Polish dinner he reveals the gulf between himself and the family of the girl he loves as he tucks in his napkin and raises his eyes in alarm. He courts, flatters and tries to seduce her by saying: "Don't be so moral; it doesn't go with those eyes." Brooding and bitter about his wife's interference, he bites the inside of his mouth, presses his lips together and pulls them back. Ralph Bellamy, recalling his sensitivity to other actors, said that when Cooper "played a scene he'd look you in the eye while speaking—straight in the eye—for a second, then he'd drop his head and stare at the floor almost as if apologizing for having intruded."

Cooper's co-star, Anna Sten, born in Kiev and trained at the Moscow Art Theater, had appeared in Russian and German films, but had trouble with English and failed to live up to Goldwyn's high hopes. She had been brought to Hollywood as a new Dietrich or Garbo, but was wholesomely pretty, not decadent or sultry. For some unaccountable reason—in her role as Polish peasant girl—she had to read a difficult line from Robert Browning's poem "Love Among the Ruins"—"Earth's returns / For whole centuries of folly, noise, and sin!"—and kept saying, with a strong Russian accent: "Earse returzs." Notorious for mangling the English language himself, in one of his pep talks on the set Goldwyn exclaimed: "if this scene isn't the greatest love scene ever put on film the whole goddamned picture will go right up out of the sewer."[1] in "Anything Goes," Cole Porter mocked Sam Goldwyn, with great conviction, instructing Anna Sten in diction. But *The Wedding Night* has been underrated. The film gives some idea of Polish life in rural New England, and transforms a major theme during the Depression—escape from the corruption of the city to an idyllic life in the country—into a moving pastoral tragedy.

The Lives of a Bengal Lancer (1935) was an immensely popular and successful adventure movie. Set near the Khyber Pass on the Northwest Frontier of India, it used sets left over from De Mille's *The Crusades* (also 1935). Its authentic footage, shot in India in 1931, conveyed a vivid sense of regimental life. Adapted front P.C. Wren's novel, it had a great many Kiplingesque elements: pigsticking, venomous cobras and roach races; a stiff old English colonel who's terribly strict when his son joins the regiment; friendly rivalry and a strong male bond between Cooper and Franchot Tone; an oily emir, a treacherous native girl and fierce Pashto hill fighters; troops picked off by snipers and an enemy ambush; torture scenes, ammunition explosions and a British column marching to the rescue; officers going native (as in Kipling's novel *Kim*) and stirring patriotic quotes front W.E. Henley's "England, My England."

Cooper plays the brave, impulsive Canadian Lieutenant McGregor, an old pro among the new officers. He smokes a pipe and has a brief flirtation with a mustache. He does a comic imitation of his ramrod colonel, rescues Tone from the cobra and the young officer from a wild pig. In a character as stereotyped as any gangster or cowboy, he pushes out his lower jaw and widens his eyes when taken by surprise, speaks the native lingo, disobeys restraining orders ("There's been enough thinking, and talking, too. I'm going"), tightens his fists but stands up under torture, sacrifices himself in the final battle and wins a posthumous Victoria Cross: all in all, a jolly good chap!

II

Throughout his career Cooper gave sturdy performances as a dashing fellow, a tough cowboy, a courageous man of action. But in 1936 he made two of his most impressive films: *Desire*, a romantic comedy, and *Mr. Deeds Goes to Town*, a social satire, both of which offered roles perfectly suited to his talents. *Desire*, his best comedy, was made in the Paramount studio between mid-September and mid-December 1935, and a small crew was sent to Europe to film the background shots of a Parisian square and a Spanish village. The $1.2 million budget included $200,000 for Dietrich (who had become the greater star, now gets top billing and still says "tewwible"), $93,000 for Cooper and 50¢ for a gendarme's whistle.

Dietrich and Cooper are charming, the script is witty and the four supporting actors are excellent. Though Frank Borzage got the credit, Ernst Lubitsch, then running the Paramount studio, did most of the directing.

The startlingly sexy opening shot behind the titles, which vividly suggests the title's erotic and venal double meaning, shows a woman's bosom in a low-cut dress and elegant fingers caressing the pearls around her neck. Like von Sternberg in *Morocco*, Lubitsch plays off—this time for comic effect—the forthright American male against the mysterious and willful European *femme fatale*. Cooper is an automobile engineer from Detroit, working in Paris. We first see him in private, comically practicing the tough approach he plans to take when asking for a vacation. When the boss unexpectedly offers him time off and the use of the company's latest car, he beams with innocent delight.

Dietrich, meanwhile, invents an elaborate ruse to steal a precious pearl necklace. Elegant and beautiful, she poses as the wife of a famous nerve specialist and arranges for a fussy jeweler to deliver the necklace to the doctor's office. At the doctor's office she pretends that the jeweler is her husband and arranges for a consultation to cure him of various neuroses: he imagines that people owe him money and prefers to wear women's clothes. The doctor reassures her: "A few careful treatments and we'll have him out of nightgowns and into pajamas in no time." Dietrich orchestrates the fraud and makes off with the loot.

Cooper, in a sporty little car, and Dietrich, in a faster, more elegant one, are both driving from Paris to the Spanish border. Happy to be free and on the road, he sings "I'm driving, I'm driving . . ." to the tune of "*Cielito Lindo*." He stops to take a photo, and she splashes him with mud. But following the Hollywood convention, his suit is immaculate in the next shot. When he kisses her hand, he self-consciously bows, grins and says: "Continental." He gets caught smuggling cigarettes into Spain and has to pop the remaining packs out of his folded socks. But he doesn't know that she's dropped the stolen necklace into his pocket. She must now pursue and entrap him to recover it.

Reversing the situation in *Morocco*, Cooper now falls madly in love with the hollow-cheeked, metal-haired vamp. He shows boyish glee when he catches up with her, smiles and shakes his head when her car horn gets stuck. Enjoying the cat-and-mouse game, she drives off and leaves him, and then slinks away as he tracks her down in a hotel. "All I know about you," he exclaims, "is that you stole my car and I'm insane about you."

In a discussion with her "uncle," another thief posing as an aristocrat, about whether Cooper's car or his "niece" is more important, Cooper says: 'Well, I don't know." But he waves his fingers reassuringly at her as he leaves with her "uncle" to discuss the damage to his car.

Lubitsch makes the most of the amusing contrast between the ingenuous, provincial Cooper and the glamorous, duplicitous Dietrich. As Dietrich shifts dramatically between black and white outfits, her lines, as in *Morocco*, are at once amusing, ironic, passionate, parodic, sly, sexy, romantic and bitter. Following her bait, Cooper—soul mate and satyr—pursues her and reveals his seductive intent. She says, "You had it in your eyes" and he shyly replies, "I didn't know it showed." Thinking she's flirting with him as she tries to extract the necklace from his pocket, he foolishly grins when she remarks: "I see you're a kind of Don Juan."

Dietrich's early films always display her stunning cabaret songs. When she sings to Cooper, with extraordinary sexual voltage, "Can it be that tonight is the night?"—and it is!—he registers all sorts of pleasurable anticipation. He truthfully whispers, "I've never been with anyone like you before," and tells her "the Spanish moon is very becoming to you." She swoons as he first embraces her and the orchestra swells to orgasmic heights. The next morning, signaling a night of love (and somehow sneaking the scene past the censor), both are too exhausted to get out of their beds. At breakfast Cooper, as ravenous for food as for sex, asks Dietrich: "Are you eating those eggs?" Urged on by outraged organizations like the Catholic Lending Library of Holyoke, Massachusetts, which wrote, "All decent people, particularly Catholic people, are looking to you to continue to eliminate the 'nuances' and the Lubitsch touch," the Breen Office insisted that Paramount eliminate Cooper's line "I'll wake up in the morning with a Spanish comb in my hand."[2]

Cooper's small-town goodness steers Dietrich to the righteous path, but both must redeem themselves by confession and reparation before they can be worthy of each other's love. Dietrich confesses that she's not really a countess, that "I fooled you, I lied to you." Cooper, who's also deceived her about his salary and position in the firm, admits: "I'm neither a king nor a prince nor a count—not even an Elk." They return the necklace and are forgiven by the surprised and grateful victims, and Dietrich suddenly switches from siren to devoted wife. The idea of her settling down as a contented *Hausfrau* in Detroit is even more delightfully absurd than her role as camp follower in the Sahara.

Contemporary critics recognized what we have now forgotten: that

Cooper was a brilliant comedian. Graham Greene called *Desire* "one of Mr. Gary Cooper's best performances." Greene's colleague C.A. Lejeune agreed that Cooper's "quiet, informal style takes the Lubitsch suggestion well. Ordinarily too receptive to be a good actor, he becomes a very good actor in the present film by virtue of this malleability." A third English critic, John Marks, noted Cooper's development and said he had precisely the right qualities to play against Dietrich: "the bony American Apollo *de nos jours*, who had steadily improved since he played his first, flat cowboy parts . . . adds an engaging polish to his habitual humour, charm, and unobtrusive male sufficiency." In this film Cooper moves with perfect masculine grace through a world made familiar to him by the Countess di Frasso. Richard Schickel wrote that Cooper, always completely natural, was "the only truly beautiful actor who did not spoil the effect of his handsomeness by seeming vain or self-absorbed."[3]

While *Desire* was the high point of Cooper's comic performances, *Mr. Deeds Goes to Town*, written by Robert Riskin and directed by Frank Capra at Columbia, took him to quite another genre and to an important turning point in his career. Instead of redeeming one lost woman, Cooper now reforms a whole corrupt society. The extremely allusive and literate script uses Cooper's lack of vanity, his apparent unselfconsciousness, his transparent goodness to create his lasting image as a popular, even mythological folk hero. Although he remains the earnest, loving, naively good guy of *Desire*, Capra's film destroyed the irresistibly sexy lover of Crawford and Lombard, Bankhead and Dietrich. The Capra image, confirmed in *Meet John Doe* (1941), led to Cooper being cast (almost in bronze) as a series of worthy but wooden real-life heroes: Sergeant York, Lou Gehrig, Dr. Wassell and Captain Billy Mitchell as well as the intolerably good father in *Friendly Persuasion*.

Born in Sicily and educated at Cal Tech, Capra was the Charles Dickens of the cinema. A talented director, he made joyously sentimental movies with a distinct social program. He explained that he conceived Cooper as the quintessential American hero: "who in Hollywood could play honest, humble, 'corn tassel poet' Mr. Deeds? Only one actor: Gary Cooper. Every line in his face spelled honesty. So innate was his integrity he could be cast in phony parts, but never look phony himself. Tall, gaunt as Lincoln, cast in the frontier mold of Daniel Boone, Sam Houston, Kit Carson, this silent Montana cowpuncher embodied the true-blue virtues that won the West: durability, honesty, and native intelligence." Capra also described the ideas that Cooper so perfectly expressed: "*Mr. Deeds*

Goes to Town was the first film that I made in which I consciously tried to make a social statement. I wanted to see what an honest small-town man would do with $20,000,000—how he would handle it, and how he would handle all the predators that would surround him, and what good would come out of that thing, what statements you could make about a man being his brother's keeper. . . . Mr. Deeds was honest, but not necessarily an idealist. He didn't go out and really think up things to do with the money; it was forced on him."

Cooper's leading lady, Jean Arthur, was extremely neurotic. Capra, who brought out the best in her, described her tortured personality: "Never have I seen a performer plagued with such a chronic case of stage jitters. I'm sure she vomited before and after every scene. When the cameras stopped she'd run headlong to her dressing room, lock herself in—and cry. . . . Jean Arthur is an enigmatic figure because she doesn't do very well in crowds, and she doesn't do very well with people, and she doesn't do very well with life, but she does very well as an actress."[4] Comforted and reassured by Cooper's kindness, gentle temperament and quiet strength, Arthur overcame her phobias and found it easy to act with him. "With Gary," she said, "there are always wonderful hidden depths that you haven't found yet. . . . With Cooper it just seems to *happen*. I can't remember Cooper saying much of anything. But it's very comfortable working with him. You feel like you're resting on the Rock of Gibraltar."

One of Cooper's earlier films anticipates the plot of *Mr. Deeds*. In his sequence (one of eight separate stories revolving around a central theme) in *If I Had a Million* (1932), he played a soldier who thinks the $1 million check he receives is an April Fool's Day joke and gives away the fortune. *In Mr. Deeds* he's left $20 million by a long-lost uncle, doesn't want the money and also tries, with considerable difficulty, to give it away. Cooper's character, Longfellow Deeds (a tall poet who does things), is a Dickensian good man who sees how money can corrupt. He affirms the dignity of work and the value of wealth that's honestly earned. He's not out to change the world, but wants to use his money to make it a better place.

The film opens as a delegation of sleazy New York lawyers from the firm of Cedar, Cedar, Cedar and Budington (Clarence Budington Kelland wrote the story on which the movie was based) arrives in Mandrake Falls, Vermont, to bring Deeds the amazing news. The stationmaster, matching the screen persona with the real Cooper, tells the lawyers that he's "very democratic. You won't have no trouble at all. Talks to anybody." Cooper

as Deeds is earnest, slightly comic and solemnly contented. He wears a
bow tie and leather jacket, writes greeting card poetry and plays the tuba,
and has never been away from his small town. Reflectively pushing out
his lower lip and refusing to get excited, he teases the lawyers by
declaring: "Wonder why he left all that money to me? I don't need it."
Promised a visit to Grant's Tomb, he's persuaded to accompany them to
the big city. Before leaving, he slips away to join the town band and plays
the tuba at his own send-off. Employing the social remedies of
Roosevelt's New Deal, he plans to give all the money away. The villainous
lawyers, plotting to get it themselves, smugly maintain: "He's as naive as
a child."

In New York, other predators try to profit from his inheritance. The
harridan wife (Mayo Methot) of a potential legatee, wearing a satin
nightgown, fiercely orders her meek husband to sign some crooked
documents. The opera board attempts to persuade Deeds to underwrite
their extravagant projects. News editors, kept from the sensational story,
send Babe Bennett (Jean Arthur) to get it by posing as an innocent small-
town girl. Deeds' New England common sense enables him to see
through most of the crooks, though he is cruelly deceived by the young
reporter.

Set up (in both senses) in New York, he now wears a silk scarf and
dressing gown, and lives in a mansion surrounded by flunkies. The
homosexual butler says that Deeds' millionaire uncle "had all those
women. No accounting for taste." Superficially transformed, Deeds
remains essentially the same. He won't allow the butler to kneel while
helping him to dress, slides boyishly down the banister of the grand
staircase and, like a country lad, lets the rain fall on his face as he leaves
the house.

When writers mock and humiliate him in an Italian restaurant, he wins
our sympathy—and Jean Arthur's—with a little lecture on human
decency: "I know I must look funny to you, but maybe if you came to
Mandrake Falls, you'd look just as funny to *us*. But nobody would laugh
at you and make you ridiculous, 'cause that wouldn't be good manners."
The masterfully delivered speech is ironic, however, because the stationmaster at Mandrake Falls *did* make the lawyers look ridiculous by
answering all their questions quite literally and not providing the information they requested.

Describing Cooper's subtle technique in this scene, Gerald Weales
wrote: "At first he laughs with them, accepting the jokes as friendly

ragging, but as he realizes their essential snottiness, his pleasure turns to anger. His amiable grin fades, his mouth tightens, his eyes grow hard. Cooper conveys the transition without histrionics. The scene is a perfect illustration of Cooper's technique as an actor."[5] Unfortunately Deeds— who quotes Thoreau and asks: "Why do people go around hating each other? Why don't people try liking each other once in a while?"—makes his well-made point more emphatic by punching one of the writers, as he later punches the lawyer at the end of the trial.

Cooper-Deeds also reveals his sweet-natured, shrewdly simple-minded character by chasing fire engines and tying up city traffic while feeding doughnuts to a horse. Riskin was a cultured writer, and Deeds' escape from human cruelty and his kindness to the horse seems to allude to a famous episode in the life of the German philosopher Friedrich Nietzsche. Seeing an Italian cabdriver beating his horse, he flung his arms around the animal's neck, wept for the suffering animal and lapsed into permanent insanity. Misunderstanding Capra's capricious hero and the ambiguous tone of the film, Josef von Sternberg told Capra that "It doesn't make sense to have your leading man, your *hero*, Gary Cooper, keep on playing the tuba nonchalantly after they tell him he's inherited *twenty million dollars*! Your hero becomes an idiot. And you can't degrade him by letting him chase fire engines like a village half-wit, or have him feed doughnuts to a horse. . . . Heroes must be noble, not imbecilic." But Cooper is nonchalant precisely because he doesn't care about the money. The Christ-like character is an idiot in the same way as Prince Myshkin in Dostoyevsky's *The Idiot*. Both men, who hope to find (or found) a kind of heaven on earth, are idiots only if judged by the debased mores of the contemporary world, which values materialism over spiritual awareness. As Arthur announces at Cooper's trial, "that guy is either the dumbest—the stupidest—most imbecilic idiot in the world—or he's the grandest thing alive."

Jean Arthur, however, has been publicly ridiculing him in a series of secretly written newspaper articles. Unaware of her duplicity, he falls in love with her and proposes with a poem. She can't respond because she's betrayed him, and has a wounded expression and sadly forced smile when she confesses her guilt and contrition. In an absurd twist of the plot (the greatest weakness of the film), Deeds—for playing the tuba, chasing fire engines, feeding horses and rejecting the millions—is charged by his lawyers with insanity, arrested and confined in a mental hospital. But there's no reason why he should be considered insane for giving away money he didn't want in the first place. During the long courtroom hearing that provides the dramatic climax, he has no counsel. Living in a mad world, "betrayed and deceived by those he has trusted (including the girl he loves), jaundiced by the cynicism of shyster lawyers, and ridiculed by the press, Deeds no longer cares to defend himself against the charge of insanity."[6] When the psychiatrist testifies against him, Cooper's expression suggests boredom, irritation and contempt. During the first part of the trial he focuses attention on himself by moving his eyes and body while remaining completely silent.

When Arthur stands up in court, publicly declares her love and exclaims, "He's been hurt by everybody he's met since he came. Principally by me. . . . [He's] honest and sincere—and good," Deeds snaps out of his depression. After his long silence his speech is all the more dramatic. What seemed like another mad idea—he plans to give each worthy family "ten acres, a horse, a cow and some seed"—actually tries to cure present unemployment and poverty by returning to the economic ideas of the nineteenth century. John Stuart Mill's *Principles of Political Economy* (1848) had expounded the principle that "When land is cultivated entirely by spade . . . a cow is kept for every three acres of land." Deeds' defense finally convinces the judge, who concludes: "in my opinion, you are not only sane, but you are the sanest man that ever walked into this courtroom."[7]

Critics now agree that Cooper's final speech demonstrates "one of the most stunning displays of verbal and intellectual sophistication on film." It was one of the few times that grace of physique, grandeur of bearing, and preternatural attractiveness were meant to exteriorize supreme inner achievement." Yet Capra's assistant felt that the actor did not, in fact, share the director's enthusiasm for Mr. Deeds' social program. He thought "Cooper certainly respected Capra, but he was just taking it as another job. He was a cold fish."[8] Cooper's own view of his art was modest, simple and straightforward. Defining the technique that won his first Academy Award nomination, he emphasized the consistency between the personality of the actor and of the character he is playing: "Naturalness is hard to talk about, but I guess it boils down to this: You find out what people expect of your type of character and then you give them what they want. That way an actor never seems unnatural or affected no matter what role he plays." He also drew specific parallels between the accidental success, wealth and fame of himself and Mr. Deeds: "Both of us had . . . unexpected fortune dumped in our laps.

Deeds got his bequest. The movies gave me mine, by degrees." There is indeed an uncanny resemblance between Deeds' reaction to sudden wealth and fame and Cooper's own experience. At the time of his break-down he had rather bitterly said: 'Somebody is always staring at you, talking to you, or trying to sell you something you don't want," and in the movie he exclaims: "There have been a lot of [sharks] around already. Strangest kind of people. Salesmen—politicians—moochers—all wanting something. I haven't had a minute to myself."⁹

Capra later described the optimistic, conventional, even platitudinous theme—"Lamb bites wolf'—that Cooper so perfectly embodied: "A simple honest man, driven into a corner by predatory sophisticates, can, if he will, reach deep down into his God-given resources and come up with the necessary handfuls of courage, wit and love to triumph over his environment." Despite its lack of subtlety—its simplistic characterization, corny sentimentality, heavy-handed Christian symbolism and embar-rassing patriotism—the critics were delighted by both the film and Cooper's role in it. *Desire* and *Mr. Deeds* both opened triumphantly in New York in April 1936. The *New York Times* called him "one of the best light comedians in Hollywood." Graham Greene—who defined the theme as "goodness and simplicity manhandled in a deeply selfish and brutal world"—wrote that "Cooper's subtle and pliable performance must be something of which other directors have only dreamed."¹⁰

III

In this extraordinary year Cooper also made two other successful movies: *The General Died at Dawn*, a political melodrama set in China, and *The Plainsman*, a large-scale Western. *The General Died at Dawn* made between early May and early June 1936, with Count André Tolstoy as technical adviser—owes something to von Sternberg and Dietrich's *Shanghai Express*(1932). Both films have an uneasy love affair between a man and a woman, who've been involved with each other before, on a train to Shanghai that's attacked and boarded by a cruel Chinese warlord. The script was written by Clifford Odets, a major Broadway playwright associated with the Left-wing Group Theater. Fond of Cooper, as almost everyone was, Odets praised his clear vision and good manners: "He was the poet of the real. He knew all about cows, bulls, cars and ocean tides. He had the enthusiasm of a boy. He could always tell you his first vivid impression of a thing. He had an old-fashioned politeness, but he said nothing casually." Cooper said the script had "a lot of words, but I'll learn 'em," not to express his intellectual limitations, but to suggest that he'd do his best with the verbose dialogue. In Odets' sly joke, Cooper plays a character called O'Hara, named for the novelist John O'Hara, who has a bit part as a reporter on the train. Cooper dismissively remarks that (like everyone else in China) the reporter is easily bought.

Odets described the ill-fated Chinese warlord, General Yang, as "a talented man, but very, very corrupt," and modeled his speeches on recent harangues by Hitler. Yang was played by Akim Tamiroff, another veteran of the Moscow Art Theater. Though he laid it on rather thick, he was nominated for an Academy Award. Like many others who worked with him, Tamiroff assumed that Cooper's minimalist performance would not register on the screen and was astonished by the effect he produced: "For three days I've acted rings around him. I've got him stopped. Against my acting he can do nawthing. I have every scene. So I look at the rushes. On the screen I am there. Everybody else is there. But what do I see? Nawthing! Nawthing, that is, but Gary Cooper."[11]

The film was directed by the Ukrainian-born Lewis Milestone, who had achieved great success with *All Quiet on the Western Front* (1930). The titles appear on the sails of swaying junks, and the rain throughout the film creates a somber mood. Graham Greene, always a perceptive critic, noted the powerful effect of the opening minutes, in which the camera rather than the dialogue creates the oriental atmosphere and suggests the theme of political oppression: "The first few silent sequences of Mr. Lewis Milestone's *The General Died at Dawn* are as good as anything to be seen on the screen in London: the dead Chinese village with the kites circling down towards the corpses, the long pale grasses shivering aside as the troops trample through, the General with the scarred satisfied face riding along the rough road in the slick American car. After that it becomes a melodrama, though a melodrama of more than usual skill."

Cooper first appears in boots, hat and light open raincoat, colored shirt and white tie, with a chained monkey inside his coat. Accustomed to his chimp, Toluca, he was at ease with the monkey who scampers through the picture and links the characters. When Cooper's arrested, the elegant English actress Madeleine Carroll takes the monkey, and it jumps back on his shoulder when he escapes and turns up in Shanghai. An American soldier of fortune, Cooper agrees to carry a vast sum of money to Shanghai in order to buy guns to "rid the province of Yang and his locusts." Told to go by plane, he's lured onto the train by Carroll. She's acting out of loyalty to her weak and corrupt father, who wants to steal the money. When they recognize each other, Carroll whispers romantically, "the train's moving, it's night time and we're alone." She falls in love with Cooper, who's working for a noble cause, yet must betray him to save her father.

Tamiroff stops the train, interrogates Cooper and tries to find the money. Cool, brave and acting as if it scarcely concerned him, Cooper rashly laughs aloud when a servant accidentally spills tea on Tamiroff. He flicks his cigarette away to suggest indifference, rolls wet bread crumbs and casually smokes while searched with a bayonet. The relationship between the two is the most interesting aspect of the movie. Though they're complete opposites, General Yang admires O'Hara's reckless bravado, and a subtle bond grows between them. Tamiroff tells him, "you are too much interested in women," and when he's taken off the train, Cooper slaps Carroll's face in anger—the first and only time Cooper hits a woman on film. He calls Tamiroff "a heartbreaker, a headbreaker, a strike-breaker—a four-star rat," and expresses the radical theme by explaining: "You ask me why I'm for oppressed people? Because I got a background of oppression myself, and O'Hara and elephants don't forget. What's better work for an American than helping to fight for democracy?" In the midst of oriental intrigue, when everyone is trying to steal the money, Cooper is the only man who'll risk his life for principles and ideals.

Shanghaied and forced to eat "junk" food, Cooper escapes from his cell, jumps ship, is wounded and feels "like a bag of broken glass." He turns up in Shanghai and regains Carroll's loyalty. When he has to shoot her double-crossing father in self-defense, he coolly remarks: "You can't do this kind of work and die in bed." Recaptured by Tamiroff, who screams "white flesh die," Cooper tells Carroll: "You kicked out one of my lungs on the train. . . . Someday, maybe, there'll be a law to abolish the blues, maybe a constitutional amendment, for all of us." Believing they're about to be executed, he declares his love and speaks one of his most famous lines: "Darling, we could have made wonderful music together." At the last minute Cooper persuades the dying Tamiroff (shot in a skirmish for the money) to spare them so they can tell his story and ensure his fame. The picture ends as Tamiroff's loyal guards kill each other and die with their master.

The explosive political situation in China made the film subject to severe censorship. The Nationalists had been fighting the Communists; the Japanese had occupied Manchuria and were now preparing to invade northem China. The warlord Yang is presumably an evil Nationalist, but the oppressed Communist peasants, aided by Cooper, are certainly not fighting for democracy. Since America supported the Nationalists, the politics in the movie were kept deliberately obscure. Lewis Milestone noted that "a real Chinese general stalked the Paramount lot with official frowns. . . . For a time it became a free-for-all in which anyone from the Chinese consulate had a right to write a scene, and anyone from the censorship board had a right to suggest new lines and situations."

The movie is wildly improbable. Carroll, the daughter of an American father, has a strong English accent. Tamiroff speaks pidgin, and other natives confuse matters even more by mingling Chinese, English and American accents. A drunken American calls the Chinese "Rastus" and "Sambo." Frustrated and enraged, Odets complained that the studio "hired me on the basis of writing talent, but they fine-tooth-combed the script for traces of radicalism." The film was originally "full of good ideas, but in the end it was a set of clichés on which we made some good birthday decorations."[12] Though the picture is sometimes talky and static, Odets salvaged more than he realized. It has many memorable lines, good twists of plot, substantial characters, and makes a serious attempt to express political themes.

Though much inferior to Cooper's other movies of 1936, *The Plainsman*, the first of four leaden pictures he made with Cecil B. De Mille, was a far greater commercial success. De Mille, the most powerful director at Paramount, controlled his own independent unit. He used the studio's sound stages, actors and crews as well as its distribution network, but ran his own operation. He had been making films since 1913 and, like the silent screen directors, still wore jodhpurs and boots and carried a riding crop. More a director of crowds than of actors, he shouted his orders through a megaphone. Anthony Quinn, who played a Cheyenne warrior, was always grateful to Cooper for persuading De Mille to give him the part. As Quinn was rehearsing an Indian song, Cooper walked in and the director confided: "I don't think the kid's going to work out." Recognizing Quinn's authentic look on screen and pleading his case, Cooper urged De Mille to "Give the boy a chance. Maybe he's confused, it's his first picture." When Quinn tried the song again and De Mille asked how it sounded, Cooper insisted: "It sounds pretty good, C.B. This kid sounds great." Quinn looked like an Indian but was really Mexican-Irish. Once he got the part he couldn't resist pulling De Mille's leg by claiming that red men and white men made fires in different ways, and that in a realistic movie the fire made by Cooper couldn't possibly pass for one made by an Indian. Following Quinn's advice, De Mille dutifully changed the fire.

We don't know if Cooper, after his marriage, continued his affairs with Carole Lombard while making *Now and Forever* or with Dietrich while shooting *Desire*. But an Indian actor, Iron Eyes Cody, reported that Cooper resumed his old habits while on location in Lame Deer, Montana. Safely away from home, he "brought along a tall, very warm-blooded blonde, and was settled in nicely with her."

The Plainsman, Paramount's version of frontier history, begins as Lincoln tells his cabinet that the west must be opened and is then assassinated at Ford's Theater. Cooper, playing a famous scout, tries to stop the villains from smuggling guns to the Indians. Taking a ferry from St. Louis to Leavenworth and then a stage to Hays City, he turns up at cavalry headquarters and announces: "Wild Bill Hickok to see General Custer." Cooper's involvement with the gun-runners and Indians is complicated by his reluctant romance with Calamity Jane (Jean Arthur), who wields a whip, gets into fights and pursues him throughout the movie. When the Indians enter a house, talk in grunts and smash things up, she calls them "painted buzzards," "hairless coyotes" and "red hyenas." De Mille once said of Cooper, "I couldn't force him to overact even by building a fire under him," but in *The Plainsman* he did burn his hero. After Cooper and Arthur are captured by the Indians, he's tortured (as in *The Lives of a Bengal Lancer*). Unable to watch him being roasted over a fire, she breaks down and tells them where to find the rifles. The well-armed Indians, charging the cavalry, fall spectacularly off horses and into the river.

In one shootout Cooper exclaims, "You're not leaving town unless dead men can walk." Following screen conventions, he kills four villains who wait patiently for his bullets instead of drawing their guns. The final scene, though factually accurate, is therefore quite surprising. The gaucho-like Cooper—wearing a flat black Cordoba hat, loose black shirt, light trousers and high black boots—is suddenly shot in the back, just as Hickok was in Deadwood, South Dakota, in 1876, the same year that Custer's troops were massacred at Little Bighorn. The gun-runners, having armed the Indians, actually triumph over the decent, law-abiding citizens.

Cooper's performance transcends clichéd lines like "women and me don't agree," "there are things that have to be done, ma'am" and "I started this alone and I'll finish it alone." As one historian of Westerns wrote: "The role allowed Cooper to project the image of a saturnine, melancholy man, fierce in his independence, who lived by his own code of what he felt to be right, and who was a truly lonely wanderer in the world."[13] But even Cooper couldn't save the movie. De Mille spent hundreds of research hours to get authentic details and then produced fatuous characters, an absurd plot and a ponderous "epic."

IV

In October 1936 Paramount was inexplicably late in picking up the option in Cooper's contract, and Sam Goldwyn, who'd been trying to recapture Cooper ever since he slipped through his fingers after *The Winning of Barbara Worth*, offered to top any Paramount deal. Cooper secretly agreed to do six pictures, over a period of six years, with a minimum guarantee of $150,000 for each. Embarrassed by their oversight and furious at Goldwyn's treachery, Paramount sued him for $5 million for hiring Cooper away. Charging Goldwyn with "a breach of morals and ethics," Paramount claimed that Cooper had already agreed to the terms of its new four-year contract until "interference by Goldwyn and the Goldwyn company thwarted and prevented such a move." The suit was eventually settled when Goldwyn lent Cooper to Paramount and Paramount lent Hathaway to Goldwyn. Bound to Goldwyn for only one picture a year, Cooper continued to make movies for both studios, and by 1939 was earning the highest salary in America.

A month after the dispute between Goldwyn and the studio, Cooper started filming his next project for Paramount, the mediocre *Souls at Sea* (1937). Henry Hathaway built two nearly identical $20,000 boat sets, with elaborate rocking machinery, which helped to push the picture to $339,000 over budget. George Raft, always uncertain about accepting a part, originally refused the role, was replaced (at Cooper's suggestion) by Anthony Quinn and then decided to take it after all. Hathaway used special effects during the now *de rigueur* torture scene. Raft, apparently "hanging by his thumbs from a yardarm over the water . . . is really lying on an invisible mattress with a flickering movie of turbulent ocean, synchronized with the camera shutter by electrical interlock, projected a few yards beyond his feet."

In this slave smuggler versus abolitionist movie, set in 1842, Cooper (as in *Mr. Deeds Goes to Town* and several later films) is falsely accused and exonerated after a trial. In contrast to the lowbrow Raft, who wears an earring and chases low-class women, Cooper is unusually talkative, intellectual and literate. He plays chess, tells the story of the Trojan Horse, refers to the career of Sir Walter Raleigh, reads *Hamlet* aloud and quotes Romantic poetry. Cooper realized the limitations of the movie, but tried to make the best of it. Just as he never took the credit for his great films, so he attempted (with a sly dig at Raft) to praise whatever he could in his weaker ones: "Parts of *Souls at Sea* were pretty terrific, and if it had followed some of my weaker pictures it would have looked like a good thing for me. But I'd had a nice run of hits. . . . *Souls at Sea* was nothing to be ashamed of, and it had an audience. But I thought the love story with George Raft and the little French girl was more arresting than my more conventional one with Frances [Dee]. Then, too, George played part of the picture with a ring in his ear, and people thought that made him a better actor. . . . It was almost exciting, and almost interesting. And I was almost good. George Raft *was* good." George Burns quipped, "George Raft and Gary Cooper once played a scene in front of a cigar store, and it looked like the wooden Indian was overacting."[14]

Though each of his films from *Desire* to *Souls at Sea* was weaker than its predecessor, Cooper had shown great skill as an actor during these years. With Lubitsch and Dietrich he was a subtle comedian in a sophisticated, international setting. With Capra and Jean Arthur he created his quite different persona as a naive, lovable and idealistic hero, and made the too-good-to-be-true character both complex and interesting. With Milestone and the classy Madeleine Carroll he was a convincing romantic adventurer who outfoxed—and also outacted—the wily Akim Tamiroff. In *The Plainsman* he almost managed to make De Mille's absurdities believable. In *Souls at Sea*, despite his generous praise of his co-star, he was better than both Raft and the wooden Indian.

Rocky, who had a beautiful figure and was very conscious of her appearance, had at first been reluctant to get pregnant. But, impressed that Fay Wray "still appeared slim at six months, said she was inspired to have a child." Rocky stayed in wonderful shape, and went swimming with Cooper and Joel McCrea on the day she gave birth. On September 15 (the same day as Charles Cooper's birthday), both Cooper and Frank Capra brought their wives to the Good Samaritan Hospital in Los Angeles. Cooper, seeing a sign that warned, "No children admitted in the maternity wing," thought "there must be something queer about this place." Capra recalled that "Like a Mutt and Jeff team, tall Gary and I paced the maternity halls, gave passing nurses anxious, pleading looks. They ignored us. He-man 'Coop' became unglued. He had a room next to Rocky's, but he cowered in the halls and fire escapes where he could chain-smoke."[15]

Their daughter, Maria Veronica Cooper, was a pretty little girl with deep blue eyes, pink cheeks and chestnut-colored hair. Her parents (but no one else) called her Cakes, after a Swedish dessert called Maria Cakes, and that endearing nickname lasted into adult life. When she got older, Cooper once left her a note at her bedside, with a drawing of a cowboy's head, that said, "Cakes wakes! Take care of the dogs and things and most of all *yourself*. Love, Popa." Though Maria was an exceptionally charming and well-behaved child, she was capable of fierce temper tantrums. When she didn't get her own way, she'd lie on her back, hold her breath and turn purple. Grandmother Shields cured her of this habit by spraying her with a water pistol. After the kidnapping and murder of Charles Lindbergh's son had terrified parents all over America, Cooper, fearful about Maria's safety, protected her by hiring a guard and putting discreet bars on her bedroom window. When friends visited the house, Maria would be brought out, shown off and then sent back to her nanny.

Cooper, who'd got on well with Shirley Temple before he had his own child, was a patient and affectionate father. He taught Maria to ride a bike and showed her how to follow deer tracks in the snowy woods. Rocky read stories to her at bedtime, and professionals gave her lessons in the sports her parents loved, tennis, skiing and riding (though she was not allowed to jump on horseback). She cried from the sharp kick of the gun when skeet-shooting, and during her first piano lesson terrified her teacher by putting a pet tortoise on her feet. Maria was given everything, apart from a horse of her own, that she really wanted. She became a sophisticated companion, went everywhere with her parents, shared their interests and was often photographed with them. Happy to be the center of attention, she never felt lonely or asked for a sibling. She made head-lines in a Los Angeles newspaper when Andy, her pet chipmunk, escaped from his box on a plane from Aspen to Los Angeles and was found a few days later hiding behind the flight deck. In the summer of 1942, when

Cooper was making *For Whom the Bell Tolls*, the four-year-old Maria dictated a cheeky and flirtatious note to her father, written out by her nanny, Miss Brown: "I found a soldier on the beach and he is my pal. His name is Nick. I don't know which I like best, Nick or Cap Allen. Momma goes to the canteen. I am going, too, next week. But I am not going to do any jitter-bugging—but maybe I'll do a little if the soldiers want me to."

Like her mother, Maria was brought up as a Catholic. In 1946, when she was in the third grade, the Marymount School in Westwood refused to enroll her because her parents had not been married in a Catholic church. To fulfill the technicality, and get her into the school, Cooper obligingly went through a religious ceremony.[16] Maria became as close to Rocky as Rocky had been to her own mother. Cooper adored his only child, and had an unusually close and happy relationship with her.

10

"Keep Shooting"

1938–1941

I

During the prewar years Cooper enjoyed family life, his house and hobbies, his friends and travels, his holidays and summers in Southampton. Now the mainstay of both Paramount and Goldwyn, he was paid exceptionally well and made movie after movie to earn as much as he could while his salary was high. In his eagerness to accept jobs he sometimes chose a turkey. *The Adventures of Marco Polo* (1938), based on the Venetian explorer's travels to China in the Middle Ages, was one of his greatest mistakes.

Marco Polo brought out Cooper's negative feelings about acting. The rugged westerner always had reservations about putting on airs and make-up, impersonating an absurd character and playing vapid roles in the void of a studio. Modest about his own talent, he confessed that "movie acting is a pretty silly business for a man because it takes less training, less ability and less brains to be successful in it than any other business I can think of."

Compared to studio executives, who had enormous responsibilities, or to well-educated financiers like his father-in-law, Paul Shields, Cooper felt actors, surrounded by toadies and parasites, were pampered creatures. For most aspirants acting is a heartbreaking career, but Cooper had never really had to hustle to get the next job. Naturally gifted as a film actor, he tended to undervalue what he did. Only later, when he met Pat Neal and went with her to acting classes, did he see that his profession had its own body of knowledge and stage tradition, that actors had to work at their craft all their lives.

Cooper never did well with mustaches and "always made a point of avoiding beards, Roman costumes and silk tights." When he broke his rule and appeared in costume melodramas like *Peter Ibbetson* and *Marco Polo*, he felt absurdly miscast. He was dismayed to find that his Chinese robes had set a new trend in women's clothes, and felt even more self-conscious when he appeared in a bizarre photo on the cover of *Life* (February 7, 1938), manically laughing or yelling, with his mouth wide open and head thrown back. On July 24, 1937 S.V. Stewart, a friend of Charles Cooper and former governor of Montana, visited Cooper in Goldwyn's studio. Dazzled by the Hollywood glamour and surprised to see Cooper (especially during meals) in oriental attire, he wrote a friend back home: "He was all made up to represent Marco Polo, who was supposed to be disguised as a Chinaman, seeking to break into a castle. He did not take off his make-up for lunch as he was in another scene right after we ate. . . . Gary says they will not let the players in the leading parts do anything that might injure them and put them out of the cast—even for a day."[1]

The production of *Marco Polo* ran into trouble right from the start. The original director quit after five days of shooting and was replaced by the old workhorse Archie Mayo. Sigrid Gurie, who played a Chinese princess at the Peking court of Kubla Khan (the subject of Coleridge's poem), was hyped as the "the siren of the Fjords" and quickly unmasked as a native of Flatbush. Lana Turner, who had four lines as a lady's maid, hated her costumes and make-up. She recalled: "I was a Eurasian hand-maiden who had caught the eye of a warrior chief, played by Alan Hale. I wore a fancy, black Oriental wig, which had to be glued around my face with spirit gum. I didn't mind the wig so much . . . but the costumes made me feel too undressed. And, worse yet, they shaved off my eyebrows, at the insistence of Goldwyn himself, and replaced them with false slanting black ones."

No one, least of all the director and actors, knew whether the cheeky mishmash of spaghetti, fireworks and quaint European habit of kissing on the lips, written by the highbrow Broadway, playwright Robert Sherwood, was supposed to be taken straight or as a spoof, whether it was fatuous or simply not funny. Cooper, in a flamboyant Errol Flynn role, with slashed sleeves and gaucho pants, is not sufficiently dashing. He's forced to speak flat, even absurd lines—"Warnings of danger are written in my heart" and "We've got to get out of here. I've got to get back to Peking"—which he cannot make convincing.

Hoping, by some miracle, that audience response would help salvage the picture, Goldwyn handed out a printed notice at the preview: "This picture is in rough form and I have brought it to you to get your aid in completing it before its release to the world. I tender you my grateful thanks for your answers to the following questions: How did you like *The Adventures of Marco Polo*? Did you enjoy the performances of [the actors]? Was the action of the picture entirely clear? If not, where was it confusing? Have you any other constructive criticism to make?" Most of the audience, confused about everything but sure of its failure, walked out before they could make any criticism at all. *Marco Polo*, Goldwyn's biggest flop, lost $700,000.

Cooper was far more at ease in the delightful, witty and bittersweet Lubitsch comedy *Bluebeard's Eighth Wife* (1938), written by Billy Wilder. The film, in which Cooper plays a seven-times-married American millionaire, recalls *Desire* (directed by Lubitsch) and anticipates his role as the tycoon playboy in *Love in the Afternoon* (written by Wilder). The film opens with a typical Wilder touch. On holiday in the French Riviera, Cooper sees a sign in a shop window listing the languages spoken by the staff, with the addendum "American understood." In their first amusing encounter, Claudette Colbert and Cooper—who's dressed very smartly, with watch chain and vest—meet in the shop when he's trying to buy only the top of a pair of pajamas and she only the bottom. The rest of the picture is devoted to bringing the two halves of the pair—of pajamas and people—together. The theme, roughly parallel to Shakespeare's *The Taming of the Shrew*, which Cooper reads in the movie, concerns his courtship of a girl from a poor but noble French family. She seeks love and a permanent connection, and does not want to become the next in a series of disposable wives. Though she marries him, she refuses to consummate their union and extorts an enormous divorce settlement.

Serious issues—commitment and equality in marriage—underpin the comedy. Cooper's character has never matured, despite his experience, because he's always bought his way out of romantic mistakes. Colbert wants to give her love, not sell it. But she realizes that he puts a price on everything and must therefore get her own money before she can persuade him to treat her as an equal. The American businessman's hardness and shallowness are contrasted to the European woman's softness and wisdom. Colbert has to harden her heart to teach her husband to grow up and stop running away whenever his relationship with his wife breaks down.

David Niven recalled the characteristic methods of the director, whose methods were so perfectly attuned to Wilder's script and who always brought out the best in Cooper. "Lubitsch sat," Niven wrote, "like a little gnome, beside the camera, perched on a small stepladder, giggling and hugging himself at all his own wonderful inventiveness. A huge cigar was always in his mouth. He was patient, understanding and encouraging; what more could any actor ask?"[2] In one charming scene a troubled-looking Niven, Cooper's secretary and romantic rival, is typing a letter with one finger in a hotel room while Cooper, fully clothed, is dallying with Colbert on a float near the beach. Niven suddenly appears in a bathing suit, climbs on the float, earnestly asks whether to use a colon or semicolon in a sentence, gets Cooper's answer, dives into the water and swims back to his typewriter.

Lubitsch brilliantly uses the luxurious 1930s settings, and gets the maximum effect from the actors' body language. Cooper strides briskly down the wide corridors of the elegant apartment with a furious light in his eyes. Niven, dressed in his evening shirt and black tie, reclines on the huge white bed in the thickly carpeted bedroom, looking dazed without his trousers. Cooper bends Colbert over a soft chair in an elaborate kiss, which ends in a splutter as he tastes the spring onions she has just eaten to dampen his passion.

Colbert threatens to take him to the Russian ballet instead of to the prizefight if he doesn't mend his ways. Cooper, changing from hardnosed businessman to shy lover, promises to behave and tries to seduce her. He plays the piano and sings, grows and then cuts off his mustache, widens his eyes in surprise when she asks him to kiss her, sits in an antique bathtub and breaks it like a big bird coming out of a shell. Finally, after joking about psychiatrists, he snaps out of the straitjacket, in which he's been confined after weeks of frustrating celibacy, and into her arms.

The sophisticated script, which demands a certain physical dash, once again allows Cooper to display his talent for light comedy. When he embraces Colbert, he seems to delight in her real intelligence and reacts as if it were an aphrodisiac. The subtle comic effects depend on the rich, tall and handsome Cooper's being thwarted (when Colbert won't sleep with him) or mistaken (when he finds Niven in her bedroom) or foolish (when urging Niven to leave while sitting on his pants so he can't do so). Cooper has the wit and flair to look as if he's enjoying the ardent pursuit and triumph over sexual frustration.

Audiences loved Colbert, who had achieved great success with Gable in

Capra's *It Happened One Night* (1934), but after Cooper had appeared as the boyish innocent in *Mr. Deeds*, they could not accept him as a worldly philanderer. Nor did fans respond to Wilder's dark satire on love, marriage and the battle of the sexes, and the movie was a commercial failure. But the actors were admired—even by those who could hardly approve of movies about the idle rich. At the national convention of the Communist Party in 1938, the *Daily Worker*'s poll "established that the delegates' favorite movie stars were Claudette Colbert and Gary Cooper."

The unhappy genesis of *The Cowboy and the Lady* (1938) has made this movie seem much worse than it really is. The director Leo McCarey supposedly wrote the script in three days to pay hospital bills. When Goldwyn asked him to direct, he said he "wouldn't touch that crap." The director William Wyler agreed that the script was "awful, just awful," but it was patched up by several eminent screenwriters, including Anita Loos, Garson Kanin and S.N. Behrman. Despite their efforts, Wyler, known for his meticulous care, complained to Goldwyn: "I am compelled to work without a completed script. Only one sequence was ready to work when we started and I didn't get today's work (Monday) until late Saturday night." Wyler was then replaced by H.C. Potter, who got screen credit but was himself replaced by Stuart Heisler.

The Cowboy and the Lady—which seems to reflect Cooper's relations with Dorothy di Frasso—has the same basic plot as *I Take This Woman*, the film Cooper made with Carole Lombard in 1931. In both, a poor but sweet-natured cowboy courts and marries the wealthy eastern daughter of a powerful father, and lives in ramshackle quarters while he performs in a rodeo. In both the father at first opposes the union but is finally won over by their true love. Cooper—back in his familiar, stylized, undemanding role—is a rugged girl-shy Montanan who expresses, through his speech and gestures, unshakable moral values. He tips his hat and smiles modestly when they meet on a blind date, says "Yeh," and keeps chewing his chili when she exclaims: "I think I'm going to like you." Opening a dishwasher, he jumps back as steam pours out and he's "ambushed by a bunch of gadgets." He disapproves of his friends' boisterous intimacy with their girls, rushes away when he accidentally sees Merle Oberon changing her dress. He squeezes her perfume spray, plays with her powder puff and gets talc on his nose while exploring her bedroom. Cooper was effective in the role that rather naively suggested love could transcend class barriers and moral goodness would eventually triumph. But this film also lost money.

Between 1926 and 1936 Cooper had enjoyed enormous critical and commercial successes with *The Virginian, Morocco, A Farewell to Arms, The Lives of a Bengal Lancer* and *Mr. Deeds Goes to Town.* Now his career had sharply declined. Moving between Paramount and Goldwyn during 1937–38, he had four flops in a row. A star, by definition, must get good parts from the studio to sustain his career and remain at the top, but in the late 1930s Cooper's instinct about choosing the best and rejecting the worst roles seemed to fail him. Rocky confessed that "John Ford sent Gary a script of *Stagecoach.* Gary was on the fence about it. I read it, and advised him to turn it down. *Stagecoach!* It made a star out of John Wayne, but we turned it down." But Cooper, earning $150,000 per film, would never have seriously considered a risky low-budget movie in which the male star was paid only $3,000. At about the same time he also refused to play Rhett Butler in David Selznick's *Gone with the Wind* (also 1939), telling William Wellman that the picture "is going to be the biggest flop in Hollywood history. I'm just glad it'll be Clark Gable who's falling flat on his face and not Gary Cooper."[3]

II

In the next few years Cooper's career suddenly revived with more conge-nial roles in large-scale adventure and cowboy movies—*Beau Geste* and *The Real Glory* (both 1939), *The Westerner* and *North West Mounted Police* (both 1940)—and with one of his most important films, Capra's *Meet John Doe* (1941). *Beau Geste*, a remake of the 1926 silent film with Ronald Colman, combined the setting of *Morocco* and male camaraderie of *Bengal Lancer* with the public school values Cooper had learned at Dunstable: loyalty, stoicism and self-sacrifice.

It was filmed in the Mojave Desert near Yuma, Arizona, and as with *The Winning of Barbara Worth*, a special movie town was constructed in the wilderness. A plank road, bound with iron strips, was built from the main highway to the camp; ninety-six tents, with wooden floors and walls, bathrooms and hot water, were erected for the crew of seven hundred; a mess tent served food, a recreation tent showed movies and a sprinkling cart ran all night to wet down the road. Food for the camels was budgeted at $140, and an affidavit by an inspector from the Los Angeles Society for the Prevention of Cruelty to Animals swore that the beasts had been well treated. According to a story dreamed up by the publicity department, when Cooper received a message that his little daughter was ill, he rode a camel, like Lawrence of Arabia, through the blowing sand to the paved road, tied it to a post and hitchhiked into Yuma. He then called home and was relieved to find Maria had recovered.

Robert Preston, playing one of three brothers who join the Foreign Legion to cover up the theft of a valuable family sapphire, paid tribute to Cooper's talent: "Cooper doesn't have the reputation as a great actor except with us who knew him as an actor. But he was great. People used to comment on what they called his idiosyncrasies, his little foibles. But Cooper never made a move that wasn't thoroughly thought out and planned. He is probably the finest motion picture actor I ever worked with." Susan Hayward, in a small part, waves good-bye to the Geste brothers when they leave England at the beginning of the picture and is reunited with Ray Milland, after Cooper and Preston are killed in North Africa, at the end. The director William Wellman, who had made *Wings* in 1927, said: "That was a rugged picture. You had to be tough. We're out on location in the middle of the desert near Yuma. Only men. We wouldn't allow a woman in the camp. At the beginning, I ran a bus to the house of ill-fame in Yuma."

Wellman also recalled that Brian Donlevy—who earned only one-tenth as much as Cooper and Milland, but stole the picture as the sadistic Captain Markoff ("Keep shooting, you scum! You'll get a chance to die with your boots on!")—played his role both on screen and off: "Everybody hated Donlevy—because he lorded it over everybody. Everybody moved out of his tent. They wouldn't even sleep with the guy. Despised him. I've never seen a guy that could completely get everyone to dislike him." After the censorship office had strongly objected to the cruelty, Tony Luraschi of Paramount sent a memo to the screenwriter, Robert Carson, at Yuma. He explained that the sergeant could bark out orders and make dire threats, but could never actually beat or kill anyone: "Markoff will receive deserters, bawl them out, goad them, tantalize them in speeches, calling attention to the rest of the men about what happens to anybody who deserts from that company, sending deserters back out into the desert, but without resorting to water [torture] incident and without whipping them at any time."[4]

In the famous opening scene Donlevy-Markoff pushes the dead legionnaires into the crenellations of the wall to make the enemy think they are still capable of defending the fort. The fierce Tuaregs attack the Saharan

outpost exactly as the Indians attack a cavalry stockade. Cooper, staring
through the shadowy interior, exclaims: "When the shooting starts we
just shoot at everybody. It makes things simpler." Though the assault is
repulsed, he's mortally wounded, and as he hears the bugles of the troops
coming to the rescue, he regretfully says: "Lovely sound, but a little too
late." Preston, the third brother, pays tribute to Cooper's courage by
cremating him on a Viking funeral pyre. The exotic setting and high-spirited action, the vivid contrast between Cooper's boyish heroics and
Donlevy's villainy, still make the picture seem quite thrilling. The poet
Karl Shapiro may have been thinking of the fallen heroes in *Beau Geste*
when he wrote of "the sleeping soldiers all metamorphosing quietly into
. . . Gary Coopers."[5]

The Real Glory, a boy's adventure story directed by Henry Hathaway,
rescued Cooper from *The Wedding Night*, *Marco Polo* and *The Cowboy
and the Lady*, his string of failures with Goldwyn. Following the
successful pattern of *Bengal Lancer* and *Beau Geste*, this film also has a
male trio (Cooper, David Niven and Broderick Crawford) bound
together as comrades to defeat the treacherous natives. Set in the
Philippines in the early years of this century, *The Real Glory* is based on
the Moro rebellion, but tends to ignore historical fact. After victory in the
Spanish–American War, the United States bought the Philippines from
Spain. But the Philippine leaders, who had allied themselves with the
Americans in order to gain independence, felt betrayed and fought
against America as they had once fought against Spain. The Moros, fanatical Moslem tribesmen whose ancestors had converted to Islam in the
fifteenth century, were traditional enemies of the Philippine Christians,
but had joined them in fighting to overthrow American rule. The Moros
began their campaigns on the southern island of Mindanao in 1902, and
Captain John Pershing and other leaders took more than three years to
subdue them. By 1940, however, the Hollywood studios had turned their
attention to making films that encouraged the war effort. As Japan was
conquering China and the United States was heading for a major war in
Asia, it was necessary to portray American rule as humane and enlight-
ened and to justify its strategically essential presence in the Philippines.
Goldwyn built a Philippine island on the back lot of the studio and hired
two hundred Filipino extras. One writer estimated that it "cost more
money ($2,000,000) and took more time (two hundred eight-hour
working days) than the original campaign."

The movie transforms the Moro rebellion against U.S. rule into a civil

war between loyal Christian Filipinos and pagan traitors. In the film
Cooper actually says, "the independence of the Philippines rests with our
boys." The action begins as the American commander orders his troops
to leave the island and hand over power to their Filipino allies. Cooper,
a devoted doctor, Niven, a charming dreamer, and Crawford, a collector
of orchids, remain behind to guide the loyal natives. Matters are complicated by the arrival of the commander's daughter, which leads Cooper
and Niven into romantic rivalry. As in *Bengal Lancer*, the natives run
amok. The captured rebels are terrified when threatened with burial in
pigskin—a detail which only makes sense if they are portrayed as
Moslems. In the course of the movie a rope bridge snaps and a traitor
falls into a spear trap, the commander is blinded by a head wound,
Crawford is ambushed and killed. The spectacular ending of *The Real
Glory* is real gory. The dam is dynamited, the river surges and troops
arriving by raft are catapulted into the fort. Niven dies as the natives raid
the arsenal and Cooper arrives with leftover dynamite to repulse their
attack.

The *Daily Worker*, in an unusually sensible review of 1939, exposed
the movie's jingoism and crude distortion of truth: "In times like these,
we question the wisdom of rattling the bones in Yankee imperialism's
closet. To show the Moros as bloodthirsty savages is neither fair to them
or to history." Graham Greene recognized that Cooper provided a core
of seriousness in the midst of all the heroic absurdities: "Mr. Cooper as
the military doctor, who arrives with a present of orchids and a colonel's
gallstone for his friends, has never acted better. Sometimes his lean
photogenic face seems to leave everything to the lens, but there is no
question here of his not acting. Watch him inoculate the girl against
cholera—the casual lab of the needle, and the dressing slapped on while
he talks, as though a thousand arms had taught him where to stab and he
doesn't have to think any more."[6]

The Westerner (1940) was based on a colorful nineteenth-century
historical figure, Judge Roy Bean. Born in Kentucky, he took part in the
Confederate victory at Chickamauga. He became known as "the law west
of the Pecos River" (which flows into the Rio Grande in West Texas), and
made lethal decisions in his saloon with a lawbook in one hand and six-
shooter in the other. The trouble, from Cooper's point of view, was that
Bean would be played by Walter Brennan and Cooper, the nominal star,
would have a relatively minor part. "It looked like his picture," Cooper
wrote. "A cowboy ultimately rode in and exchanged a few shots to the

detriment of the judge, but that struck me as being incidental. I couldn't see that it needed Gary Cooper for the part."

Goldwyn assured Cooper that his role would be expanded and also threatened to sue him if he failed to report for work. Having read the final script, Cooper formally protested and said he couldn't take the part: "After careful and reasonable consideration I regret to advise you that the character, Cole Harden, is still inadequate and unsatisfactory for me, in my opinion, as is the story. . . . Like you, I have a position to uphold. My professional standing has been jeopardized from the beginning." When Goldwyn remained adamant about his star's contractual obligations, Cooper (in a rather stilted letter, probably dictated by his lawyer) reluctantly agreed to make the film. But he warned Goldwyn that their relations had been irreparably damaged and they would not work together in the future. Despite unprecedented intimidation, Cooper said, he would "bow to your threats since normal reasoning and friendly relations mean little, if anything, to you." He agreed "to perform my services . . . to the fullest of my ability, with the express understanding that I am doing so under protest." All this "serves as confirmation that my experience since the beginning of the contract had been consistently unsettled, insecure, lacking inspiration and enthusiasm and it is, therefore, best for you to realize that our association is incompatible, holding small hope for any mutually happy solution and I fail to see how we can profitably continue this strained relationship."

The movie was shot on location in Arizona, and a crew member recalled the extreme temperatures in the desert: "We'd get up at six in the morning and drive eight miles out of town to the set. There would be snow and ice on the ground. By ten the sun would come out and we'd bake. We'd shoot till sundown. Then we'd go back to the Santa Rita Hotel in Tucson and have dinner."[7] The screenwriter, Niven Busch, said he used Cooper's expert knowledge of western history when working on the script: "If I was stuck I ran down to Cooper's dressing room, and he would put me right. Cooper was such a fund of information about the West." While on location Cooper solidified his friendship with Brennan, a New Englander whom he'd first met when they started out as extras in 1925. Brennan, expert at impersonating Goldwyn's voice, loved to call up Cooper and rage against him, yelling: "You god-damned son-of-a-bitch, you're so lousy I want Brennan to have top billing in this picture." Brennan—playing the sinister Bean as a mischievous, comical, sentimental and rather endearing old codger—stole the picture. The Cooper character had to be a tricky and devious hero, as well as a good shot, in order to survive. The movie was directed by William Wyler, a laborious plodder with an inflated reputation, who, like De Mille, lacked the dazzling dynamism of Cooper's best directors: von Sternberg, Lubitsch, Hawks and, later on, Zinnemann and Wilder.

Cooper rides into the film with his hands tied behind his back and, in Bean's courtroom/saloon, is falsely accused of stealing a horse. He learns that Bean is obsessed with the English actress Lily Langtry, who's touring America in plays by Shakespeare and Wilde. To avoid hanging, called a "suspended sentence" (the undertaker measures him as the "jury" comes out), Cooper boasts of his friendship with Lily and promises to obtain a lock of her hair. As Cooper, like Scheherezade, spins out fantastic stories about her to postpone his fate, he becomes uncommonly attached to his oppressor. They get drunk together, and Cooper, with a terrible hang-over, shares his bed and wakes up with Brennan's arm around him. When Cooper compares him to a rattlesnake, Brennan pats him on the back, gives his trademark cracked-voice wheeze and reassuringly says: "You're all right."

As the protracted Langtry joke becomes tedious, the movie fractures and then deteriorates into a series of Western clichés: free-ranging ranchers versus fenced homesteaders, the cowboy's decision to keep roaming or settle down, the sentimental courtship of a boring girl who provides the lock of hair that passes for Lily Langtry's. To celebrate the rape of the lock and prepare for the climax, Brennan names a new town Langtry (which indeed exists). When the actress finally arrives, he buys out the whole house for a private view of her performance, but the curtain goes up to reveal Cooper instead of Lily on stage. As bullets zing into the musical instruments, the mortally wounded Brennan complains, "You stopped the show." Cooper takes him back to see Lily, and his wish finally granted, Brennan dies happy. The real theme of the fatally flawed picture is how Bean's bond with Harden undermines and replaces his obsessive sexual fantasy.

When the movie premiered in Dallas in November 1940, Cooper, on horseback and in full cowboy rig, led the parade down main street. The Hollywood gossip columnist Sheilah Graham, then involved with Scott Fitzgerald, came along for the ride and had some sexual fantasies of her own. According to Sheilah, when she became airsick and Cooper lifted her into a berth on the plane, he offered to rub her stomach and she refused. Cooper also turned up in her bedroom in Dallas: "He held my hands and looked down deeply from the top tower of his eyes into mine. I don't know how long this would have lasted, but remembering Scott, I giggled and pulled away."[8] In Sheilah's implausible, self-serving account, she has it both ways. Cooper is curiously unassertive and submissive to her wishes while she is irresistibly attractive as well as loyal to Scott. Cooper's reputation as a ladies' man was so great, Sheilah suggests, that it was quite extraordinary *not* to have slept with him.

De Mille's *North West Mounted Police* (1940) was based on a historical incident, during the Second Riel Rebellion, that took place on the western frontier of Canada in March–May 1885. Louis Riel, a French-Indian trapper, once again led his band of half-breeds against the national government. "He denounced the authority of the dominion, appealed to Indians to join his revolt, and set up a provisional government. After several armed clashes and considerable loss of life, the rebellion was suppressed by government troops" in a fierce battle near Batoche, Saskatchewan. Riel was captured, tried and hanged for treason. As in *The Real Glory*, the native rebels are depicted as dark villains, and there is no explanation of *why* they are rebelling against the law and order of their white rulers. Since Wall Street financed filmmaking, the politics of Hollywood studios were always conservative. In this picture Paramount backed the redcoats against the redskins.

De Mille, famous for his exhaustive research, discarded anything that spoiled the dramatic effect. "The trouble with filming the real thing," he said, "is that on the screen it looks sham." To achieve verisimilitude in one scene, nine horses were killed. But De Mille insisted that his female stars always had to wear high heels, and Paulette Goddard—as the saucy half-breed daughter of Corbeau ("the crow"), a rebel leader—wore wedgies hidden inside her Indian moccasins. De Mille admired Cooper's superb timing and told Goddard to "watch Coop if you want to learn how to use props." She observed Cooper carefully as she repeatedly entered the tent where he was quietly cooking breakfast. "So I'm coming into the tent and Coop's frying bacon," Goddard recalled. "And every time I'd come in and take a look at him he'd have the bacon in the air at the same time."[9]

In his first Technicolor picture, Cooper plays a Texas ranger and pursues Corbeau, who is wanted for murder in America. His rough clothes, independent quest and boldness provide a contrast to the staid Canadian Mounties, who are after the same man. When told to stay in the fort, he replies (as he did in *Bengal Lancer*): "Not me, amigo, I'm gonna get Corbeau." Hesitating, as always, when he speaks to a woman, he tells Madeleine Carroll (who's become astonishingly matronly since *The General Died at Dawn* in 1936): "You're like the scenery. Good to look at but frostbitten." He swallows hard when captured and disarmed. The Indians reverse Hilaire Belloc's adage—"Whatever happens we have got / The Maxim gun, and they have not"—and acquire the machine gun from an illegal arms dealer. Cooper, exclaiming that he came "like a bat out of Helena," tricks them and captures the gun by roping it and throwing it over a cliff. Though Carroll calls him "an angel in leather," he loses her to a rival Mountie, but captures Corbeau and brings him back to Texas to face his punishment.

Even Cooper's performance, the spectacular scenery of the Canadian Rockies and the breathless action ("blood will run like water") could not redeem the absurdities of this movie. There are also witless attempts at low comedy between the stage Scotsman who spanks Goddard and Akim Tamiroff, one of the rebels, who exclaims when dying: "The Big Trapper's got me by the neck." Most of the characters (except Cooper) overact, use exaggerated speech and gestures and seem, in both accent and manner, more like operatic Sicilians than Canadian Indians. High in the snowy mountains, the Mounties are dressed in fur caps and heavy red uniforms while the Indians (warmed, no doubt, by the spotlights) run around half naked.

Cooper is stuck with lines like "Love does funny things to people, kid." But he has "a marvelous gift for keeping his cowboy suit clean and he has certainly managed to pack quite a few of these outfits into the tiny little saddlebag." Otis Ferguson, puncturing De Mille's inflated reputation, justly remarked: "If you think this accredited master of the million-dollar pinwheel could direct traffic, let alone add to the hard-won art of pictures by so much as one stretch of the imagination, this two hours of color, killing, kindness, and magnificent country, may be your dish."[10]

III

Crude as these historical movies were, they reinforced Cooper's image as the ideal hero—the rugged individual so dear to American hearts. In *Meet John Doe* (1941), one of his finest perfomances, Cooper plays an ordinary man whose fundamental goodness gives him dignity and strength.

Once again written by Robert Riskin and directed by Frank Capra, shot in two months at Warner Bros. in mid-1940, the film is a darker and derivative version of *Mr. Deeds Goes to Town*. Both pictures have a naive, idealistic, patriotic and too obviously Christian hero and a cynical woman reporter who first exploits and betrays him, then falls in love with him. In both, corrupt lawyers or politicians try to use and destroy the hero, who sinks into depression but finally revives to defend and save himself when the girl and the crowd support him. But the populist ideals of *Mr. Deeds* are radically undermined by the more menacing vision of the later film.

In *Meet John Doe* an ambitious newspaper columnist (Barbara Stanwyck) concocts a phony letter by "John Doe." Protesting all the hypocrisy, corruption and misery in America, he promises to commit suicide by jumping off a high building on Christmas Eve. Forced to produce the real John Doe, the newspaper hires Cooper, a penniless out-of-work baseball player, to play the part, and Stanwyck then writes columns in his name. Doe urges people to deal with unemployment, misery, hunger and class conflict by helping each other, by showing kindness and generosity to their less fortunate neighbors. Moved by these ideas and eager to put them into practice, many people join the John Doe clubs that spring up across the country.

Cooper—called "Stretch" Willoughby in *The Cowboy and the Lady* and "Long John" Willoughby in *Meet John Doe*—is cast for the role of John Doe in the same way that an actor is cast for a part. "The John Doe Show," one critic noted, "is choreographed, coached, costumed, scripted, produced, and taken on the road." When Doe becomes a celebrity, the mob at the mayor's office, like the mob at a Hollywood premiere, becomes so excited that it nearly tears his clothes off. He swallows the bait of money and appears in spiffy new clothes, orders food from room service and becomes enmeshed in the rotten schemes of news editors and politicians. Doe, unlike Deeds, is not all idealist from the very beginning, and does not develop a moral conscience until after he's become a celebrity.

Walter Brennan—who had appeared with Cooper in *The Wedding Night*, *The Cowboy and the Lady* and *The Westerner*, and would go on to make *Sergeant York*, *Pride of the Yankees* and *Task Force* with him—gives his best performance in *Meet John Doe*. The sane, down-to-earth Brennan keeps his tattered clothes, warns him not to sell out and remains faithful to his old values by practicing pitching with Cooper (in baseball cap, tie and vest, and with arms and legs flailing about) in their new hotel room. Brennan acts as his moral conscience, reminding him to reject fake celebrity—which is nothing more than a giant handout—and ask for work.

Stanwyck's boss, a fascistic publisher played by Edward Arnold, insists that the American people need an iron hand and sees the growing John Doe movement as a way to further his presidential ambitions. He takes over the clubs with the help of his sinister paramilitary motorcycle corps. When Cooper refuses to cooperate in these evil schemes, he is publicly denounced as a fake and jeered at by a hostile crowd at a vast rally. Realizing that he's been cynically manipulated, and thoroughly disillusioned with the people who are now baying for his blood, he now wants to jump, to express his despair and contempt for the public. But won over by Stanwyck's declaration of love, he's finally reconciled to life.

Capra recalled that Cooper was perfect for the role and that no one else could have played it as well as he did: "For the part of 'John Doe'— a lanky hobo, an ex-bush league pitcher with a glass arm—I had but one choice: Gary Cooper. I wouldn't have made the picture without him. But I had no script for him to read when I asked him to play the part. Surprisingly, he said: 'It's okay, Frank, I don't need a script.' " Cooper's authentic performance transcends Capra's sentimentality, religiosity and clichés about the common man. His very presence suggests a decency, rectitude and goodness that remain sympathetic without becoming cloying or dull. Brennan, who worked closely with him, said that "when it comes to technique, [Cooper's] is effortless. For that reason it's one of the best. . . . Cast in the right part and in the right movie, his underacting, naturalness and casualness are effective." As Otis Ferguson noted: "His is the kind of stage presence which needs no special lighting or camera magic; he makes an entrance by opening a door, and immediately you know that someone is in the room."[11]

Cooper is brief when Capra goes on too long, subtle when Capra is painfully obvious. During the interview for the John Doe job, the hesitant, diffident Cooper fingers his battered hat and covers the hole in his pants. He looks longingly at the sandwich on the desk, faints from hunger, then smacks his lips and (like the real Cooper) wolfs down his food. When they give him money and promise to fix his pitching arm, he grins with self-satisfaction. He smiles and stares at Stanwyck when she combs her hair for a photo, then pretends to be serious and tries out angry expressions. During his crucial radio speech, which inspires his followers, he clutches the rostrum and gulps at the opening words. He reads haltingly but, as the crowd warms to him, gradually gains conviction and passion. He takes a deep breath and smiles sympathetically when he personally meets his followers and is embarrassed when a grateful old lady kisses his hand. Realizing he's gone too far, Cooper admits: "Gee whiz. I'm all mixed up. I don't get it. Look, all these swell people think I'm going to jump off a building or something. I never had any such idea." To which the hardheaded Brennan responds: "You're hooked! I can see that right now. They got you. Well, I'm through." Cooper shows his skill as an actor by moving "from initial amusement to growing involvement, regret, bewilderment and ultimate despair." At the end he smokes his last cigarette like a condemned man, and his breath, vaporous in the cold night, seems to be his last.

Cooper's repertory of expressions and gestures complements his words and conveys the film's economic, religious and political themes. Just after the Depression, when millions were unemployed and everyone was worried about poverty, both *Mr. Deeds* and *Meet John Doe* paradoxically suggest that money can make you lose freedom and happiness. In the film the usually tall Cooper poses with two midgets who symbolize the "little people" while he himself stands for a superior version of the average guy. Riskin and Capra believed strongly in the essential goodness of the common man, in the power of powerlessness that is summed up in the Sermon on the Mount. During his speech Cooper paraphrases Psalms and Matthew—"the meek can inherit the earth when the John Does start loving their neighbors. . . . Wake up, John Doe, you're the hope of the world." And like Deeds, he's directly identified with Christ: "You don't have to die to keep the John Doe idea alive! Somebody already died for that once! The first John Doe!" Democracy, then, becomes an offshoot of Christianity, a political system in which each person has value and can retain his pride in economic hard times.

But Doe is so brutally manipulated and the public so deceived by the publisher's power that the little man comes close to utter defeat. The film tries to argue that though the masses can be swayed and deceived, they will finally regain their good sense and true values. When the plot reaches its crisis, however, it lays bare, beneath the liberal pieties, "the stupidities of the average citizen and the perils of mass conformity" that will allow the evil publisher to be voted into power.[12] This insight leads Doe to the brink of suicide.

Riskin and Capra had great difficulty with the ending. To demonstrate his sincerity, conviction and courage, John Doe had to jump as promised, but could not do so in a film that was meant to be a heartwarming comedy-drama. Seeking an agreeable compromise, they refused to accept the only logical and dramatic conclusion. Cooper himself came up with a neat solution that was better than the one used by Capra, by suggesting a way for Doe to jump, fulfill his promise and follow his principles, but also to be saved. "For my money," Cooper said, "they'd have spread a net for Doe and he would have jumped off the roof at the end of the picture. That's the way I should like to have done it. Because I believe that's what he would have done. Why not? Men die, you know, for things they believe in."

Riskin and Capra, horribly confused about what to do, vainly hoped that a preview would provide a miraculous solution: "At one time we had three different endings playing at various places . . . trying to see if the audience would tell us which they preferred. None of those three was satisfactory, either to the audience or to me. When, all of a sudden, here comes a letter from the outside, signed 'John Doe.' And it said, 'The only way you can keep that man from jumping off that City Hall on Christmas Eve is if the John Does themselves come and tell him he'll be much more use walking around than dead.' " In fact, neither Cooper's idea nor Capra's sentimental conclusion really solved the question. The film portrayed an ignorant and corrupt society that was ripe for dictatorship, and showed how powerful men in control of the news media could undermine and destroy democracy. The ending pushed the genie of Fascism back into the bottle of comedy. In Hollywood a kiss is never just a kiss—it's the answer to everything.

Recognizing the radical weakness in the conclusion, Capra admitted that *"Meet John Doe* missed becoming a lasting film classic because *we couldn't end it!* For seven-eighths of the film, Riskin and I felt we had made The Great American Motion Picture; but in the last eighth, it fizzled into The Great American Letdown." Hedda Hopper, rather quaintly ignoring the darker aspects of the film, said it provided "a much-needed dose of optimism to lift us out of the slough of defeatism everyone's wallowing in."[13]

For Cooper, however, it was a complete triumph. He appeared on the cover of *Time*, with a flattering story, on March 3, 1941 (exactly as John Doe had in the film), and received superb reviews. Howard Barnes, defining the various moods in the picture that made his character complex and convincing, wrote in the New York *Herald Tribune* on March 13: "He has given fine performances in the past, but none to touch this superbly modulated characterization. Whether he is toying with the idea of double-crossing the sob sister, is becoming involved with a fervent zeal for the John Doe movement, or is standing in pitiful lonely debasement when the Fascist publicist exposes the whole hoax, his is the utterly realistic acting which comes through with such authority on the screen."

11

Homespun Killer

1941

I

Sergeant York, an enormously successful film and masterpiece of military propaganda, won Cooper his first Oscar. He had played historical figures, like Marco Polo and Wild Bill Hickok, but this was his first impersonation of a contemporary hero. A classic hillbilly, Alvin York was born in the Cumberland Mountains of Tennessee in 1887. Built like Cooper, he was six feet tall and weighed 170 pounds, had red hair and green eyes. The life of this deeply religious farmer, who first refused to serve in World War I and then became a heroic fighter, was well documented in a *Saturday Evening Post* article of April 26, 1919, in his ghostwritten autobiography of 1928 and in a biography by the ghostwriter two years later.[1] Though the screenwriters used dramatic license to highlight the main events of York's life, and exaggerated the contrast between his religious background and his hell-raising youth, they had to keep fairly close to the facts. York was still alive in 1941 and had to approve the way the film was made.

Sergeant York emphasized two crucial transformations: from inebriated hellion to fanatical Christian and from gentle pacifist to superkiller. We first see York drunk, brawling and shooting off his gun right outside the local church. He's brought home and shamed before his decent mother, courts a girl and falls in love. He buys a good piece of land, wins a turkey-shooting contest and becomes enraged when another buyer swindles him out of the property. Coming home from a hard-cider spree,

165

he gets religion (to the sound of swelling organ music) during a thunderstorm. In a scene invented by the writers, his rifle is struck by lightning and twisted into a molten mass. He asks his enemies' forgiveness and decides to teach a Bible class.

York's religious principles inevitably force him to oppose the Great War. But he's denied an exemption and drafted against his conscience. In training camp he argues the meaning of the Bible with his officers and displays his skill in marksmanship. During his furlough he ponders the conflict between duty to God and to country. Ignoring the Sixth Commandment, "Thou shalt not kill," York seizes on a passage in Matthew—"Render therefore unto Caesar the things which are Caesar's; and unto God the things that are God's"—and has a kind of reverse conversion to war and violence. The Sunday School teacher decides to stay in the army, is promoted to corporal and becomes a rifle instructor.

York became a hero in the Battle of the Argonne, which was supposed to end the war before the onset of winter. On October 8, 1918, in the midst of this big push and a month before the end of the war, York, armed only with a British Enfield rifle and a .45 pistol, went on a rampage. Ignoring the overwhelming danger, he wiped out a whole sector of machine-gun nests, and single-handedly "killed 28 Germans, captured 132 prisoners, including a major and three lieutenants, put 35 machine guns out of business, and thereby broke up an entire battalion which was about to counterattack against the Americans on Hill 223 in the Argonne sector near Châtel-Chéhéry'."[2] This episode, the greatest individual achievement in military history, made him the outstanding American hero of the war. The most bizarre aspect of this well-documented exploit was York's cold-hearted, bloodthirsty enjoyment of the battle. "Got the lieutenant right through the stomach," he wrote in his diary, "and he dropped and screamed a lot. All the boches who were hit squealed just like pigs."[3]

How, then, did York manage to survive a machine-gun barrage, a bayonet assault and a German lieutenant's attempts to kill him without missing a shot? He had courage, bravado, luck, skill, marksmanship and a backwoodsman's knowledge of the terrain as well as a sense of divine mission and the belief that he was protected by the Delty. Like most war heroes, he must also have been a little crazy to take on a whole German company. In addition, German resistance was weakening, morale very low and the enemy keen to surrender before imminent defeat. Some of their troops deserted, and others refused to fight. York pushed recklessly into this pocket of weakness and emerged triumphant.

II

York's exploits, which would be compared to a Western gunfighter's, surpassed Cooper's most fantastic shootouts on film and seemed custom-made for the movies. In 1919 Jesse Lasky, one of the founders of Paramount, had offered $50,000 for film rights to his story and a deal that promised $150,000 more. But York—who was personally modest, disliked publicity and didn't want to profit from his carnage—rejected the offer. After Paramount's bankruptcy Lasky, a well-liked figure and Sam Goldwyn's brother-in-law, lost his company and his job. He became an independent producer at Warners, and by 1940 he was on his uppers.

The director Howard Hawks became interested in the project, wanted to help Lasky and approached Cooper (who'd actually been given his first start by Goldwyn). Hawks asked: " 'Didn't Lasky give you your first start?' Cooper said, 'Yeah.' I said, 'Well, he gave me mine as well, he's got a story that won't hurt either of us to do. He's broke, needs a shave.' So, I said, 'Coop, we've got to talk about this thing.' 'What's there to talk about? You know we're gonna do it.' 'Okay, let's go and talk to Warner Brothers. We'll do it if they won't bother us.' And they offered us 80 percent of the picture, I think it was. And we said, 'No, we want your usual thing.' We wanted Lasky to have it and he made about $250,000 and Coop got an Academy Award, everything worked out. So the good guys won."

Things were not quite as casual or straightforward as Hawks suggests. It took some subterfuge on Lasky's part as well as an exchange of actors to close the deal. In order to arouse Cooper's interest, Lasky sent him a telegram, supposedly from York, saying he was the only actor he wanted to play the part. He then sent York a reply, supposedly from Cooper, saying he'd be delighted to do the film. This flurry of artificial admiration clinched the agreement. Warners then loaned Bette Davis to Goldwyn to make *The Little Foxes*, Goldwyn loaned Cooper to Warners for *Sergeant York* and the way was clear for Hawks to direct the picture.

Lasky's deal with York in 1940 was close to the terms he had originally offered in 1919, when York was a much hotter property: $25,000 in advance, another $25,000 on release and a percentage of the gross earnings. The studio also agreed to meet York's special conditions: the undisclosed sums of money would not be paid to him directly but would be used to build a Bible school in his village, Cooper would play the lead and an actress who didn't smoke cigarettes would play his wife. All the living people portrayed in the movie, from General Pershing to York's immediate family, had to sign legal waivers. When York's father-in-law refused to sign, he was cut from the film and lost his chance at immortality.

Hawks, ignoring York's wishes and courting disaster, thought York's wife should be like Lil Abner's Daisy Mae. He wanted the bosomy Jane Russell to play the part as a voluptuous backwoods tramp. Though Hawks' idea would certainly have made the movie more interesting, the producer Hal Wallis brought him back to reality with a hardheaded memo: "Any attempt to make her a sultry, sexy, wild creature of the type that might be played by Paulette Goddard will, I am sure, be met with violent objections from the Yorks." Instead of Jane Russell, they settled on the fifteen-year-old actress Joan Leslie for the role of Gracie Williams, who was fifteen when the twenty-eight-year-old York first met her. Red-haired, freckled, lively and energetic, Leslie also had a sensual figure, but her air of virginal innocence was just right for a girl who's courted and falls in love for the first time. Hawks introduced Cooper to Leslie, a cute teenager who wore bobby socks and carried schoolbooks, and mischievously said, " 'You'd better like her, she's going to be your leading lady.' He said, 'Aw, you're nuts.' I said, 'No.' He said, 'How will I play scenes with her?' 'Exactly the way you just did when you talked to her. Can you remember what you did?' And we went over and repeated the things that he did, and that's the way he played scenes with her."[4]

Dickie Moore, a leading child star who played York's younger brother, called Margaret Wycherly, York's mother in the film, "a pain in the ass." She came from the New York theater, thought she was too good for the movies and condescended to Hollywood. (In 1949 she abandoned her homespun image and played the possessive mother of the crazed and murderous Cagney in White Heat.) Cooper, in contrast, took an interest in the boy, as he had in Shirley Temple. To pass the time between setups, Moore recalled, Cooper would open his wallet and slowly count a wad of one-dollar bills. Cooper taught him to throw a knife—" 'Good thing to know,' he said"—and advised him about buying his first rifle: "I'd get a Winchester 62-A pump. It's lightweight, easy to take apart, and the hammer is exposed so you always know when it's on safety. Costs less too." Cooper also introduced Moore to the outdoors, got him interested in animals and taught him about falconry. "Basically," Moore said, "he oriented me to the things I'm most interested in today, and probably will be for the rest of my life."

York's decent, homespun piety seemed to exemplify the nostalgic agrarian belief, beloved by Hollywood, that life was simpler and more virtuous in the country than the city. York's personality seemed a perfect match for the image Cooper had created in his action movies—gentle but dangerous when provoked—and refined in *Mr. Deeds* and *Meet John Doe*. As George Pattullo wrote in the first important story about York: "Have you ever seen a gunman of the old Southwest? . . . Well, that's York. The same rather gentle voice in ordinary conversation, with a vibrant note when he is stirred that fairly trumpets danger."[5]

In *Sergeant York*, Mr. Deeds goes to war. Like Deeds and Doe, York expresses the virtue and fortitude of the ordinary man in the face of adversity. Howard Koch—who did the screenplay with John Huston and two others and went on to write *Casablanca*—said that Cooper, in knobby boots, bib overalls and a battered hat, "was ideal casting for the central role of a mountaineer character, a lanky outdoor man with a winning simplicity, combined with a Yankee [from Tennessee!] shrewdness." Cooper himself, fearing he might disappoint York, was doubtful about his ability to play this plum part: "In screen biographies, dealing with remote historical characters, some romantic leeway is permissible. But York happened to be very much alive, his exploits were real, and I felt that I couldn't do justice to him. York himself came to tell me [via Lasky's telegram] I was his own choice for the role, but I still felt I couldn't handle it. Here was a pious, sincere man, a conscientious objector to war, who, when called, became a heroic fighter for his country. He was too big for me, he covered too much territory."

Cooper's visit to York in the Tennessee hills convinced him that he *could* play the part of an American icon. The two quiet men had mutual interests, established an immediate rapport and found they had quite a lot to say to each other. They talked for hours about guns and hunting while Cooper absorbed York's "faith and philosophy." Cooper, who called Sergeant York the role he liked best, realized after their meeting that "Sergeant York and I had quite a few things in common even before I played him on the screen. We were both raised in the mountains— Tennessee for him, Montana for me—and learned to ride and shoot as a natural part of growing up. Physically, I looked pretty much as he did when he became the outstanding hero of the first World War. And I managed to pick up a fair Tennessee dialect." Cooper always kept fit and loved strenuous exercise, and was also attracted by the physical effort required in this role. It reminded him of his work on the ranch, when his own life seemed purer and simpler, and suited him much better than drawing room comedy: "I like the physically gruelling schedule playing this part calls for. Quite apart from any acting requirements, here are some of the things the script calls for me to do: mix in rough and tumble mountain fights, shoe a mule, plough a hillside field, chop wood, split rails, dig stumps, haul rocks, hunt fox and wild turkey, dig trenches, topped off by killing 28 movie Germans and capturing 132 more."[6]

III

Howard Hawks—who'd directed *Today We Live* and would go on to make *Ball of Fire* with Cooper—got on wonderfully well with his star. They went shooting and riding during setups, and Cooper was best man at Hawks' wedding to Nancy "Slim" Gross in 1941. Unlike the tyrannical von Sternberg or the imperious De Mille, Hawks (like Cooper) was a well-bred man with good manners. Howard Koch wrote that "his manner was relaxed, restrained, unhurried. I never heard him raise his voice. When he wanted to convey or correct an interpretation of some role, he would draw the actor aside to make his suggestion in private. . . . He gave me the impression of a cultured gentleman."

Like Akim Tamiroff and many other professional colleagues who'd worked with Cooper, Hawks was deceived at first by his apparently casual and effortless performance, and surprised by his uncanny ability to register his thoughts through the expression on his face: "He worked very hard and yet he didn't seem to be working. He was a strange actor because you'd look at him during a scene and you'd think, this is never gonna do, this isn't going to be any good. But when you saw the rushes in the projection room the next day you could read in his face all the things he'd been thinking." York's moral struggle and inner goodness shone through on Cooper's face.

Sergeant York was shot on the Warners ranch in the San Fernando Valley, on a budget of $1.4 million, between early February and late April 1941. The daily pink memos from the unit manager Eric Stacey, who was on the set, to the studio production manager T. C. Wright at the headquarters in Burbank, describe some of the problems they encountered during filming. On the first day of shooting, "Cooper reported a half-hour late, which is nothing unusual for Cooper, I assure you." Two months later the star "developed a rash on his face, under the nose and upper part of his lip, which might prevent him from being photographed today." By February 21, when there were still more scenes to be written, Hawks ran out of script. The producer gave free rein to the director, who altered the screenplay as soon as he got it: "[Lasky] wants Hawks to look it over and is afraid to send it out without his approval since he will change it all anyway." On April 5 the crew was idle all morning: "Hawks did not give the boys a set-up until 11:30 as he was working out the action."

In the crucial scene where York spends a day alone on a mountaintop struggling to resolve the conflict between his religious beliefs and patriotic duty, the rushes "showed the one long shot that they made of the Rock where Cooper walks in. Hawks is very disappointed with this and thinks it looks phony." Though Cooper could handle animals, they were less amenable than actors and always caused trouble. On April 1 Stacey reported: "Company spent the entire morning, and well into the afternoon, working in the rain and lightning with mule that was supposed to be knocked out by a flash of lightning. As was expected, this took a long time on account of the animal." Hawks was more interested in horses than mules. When the weather put the production behind schedule, he arranged for Warners' "B" director Vincent Sherman to direct the last day's shooting and simply took off to see the Kentucky Derby.[7]

The realistic battle scenes, in which American troops advance against German machine guns, were the most difficult to film. The cameraman "constructed a pit clear across a battlefield to accommodate a truck with four cameras. Two of the cameras were on the floor shooting up at sharp angles, one shot at normal eye level, and one very high-up camera shot down as Gary Cooper advanced across the battlefield with explosives dropping all about him. Several cameras often had to be used simultaneously because the action was too dangerous and too expensive to be restaged." In the battle scenes York is methodical and businesslike rather than (as in real life) savage and bloodthirsty. At home in Tennessee, the film showed him imitating a turkey gobble to get the birds to raise their heads. After wetting the gun sight to make it stand out clearly, he picked them all off and won the turkey shoot. Cooper said: "I've never heard of anyone having any success with this method off the screen, but in the movie it looked very effective."[8] In the battle scene, Cooper repeats the gobbling sound when sniping Germans, dehumanizes them by picking them off one by one like a flock of turkeys and concludes: "I reckon the Good Lord was a-protectin' me."

Proud when awarded the Congressional Medal of Honor, embarrassed when kissed on the cheeks by a French general decorating him with the Croix de Guerre, York returns to America for a hero's welcome. The movie shows him greeted by Tennessee Representative Cordell Hull (who was Roosevelt's secretary of state when the film came out), being given a ticker tape parade (using newsreel footage) and put up at the Waldorf. Ignoring the complex issues that had propelled him into war, he states, "what we done in France we had to do," and explains that he killed the Germans "to save lives"—that is, killed them to save us. Refusing all commercial offers, he goes home to his ma and girl. When he sees his new farm, he attributes that gift to the Deity. Quoting William Cowper's "God moves in a mysterious way / His wonders to perform," he exclaims: "The Lord sure does move in mysterious ways."

The overlong 134-minute film takes a great deal of time to establish York's background and character, which are neither inherently interesting nor made so in the movie. As the writers roll out all the hillbilly clichés and offer pious solemnity unrelieved by irony or wit, the first hour becomes extremely tedious. Ma spins in the cabin, Zeb whittles in the store and everyone speaks in the familiar down-home manner—"a-buildin'," "rightly reckon," "he be here"—that we've learned to expect from Hollywood. The military action takes only fifteen minutes, and it was difficult to sustain the audience's attention both before and after the climactic battle scenes. But Americans, gearing up to fight a war, loved *Sergeant York*. The film showed them how a simple man could overcome the brutally entrenched enemy they would soon have to face for the second time.

Cooper transcended the moral and dramatic limitations of the movie—the simplistic characters, the leaden pace, the trite conflicts and sudden conversions. Despite his achievements, wealth and fame, he thought of himself as an average guy. He always tried to play himself, to live up to the image he had created and built on from picture to picture: "I wanted to do stories that were credible, that fitted my personality on the screen, and that didn't clash with the beliefs people held of me." He did not have the typical egoism of a big star, and prepared for his role in a self-effacing way by thinking in terms of the author and character rather than of the actor: "When I have emotional scenes to do, I try to figure out the mental processes of the thing. What the scene *means* to the man, what the writer meant when he wrote it, rather than what I should *do* about it." Joan Leslie remembered how Cooper's body movement conveyed meaning. He added an effective touch at the end of the film by glancing back in wonder at the new farmhouse that the grateful citizens of Tennessee had built for their hero. As Sergeant York Cooper, using the long legs of a mountaineer to step rather than climb over the fences, suggests he can easily overcome obstacles. His lanky diffidence recalls tough frontiersmen in the tradition of Daniel Boone and Andrew Jackson; his slow speech suggests thoughtfulness and wisdom; his clod-kicking shyness masks courage and virtue.

Lee Strasberg, director of the Actors Studio and teacher of the wrought-up and self-absorbed Method acting, would seem to represent the antithesis of Cooper's objective ideas and restrained technique. But he recognized Cooper's talent and tried to absorb him into his own tradition: "The simplest examples of Stanislavsky's ideas are actors such as Gary Cooper, John Wayne, and Spencer Tracy. They try not to act but to be themselves, to respond or react. They refuse to say or do anything they feel not to be consonant with their own characters."[9] The film critic David Thomson also explained how Cooper achieved his remarkable performances: "He lived with the fan magazine legend of someone bewildered at getting away with doing so little. Yet on film he was riveting and dignified. . . . Cooper never played a bad man yet he managed without sanctimoniousness and with such honesty that his integrity seemed the result of exhausting effort." François Truffaut, one of the finest French directors, placed Cooper in his pantheon and simply said "the greatest actors . . . emerge triumphant without direction . . . Cooper, Stewart, Fonda, Bogart."

IV

Alvin York admired Cooper's performance, liked the film (released the same year as *Meet John Doe*) and agreed to descend from his mountain retreat and participate in the publicity campaign organized by Hollywood. *Sergeant York* opened in New York on July 1, 1941 at the Astor Theater, which was decorated with a huge caricature of Cooper and had fifteen thousand flashing lights in red, white and blue. Eleanor Roosevelt, Wendell Willkie, Henry Luce, General John Pershing and

General Lewis Hershey of the Selective Service attended the premiere. On July 30, after the Washington premiere, Cooper met Franklin Roosevelt at the White House. York also attended several openings of the film and spoke at the Tomb of the Unknown Soldier. He attacked American isolationism and compared Senator Gerald Nye, father of the Neutrality Act, to Neville Chamberlain, who'd sold out the Czechs to Hitler in 1938.

The publicity campaign paid off. *Sergeant York* became the top-grossing film of the year and by March 1942 had carried $4 million. Nominated for eleven Academy Awards, it moved audiences and won Oscars for best actor and best screenplay. James Stewart, wearing his military uniform, presented the award in February 1942—two months after America had entered the war. Cooper, rather nervous, fumbled and almost dropped the golden statue, then lifted the microphone a foot off the ground to give his speech: "It was Sergeant Alvin York who won this award. Shucks, I've been in the business sixteen years and sometimes dreamed I might get one of these things. That's all I can say. . . . Funny, when I was dreaming I always made a good speech."[10] He then bowed and walked off, leaving his Oscar on the podium.

Europe had been at war for nearly two years when *Sergeant York* was released, and on June 22, 1941—nine days before the opening—seventy-nine Nazi divisions invaded the Soviet Union and put America's potential ally in mortal danger. The Japanese attack on Pearl Harbor was only five months away. Politicians who saw that America would inevitably be drawn into the war used the film to arouse patriotic feelings and combat isolationism. During all the celebrations and triumphs few people realized that the slow development of York's character in the movie—from religious redneck to one who sees the military light—denies rather than affirms his Christian principles. York became an outstanding example of individual initiative in the face of static trench warfare and anonymous slaughter, and personified the need to fight the enemy in order to maintain democracy and freedom. In 1941 the notable pacifist launched the most effective war propaganda ever turned out by Hollywood.

12

New Guinea

1942–1943

I

Cooper had been a top star for many years, but the enormous popularity of *Sergeant York* and his first Academy Award crowned his success. For the first time he hired a public relations firm—Rogers, Cowan and Jacobs—to look after his image. On screen, especially after *Mr. Deeds*, he played the corny, naive and innocent Everyman. As he approached forty, his films no longer promoted the glamorous actor, but the sturdy all-American hero: laconic, tough and good. Regarded by the public with affection and admiration, Gary Cooper had almost become a brand name. Wholesome and handsome, he was now a complete "celebrity," in demand on magazine covers and in advertisements, on radio and later on television. On a USO tour to entertain American servicemen in the South Pacific, he performed as a screen hero yet presented himself to the troops as an appealingly ordinary man.

Cooper appeared again on the cover of *Life* (October 7, 1940), this time in cowboy garb, and on the cover of *Look* (July 28, 1942) as Lou Gehrig when *The Pride of the Yankees* came out. On skis he was the cover story in *Skier's Informant* (February 20, 1947). On his travels to Europe he was constantly in the pages of the photo magazines. He appeared on the cover and was the subject of the lead article of the *Billed Bladet* in Copenhagen (November 13, 1959). He also earned high fees and kept his image before the public with a wide range of full-page endorsements. He advertised Ammen's skin powder and Calox tooth powder, Chesterfield cigarettes and Pabst beer, Royal Crown cola and Royal 76 gasoline, and the Insured Savings and Loan Association.

Despite all his experience in the public eye, Cooper was never an extrovert. Unlike many actors who came to Hollywood from Broadway and periodically returned for more serious work in drama, he had no stage experience or desire to appear in plays. He felt freer as a film star and said of the theater: "I wouldn't want to live that kind of a life. In a city, I mean, working every night, doing the same thing over and over. *Couldn't* live that kind of life." His inexperience with live audiences gave him stage fright. In personal appearances to publicize movies from *Beau Sabreur* (1928) to *You're in the Navy Now* (1951) as well as on his USO tour and live television appearances, he was "scared stiff and miserable."[1]

In a defensive mode that was part calculation, part instinct, he relied on his cowboy persona to forestall the expectation that he'd be dashing and articulate. This clever strategy accomplished two things: it disguised his nervousness and reinforced his screen personality. Cooper said he'd "learned that people don't expect too much from a man with a one-word vocabulary," and first used his indelible self-parody on Edgar Bergen's radio program of March 22, 1942 by saying only "yep" and "nope." The studio encouraged this engaging public image, which matched most of his movie roles. In Cooper's guest appearance in the movie *It's a Great Feeling*, made at Warners in 1949, the second-string actor Dennis Morgan comically complains that he's agreed to appear in a picture directed by the inept Jack Carson. Cooper, dressed in cowboy clothes and drinking soda pop at a lunch counter, listens to Morgan's lament, keeps repeating the word "yep" and is warmly thanked for having been a great help.

Cooper justified the split between the simple character he played and the sophisticated man he really was by stating that an actor was paid to deceive the public. He saw nothing wrong with playing down or concealing aspects of his life that contradicted the screen personality: his English education, his wealth, his socialite connections and his frequent extramarital affairs. In part he was instinctively modest. He still insisted that he was just an ordinary-looking, tongue-tied, awkward cowboy from Montana. (He falls over a stack of baseball bats in *The Pride of the Yankees* just as he fell over a row of garbage cans in *Mr. Deeds Goes to Town*.) He honestly did not believe he was, and did not want to seem to be, superior to other people in life or in films. This sincerity and dignity helped defuse professional jealousy and kept him at the top throughout his long career.

His studied blankness and almost wooden personality in public also guarded his privacy and protected him from probing journalists. Later on he explained his technique for politely evading personal questions. "I did have a reputation of not getting along too well with interviewers," he said. "The Hollywood fan magazine people really slip you a hot question every once in a while and I just never did answer them and so I got a sort of reputation for saying yep or nope."[2] Eventually he became tired of being an American icon and in his last decade took on darker and more complex films. But his next two roles—the virginal professor in *Ball of Fire* and the sentintental hero in *The Pride of the Yankees*—were very much business as usual.

II

Sam Goldwyn paid Billy Wilder $7,500 for the witty script of *Ball of Fire* (1941) and promised another $2,500 if the picture was made. Like most studio executives, Goldwyn was a tough, often unscrupulous busi-nessman who had little respect for writers. When Wilder asked for the rest of the money, Goldwyn forgot his promise and asked if they had a written agreement:

> Billy shouted, "Forget it, Sam. And if the two of us ever meet again—let's pretend we don't know each other."
>
> He slammed down the phone.
>
> It rang in a few moments. Goldwyn said, "Now, Billy, I just talked to Frances. She don't remember it, either."
>
> "Now we both know you said you would pay me a balance of twenty-five hundred. So if you don't remember it, and Frances doesn't either, the hell with both of you."
>
> He slammed down the phone.
>
> Goldwyn rang him up at once. "Please, Billy," he moaned, "listen to me.—I don't want a person going around Hollywood talking angry against me. All right, come over and pick up the . . . fifteen hundred!"

Directed by Howard Hawks, the movie reflects the Austrian-born Wilder's fascination with American slang. Barbara Stanwyck (Sugarpuss

O'Shea) is a burlesque stripper in trouble with both the mob and the law. She seeks refuge in a house that Cooper (Bertram Potts), who's writing an encyclopedia article on slang, shares with seven rather cumbersome scholarly colleagues. The rich cast includes Dana Andrews and Dan Duryea as the gangsters Joe Lilac and Duke Pastrami, and the European character actors—Oscar Homolka, S.Z. Sakall and Leonid Kinskey—as the old professors. Stanwyck, who's brash rather than sexy, readily supplies the current slang as Cooper—celibate, unworldly and hesitant— falls in love and rescues her.

The bumbling scholars, who mess about and never actually do much work, parody the Seven Dwarfs. Stanwyck, an inverted Snow White, has all the snappy lines. Cooper, a gentle giant, is a passive, reclusive man who graduated from Princeton when he was thirteen, has been out of touch with ordinary life and jumps at the chance of love with a highly improbable dame. Taking the aggressive role, Stanwyck flirts outra- geously with Cooper and remarks that after he's seen a little sunlight on her hair, he'll have to water his neck to cool off. When she stands on a pile of books to give him a meltdown kiss, he responds eagerly with "Would you 'yum' me just once more?" He's charming when love-struck, poignant when deceived and humiliated, bold when confronting the gangsters and delightfully pleased with himself when he finally wins the girl. Well aware of his limitations, she says: "He can get drunk on butter- milk, blushes up to his ears and doesn't even know how to kiss, the jerk. . . . He looks like a giraffe and I love him."

Cooper had offhandedly quoted Shakespeare in *Souls at Sea*. In *Ball of Fire*, Wilder borrows Richard's seductive words to Queen Anne in the first act of Shakespeare's *Richard III*. (He ignores the grisly context, for the murderous Richard later succeeds her dead husband as king and finally marries her.) As Cooper gives Stanwyck an engagement ring at the end of the movie, he turns the malevolent speech into a gentle scholar's homage to his lady:

> Look how this ring encompasseth thy finger,
> Even so thy breast encloseth my poor heart.
> Wear both of them, for both of them are thine.
> And if thy poor devoted suppliant may
> But beg one favour at thy gracious hand,
> Thou dost confirm his happiness for ever.

Wilder's inventive comedies romantically link the unlikeliest characters. The scholar and the gangster's moll are both caricatures, but when Cooper courts Stanwyck's brassy tart with Elizabethan poetry, the effect is charming and the verse sublime enough to convert the girl from bar to books.

The Pride of the Yankees (1942), based on the life of the baseball star Lou Gehrig, was another vehicle for Cooper-as-American-hero. Gehrig had died the previous year, at the age of thirty-seven, of the rare paralytic disease that now bears his name. He came from a poor German immigrant family—his father was a janitor, his mother a cook—and worked his way through Columbia University. His rise to greatness from humble origins followed the classic pattern of American success. As first baseman for the New York Yankees from 1925 to 1939, he established a record by playing 2,130 consecutive games. The "Iron Horse" batted over .300 for twelve straight seasons, had a lifetime batting average of .341, hit .361 in seven World Series and won the Most Valuable Player award four times.

Sam Goldwyn paid $30,000 for the rights to Gehrig's story, and publicized the picture by offering each of Gehrig's teammates and their wives $500 plus travel and hotel expenses to spend a week in Hollywood. Babe Ruth, Gehrig's rival and sometime friend, plays himself in the picture, which conveniently ignores their long-running feud. Ruth, eight years older, a lavish spender with a flamboyant, bombastic personality, patronized the frugal and modest Gehrig. Ruth drank and whored; Gehrig took his mother on road trips. They fished, hunted, played cards and went to football games together. But Gehrig wouldn't back Ruth when he held out for a higher salary, and their rivalry intensified when Gehrig's career took off as Ruth's declined. When Gehrig's mother criticized Ruth's second wife, Ruth's anger and resentment boiled over. He stopped speaking to Gehrig, and their friendship came to an end.

Ruth was deeply moved by Gehrig's brave response to his fatal illness, which brought the two old friends back together. Shocked by the terrible change in his old companion, Ruth said: "He had always seemed the last word in muscular strength to me. He could have broken an oak tree in two with his hands. Now here he was, dragging himself along, losing his balance and clutching at the air—and, in the end, becoming too weak to light a match." Ruth recalled that on Lou Gehrig Day, July 14, 1939, when the Iron Horse said farewell to sixty-two thousand fans in a moving speech at Yankee Stadium, "the Dutchman spoke of Mom and Pop Gehrig, and Eleanor, his wife, and what the Yanks had meant to him, and when he said, 'I consider myself the luckiest man in the world,' I couldn't stand it any longer."[3]

The film editor, Daniel Mandell, said the director, following Hollywood conventions, tried to change Gehrig's climactic farewell. But the editor, closely following the newsreels, managed to save the scene in the cutting room: "Sam Wood tried to add things that never happened, to make it more dramatic. How could you make a thing like that more dramatic? I got all the newsreels that I could on Gehrig Day, and I cut the whole thing just the way it was in the newsreel, with the exception that they never showed the mother and father. I had establishing shots of the band marching around, the lineup of players and all that, which I used. And I inserted close-ups of Cooper making the speech, just as it was in the newsreel. There couldn't be anything more dramatic than that."

Though the role seemed perfect for Cooper, who had been a baseball player in *Meet John Doe*, he was as reluctant to play Lou Gehrig as he had been to play Sergeant York. He knew nothing about baseball and felt he could not effectively impersonate such a popular and well-known man. But in both cases the family, who were portrayed in the film, wanted him to take the part and were pleased with his performance. "Gehrig," Cooper said, "that's no cinch. Quite a responsibility, in fact, when you think of all those millions of people who knew him, watched him, knew just how he handled himself. You can't trick up a character like that with mannerisms, bits of business. I honestly didn't want to take the part but Mrs. Gehrig came out and she told me that's the way she wanted it. Made it kind of hard for me, not being a ballplayer, not even being left-handed." Both *Sergeant York* and *Pride of the Yankees* emphasized the sentimental courtship of the couples as well as the virtuous character and impressive performance of a shy, quiet man. But Gehrig comes from good German stock while York fights the bad German enemy. York is a religious hero who shows courage in war and triumphs in the end; Gehrig is a secular hero who shows courage when fighting disease and dies in the end. Cooper developed his screen character from movie to movie, and his appearance as Sergeant York enhanced his portrayal of Lou Gehrig.

Cooper's numerous falls as a stuntman had permanently injured his right shoulder, and he was no longer able to raise his arm above his head. His coach, Lefty O'Doul, told him: "You throw a ball like an old woman tossing a hot biscuit,"[4] but he developed Cooper's baseball swing by having him chop down trees with a long ax. Since Cooper couldn't hit left-handed, the technicians devised an ingenious method of getting around the problem. They reversed the number on his uniform, had him run to third instead of first base and then reversed the print of the film. Babe Herman, a professional ballplayer, stood in for Cooper in some of the batting sequences. Cooper got his usual fee of $150,000—four times more than Gehrig's final salary.

Teresa Wright played Cooper's wife, and like him was nominated for an Academy Award. She recalled his cool professionalism, intuitive and spontaneous approach to acting, and taste for solitude. Like Joel McCrea, she found him quite talkative and well informed about politics:

I wasn't aware of learning anything from Cooper particularly, but I recall certain specifics on the set. He prepared very quietly. He didn't make a point of working up an emotion. He did it, and when he was finished, it was finished. Although to the eye it wasn't right, he was instinctively right for the film, which was something else again.

He was very easy to work with. He knew his lines. He didn't like to rehearse a lot. He wasn't one to talk over a scene for its meaning.

When he wasn't working, he liked to go off by himself. He used to whittle, making things out of light balsa wood, like airplanes. . . . He'd sometimes go off between takes and ride his bike around the lot.

When he did talk, it wasn't inarticulate. He was very positive about his opinions. When he had something to say, he said it at great length, with great conviction. On politics, you couldn't call him right-wing. I would say he was conservative. Whether you thought that way or not, you respected his beliefs.

Gehrig's wife let Teresa Wright wear in the film the charm bracelet Lou had given her, and each night it was stored in the studio's vault.

Sam Wood, confirming what Howard Hawks had said about Cooper's apparently offhand but extremely effective performance in *Sergeant York*, observed: "What I thought was underplaying turned out to be just the right approach. On the screen he's perfect, yet on the set you'd swear it's the worst job of acting in the history of motion pictures." As the young Gehrig, Cooper is all modest hesitancy and gulping swallows, shy chuckles, foot-shuffling humility and boyish innocence. But his subtly modulated facial expressions, especially during the course of Gehrig's illness, are moving and convincing.

The picture opens with a few scenes of Gehrig's childhood, then jumps ten years to Columbia University, where he joins a fraternity in which his mother is cook. He rejects an offer from the Yankees because his mother wants him to be an engineer like Uncle Otto. But he secretly joins the team when she becomes sick and he has to pay her hospital bills. During his corny courtship of Teresa Wright, a society girl from Chicago, he's the Prude of the Yankees. Like Cooper's other on-screen wives—from *One Sunday Afternoon* (1933) to *Friendly Persuasion* (1956)—Wright's character stands for conventional sentiments and decent values. Apart from the rebellious Claudette Colbert in *Bluebeard's Eighth Wife*, they are flat, wooden and dull.

Walter Brennan, who specialized in sidekick roles, plays the sports reporter who supports and idolizes Gehrig. He tacitly contrasts him to Babe Ruth and emphasizes his virtuous (if slightly dull) reliability. "His debate with a doubting reporter Hank . . . frames Gehrig's single-minded devotion to baseball as itself a kind of showmanship. . . : 'Let me tell you about heroes, Hank. I've covered a lot of 'em, and I tell you Gehrig is the best of 'em. No front-page scandals, no daffy excitement, no hornpiping in the spotlight.' 'No nothing.' 'But a guy who does his job and nothing else. He lives for his job, he gets a lot of fun out of it, and fifty million other people get a lot of fun out of him, watching him do something better than anybody ever did it before.' "[5]

When the first sign of his disease appears as he's playfully wrestling with his wife, Cooper's brave restraint seems more powerful than a forceful expression of emotion. "His eyes seethe with rage and hurt as the fickle crowd [like the one in *John Doe*] boos his errors in the park. Later, in the locker room, he tries to tie his shoelaces with half-paralyzed fingers and falls on the floor, looking around for any witnesses to his humiliation." Finally, realizing the Iron Man is made of flesh, he's forced to tell the manager: "Better send someone in for me. I can't make it any more." In the doctor's office, where the misty background suggests sorrow, he uses a baseball metaphor to ask: "Is it three strikes, Doc?" The doctor evades his question, but tells his wife the truth, and she promises: "I'll never let him know I know."

Gehrig had hit two home runs in one World Series game to keep his promise to a sick kid who foreshadows his fate. The kid, now recovered, greets him as he enters the stadium to make his final speech. In his farewell address Gehrig looked back with understandable nostalgia at a career that was not without hardships. He had suffered through the quarrel with Ruth and endured the taunts of the crowd when his undetected illness had ruined his game. In the film the screenwriters revised

and shortened the actual speech that Gehrig wrote and delivered.
Choked with emotion and making long dramatic stops between phrases,
as Gehrig had actually done, Cooper thanks his teammates, manager,
fans, press, parents and wife:

> I've been walking on ballfields for sixteen years, and I've never received
> anything but kindness and encouragement from you fans. I've had the
> great honor to have played with these veteran ballplayers on my left—
> Murderers' Row—our championship team of 1927. I've had the
> further honor of living with and playing with these men on my right—
> the Bronx Bombers—the Yankees of today.
>
> I have been given fame and undeserved praise by the boys up there
> behind the wire in the press box—my friends—the sportswriters. I've
> worked under the two greatest managers of all time—Miller Huggins
> and Joe McCarthy. I have a mother and father who fought to give me
> health and a solid background in my youth. I have a wife—a
> companion for life—who has shown me more courage than I ever
> knew. People all say that I've had . . . a bad break, but—today—today
> I consider myself the luckiest man on the face of the earth.

He then slowly walks off the field as if going to face a firing squad.

The Pride of the Yankees is an athletic tear-jerker, with an intensely
sentimental plot: a flawless hero who comes up from poverty to achieve
a great career, old-world parents, loyal teammates and devoted wife, a
tragic disease, stoic response and weeping all around. But it's redeemed,
like *Sergeant York*, by Cooper's outstanding performance. Eleanor Gehrig
said the film "was all she could hope for and that she was 'completely
happy with it.' "[6] It was one of the top ten movies of 1942, and ended
Cooper's contractual relationship with Goldwyn. Over the next five
years Cooper would make lucrative deals one at a time and form his independent production company before signing another long-term contract.

III

Like many movie stars, Cooper did some war work. In June 1943 he
drove down the coast to visit the military hospitals in San Diego. A few
months later, in November and December 1943, he took a five-week
twenty-three-thousand-mile tour of the South Pacific. On October 26

orders came through from the headquarters of the Army Service Forces for Cooper, the actresses Una Merkel and Phyllis Brooks, and the accordionist Andy Arcari to proceed three days later "by rail from Los Angeles to San Francisco thence by air to Brisbane, Australia . . . in connection with the War effort for the purpose of entertaining military personnel."

Una Merkel, born in Kentucky in 1903, began her career as a stand-in for Lillian Gish in silent films. She acted on Broadway, played mainly comic roles in movies and took part in the famous saloon brawl with Dietrich in *Destry Rides Again* (1939). Phyllis Brooks, an extremely attractive blonde who'd been a model before playing leading roles in low-budget films, was born in Idaho in 1914 and had a long affair with Cary Grant in the 1930s. Cooper couldn't sing or dance, or act very much in that restricted setting. He went primarily to show the flag and bring the troops a breath of home, to represent the tough cowboys and all-American heroes he had embodied on screen. He also went as himself, the "ordinary" nice guy who asked no special favors and got along with everyone.

The journey to Brisbane was long and circuitous. They flew on a B-24A Liberator bomber from San Francisco to Honolulu. Then, stopping along the way, they went south to Christmas Island and Tongareva in the Cook Islands, west to Fiji and New Caledonia, and south again to Townsville and Rockhampton in Queensland before reaching Brisbane, where Douglas MacArthur had his headquarters. The general told Cooper that in January 1942 he "was in a Manila theatre seeing *Sergeant York* when the bombs began falling." In a newsreel about his arrival in the sun-baked tropics (where it was summer in November), Cooper thanked everyone for a friendly welcome and compared the climate of Australia to the warmth of southern California. They then flew to Darwin in northern Australia, where General George Marshall saw them perform, and on to Papua, New Guinea (then under Australian rule). They stopped in Hollandia (now Jayapura) on the north coast, in Buna, Goodenough Island and the Kiriwina Islands off the southeast coast, in Milne Bay on the southeast tip of the huge island, and in Port Moresby, the capital, on the south coast.

The Japanese had occupied Indochina and most of China before the attack on Pearl Harbor on December 7, 1941, which brought America into the war. In early 1942, moving south with astonishing swiftness, the enemy conquered Hong Kong, the Philippines, the Netherlands East Indies, Malaya, Singapore and Burma. The advance on Australia was checked in the jungles of New Guinea in March 1942, the month MacArthur took command of Allied forces in the Pacific. The Americans won bloody but decisive victories in the Solomons and Guadalcanal in August 1942, and by July 1943, four months before Cooper arrived, had launched a major offensive.

When he reached New Guinea, the tall actor obligingly clowned for the Australian photographer Damien Parer. Struggling out of a tight cockpit, he got stuck in the door as he tried to exit and slid off the wing of the plane. With his photographer's eye Parer observed that Cooper, for all his celebrity, was the real thing. His extraordinary charisma on film was at one with the real man: "Cooper is wholly a product of the cinema. His outstanding ability to register his boyish shyness and pleasing personality is completely cinematic. He has no stage personality, no stage artifice—his medium is the screen. He is an object lesson to aspiring screen stars. Sincerity must be there."[7]

New Guinea was still inhabited by primitive tribesmen, and conditions were perilous near the battle zone. Brooks wrote that the headhunters and cannibals have "strings of human teeth around their necks, and bones through their noses and ears. . . . Many of the tribes dye their hair pink with lime. The men wear hip sarongs and the girls wear grass skirts that are suspended on the edge of their hips. . . . On every side is the evidence of war, gaping craters, bomb-strafed trees, empty trenches." They felt the danger of Japanese infiltration, heard frequent explosions of gunfire and mortars, and experienced enemy bombing attacks.

The jungles were infested with snakes, spiders and giant red ants. Cooper and his colleagues endured drenching rain as they trudged through the mud and bounced in jeeps over incredibly rough roads. They had poor housing and sometimes slept in blankets on the floor. In combat areas, Brooks reported, they ate "K-rations; malted milk tablets, vitamin capsules, powdered lemon for a drink, a rich chocolate bar for energy and a tiny tin of scrambled eggs and meat." Cooper's prodigious appetite had little scope on this spartan diet, and he lost fifteen pounds. In June 1945, sympathizing with his nephew, then in military service, he wrote that "in '43 I got a good load of 'bully beef' and dehydrated potatoes."

Nervous at first and afraid he wouldn't have anything to give the boys, Cooper took part in matinee and evening performances, and in between shows ate, drank and swapped stories with the troops. When visiting injured soldiers in the hospitals, he asked where they came from and how they were, and his naturally friendly manner put everyone at ease.

Audiences of fifteen thousand, sometimes as close as twelve miles from the Japanese lines, sat patiently for hours in the rain and mud, waiting for the show to begin. Cooper told the Los Angeles *Times*: "I'd open the show with a few Benny and Hope gags and then introduce the girls. . . . Then we'd do some comedy skits, Andy would play the accordion . . . and [following popular demand] I gave the Lou Gehrig farewell speech. Finally, we all gave them 'Pistol Packin' Mama.' "[8]

Cooper made fun of his height and told some mildly sexy jokes: "All in all it was a very nice trip. Part of the way I traveled in a submarine— lengthwise! . . . Take a girl like . . . well, take a girl like Lana Turner. Take away her sweater and what have you got. But, then, why bother you boys with that . . . you've got your hands full already." Merkel and Brooks, standing in for Lana Turner, sang songs like 'I Cain't Say No" from *Oklahoma!* "We were the first white women," Merkel said, "to go to New Guinea. Some of the men had been there two years, and they didn't even have female nurses"[9]—so the troops went wild when the actresses performed. The show concluded on a somber note as Cooper recited Gehrig's speech. The baseball hero's courage in the face of adversity inspired the troops and raised their morale.

Cooper brought back a Japanese sword, and visited military hospitals all over the country. He had not fought in either world war, and took great satisfaction in doing his patriotic duty, sharing the hardships and cheering up the troops. This wartime experience enabled him to observe the speech and behavior of officers and men, invaluable when playing military roles from *The Story of Dr. Wassell* to *The Court Martial of Billy Mitchell*. The exposure to the action and excitement of war would also intensify his comradeship with Ernest Hemingway.

13

Hemingway and
For Whom the Bell Tolls

1941–1944

I

Cooper was intensely involved with other people during his working life, and received constant attention from the public and the press, but he was a reticent man and had few intimate friends. When relaxing, he liked to pursue sports and go hunting, to be alone in the open countryside. He first met Ernest Hemingway, another celebrity sportsman, in Sun Valley, in September 1940. He discovered they had a good deal in common, and Hemingway became his closest friend. Born at the turn of the century, sons of professional men, they had achieved early fame in their twenties. *The Sun Also Rises* and Cooper's first important film, *The Winning of Barbara Worth*, both appeared in 1926. Tall, athletic and extraordinarily handsome, they loved the American west. Cooper kept up his connections with Montana, and Hemingway, beginning in 1928, spent part of every year in Wyoming and Idaho. They shared a passion for rifles, hunting and sports, and decorated their houses with stuffed trophies. Both men had suffered numerous injuries: Hemingway, from trying dangerous exploits while drunk; Cooper, from stunt riding and heroic exploits in films. Their twenty-year friendship, sustained by Cooper's amiable temperament, was unusual for Hemingway, who became impatient with old friends and tended to break with them. For Cooper, Hemingway had a rare combination of qualities. Quite outside the world of Hollywood, he was an intelligent man who understood him and could talk about personal matters.

Cooper starred in the first two films based on Hemingway's work: *A Farewell to Arms* in 1932 and *For Whom the Bell Tolls* in 1943. Though Hemingway admired Cooper's restrained yet heroic performance, he had hated the screen version of *A Farewell to Arms*. He deplored the fake morality that demanded the lovers go through a marriage ceremony and the screenwriters' creaky plot devices: Rinaldi's withholding of the lovers' letters and Frederic Henry's preposterous desertion from the army. In a letter to a journalist, Hemingway said "the movie hero deserts because his girlfriend wouldn't write him any letters. When he goes to look for her, the entire army tags along so he won't get lonely." He was equally disgusted when the studio's press agents tried to sell the movie by publicizing his own exploits in the boxing ring and battlefield.

Sun Valley, a ski resort surrounded by the spectacular scenery of the Sawtooth Mountains of Idaho, had been opened in 1936 by Averell Harriman's Union Pacific Railroad. The company, eager for publicity and well aware of Hemingway's reputation as a sportsman, paid all his expenses there, beginning in 1939, in return for using his name in their advertisements. Many film stars—including Clark Gable and Ingrid Bergman—soon followed in his wake, and it seemed at first like a celebrities' club. Idaho had excellent shooting and fishing, and offered a stimulating change from the hot and humid weather of Cuba and Los Angeles. Hemingway and Cooper spent part of the winter in Sun Valley just before and after the war, as well as many autumns, for hunting, drinking, carousing and good talk, in the 1950s.

Sun Valley reminded Cooper of his boyhood in Montana. Hemingway brought him to Bud Purdy's ranch for jump and blind duck shooting and for trapshooting magpies like live pigeons. After hunting, Cooper would come into Purdy's general store, cut open a can of salmon and eat it on the spot. A bit of a loner, he liked to speed along the country roads in his fast car, and when he hit a tasty sage grouse, he'd give it to Purdy as a gift. One day, when they were eating breakfast in Boise, a waitress spotted Cooper and a crowd gathered around him. Though not pleased by this unexpected attention, the good-natured Cooper was friendly to his fans.

Hemingway and Cooper also loved the big open lava flats near the Craters of the Moon, southeast of the resort, which were filled with jackrabbits, bobcats, crows and golden eagles. The landscape of the Rockies put them in touch with the quintessential characteristics they had known in their youth: virgin land, heroic origins, primitive Indians, pioneer solitude and individualistic triumph. Both loved, as Hemingway wrote in a flashback in *The Snows of Kilimanjaro*, "the ranch and the silvered gray of the sage brush, the quick, clear water in the irrigation ditches, and the heavy green of the alfalfa. The trail went up into the hills and the cattle in the summer were as shy as deer."[1]

In October 1940, two weeks after they met, Hemingway told his editor that Cooper's character matched his screen persona. Always intensely competitive, Hemingway could beat Cooper—still bothered by his old hip injury—in tennis. He also threatened to get his friend, who weighed forty pounds less, into the boxing ring, but Gary, valuing the fine bone structure of his face, wisely declined. Patrick Hemingway recalled that his father asked Cooper about how they staged fistfights in movies and made them look real, and the actor explained that the realistic sound of a punch came from the blow of a mallet on a grapefruit.[2] "Cooper is a fine man," Hemingway wrote, "as honest and straight and friendly and unspoiled as he looks. . . . Cooper is a very, very fine rifle shot and a good wing shot. I can shoot a little better than he can with a shotgun but not nearly as good with a rifle due I guess to drinking too much for too many years." Hemingway coveted Cooper's favorite rifle, a .22 Hornet with a German telescopic sight, and asked: "Coop, if you die before I do, are you going to will me that Hornet?" Cooper promised to do so, and then said: "Hell, I might just decide to give it to you now so I can watch you enjoy it."

They also had a powerful bond from their experience of hunting big game in East Africa. In his five months in Kenya and Tanganyika in 1931, Cooper had sixty kills, including two lions. On a two-month safari two years later, Hemingway had shot three lions, a buffalo and twenty-seven other beasts. They loved to recall their adventures (one paid for by Hemingway's rich uncle-in-law Gus Pfeiffer, the other by the Countess di Frasso), and Hemingway claimed his lesser kudu was greater than Cooper's greater kudu. Inscribing a copy of *Green Hills of Africa* (1935), now owned by Cooper's wife and daughter, the author wrote: "To Gary Cooper, hoping it will remind him of Tanganyika. With very best wishes. Ernest Hemingway."

Both men were targets of ambitious women, who often pursued and sometimes seduced them. Hemingway's glamorous third wife, Martha Gellhorn, who unkindly called him "The Pig," urged him to smooth his rough edges and follow Cooper's elegant example. "Since Marty has been around with the Coopers," he told his editor Charles Scribner, and "seeing that Gary, she wants me to have clothes and be handsome and that sort of thing." The Sun Valley photographer Lloyd Arnold reported that Hemingway (like an eastern dude) imitated Cooper's role as Wild Bill Hickok in De Mille's Western of 1936: "He went all out, had several things made, including a white capeskin hunting shirt—'going Hollywood' to quote him—'don't you think I'm as handsome as Plainsman Hickok Cooper in this fancy shirt?' "

Toward the end of his life Cooper recalled one of Hemingway's indelicate aphorisms: "Always stand in the back of the man who fires a gun and in front of the man who shits. Then you won't get shot at or shit on." He also described a shooting expedition in the fall of 1941, commanded by Hemingway, who could not resist the opportunity to take unsporting advantage of his famous guests:

> The party included Hemingway, Martha Gellhorn, Bob Taylor, Barbara Stanwyck, Rocky and me. Pheasant was our objective, and Hemingway so impressed Bob and me with his knowledge of pheasant hunting that we didn't have a word to say. He deployed us like a general directing maneuvers. . . .
>
> "Martha and I will take the upper corner," Hemingway said. "I know this field, and it's real good. Don't shoot if you flush a bird or two. In fact, don't shoot until you hear me holler. Is that clear?"
>
> We started out. Bob and Barbara got to their patch of brush just as Rocky and I reached ours. As I looked at Bob to see how he was coming, the air around him exploded with birds. If he hadn't been holding his gun, he could have caught a dozen in his bare hands. Rocky made a move, and there was another explosion of pheasant all around us. I held my gun poised, waiting for Hemingway.
>
> He knew his pheasant, all right. Far beyond Bob's or my range, the two flocks joined and swung right over his head.
>
> "Fire!" he yelled, and let go with both barrels. It took a minute for the air to clear of feathers.
>
> I looked down at Bob and he looked back at me. The Nebraska boy, and the Montana boy, raised in pheasant country, had been took.[3]

Cooper kept a copy of "If" in his dressing room, and Kipling was also a major influence on Hemingway's work. Both men retained in adult life Kipling's taste for boyish adventure as well as a streak of his cruelty. Joel McCrea said that when deep-sea fishing Cooper liked to tie pieces of meat on both ends of a string. He would then "throw them overboard and chuckle quietly to himself as he watched the squabbling of a couple of outraged seagulls who have gobbled them up and are, therefore, 'tied' together." Durie Shevlin, who spent her 1947 honeymoon aboard Hemingway's boat the *Pilar*, recalled Hemingway's callous treatment of two turtles mating on a Caribbean beach. He "rowed ashore in a dinghy, disturbed their congress, captured one for cat food and carried it aboard. He turned the turtle on its back; and it became pink, then purple, smelled horrible and died slowly."

Ingrid Bergman's first husband, Petter Lindstrom, on a hunting expedition with Hemingway, Cooper and Clark Gable in the spring of 1946, was shocked by the unsportsmanlike and indiscriminate slaughter of precious birds: "We drove along the power lines in a jeep, and they shot eagles off the power lines using telescopic sights and rifles resting on tripods. Another day we went rabbit hunting. They engaged these farmers to ride in trucks chasing the rabbits towards them. I didn't shoot a single shot, either day. They killed maybe fifty rabbits. Nobody wanted them."[4]

Hemingway told a friend, early on, that "if you made up a character like Coop, nobody would believe it. He's just too good to be true." But as his initial enthusiasm wore off, he became more critical of his gentle friend. "Cooper is wonderful and fine company to hunt with," he wrote his editor in 1941, using a down-home Arkansas expression. "Also as tight about money as a hog's ars in flytime." Hemingway hated the Right-wing Sam Wood, who directed *For Whom the Bell Tolls*, and told Cooper that Wood "was an ignoramus, devoid of both intellect and charm." When Cooper tried to defend him, saying, "Well, Sam's a lot like me," Hemingway tartly replied, "No, Coop, you *do* have charm." He thought Cooper was naive about politics and tried to avoid the subject.

Hemingway's youngest son, on the scene at Sun Valley (where, as a boy, he ran up an enormous bar bill), observed that Cooper had a soothing effect on his belligerent companion: "Though they had little in common intellectually, a kindness and gentleness seemed to exist between them." Both had healthy but discriminating appetites (though Hemingway once made Maria Cooper try gristly beaver tail as an hors d'oeuvre), and their feast of smoked goose and Chablis, devoured when they were locked in by a blizzard, inspired Cooper to observe: " 'Ain't this Mormon country wonderful! They know how to live.' 'I'm practically one myself,' Ernest said. 'Had four wives, didn't I?' "[5] They swapped barbed jokes, revealed amorous intrigues and struggled against the depredations of time.

It was good for the careers of both image-conscious men (as it also was for Hemingway and Dietrich) not only to be together but to be seen together by millions of their fans, who could vicariously participate in their glamorous experience while admiring Hemingway's masculine comradeship and Cooper's fine clothes. A four-page spread in *Life* magazine of November 24, 1941 had twelve photographs, by Hemingway's Spanish Civil War comrade Robert Capa, of the two handsome men and their almost-as-handsome wives hunting, fishing, eating, drinking, dancing and loafing in Sun Valley. This kind of valuable publicity continued into the 1950s. After Hemingway had won the Nobel Prize and Cooper his second Oscar, *Newsweek* of March 12, 1956 ran a photo of a valet-like Hemingway helping the bare-chested Cooper into a Cuban shirt. Three years later, on February 16, 1959, *Life* showed Hemingway, at a Sun Valley cocktail party, playfully tossing an olive into Cooper's open mouth.

II

Hemingway had lived the life of the romantic hero of *A Farewell to Arms*, and Cooper had portrayed him on film. Before they met, Hemingway had heard about Cooper from Marlene Dietrich and read about him in the newspapers, and he drew on his impression of Cooper's face and character when he wrote *For Whom the Bell Tolls*. He describes the hero—a lean, laconic native of Montana—as a "young man, who was tall and thin, with sun-streaked fair hair, and a wind- and sun-burned face." When the novel was published, a month after he met Cooper, Hemingway told the Kansas City *Times* that "Cooper rather fitted the character of Robert Jordan." Presenting the work to the model, he inscribed one of the advance copies: "To the Coopers, to make something to supplement the *Idaho Statesman* as reading matter. With good luck always. Ernest Hemingway. On the day we got books. October 5, 1940."

Hemingway naturally urged Cooper to play Jordan in the movie version. He sold the rights (for $150,000) to Paramount so Cooper would have the part and author and star would have some influence in choosing the director. In January 1941, en route to report the war in China, Hemingway stayed at Cooper's house while conferring with

Paramount executives. Hemingway particularly wanted Ingrid Bergman, despite her Swedish blond hair and blue eyes, to play the Spanish heroine. David Selznick, who had her under contract, telephoned her on a ski vacation in Sun Valley and asked whether it would be possible for her to lunch with Hemingway in San Francisco before the novelist left for China. "Is it possible? Possible? I am already on my way," she responded. After she'd been skiing in the sun for a week, her face was very tanned, her nose was sunburned and she had a rugged outdoor look.

On January 30 Hemingway met Bergman and liked her immediately. After telling her that her hair would have to be cut short, he asked to see her ears (Cooper would get to see much more than this) and found them as delightful as the rest of her. Gregory Hemingway said that when Bergman confided, "I always carry an extra pair of stockings in my bag," Hemingway, "whose only possible interest in her lingerie was how to get it off her," would say, "Yes, Ingrid, that's a very practical thing to do."[6] He inscribed a copy of the novel "For Ingrid Bergman, who is the Maria of this story," and told her she'd get the part. After casting the leading roles, he flew off to the "bad earth" of China.

Both Hemingway and Cooper wanted the sportsman Howard Hawks (who had directed Cooper in *Sergeant York* and would later do a brilliant version of Hemingway's *To Have and Have Not*) to direct *For Whom the Bell Tolls*. So in October 1941, Hemingway's third consecutive season in Sun Valley, the three men met to discuss the project, formulate a clear interpretation of the novel and try to convince the studio to hire Hawks. Resisting the pressure of author and actor, Paramount first chose De Mille and then gave it to the stolid Sam Wood. Completely out of sympathy with Hemingway's political views, he produced a slow-paced version of 170 minutes, which one critic called "a studio-bound and mock Spanish rendering of Hemingway." Even worse, the role of Maria was given to the Norwegian ballerina Vera Zorina.

The film was shot from July to October 1942, partly on location at the Sonora Pass in the Sierra Nevada of California. On July 14, writing to Rocky from the Douglas Lodge at sixty-one hundred feet, Cooper described the spectacular setting and gave his first impression of his leading lady: "I'm on the porch of the lodge where we eat. I've just consumed five trout about as long as this paper. The sun now hits only the high peaks, making them pink and blue, and a slight breeze from them gives a little nip to the air. . . . Shot the first scenes with Zorina. She seems O.K."

Two weeks later he reported a case of suspected espionage, and said that Zorina had been disappointing and might have to be dismissed:

> Last night a waiter and waitress left suddenly and afterwards Mrs. Nelson turned their names, description and car number in to the FBI. It seems she overheard conversation in German between them and a mysterious stranger one night, and their comings and goings all night long in their cars look very unusual for up here. There is supposed to be a huge amunition dump way up in the mountains somewhere. . . .
>
> Perhaps you've seen by this time in Louella's column about tests on Bergman. They are taking tests today or tomorrow of her and Sunday they'll run all the tests of Zorina and Bergman and decide. They want Sam [Wood] to go down again Sunday to sit in on the look see but he tells me he knows the Zorina dame is hopeless for a performance and feels whether this other gal looks it or not he thinks he can get the necessary acting job out of her.

Selznick felt that Paramount "had destroyed Zorina's looks with a murderous haircut." After two weeks of shooting, Cooper and Wood threatened to leave the film, Zorina was suddenly replaced and the big shots blamed each other for the costly mistake. Sam Wood said the film's producer, Buddy De Sylva, had insisted on Zorina; De Sylva and Y. Frank Freeman, the head of the studio, claimed it had been Wood's decision. ("Y. Frank Freeman," Billy Wilder quipped, "is a question no one has ever been able to answer.") Zorina, humiliated by her dismissal and enraged by the bad publicity, threatened to sue, and Paramount paid her full fee of $25,000.

In the summer of 1942 Rocky kept Cooper up-to-date with news about the social and sporting life of the idle rich in Southampton. She also reminded him that she attracted other men, but eagerly looked forward to their reunion: "During tennis week one drunk soldier grabbed me and kissed the hell out of me. He was immediately thrown out. . . . Soon, soon, I'll be boarding the train and, whoopie, into my lover's arms. . . . I love you—with all I've got."[7] Given Cooper's randy track record, Bergman's notorious sexual history, the impossibility of competing from a distance with a beautiful new woman, especially in the romantic setting and mood of filmmaking, Rocky was reduced to a futile plea for fidelity. She could only promise sexual pleasure when he returned.

III

Bergman tested well for the role of Maria, and Cooper and Hemingway got their way after all. Paul Henreid, who played Bergman's husband in *Casablanca*, wrote that as they were completing the film at Warners in early August 1942, "she went to the telephone and said, 'Yes, yes . . .' then let out a yell I can only compare to that of a tigress who had made a kill, a yell of such joy and triumph that I was stunned. . . . She put down the phone and yelled, 'I got it, Paul! I got it!' "

Bergman came straight from the chaotic set of *Casablanca* in the Warners' studio to the High Sierras setting of *For Whom the Bell Tolls* and was struck by the atmosphere on location: "It was so primitive and romantic up there among the stars and the high peaks before the winter snows cut off the whole region." She had often told her accommodating first husband that "she couldn't work well unless she was in love with either the leading man or the director." She soon fell in love with Cooper, and later praised his physical beauty as well as his acting: "The personality of this man was so enormous, so overpowering—and that expression in his eyes and his face, it was so delicate and so underplayed. You just didn't notice it until you saw it on the screen. I thought he was marvelous; the most underplaying and the most natural actor I ever worked with." Cooper returned the compliment. "She is one of the easiest actresses to do a scene with," he said. "She lifts the scene. That's because she is so completely natural." Bergman was superb in the close-ups; her passion for Cooper shone through on the screen and their love scenes were as rapturous as the ones with Dietrich in *Morocco*.

Bergman's adoration of her leading man was all too apparent to her confidante, who warned her: "Really, Ingrid, you must stop looking at him like that. You sit there just looking! I know you are supposed to be in love with him in the picture, but not too much in love with him!"[8] She spent all her free time with Cooper, eating evening meals and preparing their roles together. Since the film was shot far from the prying eyes of Hollywood, she escaped scandalous rumours in the gossip columns. Cooper's liaison with Bergman, as with Dietrich, intensified Hemingway's competitive instinct. As Hemingway (who fantasized about Dietrich in *Islands in the Stream*) longed for the two beautiful women Cooper had so easily taken to bed, he became increasingly critical of his friend.

Bergman recalled that "we worked twelve weeks in the mountains and later twelve weeks in the studios, Paramount spending three million dollars on their biggest film." In the finished product the unbelievably healthy, radiant actress didn't look as if she had recently been raped by a gang of Fascists and was living a primitive existence in a remote fastness of the Spanish mountains. In the novel Maria is innocent about love and sex. She asks Jordan where the noses go when people kiss, and expresses the wonder of her first sexual experience when she tells him "the earth moved." Yet, rather perversely, her violation ("a bad time, the worst time a woman can have") makes her more exciting, and she retains her essential innocence without losing her magnetic sexuality.

The action of Hemingway's novel takes place during three days in late May 1937 in the Sierra de Guadarrama, northwest of Madrid. Concentrating on the fate of a small guerrilla band—the brave Andrés, the gypsy woman Pilar, old Anselmo, the deaf El Sordo and the treacherous Pablo—Hemingway depicts the doomed struggle of the Republicans (the Left-wing and Communist supporters of the legally elected government) against the superior forces and firepower of the Nationalists. Maria has survived a vicious rape at the hands of Nationalist troops and been rescued by the guerillas. Robert Jordan, an American fighting on the side of the Republicans, must blow up the bridge over a high gorge as soon as the Republican attack starts, but not before, so that Nationalist reinforcements cannot use the road. The precise timing of the mission makes it especially dangerous, and the tension of the plot is heightened by several conflicts within this isolated group. Pilar issues a fatal prophecy; Maria and Jordan fall in love, which arouses Pilar's jealousy and the men's hostility to Jordan; a late snowfall reveals their tracks; Nationalist planes spot and attack them; El Sordo's gang is massacred; Pablo betrays them by destroying the detonators; rumors of their plans reach the enemy, who send out cavalry patrols to pursue them. Jordan discovers the bridge is strongly defended and tries to cancel the attack, but Andrés is unable to reach headquarters and deliver the message.

At the exciting climax Anselmo is killed by an explosion, Pablo shoots some of his own men to get horses for the survivors and the remaining guerrillas have to cross through enemy fire to escape. Jordan is shot, his leg is broken and he can't ride. He urges Maria to leave him, just as Bogart did to Bergman at the end of *Casablanca*, and argues that the struggle against Fascism is more important than their love. Bogart says, "I've got a job to do. Where I'm going you can't follow. What I've got to do, you can't be any part of." Cooper's Jordan, who's going to die in the struggle, also says he'll be with her in spirit: "What I do now I do alone. . . . If you go then I go, too. . . . Go now. Be strong." He's left behind with a machine gun to hold off the enemy and protect the guerrilla retreat. Though we don't actually see his death, we know he'll give his life for the cause.

A plot like this was made for movies. It had spectacular scenery, emotional conflicts, a romantic story, heroic self-sacrifice and stirring battles. But Hemingway was more scathing about the result than he'd been about *A Farewell to Arms*. Since America was fighting German and Italian Fascism while the film was being made, Hemingway naturally believed the political theme of his novel was more urgent than ever. But the Fascists under Franco had won the Civil War and had been in power for several years. The U.S. State Department advised Paramount to get the approval of the Spanish dictatorship, which naturally tried to prevent the production of the film. Though Paramount did not cave in completely, the studio tried to avoid a boycott by the Spanish government by softening the political message. The film critic James Agee quoted Adolph Zukor, the head of the studio, who fatuously asserted: "It's a great picture, without political significance. We are not for or against anybody."

With all this political pressure, the screenplay was inevitably muddled and weak. The first draft, written by the popular novelist Louis Bromfield, was discarded. The final version, by Dudley Nichols, virtually ignored the political ideas. It stressed Jordan's conflict with Pablo and his love for Maria, but omitted his poignant recollections of his father and grandfather, which were based on Hemingway's family and had made Jordan a flesh-and-blood character. The flashback to Pablo's taking the Nationalist town, beating the mayor as he runs the gauntlet and flinging him into the gorge, which Hemingway included to show the cruelty on both sides, lacks context and meaning in the film. Nichols, a committed liberal, did manage to quote the Communist leader La Pasionaria when a Republican fighter says "it's better to die on your feet than to live on your knees." And Jordan, relating the Spanish war to the coming conflict with the Axis powers, expresses ideas that were shared by all pro-Republican and Left-wing liberals: "A man fights for what he believes in. The Nazis and Fascists are just as much against democracy as they are against the Communists. . . . If the Fascists aren't licked right here, it's going to be a tough war."[9]

But the "political castration" of the movie infuriated Hemingway. Paraphrasing an unpublished letter, a biographer wrote that when Hemingway first read the script, "Nichols's love scenes struck him as astonishingly inept, while his picturesque conception of the appearance of the Spaniards could only have been derived from fourth-rate productions of Bizet's *Carmen*. . . . In place of the red bandannas prescribed by Nichols, the actors must all wear grays and blacks, and the whole emphasis must be on the native dignity of the Loyalists." The movie of *For Whom the Bell Tolls* parodied rather than portrayed Hemingway's characters, and no Spanish actors were used. Most of the Republicans and Nationalists were played by Russians with fake accents, and the cast also included a Swede, a Hungarian, a Greek, a Maltese, a Mexican, a Cuban and several Italians. To make matters worse, the studio released an abridged version of the film during the Cold War in the 1950s. All the political references were deleted, and there was "no explanation for Jordan's fighting in Spain, no reference to German and Italian planes, no flashback dramatizing Pablo's killing of the Civil Guards" and no Russian agents Karkov and Marty.

One shudders to think what the film version of *For Whom the Bell Tolls* would have been like as originally conceived, scripted by Bromfield, starring Zorina and directed by De Mille. But even with superior replacements it still had serious problems. Sam Wood, describing his efforts to make the setting authentic, said he tried in true Hollywood fashion to "improve" the natural landscape: "I never experienced anything as difficult as filming under the conditions we had, at an elevation of ten thousand feet, scrambling over rocks. We even uprooted wildflowers and greenery to prevent the harsh landscape from becoming 'pretty' for the Technicolor camera; and we substituted ancient, gnarled tree trunks instead." Though the film gets better as the action intensifies toward the end, it suffers from shadowy photography and garish Technicolor, portentous dialogue and the melodramatic acting of the supporting players. Under Wood's leaden direction, the pace drags and every scene goes on too long. As James Agee observed: "Properly conceived and cut, it could have been ten times as exciting in half the footage. The rhythm of this film, in fact, is the most defective I have ever seen in a super-production." He also recognized that the stars had saved the picture: "Gary Cooper is self-effacing and generally a little faint, like the character he plays, but the faintness has its moments of paying off, and his general support of Miss Bergman is nearly as good as the law will allow. . . . She really knows how to act, in a blend of poetic grace with quiet realism which almost never appears in American pictures."

Though the stars' performances—which earned Oscar nominations for both of them—made *For Whom the Bell Tolls* "a little less awful" than *A Farewell to Arms*, Hemingway mocked the all-too-discreet love scene in which Cooper, bowing to the prevailing censorship, didn't even "take off his coat. That's one hell of a way for a guy to make love, with his coat on—in a sleeping bag. And Ingrid, in her tailored dress and all those pretty curls—she was strictly Elizabeth Arden out of Abercrombie and Fitch."[10] Hemingway felt Cooper and Bergman had saved the film from complete disaster. He was glad to leave the movies to Cooper, and could never be tempted to write for Hollywood.

IV

Saratoga Trunk was made with Cooper and Bergman, right after *For Whom the Bell Tolls*, between late February and late June 1943, but the current demand for war movies held back its release until 1945. Warners' budget of $1.75 million (about half the cost of the previous film) included $175,000 for the rights of Edna Ferber's best-selling potboiler and funds for research in both locales: New Orleans and Saratoga Springs (the title refers to a railroad line near the New York spa).

Cooper made the movie, a complete dud, only to continue his love affair with Bergman. Their passion was still intense, and they were "full of high spirits. He called her 'Frenchie' and she called him 'Texas,' as if they had become their characters. They were seen driving together down Sunset Boulevard, and there was considerable gossip about their relationship, gossip that may have reached the ears of Cooper's wife. But Ingrid was sacrosanct in the columns and movie magazines, and no conjecture about a romance appeared in print."

The director and both stars caused many expensive delays and brought the movie in forty-two days behind schedule. Eric Stacey's alarming memos to T.C. Wright described Sam Wood's lack of planning and maddening indecision: "on many occasions he is very vague about how he is going to stage scenes, and after he has done a scene, goes home and sleeps on it, gets another idea and does it again the next day." Cooper, who had a dialect coach for his Texas accent, came down with an eye infection and couldn't do close-ups for several days. Bergman missed a week because of illness, and started messing about with the script when she returned to the set. "This scene was changed around," Stacey wrote, "and Miss Bergman, as is her practice most all of the time, has injected certain dialogue from the book into this scene."

Saratoga Trunk begins as Bergman, accompanied by her faithful mulatto maid and white dwarf servant, returns from Paris to her crumbling ancestral home in New Orleans. The English stage actress Flora Robson, in blackface, is ridiculously miscast as her servant. The research department did not seem to realize that in the 1880s (and into the 1960s) a black could not sit at a table with a white in a Louisiana restaurant. Jerry Austin, the three-foot six-inch, eighty-five-pound dwarf, is the only animated character in this tediously slow picture. Though he's ugly and tells one Negro, "I come from New Orleans; not like you, Congo," he worships Cooper and is brave and sympathetic.

Bergman wants to achieve wealth and respectability to compensate for an old family scandal, but winds up marrying Cooper for love. He first appears as the camera moves upwards from his shiny boots, along his long legs and torso (a striking contrast to the dwarf), to his black bow tie and large Stetson. Bergman—who does not look good or act well in frilly Victorian clothes—stares away when he first speaks, then turns slowly toward him. She invites him to her table, and he shows his humble origins by calling for ketchup. He shyly puts his finger on his nose and blinks when she stares at his hand on her knee. But he's really a simple man, puzzled by a wily woman, and asks himself: "What am I doin' in a house like this, la-dee-da-ing around?"

When the movie suddenly shifts for no good reason to Saratoga, and Cooper and Bergman meet again at a fashionable hotel, he rubs her feet while she sips champagne to suggest their decadent life. Cooper seems stiff and awkward, as if trapped in an uncongenial part. His character fails to develop, and he's reduced to a series of meaningless gestures. After clinching a railroad deal, he smiles with satisfaction and jams a thin cigar into his mouth. During the fight for the railroad—in the third disconnected section of the movie—Cooper's western hat contrasts to the derbys and flat caps of his eastern enemies. Trains collide and explode, the dwarf is badly beaten and Cooper carries the loyal little fellow into the hotel ballroom. The mindless movie was much more enjoyable for the principal actors than for the audience. The English critic James Agate "found Gary Cooper

. . . as tall and quizzical as ever and still wearing that sun-tanned smile and white cowboy hat which must surely make him laugh if he ever stops to think."[11]

V

Hollywood was a small town with flourishing gossip columns that serviced the local and trade press as well as the national newspapers. Cooper, a popular actor, was undoubtedly shielded by the leading gossip writers. But since he had been seen in public with Bergman, Rocky must have heard about their affair—if not about the "warm-blooded blonde" whom Iron Eyes Cody had seen on location for *The Plainsman*. The summer of 1943 was therefore a major turning point in the Coopers' marriage. After Rocky first discovered Gary had been unfaithful, and knew that people were talking about the liaison, she began to distrust him—though she still loved him. The crucial question, then, is how and why his proud and beautiful wife tolerated Cooper's infidelities.

Rocky had been warned before her marriage about his notorious philandering. But she was young and idealistic, and believed the rake would reform when they married. At the time of his affair with Bergman they had been married for nearly ten years, and Rocky, now thirty years old, was the mother of their five-year-old daughter. At forty-two Cooper was one of the most charming and handsome men in the world, constantly surrounded by attractive and seductive women who were eager to sleep with him and to take him away from his wife. He had had a promiscuous life before marriage, and gradually resumed his old habits. In his acting life he had soon learned that it was only a short way from the restraints of embracing on camera to the delights of touching in private, and an even shorter step from there to bed. As his friend Virgil Sherrill put it, "the plate of delicacies was offered and he partook."

Several writers have commented that Cooper and Rocky "had been going their separate ways since the mid-1940s and only continued to reside together for the sake of their daughter," that their "marriage was endowed with an extraordinary *laissez-faire* attitude on both sides that allowed Coop and Rocky to roam alone pretty much as they wished." But the situation was more complicated and the bonds much stronger than this. Rocky did not go her separate way, emotionally or sexually, until their three-year legal separation in 1951. Until then most of the *laissez* was on her part and the *faire* on Cooper's. A studio executive vividly recalled seeing her publicly humiliated when Cooper suddenly left a social occasion for one of his liaisons: "We're all sitting around after dinner and Gary glances at his watch and nonchalantly strolls out the door with a polite good night. And Veronica watches him go, knowing full well his heart belongs outside the home and seemingly she couldn't care less."[12]

Rocky enjoyed her status and privileged life. She managed the servants and the house, which she furnished with taste, and was always a lively and immaculately dressed companion at Hollywood parties. Whatever compromise they arrived at, spoken or unspoken, the contemporary double standard would have prevented her from having the same freedoms that he enjoyed. When she married him, she may have sensed his weakness—he had had a breakdown two years before they met—and hoped she would give him stability. It was almost as if her strong, sustaining character enabled him to go off the rails from time to time. Cooper liked "loose" women, so different from his well-brought-up and self-controlled wife. He enjoyed the sensation of falling in love and being adored, and he knew he could always rely on domestic security with Rocky.

Friends thought her tough and indestructible, made of granite with a streak of iron. She could take it, and didn't cut and run when things got difficult. Over the years constant competition with ever-younger movie stars and celebrities turned her into a colder, harder woman. She had a famous husband and had "bought the whole package." Realistic about sexual life in Hollywood, she accepted the more tolerant European tradition and allowed his transgressions, recognizing that his numerous affairs, with one notable exception, were either one-night stands or brief encounters that lasted only as long as it took to make a film. "Rocky handled everything beautifully," said her friend Connie Wald, "held her head high and hid the hurt."[13]

Cooper didn't lie to her and was open about his affairs. But he refused to argue with her (Maria said) and warned Rocky: "If you want to fight, I'm out of here." He meant this matter was not negotiable, that he'd continue to do as he pleased and would leave her if she quarreled with him about it. In return for his infidelities, she demanded her pound of flesh. She got her way in most other things and seemed to lead him through the social rounds of Hollywood like a tame bear. Though they maintained a friendly demeanor in front of Maria and rarely argued in public, the actress Suzy Parker often saw them talking to each other between clenched teeth. The actor Rod Steiger found the tension in their house almost unbearable, and compared the adolescent Maria to a taut wire about to snap.[14]

Arlene Dahl, who knew the Coopers well, was shrewd about matters of the heart. Rocky, she said, had married one of the great romantic idols of our time and knew quite well that he had human frailties. She also realized that Hollywood wives had to be bit players, not co-stars, and remain (at least outwardly) subservient to their husbands' wishes. Rocky was too proud to discuss Cooper's infidelity, the unmentionable elephant in the middle of the room. He was like a naughty boy who came home to mama, was scolded for his bad behavior and went forth to sin again. Rocky wanted to be Mrs. Gary Cooper, and would endure almost anything to remain so.[15] Most important of all, she was deeply in love with her husband.

Rocky stoically believed that people should deal with their own problems and not depend on others for help. Though she was a loyal confidante, if friends complained to her about their lives, she'd sometimes dismiss them with "Next case!" Always sustained by her religion, she believed that marriage is a sacrament, that divorce is not possible, that human imperfection demands charity. In the traditional Catholic view, this world is a place of suffering, a preparation for a better life. Rocky criticized, complained, lamented, cried, attacked and threatened, and prayed for her cup of bitterness to pass. She had the strength to endure and accept Cooper's infidelities, and ultimately she prevailed.

Paul Shields, who had love affairs of his own, said Cooper was both a "man's man and a woman's man." Defending Cooper within the family, he thought Rocky was too hard on him and made him suffer for his transgressions. Outside the family, Cooper was protected by the Hollywood press, which adored him and sanitized his life. Until the more ruthless *Confidential* magazine appeared in the 1950s, gossip writers were reluctant to report the dalliance of a married man. Lupe Velez had shown Cooper what horrors could occur if emotions got out of control, and after his marriage he tried to behave with discretion. The affairs of other actors often seemed sleazy, but his never did. The press was always reluctant to soil the reputation of a well-liked man who embodied the American dream. Compared to the many stars who constantly married and divorced, the Coopers remained, through many vicissitudes, a couple. Rocky's loyalty as well as his natural modesty, grace and air of boyish innocence helped steer him through the shoals of scandal.[16]

14

Hollywood Politics

1944–1947

I

In the early 1940s Cooper had made five important films in a row—
Meet John Doe, Sergeant York, Ball of Fire, The Pride of the Yankees and
For Whom the Bell Tolls—and was at the peak of his career. But of his
next thirteen movies after the Hemingway film only two—*Cloak and
Dagger* and *The Fountainhead*—are worth a second look today. The rest
are adventure stories, war movies or "heartwarming" comedies in which
Cooper plays familiar versions of roles he had done much better in the
past. He made a lot of money—in the mid-1940s he even formed his own
production company—but had as little success in finding interesting and
challenging material as he had at Warners or Paramount. In 1947 he was
briefly caught up in the decade-long anti-Communist fever that gripped
the nation and appeared as a "friendly" witness before the House Un-
American Activities Committee. In the prime of his life he found himself
marking time instead of going forward. It was Cooper's downtime, a
period in which his malleable nature and oddly passive temperament
betrayed him into poor films and bad influences.

The Story of Dr. Wassell (1944), Cooper's third movie with De Mille,
was based on a true story from recent history. In early March 1942 the
Japanese had landed near Batavia, defeated the Dutch forces and
completed the conquest of the Netherlands East Indies. Corydon
Wassell—a doctor from rural Arkansas who had been a medical
missionary in China—had cared for twelve wounded American sailors,

evacuated from cruisers under Japanese bombardment, in a remote hospital. Ordered to abandon his patients to the advancing enemy, Wassell stayed with them, got them through the jungles of Java and put them on a small ship that took them to Australia. As in *The Real Glory*, Cooper played a noble American doctor caught up in an Asian war. In *Dr. Wassell*, as in *Sergeant York*, Cooper once more impersonated a deeply religious man reluctantly drawn into battle, a backcountry soldier as national hero, in a movie that was little more than patriotic propaganda.

De Mille's view of the project was as supercolossal as ever. He used voluminous research to produce fake-looking scenes and produced an episodic narrative that included flashbacks to every aspect of the hero's life: his country medical practice in Arkansas, where he had a kind word for everyone; his rivalry with another doctor about a major scientific discovery; his flight from a supposed scandal in China; the impediments to his marriage, which are finally overcome. Developments in the plot and changes of scene are clumsily engineered by the arrival of letters, orders and telegrams, and the movie attempts to lighten the somber rescue-of-the-wounded-in-war theme with intolerable interludes of comedy, dance and romance. The picture is laden with every sort of cliché, predictably beginning with "Anchors Aweigh" to signal its naval theme and ending with medals pinned on Wassell's chest.

De Mille had a ninety-five-day shooting schedule and a $2.72 million budget that included $200,500 for Cooper, $10,000 for his co-star, Laraine Day, and $3 for one red pig. He used a great deal of war footage from the army and navy, but insisted that the movie was "not a war story." Emphasizing its sentimental box-office appeal, he made a far-fetched comparison to the nostalgic novel about an elderly English schoolmaster by James Hilton (who wrote Wassell's biography in 1943). "It's a *Goodbye Mr. Chips* of the Navy," he said. "The reason the story is great and different [is that] while it is war, it isn't a question of killing; it's a story of life saving rather than life taking." In a statement written by the studio publicist to emphasize the romantic aspect of the film, Laraine Day praised Cooper as a lover: "It was like holding a hand grenade and not being able to get rid of it! I was left breathless. Gary kisses the way Charles Boyer looks like he kisses."

Cooper's Dr. Wassell stands for goodness and gallantry, humility and humane concern. As flat as all the other characters, the doctor is a noble bore, scarcely made of flesh and blood. A muscular Christian, he prays mightily before the arrival of the enemy, exclaims "hogs ran me out of Arkansas and snails ran me out of China," and reassures his dispirited followers: "Don't make any mistake, we're gonna get out of this." A paragon of courage and persistence, he forces his way onto a ship with his patients and performs an emergency operation at sea. He's also praised by the president, wins the Navy Cross and gets the girl. Even Cooper's charismatic personality can do little with a character as stony and idealized as a piece of Soviet sculpture.

After the war the power of the studios—forced by the government to sell their chains of movie theaters and battered by intense competition from television—began to decline. At the same time, leading actors began to realize that they could keep more of their money if they formed their own independent film companies. As an actor Cooper was in the 90 percent income tax bracket; as a producer, taking a percentage of the profits, he paid only 25 percent of his capital gains.

In 1944 Cooper formed International Pictures with three powerful figures in Hollywood. Leo Spitz, an able lawyer and meticulous businessman who had been president of RKO, managed the finances. William Goetz, a witty, lovable man, who'd married Louis Mayer's daughter Edie (a reigning Hollywood hostess), had been head of production at 20th Century-Fox. Nunnally Johnson, a clever fellow and highly successful screenwriter at Fox, had recently written *The Grapes of Wrath* and *Tobacco Road*. The infant company rented offices and a sound stage at Goldwyn Studios, which provided production facilities in return for a standard overhead charge of 25 percent of the budget. Johnson wrote and produced *Casanova Brown*, which lost money, and wrote *Along Came Jones*, which did very well. In 1946 the partners sold their short-lived and not very successful company to Universal, and Goetz became head of production for Universal International.[1]

In contrast to *Dr. Wassell*, where he's serious, dignified and brave, in *Casanova Brown* Cooper is a sweet-natured, naive and awkward fellow who sets a house on fire when he tries to hide a cigarette. Cooper and Teresa Wright play a young couple whose marriage has been annulled. Too proud to contact him when she discovers she's pregnant, she has the baby and then discovers he's about to marry someone else. She pretends to put the infant up for adoption to lure him back on the eve of his wedding. Cooper kidnaps the baby, and all kinds of broadly comic complications ensue as the distracted father tries to feed, diaper and care for the infant in a hotel room. Sentimental, obvious and painfully unfunny, the movie reverses the traditional roles of parents and satirizes the modes of nurturing infants in the 1940s.

Wright felt that Sam Wood, an incompetent director who had little understanding of actors, wrecked Johnson's script. In scenes where everyone was supposed to talk at once, with overlapping dialogue, Wood had them all speak separately and lost all the comedy. After Cooper had spoken his lines in the love scenes, to accommodate the star Wood allowed him to leave the set. Putting the actress at an enormous disadvantage, Wood had Wright play her scenes alone, with a lamp standing in for the actor.

Compared to *Now and Forever*, in which Cooper had played the feckless father of a little girl, the later movie seems quite weak. Though also sentimental, *Now and Forever* has a dark edge to it. In contrast to the rather blank and cute Teresa Wright, Carole Lombard has a bruised, unhappy look that suggests the pain of loving someone who's completely unreliable. In the earlier film Cooper's charming and selfish character has some complexity, and his behavior is partly driven by his love for his child. *Casanova Brown* needed some sharp-edged acting to make Johnson's clichéd script effective on screen. But Cooper, unable to balance sentiment and realism, resorts to a set of grimaces in a series of slapstick scenes. The movie flopped—and still looks pretty bad. Even the most popular actors had to take some inferior roles to keep working and earn money.

Cooper rashly became the producer as well as the star—an unsatisfactory combination of duties—of *Along Came Jones* (1945). He soon discovered that he lacked talent as a planner, financier and organizer. Not realizing that Loretta Young's plain cotton dress had to be cut properly to show off her figure, Cooper suggested that they buy one off the rack for $7.50 instead of having it handmade for $175. When the designer tentatively agreed to this but insisted that Cooper himself inform Loretta about the new arrangement, the good-natured Cooper quickly changed his mind and approved the expensive dress.

Johnson had to raise the more delicate issue of Cooper's lack of interest and sloppy performance in this superficial and undemanding role. As Johnson recalled:

In the middle of the picture, the production manager . . . said, "We're running behind on money and on time. Every day we're a little bit more in the red." I said, "Why?" . . . He said, "Cooper. He's not prepared when he comes in. He doesn't get his lines the night before. He's learning them on the set. . . . We have to have a lot of takes." I said, "Why don't you tell him?" . . . What he was saying was, "You tell him. He's the star. He's the producer. Tell him."

"All right, I'll tell him," [I said] though I didn't know how to because I was as uneasy about this as he was, but finally I went out to Cooper's dressing room. . . . I said, "Do you know we are behind, running in the red? All on account of one actor." Very innocently. He tried to think of who it was, I am sure he was thinking of the others. I said, "He's not ready with his stuff and he's having to have more takes." He said, "Who is he?" I said, "You," and I walked out. I'd never stay to argue with a star about this matter. Now he never got mad, but I didn't know him too well. It's awfully hard to go to a big star like that, and he was my boss too, and say, "You're screwing things up." After that he picked up. He realized it then. He was a nice man.

Cooper couldn't deliver rapid dialogue. When Johnson suggested he pick up the pace a bit and not hesitate so much in his speeches, Cooper explained that his slow speech was not based on his style of acting: "it's really because I can't remember my lines." But hesitation had become his trademark, and the audience loved him for it. Johnson emphasized that the picture, despite the languid pace, came in on schedule and under budget. He also quoted Cooper's self-deprecating response to his brief, uneasy role as movie mogul: "My next step will be to master the cigar. The cigarette makes a very good smoke but it simply doesn't carry authority."[2]

Cooper and Johnson were very fond of Goetz, who put up the money and helped make the deals. But Johnson did not have much respect for his taste and talent as a filmmaker, and felt Goetz contributed very little to the content of the movies they made: "Bill wasn't a picture maker in that sense. He fancied himself for making up titles. Seems to me a rather hollow distinction, but he named both of those pictures, *Casanova Brown* and *Along Came Jones*. They were all right. No, he didn't get into the contents of the script. I guess he just wanted to see them keep moving and come out happy at the end. That was the extent of his production supervision."

Johnson also observed that despite Cooper's *laissez-faire* attitude about Loretta Young's dress, both International movies had limited budgets. They were made as economically as possible and then cunningly disguised so they wouldn't look cheap. Johnson's resigned, cynical tone emphasized the seamy side of the deceptively glamorous business. "There were a few farmhouses, a little fort in the west in 1890. . . . I suppose we shot *Along Came Jones* in that same saloon that everybody got shot in on the lot. Every star in the business has died in there or killed somebody there, one time or another. God, the things you had to do to keep it from looking like it: another sign up there, put some little scroll work around here, three steps instead of two steps, anything. But outdoor pictures are by their very nature cheaper to do. There's nothing to put up and show them." Johnson was amused when "Wild Bill" Elliot, the star of assembly-line Westerns, came to visit their shabby set in his brilliant costume and provoked Cooper's joke about the contrast between them: "He was really a sight to behold. Cooper was wearing a worn cowhand's outfit and was really a dilapidated looking fellow as he talked to Elliot and inspected his paraphernalia. Presently Elliot galloped off handsomely and Cooper came back to me and stood with his eyes on the ground for a moment. Then he said sadly, 'They gave him *two* guns.' "

In *Destry Rides Again* (1939) James Stewart had played the mild-mannered sheriff who refuses to carry a gun; in *Along Came Jones* Cooper is a comically inept cowboy who can't shoot one. In *The Westerner* Cooper was mistaken for a horse thief and nearly hanged; in *Along Came Jones*, a lighthearted parody of all his cowboy heroes, "Melody Jones out of high Montana" is absurdly mistaken for a killer and nearly shot. Proud of his newfound notoriety, and fear-inspiring presence, Cooper boasts in the film: "I ain't hardly said ten words in this town, and already I got a certain . . . standin'." In this picture he deliberately exaggerates all his western mannerisms. He sings when he moseys into town; eats canned tomatoes with a knife (as he had done in Sun Valley); gulps and smiles when he first sees Loretta Young; wipes his lips, turns slowly and gives her a big kiss; takes a deep breath, narrows his eyes and puts his chin down as he struts into the bar. When he draws his gun, it flies out of his hand, and he's finally saved when his sharpshooting girl drills the villain in the head. Though a single joke is usually not enough to sustain a whole film, Cooper carried it off. Joel McCrea called him "the greatest exponent of the manure kicker school of acting. . . . The idea is to scuff around barnyard dirt while muttering some phrase like 'Aw shucks, Miss Nancy.' "[3]

Though De Mille had subjected Cooper to many absurdities in the epic mode, he strongly objected to seeing him in a role that mocked the Western hero. "You shouldn't do that sort of thing," he told Cooper.

"Playing a man on the screen who can't shoot. You are the guy who is supposed to know how to do such things. . . . Never play anything that lets the public down, your public. If you kid a Western, if you kid a hero, you are doing yourself damage. . . . You can let down your public once, Gary, and be forgiven. But don't try it a second time." Johnson used comedy to challenge the myth of the west, and saw Cooper as an idealistic and naive cowboy Quixote: "I was using the cold, unflinching eye of the camera to probe a sick Society. Never for one second did I think of Cooper as a tramp cowhand; to me he was Western Man, eternally gallant, eternally defeated, and the picture itself one long bitter laugh at life."[4] Though the script certainly doesn't substantiate Johnson's claim, the movie didn't harm Cooper's image. When it opened in July 1948, Norman Rockwell depicted him as a Western hero on the cover of the *Saturday Evening Post*.

II

Cloak and Dagger (1946), made at Warner Bros., was much more serious and ambitious than Nunnally Johnson's two comedies. Cooper had successfully played a doctor in two movies. In this film he's an atomic scientist, Alvah Jesper, hired by the OSS to rescue a colleague held captive by the Nazis. He impersonates the professional man, but conveys no inner sense of his character.

Fritz Lang, the irascible Austrian director, was famous for his classic thriller *M* (1931), with Peter Lorre, about a child murderer in Düsseldorf. Lang stated that "Cooper's part was based on J. Robert Oppenheimer, whom I had met and who had given me a certain insight into the experiments at Los Alamos and the first atomic bomb." But Ring Lardner, Jr., co-author of the script with Albert Maltz, said they did not have Oppenheimer in mind as a model for Jesper. Oppenheimer was far too knowledgeable, too important and too well known to be taken out of the atomic program and sent into enemy territory in wartime. Oppenheimer's safety would be far more important than any information he could obtain by spying against the Nazis, and no cloistered scholar would have the necessary survival skills to be an effective undercover agent. The original idea, Lardner said, was that only a nuclear physicist would be able to find the Italian scientist, question him about technical matters and discover what projects he was working on.[5]

Admitting it was an odd role for Cooper, Lang explained: "To cast him as a top scientist is already unusual. . . . I am casting against image which I like to do. . . . You have to *use* him, but you try *slightly* to change some things." Cooper met Lardner twice before the film went into production and told him that he "might get away with it, provided you keep the lines pretty short and don't give me too much intellectual stuff." Favorably impressed by Cooper's unpretentious attitude and awareness of his limitations as an actor, Lardner shortened his lines and simplified the dialogue. According to Warners' publicity department, Cooper prepared for the role by spending a week at Cal Tech in Pasadena "to orient and indoctrinate himself in correct techniques in a physics lab and familiarity with terms and phrases." Cooper described it less pretentiously: "We familiarized ourselves with basic data about atom splitting—well, at least I tried. And they took pictures for set construction and dressing."[6]

The film was hampered from the start by Lang's disputes with the producer. Lang and the writers wanted to warn the audience about the danger of nuclear weapons. Warners wanted to make the usual spy melodrama. The studio, which had final control, cut the script and eliminated the main theme. In doing so, they gave Cooper some innocuous lines and turned him into a conventional scientist–hero. According to Lardner, "a running battle developed, during the preproduction period, between the autocratic Lang and the film's producer, Milton Sperling. At a script conference two days before shooting was to start, Sperling said to Lang, 'Fritz, you and I have had a lot of words, but let's let bygones be bygones, and I will see you on the set on Monday.' 'That,' Lang countered, 'will not be necessary.' " The unit manager Frank Mattison reported that the director refused to be hurried: "Lang is opposing all our efforts to eliminate anything or condense scenes. He was sulking last night because we told him he would have to finish on location today." Lardner felt the picture didn't turn out very well.

As overbearing as Josef von Sternberg, Lang vented his frustration on the leading lady, as well as on the producer. Lilli Palmer, a German actress playing an Italian partisan in her American film debut, threw her shoulder out of joint, was taped up and gallantly continued to work, but couldn't drive home. She also had to leave the set and go to Mexico to have her American visa extended. When her difficulty firing a machine gun coincided with Lang's bladder problems, there was "a mutual blow-up." Palmer later complained that Lang "made a point of speaking only English and was reasonably friendly, in curt sort of way. Authoritarian, though. Even moving my head from left to right turned into a third degree." Lang cuttingly remarked: "It was very difficult to work with her. I was very unhappy with her, and the producer was very unhappy. . . . But when I saw the picture in Washington two or three months ago, I realized how extremely good she was in the picture. She has no heart, but that is something else."[7]

Despite alterations to the script, Cooper remained uneasy with his role. He had delivered long speeches perfectly in *Mr. Deeds* and *Meet John Doe*, but still had trouble with these learned lines. Frank Mattison, in critical memos to T.C. Wright, wrote that "Cooper had a difficult day with dialogue, as this scene is almost continual talking for him. . . . The fight was the only thing he did well because it did not require his memorizing lines." On June 6 Mattison reported that Cooper had stomach troubles from a surfeit of fruit: "Mrs. Cooper phoned in and said that Gary Cooper would positively not be in to work this morning, but possibly might be able to make it this afternoon. We had a scene on Tuesday wherein he was eating apples all day and he was suffering from it yesterday." He also noted that Cooper, who'd been excellent in the action scenes, could use a day "to recuperate as he put in a very hard four days at the end of last week in fight scene which is very spectacular." Though Lang was difficult to please, he praised Cooper for taking part in these scenes despite his back and hip injuries: "All of it—I'm very happy to say—was done by Cooper. He had a double because of a dislocated hip, but I asked him, 'Look, Gary, I will be very careful . . . and then I can do it in close-ups.' He was very cooperative and there is not one shot in the fight made with the double. Cooper was wonderful—he tried very hard. I liked him very much."[8]

In the film the professorial Cooper moves slowly and speaks deliberately. When the OSS asks him for a scientific explanation of Nazi atomic research, he reflectively pushes out his lower jaw and rubs his lips with his finger as he talks. Impressed by his skillful timing, Palmer wrote that "Cooper could deliver a long speech on camera while rummaging in his pocket for a cigarette, continue talking while he fussed with the matches, pause for a moment of what looked like intense concentration, pick up where he left off, put the matches away, rub his nose, and go on talking as if the camera didn't exist."

Lang managed to give *Cloak and Dagger* some characteristically brutal touches. During a rescue operation a physicist is casually shot by the woman who's guarding her. While a tenor sings in the street, Cooper, in a deserted alley, beats a Nazi henchman to death. Though the film was made at the beginning of the Cold War in 1946, the enemy was not Russian, but German. As a partly Jewish anti-Nazi émigré Lang was emotionally committed to portray the Fascist mind. But the studio had the last word in its disputes with the troublesome Lang. The last reel originally showed "Nazi atomic production plants housed in caves, on the order of the underground rocket research center at Peenemünde. Three of the plants were located and destroyed, the fourth transferred piecemeal either to Argentina or Spain." It also had a thematic speech that criticized the bombing of Hiroshima and warned about America's ability to control the power of atomic weapons. "Peace? There's no peace!" Cooper's Jesper had originally said. "It's year one of the Atomic Age and God have mercy on us all . . . if we think we can wage other wars without destroying ourselves."[9] The studio threw out the last reel, gave Jesper a bland speech advocating "a free science in the service of humanity" and substituted a happy ending ("I'm coming back for you, Gina") for a doom-laden one. These crude alterations turned the potentially significant film into a routine war movie.

On September 18, 1946—three months after Gary completed *Cloak and Dagger* and three days after his father's eighty-first birthday—Charles Cooper died after a long illness. In 1934 the judge, walking with a cane, had been crossing the intersection at Hollywood and Vine when a woman driver ran a red light and hit him. She had no money, so he couldn't sue, and Gary paid all the medical bills. But Charles suffered serious back and knee injuries, soon retired from his law practice and remained in poor shape. During World War II, while confined to a wheelchair, he visited wounded soldiers in hospitals, recited passages from Shakespeare and treated them to ice cream. On October 9 Cooper wrote their old friend Wellington Rankin: "Father caught pneumonia quite suddenly and passed on with very little suffering. Though his health had not been very good these last few months, he was able to enjoy things, particularly the baseball games which he attended regularly until a few days before his illness. Mother is quite well and is taking it like the good soldier she is."

Alice stayed healthy and active. An expert guide to Hollywood, she had impressed a former governor of Montana who came to movieland in 1937. On his visit S.V. Stewart wrote: "Mrs. Cooper drove. She knows the answers to everything. Showed us where all of the actors live. . . . She knows every street and alley, and who lives there, and she can dodge through the traffic like a taxi-driver." Alice had done her bit for the war effort by running a canteen in Beverly Hills.

Hedda Hopper, always eager for news about Cooper, had kept in touch with his mother. On October 1, 1946, shortly after her husband's death and still living at 529 North Cahuenga, Alice graciously thanked Hopper for her condolence letter: "It's hard to say what is in our heart, but many thanks for the lovely flowers. My family joins me in expressing appreciation. Lovingly, Alice L. Cooper, Mrs. Charles H. Cooper." Six years later, still going strong, Alice again thanked Hedda for her birthday greetings: "Lovely, in your busy life, to think of me. I love the hat—wear one like it. Am 79 now, getting on. Love to you dear, Alice L. Cooper."[10] Her favorite Gary Cooper movie, *The Pride of the Yankees*, emphasized the son's devotion and the mother's profound influence on his successful career.

III

Unconquered (1947), Cooper's most lucrative film, cost nearly $5 million ($394,000 over budget) and was partly shot on location in Idaho and western Pennsylvania. It had 25 name players and 4,325 costumed extras. Cooper had been earning $150,000 for each film, but made at least double that fee for this picture. Like many actors in the postwar era, he now got a percentage of the profits: 5 percent of the gross to $6 million and 10 percent above $6 million, with a minimum guarantee of $300,000. His co-star, Paulette Goddard, made a respectable $112,000.

Cooper's three Westerns with De Mille—*The Plainsman, North West Mounted Police* and *Unconquered*—"all reflect one another: they share the military, an independent hero, his gutsy girl, and rogues selling guns and hooch to the savages." The title *Unconquered* describes the American settlers in the New World. The movie was based on the 1763 Indian rebellion led by Pontiac, chief of the Ottawas, against British control of what was then the northwest frontier. After his surprise attack on Detroit had failed, Pontiac destroyed most British forts west of Niagara.

The plot revolves around the attempt of Cooper, playing a Virginia militiaman, to rescue Goddard from the dastardly gun trader Howard Da Silva, who's always about to have his way with her. Goddard's also scrubbed clean by Cooper in a wooden bathtub, and saved from whipping (though her shirt's torn off her back) as well as from torture at a fiery stake. As the tanned, dashing and self-assured Cooper takes Goddard to the king's ball and tells her, "the moonlight is turning your dress into green fire," he too looks gorgeous in a tricorn hat and red British uniform trimmed with gold.

In the most memorable scene Cooper and Goddard, chased by Indians, rush down the rapids in a canoe and shoot madly over a waterfall. Cooper, with Goddard tied to him, saves them by grabbing a conveniently overhanging tree branch and landing safely on a rock ledge. The scene took two weeks of special shots on the Snake River in Idaho, which were then matched with a week of shots on the Paramount lot. In his book on special effects John Brosnan explained the enormous technical skill required by this absurd but spectacular scene:

> The production crew found a river that had rapids but no falls and another river that had falls but no rapids. So each river was photographed separately, and the two rivers matted together to look like one stream. . . . Cooper and Goddard [were] filmed while being dropped five feet over a studio-made waterfall that blended in with the projected background. At the bottom of this drop the stars were supposed to grasp an overhanging tree limb and swing themselves under the falls to the safety of a hidden ledge. As there was no tree growing near the originally photographed falls artists had to matte paint a tree limb into each frame of the film. Then a live "double" for the limb was installed on the studio tank stage and a stunt man and woman, doubling for the stars in a canoe, slid down an invisible piano wire track through the studio-made waterfall and grabbed, as it were, a tree that was not there.

De Mille's bias prevented him from making a movie that had any genuine understanding of the Indians or the historical struggle his picture ostensibly portrayed. To De Mille, the redskins merely blocked the advance of civilization and interfered with the concept of Manifest Destiny. A narrator opens the picture by stating: "To the Indians, all men came as invaders." Cooper says "no one can control the Indians," but when trouble starts he must carry an offer of peace. After he kills one of them, his friend, following the conventional formula, exclaims: "Well, that's one good Injun." Duped by a cheap trick with a compass, the treacherous primitives massacre a village, prompting Goddard to observe: "The Indians will always burn, torture and kill to get back the wilderness." The best thing in this static, cliché-ridden movie is the appearance of Boris Karloff as Guyasuta, chief of the Senecas—barechested, beaded, braided and with a campy lisp. Weak on pronouns and definite articles, he prophetically declares: "White man forts burn—all die." Howard Hawks once asked Cooper "how on earth he could read those goddam lines. 'Well,' he said, 'when De Mille finishes talking to you, they don't seem so bad. But when you see the picture, then you kind of hang your head.' "[11] Cooper, who had played with Indian children as a boy and observed their life in Montana, knew De Mille's depiction of their culture was fake. But it was not his way to quarrel with the director, so he compromised his values, took the money and played the role.

Good Sam (1948), written and directed by Leo McCarey, is a weak imitation of *Mr. Deeds Goes to Town*. Instead of being naive and idealistic, Cooper is now merely goofy. In this labored, repetitive, one-joke movie, one of Cooper's worst, the hero, Sam, has too much faith in people and does a number of disastrous good deeds. Sinclair Lewis, who thought people wouldn't be able to identify with the character and refused to work on the script, told McCarey that "a man who tried to lead in our times the life of an apostle would be an idiot and would be considered by others to be one." Ann Sheridan, good in sassy roles and miscast as Cooper's bland wife, suspects his motives, and complains about the way he's ruining their lives: "You're nothing but a doublecrossing, two-faced, sneaking Samaritan." Crushed by her outburst and torn between his spiritual yearnings and the crass materialism of the real world, he goes on a binge and (rare in a Cooper movie) gets horribly drunk. Having overdone his gestures to compensate for a poor script, Cooper was harshly criticized by a reviewer in *Cue* magazine: "Mr. Cooper is now a grown man and his boyish bashfulness, sheepish grins, trembling lip and fluttering eyelids are actor's tricks he can surely do without."

A free agent since leaving Goldwyn and Paramount in 1942, Cooper had briefly formed his own production company. But he knew he'd been making mediocre movies for big money and was worried about the decline of his career. He had done *Saratoga Trunk* and *Cloak and Dagger* at Warners, and now thought he could do better with a long-term agreement at one studio. On October 22, 1947, Warners drew up a twenty-seven-page contract, approved by his lawyer, I.H. Prinzmetal, which gave Cooper approval of script and director and (after a revision in 1949) guaranteed him $295,000 per picture. The contract also had the standard morals clause: "Artist shall conduct himself with due regard to public convention and morals. Producer may, at its option, upon five days notice to artist, cancel this agreement in the event of a breach hereunder." Though Cooper flouted this clause, his affairs were not public knowledge, and he was far too valuable a property to be dismissed. One writer estimated that by June 1955 Cooper had made eighty films, from which the studios had earned $250 million and he himself $6 million in salary and percentages. Well worth that money, Cooper made astronomically more than the average American and had become a millionaire. But he had invested conservatively, had not done especially well in real estate and was still in the highest tax bracket. Wary of arousing envy, he said he did not feel like a wealthy man: "I'm not rich; I don't own oil wells, like Bing Crosby and Bob Hope. I couldn't afford to retire and take up painting."[12]

IV

In the same week that Cooper signed his new contract with Warner Bros. he appeared before the House Un-American Activities Committee (HUAC) in Washington as a "friendly" witness. A conservative Republican, like his father, he had voted for Coolidge in 1924 and for Hoover in 1928 and 1932, and had actively campaigned for Wendell Willkie in 1940. But it was most unusual for him to be in the political spotlight.

At the time of his brief association with a group called the Hollywood Hussars, Cooper was rumored to be a Fascist sympathizer. This notion originated in a widely read and frequently quoted article by the California journalist Carey McWilliams, "Hollywood Plays with Fascism," published in May 1935 in the left-wing journal the *Nation*. Hitler had taken power in 1933, and McWilliams, fearful that Fascism in Europe would spread to this country, warned that the actors Victor McLaglen, George Brent and Gary Cooper, "distinguished as a movie-lot Bengal Lancer, have permitted their names to be used as sponsors for fascist groups in Hollywood. . . . When these warriors-in-make-up are financed by powerful interests, backed by civic organizations, blessed by the local ministry, and drilled by army officers, the burlesque of fascism warrants careful consideration. . . . The [Hollywood] Hussars, it seems, were founded by Mr. Cooper to 'uphold and protect the principles and ideals of true Americanism.' "

McWilliams also revealed that the newspaper tycoon William Randolph Hearst was the powerful interest who backed the Hussars: "Mr. Hearst induced Gary Cooper to try his hand at the game, promising liberal backing and support. It will be recalled that Mr. Cooper is friendly with Hearst's ménage, having recently appeared as leading man for one of Hollywood's most charming actresses [Marion Davies in *Operator 13*]. . . . The primary purpose of these fascist units in the industry was therefore to counteract the agitation and influence of liberal groups [like the Writers Guild of America]. But the Hussars and their allies have other uses. They are designed to advertise the charms of fascist organizations to the American public."

McWilliams first states that Cooper permitted his name to be used as a sponsor, then leaps to the conclusion that the Hussars "were *founded* by Mr. Cooper." He categorically calls the Hussars a fascist group, then more accurately defines them as a "burlesque of fascism." But the stated aims of this organization—to "protect the principles and ideals of true Americanism"—have no connection to Fascism, and one of the local ministers who "blessed" the Hussars, "Rabbi Isadore Isaacson, of Temple of Israel, Hollywood," was not likely to give his benediction to a pro-Nazi movement. Despite its reckless assertions, modified by later writers, McWilliams' article branded Cooper as a Fascist.

Though they cite McWilliams in *The Inquisition in Hollywood* (1980), Ceplair and Englund omit the word "fascist" when describing the Hussars' activities: "They drilled in their spare time, received instruction in military tactics from retired army officers and active police officials, and generally basked in the friendly sunshine radiating from the Hearst press." In *The Hollywood Writers' Wars* (1982), however, Nancy Schwartz, using words like "vigilante" and "guntoters," gives a more menacing account. According to Schwartz, Gary Cooper was known to be "one of the most politically naive reactionaries in Hollywood. During the late thirties he had gotten caught up with Arthur Guy Empey's Hollywood Hussars, a reactionary vigilante army that was preparing, with the help of guntoters like . . . Victor McLaglen and Ward Bond, to do a little housecleaning in their community—their targets, preferably, anyone slightly pink. Cooper's agent had pulled him out of the Hussars."[13] She does at least identify "Colonel" Empey—who fought with the British as a private in 1916 and wrote a realistic account of trench warfare in his memoir *Over the Top* (1917)—as the real leader. Although Schwartz describes Cooper accurately—he was a member only from

March to June 1935, was "politically naive" and didn't realize the serious
implications of belonging to a paramilitary group—the Hollywood
Hussars were actually quite harmless. A similar organization, Victor
McLaglen's Light Horse Cavalry, actually played the newspaper tycoon's
black-clad motorcycle corps in Cooper's *Meet John Doe* and in 1941,
when such groups seemed more dangerous, were portrayed in a negative
light.

A third writer, Anthony Slide, following McWilliams, wrote a more
wide-ranging article about "Hollywood's Fascist Follies" for *Film
Comment* in 1991. Taking Hollywood hyperbole for solemn fact, Slide
quoted a statement in the *Motion Picture Herald* that the Hussars were
"armed to the teeth and ready to gallop on horseback within an hour
to cope with any emergency," including "Japanese 'invasions,'
Communistic 'revolutions,' or whatnot." Like McWilliams, Slide
quoted Cooper's statement of principles and claimed these patriotic
banalities were sinister and fascistic: "Americanism is an unfailing love of
country; loyalty to its institutions and ideals; eagerness to defend it
against all enemies; undivided allegiance to the Flag; and a desire to
secure the blessings of liberty to ourselves and posterity. Therefore,
Americanism is the foundation upon which we are building the
Hollywood Hussars." More recently, however, Garry Wills has surveyed
all references in the Los Angeles *Times* to Victor McLaglen's group and
found nothing more menacing than "social and charitable events
attended by his troop."[14] During Cooper's brief association with the
group, the Hollywood Hussars did little more than dress up in handsome
uniforms, practice military drills, go horseback riding and enjoy aggressive male camaraderie.

Charles Higham, the most unreliable writer on Hollywood politics,
also condemned Cooper as "pro-fascist" for meeting Georg Gyssling, the
Nazi consul general in Los Angeles, Mussolini's son Vittorio (on October
2, 1937) and the SS general the Duke of Saxe-Coburg-Gotha (on April 5,
1940). (The duke, a member of the German and British royal families and
an old Etonian, had tried in January 1936 to arrange a discussion
between Hitler and the British prime minister in order to prevent war in
Europe.) These meetings were attended by many other prominent
conservatives: Hearst and Marion Davies (who probably persuaded
Cooper to come), Harrison Chandler of the Los Angeles *Times*, the sugar
king Adolph Spreckels, the president of USC, Will Hays of the censorship
office, Walt Disney and Winfield Sheehan, the Fox production chief.[15]

Though ill advised, even foolish, these gatherings had taken place before America entered the war.

In his biography of Cary Grant (1989) Higham stated that in 1938 Cooper "Would go to Berlin and be entertained by Hitler." In fact, Cooper did not go to Berlin in 1938, did not meet Hitler and was not entertained by him. Higham claimed that his source was Anthony Slide, who when challenged said "the first he had heard of Nazi connections of Gary Cooper came from Higham." Undeterred by Slide's denial, Higham changed his tack and in his life of Louis Mayer (1993) wrote that in 1938 Cooper had "been a guest of Albert Göring, industrialist brother of Hermann Göring and of Hitler's close friend, Karl Ritter, of UFA studios in Berlin."[16]

Cooper did meet Albert Göring in 1939, not 1938, and the purpose of his visit was not to socialize with Nazis, but to accompany his father-in-law, Paul Shields, an economic adviser to Roosevelt and liberal in politics, on a U.S. government mission to investigate German finances. Albert Göring, far from being pro-Hitler, was staunchly anti-Nazi and often had to be saved from arrest by his powerful brother. As David Irving wrote in his biography of Hermann Göring: "Albert remained the black sheep of the family. He became a thermodynamics engineer, fell out with Hermann as the Nazis came to power, and moved to Austria, where he applied for citizenship in the hope that this would put a safe frontier between himself and his domineering brother." Albert did not change his political views during the war: "Invited in 1944 to a dinner in Bucharest with the ambassador Manfred Killinger, he had refused to 'sit down with a murderer.' . . . More recently, Albert had provided funds for Viennese Jews who had emigrated to Trieste." Unlike most Americans, Cooper actually saw for himself the menace of German militarism—very different indeed from the posturings of the Hollywood Hussars and the Light Horse Cavalry. Instead of sympathizing with Fascism, he was appalled by the war-mongering atmosphere in Berlin in 1939. When he returned to America, he warned his countrymen about the danger of conflict with Germany: "There's no question in my mind that those people want to have a war. They're determined to be a world power and seem to feel that's the only way to become one. Those storm troopers are awesome. The atmosphere in Berlin—well, I've never sensed such tension." Dismissing Higham's irresponsible charges against Cooper, the Columnist William Safire has recently concluded: "From the testimony to date, I'd say Coop is clean."[17]

Rocky and most of Cooper's social and professional friends were conservatives and anti-Communists: his wife's uncle Cedric Gibbons, the directors Sam Wood, Victor Fleming and King Vidor, and actors like Clark Gable and Adolphe Menjou. In February 1944 Gibbons and Sam Wood (who had helped delete the Left-wing political content from *For Whom the Bell Tolls*) persuaded the rather passive Cooper to join the Motion Picture Alliance for the Preservation of American Ideals. The Alliance's statement of principles and its desire to cleanse the film industry of Reds were announced in a full-page ad in the *Hollywood Reporter*: "We resent the growing impression that this industry is made up of, and dominated by, Communists, Radicals and crackpots. . . . We refuse to permit the effort of Communist, Fascist, and other totalitarian-minded groups to pervert this powerful medium into an instrument for the dissemination of un-American ideas and beliefs. We pledge to fight, with every means at our organized command, any effort of any group or individual, to divert the loyalty of the screen from the free America that gave it birth." In a brief speech at a meeting of the Alliance on March 28, Cooper endorsed these principles. He scolded " 'the lukewarm Americans who dally with sedition in the guise of being liberals' and suggested that they would benefit from careful study of the pledge of allegiance to the flag."

Cooper had been invited to meet Roosevelt in the White House after the showing of *Sergeant York* in 1941. But on October 31, 1944, as Roosevelt was running for an unprecedented fourth term, Cooper bought his own radio time to campaign against the president and on November 6 took out an ad for Dewey in the *New York Times*. In his radio speech he vaguely criticized Roosevelt for dishonesty and for failure to keep his word, for maintaining friendships with dubious types and—darkly hinting at the excessive influence of Jewish advisers like Bernard Baruch and Felix Frankfurter—for adopting "foreign" ideas: "I am going to vote for Governor Dewey because he's efficient—and, because he's honest. That's terribly important, I think, his being honest. Matter of fact, I've been for Mr. Roosevelt before—but not this time. There's been too many broken promises to suit me—and too much double talk. . . . I don't like the company he's keeping. I disagree with the New Deal belief that the America all of us love is old and worn-out and finished—and has to borrow foreign notions that don't even seem to work any too well where they come from."[18] Cooper's attack was as unpopular as Bogart's public endorsement of Roosevelt in November 1944. The studio strongly

warned both actors not to hurt their standing at the box office by antag-
onizing fans who did not agree with their political views.

V

Cooper's membership in the Right-wing Motion Picture Alliance put him
squarely in the anti-Communist camp. When the Alliance pressured
HUAC to start an investigation to drive the Reds out of Hollywood and
"remove the label of communism that had been pinned on the industry,"
he became caught up in the hysteria that gripped the nation in the early
years of the Cold War. The Russians had been our allies in the struggle to
defeat Hitler, but were now sinister enemies in the fight for political and
economic power in Europe and Asia. In that atmosphere it was
commonly assumed that anyone who opposed Right-wing thought was
pro-Communist.

HUAC, chaired by J. Parnell Thomas, a New Jersey Republican,
looked for political conspiracies in government and industry. The
Committee had turned its attention to Hollywood as early as 1940, when
informers tried to incriminate writers and actors. In its view, artists and
intellectuals were always suspect and films were a dangerous propaganda
weapon. There had been some pro-Russian propaganda in wartime films
like *Mission to Moscow* (1943), based on a book by Ambassador Joseph
Davies and made at Roosevelt's request, but the conservative studio heads
controlled the content of films. In 1947 HUAC, through FBI investiga-
tions, already had all the names of known or suspected Communists. But
the congressmen wanted to gain valuable publicity and advance their
political careers (Nixon first gained prominence as a member of this
committee) by a public demonstration of their power. Now "the Alliance
opened the door for HUAC, and the reactionaries began casting about for
some CP informers to make their picture complete" by identifying the
Reds the Committee was so eager to expose.

The investigation of Communist infiltration in Hollywood began on
October 20, 1947 in the crowded Caucus Room in the Old House Office
Building in Washington. The large, drafty stone hall, with its mass of
bright lights and whirring cameras, its persistent interrogators, screaming
hostile witnesses and angry gavel pounding right next to the microphone
created a theatrical atmosphere. It had fierce dialogue, intense drama and
a highly emotional audience. During the first week of the hearings

Cooper was one of the "friendly" witnesses, who included the actors Robert Taylor (his hunting companion), Adolphe Menjou (who had appeared with him in two films), Ronald Reagan, George Murphy and Robert Montgomery as well as the writer Ayn Rand and studio executives Louis Mayer, Jack Warner and Walt Disney. These figures named prominent Communist sympathizers and "cast themselves in the role of 'concerned patriotic citizens' defending a shrinking studio beachhead against an invading Bolshevik menace. . . . [They] related how they had vigilantly scrutinized prospective scripts for their 'Communistic' content, tried to warn their colleagues and superiors of 'subversive' activity, and generally tried to set a high standard of patriotic Americanism."

When Cooper and Taylor appeared, a thousand women mobbed the Caucus Room and tried to tear off pieces of their clothing. Taylor, declaring it was his duty as a citizen to state his political views, went on to destroy a number of careers. *Variety* noted that like other "friendly" witnesses, he was allowed to "read prepared statements, use notes and ramble widely in offering testimony of strong nature without supporting evidence."[19] Taylor named Howard Da Silva, who'd recently played the villain in Cooper's *Unconquered*. Sam Wood, president of the Motion Picture Alliance and most fanatical of the anti-Communists, named his fellow directors John Cromwell and Edward Dmytryk, writers Dalton Trumbo, John Howard Lawson and Donald Ogden Stewart. The first two writers were among the "unfriendly" witnesses, known as the Hollywood Ten, who were called the following week. Mayer named Lester Cole as well as Trumbo and Stewart.

Cooper himself had been dragooned into Communist Party propaganda campaigns in Italy and Yugoslavia in May and July 1947. As a result, Communist newspapers around the world, including the *Tribuna Popular* in Rio de Janeiro, published fantastic stories about him: "Gary Cooper, who took part in the fights for the independence of Spain, held a speech before a crowd of 90,000 in Philadelphia on the occasion of the consecration of the banner of the Philadelphia Communist Federation. Between other things he said: 'In our days it is the greatest honor to be a Communist. . . . To be a Communist means having sun and light in one's spirit.' " These statements were quoted in *Newsweek* of August 18, 1947 and again, at greater length, during his testimony. Forced to defend himself against these absurd statements, Cooper reassured the public that 'I'm no danged Red, never have been a Red, don't like Reds, and never will be a Red."

Cooper was subpoenaed because his association with the Hollywood Hussars and membership in the Motion Picture Alliance had made him the most famous conservative in Hollywood, but his political attitudes played little part in his professional or private life. He had worked with Ring Lardner, Jr. and Albert Maltz (also among the Hollywood Ten), who had written the script of *Cloak and Dagger*, and with Da Silva on *Unconquered*, without objecting to their political views. But he disliked Reds and went along with rabid friends who assured him that he was doing the right thing.

Cooper's testimony—which took place on October 23 and interrupted the filming of *Good Sam*—was very different from the statements of the other "friendly" witnesses. While they were full of passionate intensity, Cooper seemed diffident, even embarrassed. He resorted to his engaging "shitkicker" image—boyish, naive and soft-spoken—and twice had to be urged to speak louder. Asked his present occupation, Cooper—as if on screen—smiled shyly, chuckled, rubbed his nose, hesitated, blinked, looked down and modestly whispered "actor." In a reprise of *Mr. Deeds Goes to Town*, he equaled his finest film performances and had the Committee—and the public—eating out of his hand.

When questioned about Communist influence in Hollywood, Cooper was deliberately vague. He used a provocatively humorous tone when recounting some unpatriotic remarks: "Well, I have heard tossed around such statements as, 'Don't you think the Constitution of the United States is about 150 years out of date?' and—oh, I don't know—I have heard people mention that, well, 'Perhaps this would be a more efficient Government without a Congress'—which statements I think are very un-American." Despite his deceptively offhand manner, Cooper did believe that the Constitution was sacred. In July 1917, when he was a sixteen-year-old boy in Montana, a headline in the Butte *Post* had proclaimed of an IWW union organizer: "In A Treasonable Tirade [Frank] Little Says Constitution Is Mere Scrap of Paper." The conservative Montanans who used patriotism to crush dissent and oppose social change, took such inflammatory remarks very seriously. On August 4, four days after his speech, in a notorious episode that made a lasting impression on Cooper, Little was lynched by the mob and hanged.[20]

The chairman then queried Cooper about "communistic information" in his film scripts. The actor, while allowing as he had seen some, deftly evaded specifics and persuaded the committee to accept an absurd explanation of his failing memory:

Cooper: I have turned down quite a few scripts because I thought
they were tinged with communistic ideas.
    —Can you name any of those scripts?
Cooper: No, I can't recall any of those scripts to mind. . . .
    —Will you think it over, then, and supply the committee
with a list of those scripts?
Cooper: I don't think I could, because most of the scripts I read at
night, and if they don't look good to me I don't finish them
or if I do finish them I send them back as soon as possible
to their author.
    —I understand. I didn't understand you before.

Asked if the Communist Party had ever attempted to use him, Cooper
responded, more frankly and colloquially: "They haven't attempted to
use me, I don't think, because, apparently, they know that I am not very
sympathetic to Communism. . . . I could never take any of this pinko
mouthing very seriously, because I didn't feel it was on the level." Finally
Cooper, who couldn't tell Karl Marx from Groucho Marx, agreed with
the chairman that the Communist Party in the United States should be
outlawed and based his arguments on ignorance: "I think it would be a
good idea, although I have never read Karl Marx and I don't know the
basis of Communism, beyond what I have picked up from hearsay. From
what I hear, I don't like it because it isn't on the level."

On the following day, October 24, 1947, a headline in the Los Angeles
Times proclaimed: "Four Film Actors Hit at Reds in Hollywood." Cooper
and his colleagues believed their testimony would defend the film
industry from congressional attacks by focusing their investigation only
on known Communists. "Their function was not to provide the
Committee with information, but with luster."[21] Sam Wood, misunderstanding the point of Cooper's performance, said: "He came across badly.
Stupidly. He emphasized hearsay and couldn't remember the names of
scripts he turned down because of an anti-American theme. He was just
as opposed as the others, but could not get himself to label anyone. " In
fact, Cooper acted wisely when he found himself in a dangerous scenario,
and fell back on charm and cunning. He was not a rabid conservative,
like Wood, and instinctively shrank from naming names. Walter
Goodman, in his book on HUAC, also misunderstood Cooper's strategy,
and wrote: "The most pointless testimony came from Gary Cooper, who
had been invited to Washington for show, and whose appearance (in

double-breasted suit, light blue silk necktie, and white shirt) brought sighs from the spectators."

Cooper's testimony was an "appearance" in both senses—he obliged his friends by *appearing* to support HUAC, but made no specific accusations. This explains why Wood was loathed afterward by most people in Hollywood while Cooper, despite his testimony, was respected and even loved. Ring Lardner, Jr. and Edward Dmytryk, two of the Hollywood Ten, understood what Cooper was up to. Lardner thought him a valuable, malleable figure who didn't really know many names. He was the "least effective witness" and did "very little damage" at HUAC. Dmytryk agreed that "Cooper, for all his cooperation with the committee, did not yield to them a single name nor a solid lead to any script that might be investigated."[22]

But Cooper and the others did lend dignity to the proceedings, softened up the public and prepared the way for the violent attacks on the "unfriendly" Left-wing witnesses. They actively encouraged an investigation that harmed their industry in ways they couldn't foresee. The "friendly" witnesses confirmed the existence of Communist infiltration in Hollywood; the "unfriendly" ones were accused of subversion. The former didn't know the names of Communist Party members; the latter refused to give them. The former were allowed to read speeches and testify at great length; the latter were cut off before they could speak and dragged from the room by armed guards.

Membership in the Communist Party was and still is legal—though generally covert—and its influence was extremely limited. The charge that Hollywood writers planned a violent overthrow of the government was ridiculous, but HUAC claimed Hollywood was full of subversives who used movies to indoctrinate a gullible public. During the second week of the HUAC hearings, a riveting public spectacle on radio and newsreels, leading writers and directors were accused of being Reds or Communist sympathizers. They appeared before the cameras, blinked in the glaring lights and were shouted down by the chairman. After the hearings, present and former members of the Party—without evidence, trial or a chance to defend themselves—were condemned as pariahs and deprived of their jobs.

In his definitive book on HUAC Robert Carr emphasized the contrast between the Committee's aims and its achievements: "From the beginning it was evident that the investigation would show that Communists or fellow travellers held jobs in the motion picture industry. But whether the Committee could prove its oft-repeated assertion that those Communists had introduced Communist propaganda into films was much more uncertain. . . . While the Un-American Activities Committee repeatedly insisted that it had a list of films that contained Communist propaganda . . . no such list was ever made public." Carr concluded that HUAC could never substantiate its accusations and that the proceedings were a fiasco: "The Hollywood hearings revealed the committee at its worst. . . . No other major investigation of the committee ever ended so anti-climactically or produced so little tangible evidence in support of a thesis which the committee set out to prove."

Nevertheless, HUAC had the power to destroy its enemies without producing evidence. Despite its legal and moral defects (Parnell Thomas was later sentenced to eighteen months for padding his payroll and wound up in Danbury Prison with two of his victims, Lardner and Cole), HUAC created a terror in Hollywood that encouraged colleagues to betray each other. When it reconvened in 1951, a mass of friendly witnesses panicked to get clearance and avoid the ever-expanding blacklist. They confessed their political sins and were forced to incriminate their colleagues. By doing so, they were able to work, but they humiliated themselves and lost the respect of both inquisitors and victims. As a sense of fear and repression swept through Hollywood, screenwriters who refused to recant were ruined and forced into exile. HUAC discredited the industry and gave the impression of a deep-rooted Red conspiracy. It destroyed friendships, broke up marriages and ruined hundreds of careers.

Cooper's political behavior suggests more confusion than commitment. Much wealthier and more Right-wing than his conservative Republican father, he espoused a rather simplistic "my country right or wrong" patriotism. He opposed Communism without knowing anything about it and seemed rather proud of his ignorance. In this discreditable episode, he allowed himself to be manipulated by more ideologically motivated friends, like Sam Wood and Adolphe Menjou, into joining the Motion Picture Alliance and appearing at the HUAC hearings. Just as he hurt his own reputation by lending his enormous prestige to paramillitary organizations in 1935, so his thoughtless participation in the HUAC persecutions hurt the film industry itself.

As the witch-hunt continued, Cooper made occasional statements that revealed his political attitudes had remained willfully naive and simpleminded. After Arthur Miller, then married to Marilyn Monroe, had appeared before HUAC in 1956 and refused to name names, Cooper again fell back on blind chauvinism and attacked Miller for criticizing the ruthless aspects of American capitalism in *Death of a Salesman* (1949): "A man like Arthur Miller, he's got a gripe against certain phases of American life. I think he's done a lot of bad. Ours is a pretty good country and I don't think we ought to run it down. Sure there are people like this fellow [Willy Loman], but you don't have to write plays about them."

Yet Cooper seemed to have learned something from his unhappy involvement in politics. He realized that he'd been used by others and been out of his depth. In October 1947, the very month he appeared before HUAC, he undermined his own testimony by stating: "I feel very strongly that actors haven't any business at all to shoot their faces off about things I know we know damn little about." In his last political statement, in the *Hollywood Reporter* of November 1958, he recognized his own limitations and condemned actors' brash eagerness "to stand up and pontificate on virtually every matter from foreign policy to foreign fillies."[23]

15

The Fountainhead
and Patricia Neal

1948–1951

I

After selling his film company to Universal and signing a long-term contract with Warners, Cooper had quite a lot of money to invest. In the summer of 1948 he bought fifteen acres of land in Aspen, then a pristine ski resort in the Rocky Mountains of western Colorado. While living in the Jerome Hotel, he began to build a four-bedroom, five-bathroom house, with an eighteen-by-thirty-eight-foot living room, an aluminium roof to "slide" the heavy snow, a view of the ski runs on the nearby mountain and plenty of space for guests. The house was completed in 1949, the first year of the Aspen Institute, when distinguished musicians and intellectuals—Artur Rubinstein, Albert Schweitzer, José Ortega y Gasset—brought culture to the wilderness.

Rocky brought in sand and made a little beach around the pond where they went swimming. A stream ran past the other side of the house where, Cooper told Louella Parsons, "a man just has to sit and draw the fish in." In an article called "The Place I Like Best," he described their idyllic existence: "On April days when we don't feel like skiing, we can still take a dog sled through snow pockets in the hills. At night we walk through the town or loll in front of the fire in old clothes." But the Coopers' life in Aspen was not, in fact, very happy. The construction of the house coincided with his love affair with Patricia Neal, which caused tension, misery and domestic discord. The house took on bad associations, the family spent very little time there and even their tenants disliked it. In the mid-1950s, before building his mansion in Holmby Hills, Cooper sold the "bad luck" place (which would now be worth millions) for $70,000. Later owners tore it down and built another house on the site.

The Fountainhead (1948), Cooper's first film with Neal, was based on a novel by Ayn Rand. Born in Russia in 1905, she had graduated from the University of Leningrad and come to America in 1926. Her long and turgid book, published in 1943, was written in a bodice-ripping, hothouse style. In its most famous scene, the pathological and perverse Dominique Francon (Neal) catches sight of Howard Roark (Cooper) drilling stone in a quarry: "She saw his mouth and the silent contempt in the shape of his mouth; the planes of his gaunt, hollow cheeks; the cold, pure brilliance of the eyes that had no trace of pity. She knew it was the most beautiful face she would ever see. . . . She felt a convulsion of anger, of protest, of resistance—and of pleasure. . . . She was wondering what he would look like naked."[1]

Like the novel, the film (also written by Rand) glorifies selfish individualism. Roark, an idealistic and uncompromising architect, is a blend of romantic hero and stern intellectual. He believes "the world is perishing from an orgy of self-sacrificing" and tells his astonished patrons: "I don't work with collectives, I don't consult, I don't cooperate, I don't collaborate. . . . My work's done my way. A private, personal, selfish, egotistical motive. That's the only way I function." Though the title is not specifically mentioned in the film, Rand's book argues that selfishness—a kind of divine egotism possessed by artists—is the fountainhead, the true source of originality, knowledge and all that is good in the world. Roark's glorification of individual genius and scorn for the common man ran counter to the ideals of American democracy, but Rand's fanatical opposition to her native Communism went over extremely well during the Cold War. By 1962 her novel had sold almost half a million copies in hardcover and more than a million in paperback.

Rand was paid $50,000 for the movie rights and $13,000 more for her screenplay. In an unusual deal, she had complete control of the script and final approval of all changes. Using her hero's tactics, she threatened to blow up Warners' studio if it altered one word of her work. In her visual instructions for the screenplay, Rand wrote: "Among present day architects, it is the style of Frank Lloyd Wright—and only Frank Lloyd Wright—that must be taken as a model for Roark's buildings." In the film

Roark's teacher quotes the famous adage of Louis Sullivan, who'd been Wright's mentor: "The form of a building must follow its function."

Asked to do the drawings and design the buildings for the picture, Wright treated it like an architectural commission and demanded 10 percent of the budget: $250,000. After Warners refused to pay that astronomical fee, its art director, Edward Carrere, designed more than three hundred buildings for the film. Wright later said the movie was "a grossly abusive caricature of his work ... an architectural (and cinematic) disaster." "I think she bungled it," he told a reporter. "It's a treacherous slant on my philosophy. She asked me to endorse [it], but I refused."[2]

Warners originally planned *The Fountainhead* for Humphrey Bogart and Barbara Stanwyck, though Bette Davis, Ida Lupino and Eleanor Parker were also considered for the female lead. Bogart, though not as good as Cooper in love scenes, would have made the lofty, monomaniacal hero more arrogant and abrasive, more bitter and fanatical. Rocky Cooper had read the novel when it first appeared and thought Gary might want to do it. His lawyer, I.H. Prinzmetal, thought the part was wrong for the man who had epitomized democratic ideals in *Mr. Deeds* and *Meet John Doe*, and told the studio: "Cooper's audience was not intellectual, and if they heard him say such selfish things they'd hold it against him. It might damage his reputation and career." But the strong-willed Rand thought Cooper looked like her hero and wanted him for the part. "He is my choice for Roark," she said. "His physical appearance is exactly right."

Cooper overruled Prinzmetal and secured *The Fountainhead* as the first picture under his new contract. He was stiff and wooden in most scenes, but Rand felt "satisfied with his performance, even though the real Roark of the book should have been stronger, [for] there is no actor in Hollywood who could have come closer to being the right type for it than Gary Cooper. I would rather see the part underplayed than overdone by some phony-looking ham." King Vidor, agreeing with Rand and defending his stylized direction of Cooper, also praised his acting: "The camera and the microphone are such penetrating instruments that it is unnecessary to project oneself toward them. Instead, they almost get inside the performers and exhibit what is really inside. In the case of Cooper, a highly complex and fascinating inner personality revealed itself."[3]

When Warners wanted a new face, Neal beat out her rivals and got the female lead. Born in Kentucky in 1926 (and twenty-five years younger than Cooper), the daughter of a coal company bookkeeper, she had studied drama at Northwestern University and been a model. She had made her Broadway debut at the age of twenty in John Van Druten's comedy *The Voice of the Turtle* and had the leading role in Lillian Hellman's *Another Part of the Forest*. Warners brought her to Hollywood for *John Loves Mary*, a weak comedy with Ronald Reagan, and *The Fountainhead* was her second film.

Neal had an engaging personality, an interesting wide, flat face, a voluptuous figure and a husky voice. She got $25,000; Raymond Massey, who played the overbearing newspaper tycoon, made $65,000; King Vidor, who'd directed *The Wedding Night* in 1935, earned $150,000; and Cooper was paid $275,000. The fifty-nine-day shooting schedule ran from July 12 to October 8, 1948. The exuberant twenty-two-year-old Neal could not resist enjoying her new life in Hollywood. The unit manager, Erie Stacey, had some complaints about her nightlife and lateness, which caused delays and cost money: "Neal is, I'm afraid, starting to 'play' at night, and, of course, the company can do nothing about this officially. But this in turn is apparently interfering with her work and her ability to remember her lines. This is in addition to getting too pally with the hairdressers. . . . Pat delayed the company one hour and ten minutes, having overslept and did not report to make-up until 8:30 A.M."

In the film the Master Builder of Aspen plays an architect whose Gaelic name suggests roar and rock. After struggling against adversity, winning an important commission and then throwing away his career by scorning the foolish demands of his patrons, he refuses to compromise by adding classical ornament to his stark modern building. Too earnest, dedicated and committed to his vision, he can't get professional work and becomes a laborer in a stone quarry.

The drilling scene was shot in Knowles, between Fresno and Yosemite National Park, at the largest and oldest quarry in California. As Roark thrusts his vibrating jackhammer into a tight hole in the granite wall, Dominique Francon (whose name suggests frank domination) suddenly appears and stares down at him from above. When Roark rejects her advances she returns to the quarry on horseback, obsessed and transformed by her vision of sexual energy. As Roark stares wildly at her, she strikes him in the face with her whip. The violent embrace and balletic seduction that follow this bit of sadism are accompanied by a crescendo of Wagnerian music. In contrast to the rest of the film, where he's rather restrained, Cooper expresses a kind of caveman passion in these love scenes. Powerful yet self-possessed, he kisses Neal as if he really meant it (and he did). The censor got quite worked up about this and insisted: "The action in scene 66 is completely unacceptable. As presently written, this scene seems to suggest a sex affair. Moreover, this sex affair has about it a flavor suggestive of a not-too-strenuously resisted rape. . . . Here and elsewhere, the kissing should not be passionate, prolonged or *open-mouth*."[4] Dominique's sexual aggressiveness was too much for the censor, who considered it improper, even insulting, to suggest that women had such passionate feelings. Though the scene was then considered quite daring, they toned it down and shipped it past the censor.

The riveting quarry scene recalls and may have been influenced by Jacob Epstein's famous *Rock-Drill* sculpture of 1913, which has the same force and passion as Roark's character and illuminates his ultramodern buildings. Epstein's "robot, itself nearly seven feet high, stood on the drill's tripod of stilts, bringing the whole work to more than nine feet." When first exhibited in 1916, the masked, jutting head and stylized torso, with one hanging right-angled arm, were reduced in size but strengthened in power. Describing this "terrifying metal object, mindless as the machine that drills . . . and clad in the armour of a warrior," Epstein said: "I've rendered this subject in a manner that gives the utmost driving force of hard, relentless, steel-like power." In 1955 Ezra Pound named a late section of the *Cantos* after Epstein's *Rock-Drill* in order to "imply the necessary resistance" in hammering across his violent message.[5] Roark stands for Rand's ideal of mechanical, almost inhuman intellectual and physical power—a force that can and must overwhelm inferior beings.

Dominique "is by turns the destroyer, the seducer, the disciple, and finally an ally." She hurls a classical statue out of a high window to liberate herself from conventional art and express her affinity with modernism. She feels stifled, doesn't want to be tied to anything and is rather repulsive: cold and passionate, arrogant and slavish, ruthless and docile. She recognizes Roark's genius and admires his impressive erections. She loves him from the first moment she sees him and wants to marry him. But she gives herself instead to men she despises: first, to Peter Keating, a weak society architect who plays Salieri to Roark's Mozart; then to Gail Wynand, whose newspaper—prompted by its power-hungry art critic, Ellsworth Toohey—launches a violent attack on Roark's ideas. And she perversely tells Roark that before she'll marry him, he must give up the work she so admires and pursue a goal of mystical purity.

Roark secretly agrees to help Keating design a public housing project on condition that absolutely nothing be changed. When he discovers that his plans have once again been altered, he blows up the project with dynamite as if he were Robert Jordan destroying the bridge in *For Whom the Bell Tolls*. Dominique helps with the dynamiting and then slashes her wrists with shards of broken glass in order to share his punishment and suffering.

In a long, dogmatic but curiously undramatic speech at his trial, Roark—jaw thrust forward and hands in his pockets—emphasizes "inn-tég-grity." He rhetorically asks "has man any right to exist if he refuses to serve society?" and claims that the designer of the buildings has a right to destroy them: "The great creators—the thinkers, the artists, the scientists, the inventors—stood alone against the men of their time. Every great new thought was opposed. Every great new invention was denounced. But the men of unborrowed vision went ahead. They fought, they suffered and they paid. But they won." Arguing his case before a jury that resembles the ordinary people who had hoped to move into the housing project, he admits the dynamiting but is found not guilty.

The arguments in the trial scene of *Mr. Deeds* were logical, moving and persuasive. In both the novel and film of *The Fountainhead*, by contrast, Roark's ability to sway the jury (which represents the despicable masses who hate true genius) is absolutely unconvincing. By putting his architectural designs (or his own ego) before all social benefit and blowing up the desperately needed homes in the project, Roark seems not principled but insane. Even Vidor "greatly disliked *The Fountainhead*'s ending. It was silly to have an architect blow up a building just because they changed some of the facade."

After the trial Wynand commissions Roark to construct the world's tallest building as his grandiose memorial. He then kills himself for no good reason but to clear the way for Roark to marry Dominique. The picture ends vertiginously as Dominique, who'd looked down on Roark in the quarry, now looks up at him. She ascends in an open elevator while he towers above her on the steel grid of his new skyscraper. In contrast to the straightforward elevator ride to the top of city hall in *Meet John Doe*, this final scene required "a nightmare of special effects. Riding to the top of the elevator, she eventually reached a point where she is looking down on the Empire State Building. Glancing up she sees the rest of the new building she is ascending, and to make it believable, the perspective (of back projection) had to be changed constantly from floor to floor."[6]

The film has some fascinating themes: individuality, integrity and various modes of financial, sexual and artistic power. But Rand could not dramatize her ideas through credible characters. Keating, the slavish architect, Toohey, the hostile art critic, Wynand, the arrogant millionaire all seem like mechanical puppets. Everything in this Nietzschean fairy tale—Dominique's emotional somersaults, Roark's explosive violence, Wynand's unmotivated suicide and the jury's freakish decision—is determined by Rand's dogmatic thesis.

Stuck with a didactic script and stilted speech, Vidor avoided a realistic style and made the camera work, sets and acting extremely mannered and operatic. As in the classic *Cabinet of Dr. Caligari* (1919), the camera angles are tilted and the decor Expressionistic. The actors tried to commit themselves to Rand's vision and Vidor's direction. Cooper, who couldn't adapt to this unfamiliar style, was too restrained; Neal, always over the top, strained for effect; only Massey, an experienced stage actor, seemed in his proper element. At the premiere Neal felt humiliated when no one said a word to her about her performance. Finally a dancer approached her and broke the glacial silence by exclaiming: "Oh, you were so bad!"

The Fountainhead was ambitious, unusual—and rather repugnant. Condemned by the critics, it was both an artistic and commercial failure. Howard Barnes in the New York *Herald Tribune* called it "scrambled, pretentious and embarrassing."[7] John McCarten in the *New Yorker* dismissed it as "the most asinine and inept movie that has come from Hollywood in years." Bosley Crowther in the *New York Times* wrote that "Cooper seems slightly pathetic with his candor and modesty in the midst of so much pretension. . . . He is Mr. Deeds out of his element and considerably unsure of himself. His lengthy appeal to the jury is timid and wooden." *Cue* magazine's critic, who recognized its trashy content, was severest of all: "It is a hysterical mixture of frenzy and fraud—of spasmodic sincerity and sinister cynicism—of flashes of literary power and shoddy, bombastic nonsense. . . . The juxtaposition of high-sounding phrases regarding an artist's integrity with the steam-heated flashes of purple passion . . . turns this film into a story fit for the tabloids and the trash basket."[8]

Writing in the trade journal *American Cinematographer* when the film first came out, a Hollywood insider closed ranks and called *The Fountainhead* "handsomely mounted, beautifully designed, and imaginatively photographed." But the architectural critics, focusing on one of the rare pictures about their profession, were as savage as the film reviewers.

George Nelson, writing in *Interiors* and scorning "Hollywood's unerring instinct for the phony," said the buildings in the movie made no sense architecturally and would collapse if actually constructed. He concluded that even for an uninformed public, "there is still no reason for turning out such garbage." Andrew Saint, in *The Image of the Architect*, later declared that "a fantasy such as *The Fountainhead*, which glorifies architectural egoism, misconstrues constructional reality and insults the practising intelligence of designers."[9]

The head of advertising in the New York office, trying to put a brave face on a complete turkey, sent a desperately optimistic telegram to Jack Warner. After dismissing the informed review in *Interiors* as egghead criticism, he asked if they could stir up some publicity by connecting Roark to his iconoclastic model, Frank Lloyd Wright: "*Interiors*, architect's magazine, belts whiskers off sets in *Fountainhead*. From number of screenings we have had on this picture so far, we can tell that middlebrow and lowbrow audiences like it. Highbrows do not. . . . Tell me if we ever contacted Lloyd Wright as consultant architect on this picture or if he ever indicated that he wanted to work on story. Am informed that Wright did things in his life that would frighten even Roark." The critic Charles Silver shrewdly blamed the intransigent Rand for the disaster and concluded that once her screenplay was accepted, the movie was doomed: "The great problem with *The Fountainhead* arises from Miss Rand's script of which she was so proud, Warners so indulgent, and Vidor so tolerant. It was one of the worst pieces of scenario-writing in film history, so horrendous in its soft-minded polemics, blatant absurdities and tasteless excesses that it fails to achieve even camp entertainment value."[10]

The Fountainhead is a weird film, but its shoddy yet provocative argument and deliberately unnatural style still shock and engage the audience. Its ludicrous sexuality has, in fact, made it a camp classic. Rebellious students of the 1990s, like those of the 1950s, love to identify with the omnipotent artist-as-superman who puts his work above everything else, rejects the rules that govern the behavior of ordinary men and destroys whatever annoys him.

II

Like *Saratoga Trunk* with Ingrid Bergman, *Bright Leaf* (1950), Cooper's second movie with Patricia Neal, was a dud costume drama, made—

through his power at the studio—only so he could continue his love affair. Both Lauren Bacall and Neal (in their mid-twenties and in love with a much older man) wanted to play the goodhearted prostitute whom Cooper really loves, rather than the tobacco magnate's daughter whom he marries and hates. Bogart, a powerful figure at Warners, lobbied actively for Bacall, but Cooper wouldn't do battle for Neal. As Joel McCrea had pointed out, his friend was curiously passive and compliant: "In a profession wherein competition is bitter and every man is on his own, he won't fight for himself. He never has. . . . He takes what he is given and does what he is supposed to do." Resigned yet angry about losing the better part to an inferior actress, Neal said: "I desperately wanted to play the role that went to Lauren Bacall. . . . Gary could have helped, but he wouldn't fight for anybody. He didn't have the fight in him. . . . That was Gary. He hummed, nodded and was noncommittal."[11]

The Hungarian Michael Curtiz, who'd directed Bogart in *Casablanca* (1942), was tyrannical and temperamental. According to Fay Wray, he "was a machine of a person—efficient, detached, impersonal to the point of appearing cynical. He stood tall, militarily erect; his calculating, functional style made his set run smoothly, without humor. He had a steely intelligence and moviemaking know-how that made you feel there was a camera lens inside his cool blue eyes." After her tremendous success with Howard Hawks and Bogart in *To Have and Have Not* (1945) and *The Big Sleep* (1946), Bacall's film career had fallen into a sharp decline. A tough dame, she often clashed with Curtiz. When the director, attempting to put the young upstart in her place, told her it would be years before she became a great actress, Bacall coolly asked "if he'd like to hold up the picture till then." (Cooper was the only actor who appeared with three of Bogart's wives: Mary Philips in *A Farewell to Arms*, Mayo Methot in *Mr. Deeds Goes to Town* and Bacall in *Bright Leaf*.)

While making *Bright Leaf*, Neal encouraged Cooper to join her in the drama classes of Michael Chekhov, a Russian character actor, at the Stage Society of Los Angeles. After twenty years in the movie business, Cooper bravely got up before the group of stage actors and did improvisations on the play-within-a-play scene in *Hamlet*. Modest about his ability and humbled by the experience, he confessed: "I have only one or two tricks at best, and that's not enough, is it?" But Cooper taught Neal how to keep blowing undesirable lines in a script until they had to be rewritten. She later asked Suzy Parker, then acting in a Cooper film, if he was still "playing his old game."[12]

After a long series of noble and heroic parts, Cooper returns in *Bright Leaf* to the disreputable character and rough style of his old cowboy pictures. With the help of a stuntman, he takes part in a fistfight, a gunfight and a wholesale riot. He also falls down a flight of stairs and stops a runaway horse and carriage. Despite, or perhaps because of, his acting lessons, Cooper seems ill at ease in the role of a lowborn ruthless rake and self-made cigarette tycoon who throws out lines like "If your father had hound dogs, they'd be clawing on me this minute." Wanda Hale, in an unusually critical review in the New York *Daily News*, accurately predicted: "Many more pictures like his new starring vehicle, *Bright Leaf*, and his high standing is likely to drop as suddenly as an elevator with a busted cable." The more indulgent Bosley Crowther praised Cooper while condemning both Neal's hysterical repetition of Dominique and Bacall's rather prissy whore: "Although Mr. Cooper does a commendably strong and vivid job as a man wracked by agitating passions which propel him to his doom, Patricia Neal plays his female tormentor as though she were some sort of vagrant lunatic. Her eyes pop and gleam in crazy fashion, her face wreathes in idiotic grins and she drawls with a Southern accent that sounds like a dim-wit travesty. . . . Lauren Bacall is torpid and dull."[13] *Bright Leaf* unlike *The Fountainhead*, transcended the stinging reviews (Crowther's criticism of Neal's native Kentucky accent must have been particularly galling) and made a handsome profit of half a million dollars.

III

Cooper was not a cold seducer and user of women, but an enthusiastic lover who kept an eye out for the ladies and was a great admirer of the female chest. When an interview was canceled in New York, he told his press agent: "Forget it. We'll go look at the tits of the pretty girls on Fifth Avenue," and exclaimed: "Look at the knockers on that girl." Commenting on his love life in middle age, he told the actor Sonny Tufts that "as long as the little fillies want me for a good roll in the hay and not for who I am, that's okay. I'm not for chasin' much these days, though." But because he was a star, women constantly pursued him and offered themselves, and he never had to do much chasin'. Ned Nugent, a studio electrician at Paramount, observed him closely at work and noted that Cooper "never missed a trick. If he was born for the camera, he was born to make love. He was too good to be a rooster. He wanted to satisfy women . . . enjoyed looking at them, listening to them, pleasing them." Marriage had done little to diminish his capacity for loving and delight in liaisons. As Nugent commented, "a guy like that does not change."

Cooper's magnetic attractiveness and powerful sexual urge could not be confined to one woman. In a different profession he might have had a more calm and controlled sexual life. But as Nugent perceptively explained, the great movie stars worked extremely hard, often to the point of exhaustion, and their very careers depended on maintaining their superhuman image: "Guys like Coop worked twelve hours a day. They were expected to be seen dancing at the best nightclubs and to get up at five o'clock the following morning and know their lines. . . . The Gables, Coopers and Tracys needed outlets—hunting, golf or tennis, but always women. Their egos were like batteries. They needed constant recharging. They were the things dreams were made of, but they didn't believe it, so they had to find their own magic. There was no way Coop could be faithful and it had nothing to do with not loving his wife." Cooper may have cherished the idea that a casual young filly might want him for himself, but his fear that she was only attracted to his image drove him to more and more sexual conquests.

Cooper's well-known affairs with famous actresses—Clara Bow, Evelyn Brent, Lupe Velez, Marlene Dietrich, Carole Lombard and Tallulah Bankhead as well as his prolonged holiday with Dorothy di Frasso—all took place before his marriage in 1933, though he may have briefly resumed his liaisons with Lombard and Dietrich while making *Now and Forever* (1934) and *Desire* (1936). His involvement with Ingrid Bergman, who was also married, lasted only while they worked on their two films. Rocky had been hurt by this last affair but still loved him, and their new house in Colorado seemed to symbolize the renewal of their marriage.

Patricia Neal, much younger than Cooper's previous mistresses, was very different from all the others. University-educated and a talented Broadway actress, she was beautiful, warm and sensual. Her youth, freshness and adoration flattered and inspired him. She was someone he could teach and help to shape. This affair touched his deepest emotions and he fell in love. Neal became a serious threat to his marriage, and during their intense relationship Cooper left his wife. But it took three years to work out his true feelings and decide what he ought to do.

Like most women, Neal was immediately attracted to Cooper and overwhelmed by his beauty, but she also found him a stimulating companion: "His eyes were the most fabulous shade of blue and always sparkling, and he had long eyelashes that were curled more outrageously than any girl's. His hands were long and graceful and beautiful. I think his hands are what I remember most. . . . He was the most gorgeously attractive man—bright too—though some people didn't think so. I lived this secret life for years and I was so ashamed, yet there was the fact of it."[14]

Unlike Bergman, Neal deliberately held back from a love affair with Cooper till *The Fountainhead* was finished. Film actors are plunged into two or three months of instant intimacy, but on this occasion (Neal wrote), "our instincts warned us that the sexual tension being recorded on film might be lost if we went to bed." On the night they closed production everyone at the wrap party sensed that Cooper and Neal were in love. "No one spoke of it," Neal remarked, "but the energy between us radiated an excitement that brought everyone at the party into its orb. I am sure most were wondering if the affair had begun or not, but at that moment our love was still innocent. Guests finally began to drift away, but Gary and I lingered. His wife was in New York. The moment had come. I knew it and so did he." When they returned to her flat at 2146 Fox Hills Drive, near Sepulveda Boulevard and the 20th Century-Fox studio, she handed him her door key, they walked in and she led him to her bedroom.

Since he was married and scandal could damage and even ruin them (both were subject to the morals clause in their contracts), they had to be as discreet as possible and sometimes met in the house of their mutual friend Arlene Dahl. But the secrecy and danger, like the delay in consummation, merely intensified their excitement. Unlike Rand's uncompromising lovers, Cooper and Neal tried to have it all. They wanted to preserve the facade of Cooper's marriage, maintain their dignified public images and continue their careers. They'd listen to records while Neal cooked meals at home, eat in obscure Mexican restaurants in downtown Los Angeles and take long walks on the beaches of Santa Monica. One night, when Cooper was staying with her, there was a terrible car crash outside her window. Neal ran down to the street and discovered that a man had been badly injured and a woman killed. Two passing motorists stopped to help. When Neal denied she had a phone, one of them slashed his ankle while kicking in the glass door of a gas station to call an ambulance. Cooper then came down in *her* dressing gown to see what had happened. Just as Cooper once feared that he might be discovered if Lupe had an epileptic seizure and he had to call a doctor, Neal was terrified of a scandal if anyone recognized him. Her guilt about the affair and desire to protect Cooper made her lie about the phone and put the man's life in danger.

In the late fall of 1948 Neal went to England to make another film with Ronald Reagan, *The Hasty Heart*. She thought about Cooper constantly, wrote to him nearly every day and also received a great many letters from him. "I would read them over and over," she said, "treasuring each word. He was a beautiful writer and his letters were filled with a quiet, pervasive passion. I kept all of them for many years, until they disappeared at the time of my stroke" in 1965—probably destroyed by her jealous husband, the popular English children's writer Roald Dahl.[15]

When Neal visited the Brentwood house, the nervous Cooper kept tripping over everything, and she felt embarrassed when Rocky, clearly suspicious, exclaimed: "What's wrong with you, Gary, anyway?" Yet Cooper was thrilled by the idea of being with both his mistress and his wife. If he'd kept his two lives separate, he might have continued his affair with Pat indefinitely. But in July 1949, before making *Bright Leaf*, he decided to drive out with Pat and some other friends to see the new house in Aspen that had been keeping Rocky happily occupied. Though they'd been together for nine months, his affair with Neal was still secret. Cooper had seemed passive as she led him to bed that first night, but Neal said he was "a great lover – he really was," and they "made fabulous love" on the way to Colorado.

When they arrived, Rocky asked Cooper if he was having an affair with Neal and if he loved her, and he said yes to both questions. Realizing that the eleven-year-old Maria was disturbed by the unbearably tense atmosphere, Rocky thought it would be less painful for her to know the truth than to remain in the dark. She called Maria into the bedroom and told her that her father "thought he was in love with Patricia Neal." She made it clear that this serious problem had nothing to do with Maria or their love for her and gave her a kiss. Rocky also told her that Gary was very upset, that she ought to give him a hug and try to be understanding. She sent her into the adjoining room, where Cooper was staring out of the window. Maria cried at first but was greatly relieved to know what was really happening, and Rocky's comforting words helped her deal with the difficult situation.

Tired of covering up his defections and wanting everything honest and open, Rocky had blown the lid off his sexual life. It was a declaration of war, and the collision of Cooper's two worlds jolted him out of his trance. Neal, unaware of Rocky's state of mind, couldn't understand how she could have "hurt" her own daughter in this way. When she saw the Coopers at the Jerome Hotel the next morning, "Rocky's face was like stone. Maria's was stained with tears. The child looked at me and spat on the ground. Such a little girl, and she spat with so much hate."

Wretchedly jealous, Rocky resolved to treat Pat with contempt. She made weak wisecracks about the "southern cow who eats corn bread and black-eyed peas." On a later occasion, when Pat sent Gary a wire congratulating him on a radio performance, Rocky shot back a sharp reply: "I HAVE HAD JUST ABOUT ENOUGH OF YOU. YOU HAD BETTER STOP NOW OR YOU WILL BE SORRY." Pat was secretly pleased when friends told her that Rocky was icy, selfish and bitchy. But after her anger had subsided, Rocky dealt with the crisis intelligently. She did not attack Cooper in front of Maria and tried to reassure her that both parents loved her. Rocky "encouraged me," Maria wrote, "to be understanding of my father and never to blame him." Maria always blamed Neal, not Cooper, and later came to feel that his affair was "a very human thing."

Protected by her parents, Maria never saw them quarrel openly. But naturally enough, there was a great deal of anger and tension boiling up beneath the calm surface of their household. Some friends felt Rocky resented the fact that Cooper and his daughter adored each other and "took it out on Maria" when he was absent. More disturbed than she realized by her mother's visible unhappiness, Maria walked in her sleep and was once found in a trance at the edge of the pool.[16]

An armed truce prevailed until the next crisis erupted. In October 1950 Neal told Cooper that she was pregnant. He could have used this event to leave Rocky, marry Pat and have the child. Instead, after consulting his lawyer (whose brother was a doctor) and without even discussing the situation with Neal, he arranged for her to have an abortion. "There's a doctor downtown in Los Angeles," he told her. "I suppose we have to, Pat. Our appointment is tomorrow afternoon." The international furor surrounding the birth of Ingrid Bergman's illegitimate child powerfully influenced Cooper's decision and Neal's consent. In March 1950, while still married to Petter Lindstrom, Bergman had a son with the Italian director Roberto Rossellini and was immediately frozen out of work in Hollywood. Cooper knew their careers could never recover from a similar scandal.

In her chilling description of the abortion, Neal wrote that the doctor "held a needle at bay while he filled the syringe. It was the longest needle I had ever seen in my life. I closed my eyes. The needle's impaling gift was supposed to relieve pain. I thought I would die. My body began to sweat from every pore. The most agonizing hour of my life commenced. All I could hear was the sound of scraping." Cooper tried to comfort her by holding her in his arms for hours while they wept. But he also astonished Neal by telling Rocky about the abortion. A devout Catholic, Rocky must have been both horrified and relieved as well as strangely moved and tormented by the thought that her husband had nearly had a child with another woman. Consumed with guilt, Neal deeply regretted the abortion and later reflected that "If I had only one thing to do over in my life, I would have that baby." Her sacrifice had held them together, but he continued to live with Rocky.

Joel McCrea emphasized Cooper's unwillingness to confide in anyone about his personal dilemmas: "He never kicks. He never mentions, even to me, any sort of problem or difficulty he may have encountered. He never discusses anything personal with anybody." Despite his characteristic reserve, Cooper brought Pat to Cuba for the Christmas holidays in 1950. He wanted to introduce her to Hemingway and ask Papa's advice about whether he should leave Rocky and marry her. Neal recalled that Hemingway greeted Cooper by throwing punches at him, and later told her: "I'm a good writer. I'm a helluva good writer." She also knew that "Gary was telling him that he wanted to marry me. He was asking for Papa's blessing, and I was sure he was getting it. . . . Gary and I were escorted to the little guest house and found it had one double bed, which had been turned down for us to share. Years later I read that Ernest Hemingway disapproved of our affair. He did not then."[17]

Hemingway was ambivalent about Cooper's situation, which bore an uncanny resemblance to his own. In 1924 he too had persuaded his first wife, Hadley Richardson, to have an abortion. He had left the older Hadley to marry Pauline Pfeiffer in 1926 and (as he wrote in *A Moveable Feast*) felt intensely guilty about it. In 1949 he had also fallen in love with a nineteen-year-old Italian girl, Adriana Ivancich, but had managed to keep that affair platonic. He certainly understood Cooper's feelings, and may have encouraged his friend to do what he himself had once done.

Hemingway liked Pat, but his wife Mary, friendly with Rocky and threatened by Adriana, was hostile.

In May 1951 Cooper clashed with Rocky. Her tolerance was wearing thin, and she felt he ought to be a loyal husband if they were to remain together. Gary wanted to be free to continue his relationship with Neal. They were legally separated on May 16, and he moved out of the Brentwood house. But he went to the Bel Air Hotel—where, as Maria told me, every estranged Hollywood husband goes—instead of moving in with Pat. Civilized, as always, Rocky even helped him rent a house in Brentwood. Whenever possible, he took Maria to the beach, movies and dinner. Hollywood was surprised that the Coopers could maintain their friendship in the midst of this crisis and even continue to spend their holidays together. But there was no tension when Rocky and Maria visited Cooper in Mexico and Paris in the early 1950s. Maria said they were all glad to see each other and had a good time. Their three-year legal separation was not a stagnant period. Rocky swallowed her pride and remained in love with him. Cooper, however much he strayed, regarded his wife and daughter as the stabilizing force in his life. Both were receptive to a reconciliation, and scrupulously avoided the bitter scenes that so often bring couples to the breaking point.

Their attempt to lead normal lives during the separation was made much more difficult by the invasive publicity and constant exposure they received in the press and gossip columns. Rocky bravely declared: "I can't say we haven't had a little difficulty, but I can say that it isn't serious." Pressed by reporters, Neal desperately—and rather hopelessly—begged: "Please! I'm from a pretty conventional family background and I don't like this kind of thing at all. I hope this kind of talk will die down, that people will find something else to talk about. I wish that everyone would just ignore this."[18] But the gossip vultures didn't dare offend Cooper's friends and fans by attacking a greatly loved figure who'd appeared in films as Sergeant York and Lou Gehrig.

Hedda Hopper, who'd performed with Cooper in *Children of Divorce* way back in 1927, liked him and tried to protect him. In May 1951 she transcribed her notes of a telephone conversation in which she officiously warned him not to let Rocky get all his money. Admitting that stardom had made him egoistic and selfish, and realizing that his wife could not tolerate his adultery forever, Cooper defended Rocky and blamed himself: "She's not like that really. . . . It's all my own fault. Too many things during our long marriage were taken for granted. It's all my doing, but I do want to be free. . . . After 25 years [in films] I've had a helluva lot of happiness and many things that have been good. Many more than most people get and many more than I deserve. Picture stars are spoiled. They get a little hoggish. They think they're the best things in the world; they're not. . . . But don't think badly of Rocky; she's a good girl."

Dorothy di Frasso also threw herself into the fray by urging Neal to "fight for him, he's worth it." When Neal replied, "but I've met Rocky, and she's tough," di Frasso replied: "I met her, too. She had me for tea with two other of Gary's ladies. She took the occasion to return the gifts each of us had given him. You're going to need all the spunk you've got, my dear."

Rocky generously told a reporter: "I don't expect Gary not to go out with girls when he's away." Legally free to do as she wished, Rocky now realized that she too could arouse jealousy by seeing other men. Her flir-tations, beaux, escorts, admirers and lovers included the Argentinian actor Carlos Thompson, who serenaded her with a guitar, and later married Lilli Palmer; Robert Six, a millionaire airline executive and former husband of Ethel Merman; and, more seriously, Howell von Gerbig, all-American athlete and Palm Beach–Old Westbury socialite, who was an "item" but didn't work out. In 1952 Rocky also had a brief fling—"no big deal"—with Barnaby Conrad, the American bullfighter and writer. Conrad found her attractive, sexy and aloof, "a tough baby." She didn't need much persuasion to go to bed, but slept with Conrad to show Cooper she could do it. Rocky talked about Gary as if he were a wayward child and was still jealous of Pat Neal. "He's still seeing that woman," she said, "I think it's still going on."[19]

Another constant companion was Peter Lawford. Neal saw them together at a party, "looking like a million dollars. Her dress was gorgeous, her hair and makeup impeccable. If there had been tears shed, there was no sign of them now. Every eye in the room gravitated toward her. Including Gary's." When Cooper returned for a visit and discovered Lawford's toothbrush, clothing and books, he didn't seem to mind. But when he found Lawford working on one of his cars, which he cared for more than any other possession, he swore at him and wittily said: "I don't mind a man tinkering with my wife, but I won't have him tinkering with my car."

Though Cooper returned Neal's love, he never led her to believe he would marry her. During his legal separation (which lasted as long as his affair with Neal and coincided with it for nine months), he never asked

Rocky for a divorce—though she might have given him one and remarried outside the church if she'd met the right man. According to Jack Warner's wife, Ann (who put up with her own husband's frequent infidelities), "Rocky was very smart. During that period, she wasn't nasty, she looked good, and she made her own life. She went out with a few boys, and she acted very cleverly. She was fighting . . . Pat Neal, who happened to be a decent woman."[20]

In September 1951, four months after his separation, Cooper went on location to film *High Noon* and had an affair with Grace Kelly. He tried to discourage Neal from visiting the set and then, to throw her off the scent, told her that the director Fred Zinnemann was having a fling with Kelly. After the initial exchange of greetings, Kelly (Neal said) gave her the Philadelphia frost. Annoyed that Neal had replaced her in Cooper's bed for two nights, she stared coldly down at her plate during dinner, refused to talk and was "horrible."

Guilty about Neal's abortion, his lack of commitment to her and his affair with Kelly, Cooper was uncommonly generous with gifts. He gave Pat a new Cadillac, a mink jacket and pair of diamond drop earrings. After Neal's marriage to Roald Dahl in 1953, he asked her to sell the earrings Cooper had given her. When she took them back to Harry Winston's, the clerk revealed that they were one of three pairs purchased at the same time (did Kelly and a third favorite get the others?). He made a very low offer to buy them back, and Neal, eager to get rid of them, accepted. At Christmas 1951, when Neal was in the capital with Van Johnson and his wife making *Washington Story* (1952), Cooper sent her the fur piece. Neal was ecstatic, but Evie Johnson thought, "Oh-oh, this is the kiss-off'—and it was.

Nunnally Johnson's wife Dorris recalled that Neal (unlike Rocky) was universally liked, that people in Hollywood approved of their affair and wanted her to marry Cooper. But there were ominous signs. Cooper, twenty-five years older than Neal and, as injuries and ill health caught up with him, looking more than his actual age, warned her: "I'm too old for you, baby." One night, after spying through her window while Kirk Douglas attempted to seduce her, Cooper was overcome by jealousy. When Douglas had left, he came into her apartment, slapped her face and bloodied her nose. After that rare outburst of violence (the only time he's known to have hit a woman), he apologized with "Baby, I'm sorry. Let's just forget about it."

In mid-1951 Cooper's health began to break down, and he had a series of surgeries for hernias and ulcers. On August 8 in Santa Monica, after playing some rough scenes without a double, he had the first of four hernia operations. Toward the end of the year he felt corroded by guilt, the conflict between Neal and his family, and his own maddening indecision. Keeping all his anguished feelings inside, he lost his appetite and began to suffer from abdominal pain. On December 8, while in New York, he had the first of two operations for ulcers. Neal spoke to him on the phone and then, terribly worried, called his mother, whom she had met a few times. Naively hoping for comfort and love, Neal said she desperately needed to see her. "See you?" Alice icily replied. " 'Why should I see you after what you have done to my son? He is sick because of you. Do you know what you are?' The ax of Alice Brazier Cooper went through my heart."

Hurt and humiliated, Neal called him back and cried: "It is over. I really mean it, Gary, I can never see you again. Your mother—I called her. She insulted me. No, she told me the truth. It is all over." Cooper, seeing a means of escape, agreed with astonishing alacrity. " 'You want it that way?' he asked. 'All right . . . if that's what you want.' " But when she received his soft mink jacket as a Christmas present, her hopes revived and she called him at Sun Valley, where he was vacationing with his family. Expecting a joyful reconciliation, Neal was again shocked and humiliated to hear he was not coming back to California. She declared her love and pleaded: "I can't bear this. What are you doing to me? Are you leaving me? What are you going to do now?"[21] Evading her question about whether he was seeing other women or returning to Rocky, he said that his plans were uncertain and he might go to Paris. Neal had had the abortion to please Cooper, but this merely prolonged his double life. In the end he left her anyway.

Disarmingly honest and open, Neal told the predatory Hedda Hopper—on the scene to pick at the corpse—that she loved Cooper deeply but had to detach herself from a family man and begin to lead her own life:

> I will not see him when I get back to Hollywood. I have been very much in love with him. And I am sure he has loved me. But I saw that it wouldn't work so I stepped out. I have a lot of life ahead of me. And I want to live it with someone who is fun and unentangled, someone with whom I can have a relationship that will be good—and permanent.

Coop is wonderful. I never knew anybody like him. But he's a very complex person, as you well know. . . . It is, I assure you, over and ended forever. Wouldn't you know it would be just my luck to fall in love with a married man?

Cooper's explanation to another gossip columnist, Radie Harris, was more disingenuous and evasive ("and with whom" sounds more like a press agent than Gary Cooper): "She came into my life at a time when I thought my marriage had reached the point of no return. I had played around before—with Clara Bow, Lupe Velez, Dorothy di Frasso—but with Pat it was very different. She was the girl I loved and with whom I wanted to spend the rest of my life. But that hope had been dashed to the ground. So we decided the only thing to do was not to see each other again." He admitted that his marriage had failed, though he returned after the point of no return, and mentioned only a few of the women he played around with before getting married. "Dashed to the ground" suggests that Rocky had refused a divorce, though that option might have been possible if they had really wanted it. The phrase "only thing to do" is illogical. They could have done many other things—carried on as before, lived together, moved abroad—if he had really wanted to stay with her.

The parallels between the break with Lupe in 1931 and with Neal in 1951 are striking. In both cases Cooper's health broke down because of the intense conflict between two women—Lupe and his mother, Neal and Rocky—who vied to possess him. His strong-willed, possessive mother was instrumental in ending both affairs. The essentially cautious and conservative, loyal and rather passive ("All right . . . if that's what you want") Cooper, confronted with intense family pressure, abandoned plans to marry Neal, as he had done with Lupe, and fled abroad.

Neal wrote that Ingrid Bergman had the "guts" to have her illegitimate child and she did not. Saddened by their breakup because she still loved Cooper, she recently reflected that he "didn't have the guts" to leave his family and stay with her. She wanted to marry him. But when "things got sticky," he turned away and decided to leave. In the end, she said, he loved his family more than he loved her.[22]

A third feminine influence—his daughter, Maria, now fourteen—also affected the outcome. Though he wanted to marry Neal, he would not do so if it meant losing Maria's love and respect. When Cooper and Neal met by chance and for the last time in New York in October 1955, she confessed: "You broke my heart, Gary. You really did." He tried to explain and justify himself by saying: "You know, baby, I couldn't have hurt Maria for the world." Maria believes that she herself was, in some ways, his moral guide and conscience.

After the break both Neal and Cooper suffered deeply. She gained a lot of weight, came close to a nervous breakdown, went to a psychiatrist and found it difficult to concentrate on her work. Despite his apparently offhand attitude, he didn't just walk away. For a time he too was a physical and mental wreck. When she saw Cooper, who was always temperate and immaculately dressed, at a Hollywood party in 1952, she was shocked at his appearance. He was so intensely depressed that he didn't care if he was seen in grubby condition: "He looked as if he'd been drinking for a long time. He was very thin and he needed a shave. I never knew Gary to go without shaving except when he was out with his dogs in the country. His tie was spotted and his coat rumpled. I spoke into the saddest face I'd ever seen. . . . We were both going to pieces and stupidly trying to hide it from each other." His nephew, Howard, thought Cooper had seemed "born again" with Pat Neal. As he drove Howard through the Hollywood canyons in the summer of 1951, Cooper seemed at his happiest, on top of the world, showing his feelings like a real human being." Only six months later, after his operations and the break with Neal, Howard was struck by the dramatic change. Cooper looked terrible, like death.

It was strange and ironic as well as symptomatic of Cooper's deep-rooted conflict that he did not move in with Neal after separating from Rocky in May 1951 or return to Rocky after breaking with Neal in December 1951. Though physically and emotionally battered at the end of that year, he was not yet ready to come home. He went out with Annabella, Tyrone Power's ex-wife, and Kay Spreckels, who would soon marry his old rival Clark Gable. He then spent nearly two years abroad, making movies in Mexico and France, where he had several other affairs. As a world-famous celebrity, Cooper was constantly hunted by the newspapers. "Everywhere I went I ran into reporters and photographers," he said. 'They pursued me relentlessly. They hounded me for bulletins on my separation from Rocky—would we reconcile or divorce? . . . I owed a great deal to the public and was obliged to grant interviews and talk at times I didn't feel like saying anything. . . . I was trying to get away from it all and all I did was stew."[23]

16

High Noon

1951–1952

I

Though *Cloak and Dagger* and *The Fountainhead* were eccentric, interesting films, they had failed at the box office, and Cooper had not had a real success since *For Whom the Bell Tolls* in 1943. His long-term contract with Jack Warner, who limited his choices and offered him poor roles, matched his series of flops with Sam Goldwyn in the mid-1930s. He made *Task Force, Bright Leaf, Dallas* and *Distant Drums*, as well as *You're in the Navy Now* with Fox, during his affair with Pat Neal, and his emotional turbulence made him lose his grip on his career. After a decade of inferior movies, many people in Hollywood thought he was washed up.

The process of making *Task Force* (1949) was far more interesting than the end product. The Long Beach shipyard lent the studio, for two months and without charge, equipment from the commander in chief's operations room. One shot, using an admiral's barge and jet planes, cost the navy $24,000 an hour. The film company of 117 worked aboard the USS *Antietam* for twenty-four days while the ship tried to operate normally. The narrow passages, loud noise, poor lighting and shifting position of the sun as the ship changed course caused many problems.

The producer, Jerry Wald, wanted to make a dramatic and well-structured story out of twenty-seven years of naval aviation, but he could never resolve the conflicting demands of history and drama. To complicate matters Wald had four different units shooting at the same time. They competed with the war footage supplied by the navy, which included the Japanese attack on Pearl Harbor, American pilots landing on carrier decks and kamikazes crashing into ships. This material was the most exciting part of the finished movie.

The production also had more than its fair share of accidents. In the middle of shooting, on November 22, 1948, a Warners truck caught fire and burned on the way up from San Diego to Burbank. Its load of cut and stock film, daily rushes, personal baggage and make-up was totally destroyed. Cooper himself was riding in a naval barge that broke down and got lost in the heavy December fog in Long Beach Harbor. It took on water and drifted close to dangerous rocks before being rescued by a naval ship. Another accident on the carrier *Antietam* nearly killed him. During gunnery practice, a robot target plane was hit by artillery from the ship's cannon. It caught fire and headed for the open deck, where Cooper, with the other actors and technicians, was standing. As they dived for cover, the flaming plane skimmed the deck and crashed into the sea.

Intensely involved with Pat Neal, Cooper also caused problems of his own. In his typically gloomy bulletins that December, Eric Stacey told T.C. Wright that Cooper's lateness and slowness were causing expensive delays. But if anybody irritated him, Stacey warned, he could play the prima donna and was liable to procrastinate even more: "Cooper out late previous nite and not well. Rocky called to say he'd come late at 10:30. . . . You know damn well that when Cooper comes back, he won't be rushing around and available. He always has been slow." That same month Stacey rather unfairly blamed Cooper for not finishing a scene that Delmer Daves, the director, wanted to include and Steve Trilling, Jack Warner's assistant, wished to leave out: "If Trilling wants this company to move faster, they should talk to Gary Cooper. . . . He is no speed demon and is invariably late for calls and very slow getting onto the set. However, from past experience with this gentleman, if anybody says anything to antagonize him, he is liable to delay the company by being even later than ever." Cooper's acting lessons had made him unhappy with the feeble script and his own performance. One day he lost patience, angrily muttered "amateur, amateur!"—and walked off the set.[1] But he was pleased with his scene in the hospital—after he's crashed and been rescued from the sea—when his fellow officers, alluding to his off-screen friendship and previous film, bring him a copy of Hemingway's *A Farewell to Arms*. Cooper retained his boyish expression, looked splendid in his blue dress uniform and could bring a one-dimensional character to life. But Radio Moscow, which recognized an effective piece of propaganda, scathingly called *Task Force* "a film which glorifies war and calls for the militarization of the country's whole life."[2]

Distant Drums (1951), about the war against the Seminoles, was filmed on location at the Castillo San Marcos, a seventeenth-century Spanish fortress in St. Augustine, and in the Florida Everglades. The technical crew had a rough time with the amphibious setting, spongy ground and deadly reptiles. Slim Talbot claimed "they let five alligators loose against me in a water fight scene." The director, Raoul Walsh, in one of his tall tales, said: "Cooper complained that he had donated a gallon of his best blood to the mosquitoes and leeches. He had brought back a rattler skin, which he claimed he had torn from its original owner in a fit of berserk rage." From the Naples Beach Hotel on the Gulf of Mexico Cooper, writing more enthusiastically, stroked the fur of Hedda Hopper: "This has been a rugged location but not so tough that we couldn't spend a little time scrounging around for shells while we were shooting on the wild Gulf coast. So with the compliments of the *Distant Drums* shell gatherers, here's a Horse Conch for your mantle. Naples is quite a spot. I couldn't think of a better place if you were looking for a rest. No big city, no noise, no bright lights. We're all going to return to civilization very healthy."[3]

Cooper's co-star, making her film debut, was the twenty-two-year-old "luscious blonde" Canadian ballerina Mari Aldon. According to Pat Neal, the two had an affair. Aldon confided to the Los Angeles *Times* that the ordeal of shooting in a swamp made her itch, and said that "Gary Cooper was an inspiration to me and a rugged trooper. Nothing was too tough; he had no double, and asked for no special favors." Cooper gallantly told Edith Roosevelt, the United Press correspondent in Hollywood, that "Mari Aldon's kisses have a fresh quality to them. You sort of feel know-all and protective towards her."[4]

II

In 1951, after twenty-five years in the business, Cooper's professional reputation declined, and he was dropped from the *Motion Picture Herald*'s list of the top ten box-office performers. Most people now thought he was "only good in a western broad-brimmed hat." The producer Stanley Kramer, who owned a small independent company that released films through Columbia Pictures, was desperately seeking a star for the low-budget film *High Noon*. After a series of elaborate and expensive flops, Cooper was receptive to a project with a good story and a complex character. He liked the script by Kramer's partner, Carl Foreman, agreed to cut his fee of $275,000 per picture and do the film (getting the same deal as the director, Fred Zinnemann) for $60,000 plus a percentage of the profits.

Kramer, Foreman and Zinnemann all thought Cooper would be perfect for the troubled character of Marshal Will Kane, whose idealism opposed indifference and evil. Gaunt and slightly stooped, with ulcers and a bad back, he rode with difficulty and walked like a tired panther. Kramer later condescended to Cooper and, emphasizing his heroic image, underestimated his skill and talent: "He was not my favorite actor, my kind of actor. But Cooper belonged in *High Noon*. That part was made for him, that pebble-kicking, nonreacting, all underneath kind of man who is tight-jawed and restrained. Cooper was interesting to me, but I don't think that what he did was necessarily acting. I think there are a certain number of actors in the world who are not actors. They are merely people who can be believed." Cooper knew otherwise. He felt that his whole background as well as acting career had prepared him to play citizen Kane: "I saw in it a graphic presentation of everything dad had taught me at home." His comments show his natural feel for the part and his grasp of the issues: "My concept of a sheriff [i.e., marshal] was that of a man who represented the people. Alone he could never do his job—he had to have help. The sheriff I was asked to play was different than any I'd ever known or heard about because Sheriff Kane had to stand alone, literally, against the lawless. It was a challenging role—and I loved it."[5]

Kramer bought John Cunningham's story "The Tin Star," published in *Collier's* in December 1947, for $25,000. In the story a murderer, unexpectedly released from prison, exacts revenge on the marshal who'd captured him by gunning him down on his wedding day. In the movie the marshal kills the gunman and his gang. The budget of *High Noon*, only $750,000, meant the film had to be made with the greatest speed, concentration and economy. Zinnemann had ten days of rehearsal and shot the picture from September 5 to October 6, 1951, on a tight thirty-two-day schedule. The cast and crew started early every day—beginning with the church scene at the Columbia Pictures ranch in Burbank—and worked late into the evening. The outdoor scenes were shot on location in Sonora, in the High Sierras, where Cooper had made *The Virginian* and *For Whom the Bell Tolls*. Zinnemann's meticulous planning enabled him to make four hundred shots in only four weeks.

The film is set in Hadleyville, population 650, in the New Mexico Territory, on a hot summer Sunday in about 1880. Though the town was fictitious, the name recalled Mark Twain's story "The Man That Corrupted Hadleyburg" (1900), a satiric attack on complacency, hypocrisy and greed in a small American town. The picture takes place between 10:35 A.M. and 12:15 P.M.—slightly longer than the eighty-four-minute running time—and observes the classical unities of time, place and action. The cinematographer, Floyd Crosby, gave a vivid description of how Zinnemann directed the dialogue, movement, camera and lighting in the film: "He would get the actors together . . . and he'd start to rehearse a scene. He'd rehearse the dialogue and get the thing going the way he wanted. Then he'd start to block out the scene to get the movements, then I would come in and the rest of the crew, and would watch how the scene was blocked out, we'd get the marks for the actors, and whatever camera moves, we'd mark where he wanted the camera. He'd very often take a [view] finder—lay it out through the finder, if he had camera moves. And then he'd turn the set over to me and we'd light it with the stand-ins."

Using black-and-white film (which was cheaper than color), Zinnemann tried to achieve the effect of old newsreels. He studied Mathew Brady's Civil War photographs, and made the flat light and bright sky duplicate the grainy texture of an austere town and windblown street, stripped to their bare essentials. The low-angle shots of the empty railroad tracks anticipated the fatal arrival of the train, and sharp cuts rather than slow dissolves intensified the pace. They wanted gritty realism and, as Crosby said: "decided right from the beginning to avoid pretty photography: not to filter down the skies, to have hot fairly white skies, and make this town look as hot and crummy and dusty and unattractive as a small western town was. . . . We tried to keep it as stark and as natural and as unobtrusive [as possible]." Zinnemann also revealed how he got the desired effects: 'We were very careful to omit all clouds in our outdoor shots. In most westerns, beautiful cloud formations are considered *de rigueur*. But we wanted to emphasise the flatness, the emptiness of the land and inertia of everybody and everything. To contrast all that with the movements of the marshal, we dressed Gary Cooper all in black, so that when his lonely figure issued forth into the stark, bright stillness, his destiny seemed even more poignant."

The director used the same stark camera work on Cooper's face as he had on the landscape. "We deliberately used flat lighting for Cooper," Zinnemann said, "to make him look as tired and as old as we could, which was a great departure for a western hero," who was always supposed to seem dashing and romantic.⁶ The extreme close-ups and minimal make-up, showing every line and wrinkle of his haggard face, revealed his fear. Zinnemann got the right performance from Cooper, an enormously experienced actor, in one to three takes, and portrayed his gradual change from a well-dressed bridegroom to a disheveled and wounded lawman.

Unlike *Task Force*, in which Cooper was late and slow, dissatisfied with the script and with his own performance, he got along perfectly with Zinnemann and cooperated fully on the picture. He worked long hours under difficult conditions, and the film remained right on schedule. Between takes the affable star would chat with the crew or snooze under a tree. He had recently had a hernia operation, and threw his back out while rehearsing the wedding scene and lifting Grace Kelly onto a ledge. Though it was difficult for him, he did the fistfight with Lloyd Bridges without a double. Cooper admired the realism of *High Noon* and contrasted it to the conventional cowboy movie in which the hero is absurdly superhuman: "Westerns get away with lots of beating up and shooting—but it's so phony, nobody believes in it. A guy can stand up and take a couple of .45 slugs in the belly, and then turn around and shoot a whole posse, or he can take a dozen punches, then roll over and beat up the other guy."

Cooper's performance impressed the director and screenwriter. Zinnemann, noting how the camera loved him, said that he was marvelous when he had the right part and could act in character. Foreman was even more enthusiastic: "His own character and integrity shone through the image he portrayed on the screen. . . . He was very likely the best *film* actor in the world. He had mastered the requirements of the camera better than anyone else I know. He *communicated*—the hallmark of a really great actor."⁷

Cooper's co-star, the twenty-one-year-old Grace Kelly, also played a character who was close to her age and background. She had had only a small role in one movie, *Fourteen Hours* (1951), and was acting in summer stock in Denver. Kramer hired her, on a hunch and without a test, for a few hundred a week. The contrast between the rough, experi-

17

Gary with Arthur Cooper, 1930s. Gary grew apart from Arthur, a conventional banker, after their boyhood years in England were over.   Howard Cooper

18

Paul Shields, 1958. "A tough, cold operator, he made a lot of smart deals."
Estate of Gary Cooper

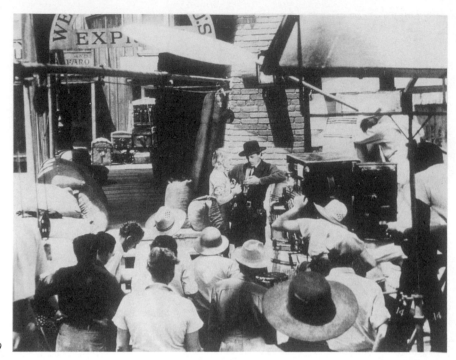

19

Filming *The Plainsman*, with Jean Arthur, 1936. Glaring lights and reflectors, supported by miles of thick serpentine wires, blazed in the actors' eyes, and the heavy camera and crane-like sound booms loomed close to their faces.
Estate of Gary Cooper

20

Cooper, with Harry Carey, Frances Dee, George Raft and Olympe Bradna, 1937. Raft had "a ring in his ear, and people thought that made him a better actor."
Frances Dee McCrea

21

Cooper, with Edward Arnold, in *Meet John Doe*, 1941. Refusing to
cooperate in the publisher's evil schemes, Doe is publicly denounced
and jeered at by a hostile crowd.

22

Ernest Hemingway, with Cooper, Sun Valley, 1939. "Cooper is a fine man, as honest
and straight and friendly and unspoiled as he looks."
Photo by Lloyd Arnold

Ingrid Bergman, 1940. She couldn't work well unless she was in love with the leading man.
Kobal Collection

23

24

Cooper on a USO tour in New Guinea, 1943. He felt the danger of Japanese infiltration, heard frequent explosions of gunfire and mortars and experienced enemy bombing attacks.
Montana Historical Society

25

Patricia Neal, with Cooper, 1948. She said: "He was the most gorgeously attractive man—bright too—though some people didn't think so."   Patricia Neal

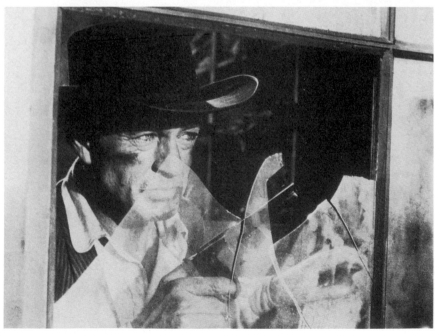

26

Cooper in *High Noon*, 1952. The extreme close-ups and minimal makeup, showing every line and wrinkle of his haggard face, revealed his fear.
Estate of Gary Cooper

27

Roberta Haynes, with Cooper and Barry Jones, making *Return to Paradise* in Samoa, 1952: "You just barely set foot on the ground here and you know why Gauguin stayed."
Roberta Haynes

28

Lorraine Chanel, with Cooper, on the set of *Vera Cruz*, 1954. "A stunning half-Mexican, half-Swedish model"
Lorraine Chanel

29

Cooper in Acapulco, wearing gun and holster, in front of a stone bridge, early 1950s
Lorraine Chanel

30

Cooper in Acapulco, early 1950s: He was "the tall, thin type of American, with pale
blue eyes of an idealistic, disappointed expression."
Lorraine Chanel

31

Cooper, with Richard Widmark and Susan Hayward, 1954. Widmark said Cooper "was catnip to the ladies."   Richard Widmark

32

Rocky and Maria, c. 1950. Cooper said of Maria: "I've never known her to do anything that wasn't right. She is my life."
Photo by Jean Howard, Estate of Gary Cooper

enced marshal and his awkward, straitlaced bride was extremely effective. She was ideal for the civilized Quaker girl, out of her element, unaware of the dangerous currents swirling beneath the surface, a foreigner in the western wilderness. "She was very, very wooden," Zinnemann said, "which fitted perfectly, and her lack of experience and a sort of gauche behaviour was to me very touching—to see this prim Easterner in the wilds of the Burbank Columbia back lot—it worked very well."

Kelly said she preferred older, more experienced men and was grateful to Cooper for his professional advice: "He's the one who taught me to relax during a scene and let the camera do some of the work. On stage you have to emote not only for the front rows, but for the balcony too, and I'm afraid I overdid it. He taught me that the camera is always in the front row, and how to take it easy." Noting that Kelly combined Rocky's wealthy background with Neal's youth and beauty, and recognizing her potential, Cooper "thought she looked pretty and different. And that maybe she'd be somebody. She looked educated, and as if she came from a nice family." Dressed in slacks and loafers, Kelly drove around the Mother Lode country with Cooper in his sleek silver Jaguar.

Kelly's prim and virginal looks belied a woman whose passion matched Cooper's. One of her acting teachers, Don Richardson, remembered that she was astonishingly eager for sex. On the night they first met, "we went over to my place. I started a fire, and within forty minutes we were in bed together. It was an amazing sight, seeing a girl as beautiful as Grace lying naked in my bed." Three years later, during the making of *High Noon*, Cooper told a friend that he was having an affair with Kelly, who was sometimes indiscreet: "when Grace came up to him, just the way she looked at him you could tell she was melting. She'd embarrass him, sometimes, by coming over and putting her arms around him and being obvious in front of other people."[8] Neal confirmed the affair with the offhand dismissal, "Listen, she slept with them all!"

When the affair had ended, Cooper, no longer impressed by her education and nice family, "imitated Grace Kelly's snooty way of speaking and would put his nose in the air—saying it was one of her gestures." He also commented rather ungallantly on the contrast between her frosty demeanor and passionate sexuality: "Looks like she could be a cold dish with a man until you got her pants down and then she'd explode."[9] In *High Noon*, however, there's a powerful contrast—as there had been with Lupe Velez and Rocky in real life—between Katy Jurado,

the dark, sensual mistress, and Grace Kelly, the restrained and elegant
bride who replaces her.

III

In Cunningham's story the marshal is called Deane, but when Jurado had
trouble pronouncing it, the name was changed. The hero's first name
suggests his will to defy his wife, face his enemies and defeat them. Kane
(Cain, the biblical murderer) suggests the dark side of his character: his
old affair with Helen Ramirez (Jurado), the men he'd killed while
enforcing the law, his capacity for violence. The film begins as three silent
horsemen ride into town behind the titles. Tex Ritter, the popular
cowboy star, sings the mournful ballad "Do Not Forsake Me Oh My
Darlin' / On This Our Weddin' Day," which sets the desperate tone and
outlines the conflict before the story actually begins.

Kane (Cooper) blinks and gulps nervously at his wedding to Amy
(Kelly) and gives her a shy peck on the cheek as the last ominous words
of the ceremony, "till death do you part," suddenly become an immediate
possibility. Frank Miller, whom Kane had sent to prison and who was
supposed to hang for murder, has been pardoned. His three gang
members have already arrived and he's coming in on the noon train to
take revenge. It's likely that Kane will not live long enough to consummate his marriage. "They're making me run," he tells Amy. "I never run
from anybody before. . . . I've got to [go back]. That's the whole thing."
Amy, a Quaker, whose father and brother were killed by guns, intensifies
the moral crisis by declaring she won't be around when the fight is over:
"I mean it! If you won't go with me now—I'll be on that train when it
leaves here."

The conflict between the woman's plea for safety and the man's sense
of honor is exactly the same as in Cooper's *The Virginian* (1929):

Molly: We can go away—I'll go with you—anywhere.
Virginian: You mean run away? Where could a man go? You can't run
              away from yourself. I got to stay.
Molly: But you can't stay just to kill—or be killed.
Virginian: You don't think I want to do this?
Molly: Everybody knows you're not a coward.
Virginian: No. Molly, there's more to it than that.

Molly: It's just your pride. Because you've got some idea about
          your personal honor.
Virginian: I don't know what you call it—but it's somethin' in the
          feelin's of a man—deep down inside. Something a man can't
          go back on.

In both films the hero is threatened by his old enemies, the decent but
cowardly townsfolk desert him, he kills the villains (one in *The Virginian*,
four in *High Noon*) in the final shootout and, as the people come out of
hiding, his sweetheart embraces him in the dusty street.

Amy goes to the station, where the gunmen also await the train.
Walking around the town, Kane tries to raise a posse to help him. But the
people, like his wife, all desert him. The judge, hoping to be a judge
again, folds up the American flag, packs the scales of justice and flees the
courtroom. Kane's deputy, Harvey Pell (Lloyd Bridges), jealous of Kane
and angry that he's not been appointed to replace him, won't help. The
others are too frightened or too old. Helen Ramirez, once the mistress of
Frank Miller, then of Will Kane and lately of Harvey Pell, decides to
leave. She darkly predicts that "Kane will be a dead man in half an hour,
and nobody is going to do anything about it. . . . And when he dies, this
town dies, too. It smells dead to me already." She also tells Amy: "If Kane
was my man, I'd never leave him. I'd get a gun—I'd fight."[10] But she's
now estranged from Kane. Sensing doom, she sells the hotel and boards
the train.

The scene in the church, where Kane vainly appeals to the congregation for help, shows democracy—in which everyone has an opinion,
but nothing gets done—in crisis. In an ironic touch, a parishioner
named Cooper convinces the initially enthusiastic crowd not to help
him. The choir establishes the apocalyptic mood by singing "The
Battle Hymn of the Republic," and the scene ends with the line "He is
sifting out the hearts of men before His judgment seat." The day of
reckoning comes as Kane's search for loyal deputies forces the people
to make a moral choice. Similarly, when Kane enters the church, the
minister is preaching from Malachi 4:1: "For, behold, the day cometh,
that shall burn as an oven; and all the proud, yea, and all that do
wickedly, shall be stubble: and the day that cometh shall burn them
up." The menacing arrival of Frank Miller, the fourth horseman,
alludes to Revelation 6:8: "and his name that sat on him was Death,
and Hell followed with him."

Rejected by the people, Kane admits he's afraid. Showing rare depth in a Western hero, the helpless marshal lacks the power to defeat his enemies. Horrified by his lack of support in the town and abandoned by his bride, who can't understand the need to fight, he knows he'll be killed before he can begin his new life. Like his wife, Kane has a crisis of conscience. As he struggles with his inner conflict, he expresses both courage and fear. After the last man has deserted him ("This ain't like what you said it was going to be"), he writes his will, buries his head in his arms and weeps in the solitude of his office.

Time itself is the dominant motif in *High Noon*. Kane desperately consults his pocket watch, and the camera frequently cuts to the inexorable clocks and their swordlike pendulums. As the minutes tick off, the clocks move more and more slowly and become larger and larger on the screen. The repeated shots of the static railroad tracks, stretching infinitely toward the horizon, are contrasted to Kane's restless motion in search of help. The sharp shadows suggest the conflict of good and evil. At the end the track is filled with the approaching train and its streaming black smoke, while windows, shutters and doors are closed all over the empty town. Helen Ramirez and Amy, the women who represent civilized life, board the train as Frank Miller, the embodiment of evil, descends.

The film excludes everything that is extraneous—Kane's past life as marshal, his dispute with Frank Miller, his affair with Helen Ramirez, the violent deaths in Amy's family, the courtship of his wife—and concentrates on the classical climax, which is as beautifully choreographed as a ballet. The shootout begins with a spectacular close-up of the marshal, Zinnemann explained, "with the camera on a boom receding into an enormous high long shot showing the entire village, empty of life, holding its breath, all windows and doors closed, not a soul, not even dogs to be seen, waiting for the impending gunfight."

After his henchmen are killed, Miller must face Kane alone. He takes Amy hostage, but as she scratches him and pushes him away, Kane shoots him dead. The townspeople pour out of their houses and fill up the street. Disgusted by their cowardice, Kane throws his tin star in the dirt, turns on his heel and (as he did in the beginning) rides off with his bride. Their bond is now stronger than before. William Faulkner, calling *High Noon* one of his favorite films, said: "There's all you need for a good story: a man doin' something he has to do, against himself and against his environment. Not courage, necessarily."[11]

IV

High Noon is about duty, self-respect, conscience, honor and the relation of character to destiny. But it's also a political allegory that reflected Carl Foreman's personal experience. Born in Chicago in 1914 and trained as a lawyer, Foreman made military documentaries during the war. In 1948–50, just before *High Noon*, he wrote the screenplays for four extraordinary films: *Home of the Brave, Champion, Young Man with a Horn* and *The Men* (Marlon Brando's debut), directed by Zinnemann.

In 1951, after a four-year hiatus, HUAC resumed its investigation of Communist subversion in Hollywood. At the height of the Cold War and the hysteria engendered by McCarthyism in America, the committee was now more popular and powerful, more vicious and destructive than when Cooper had testified in 1947. Foreman and his wife had joined the Party in Hollywood but dropped out in disillusionment in 1942. Subpoenaed by HUAC in April 1951, while he was writing the script, he was called to Washington to testify on September 24, while working as associate producer during the shooting of the film. Explaining his feelings, Foreman said: "During the so-called McCarthy period here in Hollywood, my problem was that I felt very alone. I wasn't on anybody's side. I was not a member of the Communist Party at that time, so I didn't want to stand with them, but obviously it was unthinkable for me to be an informer. I knew I was dead; I just wanted to die well."

Foreman knew in April that he'd be blacklisted after refusing to cooperate with HUAC. So he rewrote the script and transformed it into a portrayal of how fear affected people in Hollywood. In the film, he calls Hadleyville (or Hollywood) "a dirty little village in the middle of nowhere." Foreman saw himself in Will Kane, abandoned by everyone and left alone to fight the battle for law, civil rights and justice. "So much of the script became comparable to what was happening," Foreman later wrote. "There are many scenes taken from life. One is a distillation of meetings I had with partners, associates, and lawyers. And there's the scene with the man who offers to help and comes back with his gun. 'Where are the others?' he asks. 'There are no others,' says Cooper. . . . I used a western background to tell the story of a community corrupted by fear, with the implications I hoped would be obvious to almost everyone who saw the film, at least in America."[12]

Both Kramer and Cooper approved the changes that sharpened the political meaning of the film. But they adopted very different attitudes to

Foreman after he'd testified and taken what was known as "the diminished Fifth." Foreman (unlike the Hollywood Ten) agreed to answer
questions and denied he was currently a member of the Party, but he
would not state if he'd been a member in the past and refused to name
names. When Foreman was blacklisted, Kramer and the studio executives—fearful of their investments and careers—tried to save the picture
at the box office by severing their connections with Foreman. Cooper and
Zinnemann—like their main backer, Bruce Church, a prosperous
California farmer—remained loyal to Foreman.

   Though allowed to keep credit for his screenplay, Foreman was
dropped as associate producer. Kramer publicly disavowed him a few
days after he'd appeared before the committee, and later that year signed
a four-picture deal at Columbia with Edward Dmytryk. (One of the
Hollywood Ten, Dmytryk had served his jail sentence, then named names
and was "cleared" to work again in Hollywood.) Foreman, in a restrained
attack on his old friend, explained: "I got kicked out of my own company
by Kramer. We had a contract with Columbia. As a group there was no
way our films could have been attacked for being subversive. Instead
Columbia said the pressures were too great. I'm not talking only about
the right-wingers, who told Kramer ... to get me to cooperate with
HUAC. If Stanley had had the guts to ride it out we might have won—
Gary Cooper wanted to invest. But Stanley was scared. In the crunch he
said he was not prepared to have his career destroyed by my misguided
liberalism."

   In *High Noon*, when Jonas Henderson (Thomas Mitchell) tells the
church congregation, before capitulating to fear—"It's our problem. . . .
We got to have the courage to do the right thing"—he means (in political
terms) that it's not only the victim's problem, but society's as well.
Everyone urges Kane to leave town and give in to Miller's gang instead
of fighting it. Everyone is fearful and deserts him when he seems
doomed. In a similar way, people in Hollywood had rejected those associated with Communist views, not out of principle, but out of fear.
Blacklisting was the equivalent of destroying the good men and letting
HUAC, the evil outsiders, rule the town.

   During this crisis Cooper, like his father, revealed the liberal strain in
his conservative thought. In a fine consistency between screen role and
real character, Cooper—as if to atone for his appearance as a "friendly"
witness—showed considerable moral courage by supporting Foreman. By
the time of the second HUAC investigation of 1951, Foreman had "set

him straight" about many crucial political matters, and he now had a much clearer understanding of how HUAC had persecuted innocent people and destroyed many lives. Pat Neal, a liberal, also helped persuade Cooper to support Foreman. "You mustn't let him down," she said. "You must help him when he's in trouble."[13]

Foreman wrote that in 1951, the most difficult time to support an accused and then blacklisted writer, Cooper "put his whole career on the block in the face of the McCarthyite witch-hunters who were terrorizing Hollywood." After Foreman was subpoenaed in April, "Cooper was immediately subjected to a violent underground pressure campaign aimed at getting him to leave the film, and he was told that unless he agreed to do so he, too, would be blacklisted in Hollywood for the rest of his life. But Cooper believed in me. He saw it through." After Foreman had testified in September and been abandoned by Kramer, Cooper called Foreman at home and asked him how he could help. When Foreman said he was going to form his own production company, Cooper replied: "Count me in—now. Use my name. I mean it." And he publicly announced: "I like and admire Carl Foreman and am delighted to be in business with him." Cooper was then so popular that even Hedda Hopper couldn't crucify him.

But Louis Mayer and Walter Wanger warned Cooper that he might never get another decent role if he didn't back off. Foreman later explained that their partnership was also "prevented by the pressure of the Hollywood blacklist. Cooper came under severe attack from John Wayne and Ward Bond, as well as others in the so-called Motion Picture Alliance for the Preservation of American Ideals, as well as Warner Bros. and various right-wing publications, and I released him from his commitment in order to avoid damage to his career." Realizing that they could never establish a business in this hostile climate, Foreman told Cooper: "I know. Nobody can hold up against this . . . not even you." Though Cooper was finally forced to admit defeat, the grateful Foreman declared: "He was the only big one who tried. The only one."

Foreman was nominated for an Academy Award for best screenplay. He emigrated to England in May 1952 and wrote many scripts, including *The Bridge on the River Kwai*, for which he received no credit. Writing to Cooper from London in June 1957, Foreman reaffirmed their friendship and his desire to work together on another film: "You know how much I have wanted to do another picture with you. I hope this will still be possible. I have some very exciting things coming up after *Stella*, and it would be my dearest wish that one of them should be the means of our reunion."[14]

V

Despite its taut script, superb direction and effective cinematography, *High Noon* received a terrible audience response at the previews. Kramer brought in the film editor Elmo Williams to rescue it, and he gave the final form to what is now considered a flawless film. Williams took the rhythm of the picture from Cooper's slow drawl and stiff walk. He trimmed Kelly's role and cut the peripheral stories (which took place outside the town) about characters coming to help Kane, and had the idea of periodically cutting to the clocks to build up suspense. Williams explained how he also increased the importance of sound: "What I wanted to do with the end was to play lonely, simple sounds against the sudden, loud, staccato gunfire. So I have a fly buzzing around in the office, I have the scratch of Cooper's pen as he's writing his last will and testament, I have the ticking of the clock—single, isolated sounds, always with Cooper working and listening for the train." Kramer shot the film at Columbia but planned to release it through United Artists. He thought Harry Cohn, the head of the studio, wouldn't understand the picture and refused to let him see it. Cohn sent his car, with fake "instructions" from Kramer to get the film and bring it to his house for a private screening. When Kramer confronted Cohn about the theft, the mogul coolly replied: "It doesn't matter, since the film's a piece of crap anyway."[15]

The press and public were more perceptive. Though *Pravda* predictably lambasted *High Noon* as "a glorification of the individual" who triumphs without popular support, the American reviewers appreciated the film's artistry. Hollis Alpert in the *Saturday Review* wrote: "They have generated suspense . . . they have kept the talk . . . to a minimum, and the film, visually, has been put together like a carefully wrought mosaic." *Time*, agreeing that "Zinnemann's direction wrings the last ounce from the scenario with a sure sense of timing and sharp, clean cutting," called it "a taut, sense-making horse-opera that deserves to rank with *Stagecoach* and *The Gunfighter*."[16]

High Noon grossed $3.75 million in America and eventually earned $18 million worldwide, and Cooper was said to have earned $600,000 from this film. He'd been nominated three times for best actor, and won an Academy Award for his role in *Sergeant York*. *High Noon*, for which he won a second Oscar in 1953, was a far greater performance and his finest film. He'd met John Wayne by chance while making *Blowing Wild* in Mexico and asked Wayne to represent him at the ceremony. Cooper had once turned down *Stagecoach*, and Wayne, accepting the award on his behalf, now declared: "I'm going back and find my business manager and agent, producer and three name writers and find out why I didn't get *High Noon* instead of Cooper."[17]

Cooper's second Oscar finally made people realize that he was one of the most subtle actors of his time. He later said, with characteristic modesty: "My whole career has been one of extreme good fortune. I think I'm an average actor. . . . In acting you can do something and maybe . . . some people think it's fine, but you know inside of you that it can be done better. . . . You don't feel that you really attained a goal in the acting business; you always feel that you're still learning." Rocky related his restrained, low-keyed style to his fundamental shyness: "Acting embarrassed Gary. He disliked calling attention to himself. That's how he developed his slow-motion style: by perfecting the absolute minimum. Instead of laughing roguishly, he smiled quietly. Rather than yell or shout in a role, he preferred clenching his teeth and talking in a whisper."[18]

The English screenwriter Penelope Gilliatt emphasized Cooper's authoritative presence, which had evolved from his Montana background and experience as a stunt rider: "He possessed to a rare degree the instinctive physical style that is part of the heroic actor's equipment." James Harvey concentrated on the disturbing aspects of his character beneath his striking appearance: "Cooper was a man of extraordinary beauty: a troubled beauty, with expressive wounded-animal eyes, with suggestions of cold mischief in them at times, of dumb suffering sensuality at others. . . . The eyes are so stricken, the face so lean and taut and clenched at the jaw when he is young, so collapsed when he is older. In repose, the beauty seems authentically tragic." The screenwriter-director Richard Brooks stressed Cooper's authenticity and riveting self-assurance: " 'I think he's a great movie actor.' 'Why?' 'Because you're looking at *him*, no matter who else is talking, because when he reaches for a gun, if he's playing in a Western, you believe he's touched that gun before. He works at it. He has your full attention. Not only that, but he can make you feel something, something visceral, something deep, something that matters. He *is* who he plays."[19]

VI

High Noon inspired two important films that reacted against its moral and political message. *On the Waterfront* (1954) was written by Budd Schulberg and directed by Elia Kazan, who had both appeared before HUAC in 1951 and (unlike Cooper and Foreman) named names. Their political allegory justified their own betrayals by having the stevedore hero, Marlon Brando, inform on and condemn his former friends and union comrades. A friendly witness, he testifies against Jonnny Friendly and other racketeers (a false analogy to the Communists) before the Waterfront Crime Commission (HUAC) for the greater good of society. In a self-serving effort to vindicate their own behavior, the traitor becomes a hero. As Victor Navasky wrote, Schulberg and Kazan created "a context in which the naming of names is the only honorable thing to do—the maximum case for informing."

John Wayne and Howard Hawks responded more directly to *High Noon* in *Rio Bravo* (1959). Though Wayne had accepted Cooper's Oscar, he hated the film. He had also attacked Cooper for supporting Foreman, whose only "crime" was refusing to betray his friends. As late as his *Playboy* interview of 1971, the unregenerate Wayne alluded to the infamous committee and called *High Noon* "the most un-American thing I've ever seen in my whole life." Inventing a scene that was never in the script in order to impugn Foreman's patriotism, Wayne also claimed: "The last thing in the picture is ole Coop putting the United States marshal's badge under his foot and stepping on it. I'll never regret having helped run Foreman out of this country."

Howard Hawks, who'd made three films with Cooper, agreed with Wayne that *High Noon* was not authentic and that a real sheriff would never have to ask for help. Hawks exclaimed: "It's phony. The fellow's supposed to be good. He's supposed to be good with a gun. He runs around like a wet chicken trying to get people to help him. Eventually his Quaker wife saves his guts. That's ridiculous. The man wasn't a professional." Hawks also asked, in the most simple-minded way: "What did he have to have help for? Why didn't he just go out and shoot?"[20]

Rio Bravo is a derivative and grossly inferior version of *High Noon*. Angie Dickinson, in the equivalent of Grace Kelly's role, provides the love interest; Walter Brennan, talkative and with the same high cackle as in *To Have and Have Not*, brings comic relief; and there's even, like Katy Jurado, a Mexican hotelkeeper. An antagonist tells Wayne, who's called

Chance and is willing to take one, "You talk awful big for a man who's all alone." Wayne's biographers simplistically wrote: "Every inch a Hawks hero, Chance does not decry his fate or scour his town in search of help. He simply does his job, stoically and without fuss. In the process his friends respond. Without asking for it, he receives help in every crisis, and during the course of the film he is saved by a drunken friend, a crippled old man, a young gunslinger, a dance-hall girl, and a Mexican hotel operator." Wayne, all bluster and bombast, rejects offers from the frightened citizens, telling them: "This is no job for amateurs." But Cooper is *alone* in *High Noon* while Wayne has three deputies—the drunken Dean Martin, the lame Walter Brennan and the youthful Ricky Nelson—in *Rio Bravo*. Cooper asks for help but doesn't need it; Wayne doesn't ask for help but gets and needs it.

The film critic Andrew Sarris, attempting to argue the case for *Rio Bravo*, wrote that "Wayne accepts his responsibility without any of Cooper's soul-searching and without passing off responsibility to society. . . . While Cooper is upset because an old ex-sheriff (Lon Chaney, Jr.) will not join him at the barricades, Wayne refuses the assistance of Ward Bond because Bond is not good enough with a gun. . . . [Zinnemann] spends most of the film on the pathos of Cooper's helplessness, and then denies Cooper any sensible defense against three [i.e., four] gunslingers who want to kill him."[21] But Cooper's anguished soul-searching, opposed to Wayne's mindless machismo, is precisely what makes *High Noon* a fine film. Cooper's defense—successful, if not "sensible"—is his self-reliance.

Unlike Wayne, born and bred in Iowa, Cooper was an authentic westerner who didn't have to be taught to ride, carry a gun or walk like a cowboy. He had been doing these things since boyhood. Compared to the gentle but capable Cooper, Wayne was a bully and a boor. He always played a shallow, superhuman hero who solved every crisis with a punch or a shot. Wayne hated Cooper's admission of defeat, but was incapable of expressing his inner conflict and torment. *Rio Bravo*, as Cooper said of conventional Westerns, was "so phony, nobody believes in it"; *High Noon* transcended the conventions of the genre and was the greatest Western ever made.

17

The Wandering Years

1952–1954

I

Cooper had the kind of role in *High Noon* that appeared only once in a lifetime. Anything that came afterward was bound to be disappointing. In 1952 he made *Springfield Rifle*, a mediocre Western, and then decided, for tax reasons, to live abroad. Legally separated from Rocky in May 1951, and no longer attached to Pat Neal, he was free to drift around on his own. In the early 1950s producers began to realize that making pictures in foreign countries not only provided realistic, even exotic backgrounds, but also enabled them to reduce both costs and taxes. Stars like Cooper—looking for a bit of adventure, a change from the constrictions of the studio and a considerable tax break if they stayed out of the country for eighteen months—jumped at the chance to work in the South Pacific. He made *Return to Paradise* in Samoa, and *Blowing Wild*, *Garden of Evil* and *Vera Cruz* in Mexico. He had affairs with the actresses Lorraine Chanel in Mexico and Gisèle Pascal in France, but eventually grew tired of this wandering, unstable and sometimes lonely life.

Springfield Rifle (1952) was made from late April to early June in the Mojave Desert and at Lone Pine in the Sierra Nevada. The rugged Hungarian director André De Toth shot some scenes above ten thousand feet on Mount Whitney. On the first morning, during a heavy snowstorm, the landscape was eerily silent. De Toth announced "We'll shoot" and Cooper, game for anything, agreed to try it. They filmed in the storm till the sun came out on the third morning, but De Toth was furious when the producer, Lou Edelman, cut the storm scenes. De Toth also recalled that in the evenings, after a few glasses of Jack Daniel's, Cooper (as his father had done) gave superb readings of Shakespeare.

The film is set on the western frontier in Colorado during the Civil War. Influenced by *Winchester '73* (1950), it celebrates the recently invented Springfield rifle, a muzzle-loading rather than breech-loading gun, which saves the northern cavalry from southern spies and raiders. Cooper is again falsely charged—this time for desertion—and joins the enemy in order to expose them. The script is terrible, the plot confusing, the motivation unclear, mostly because of the cuts made by the producer. But Cooper confounds the Confederates, captures the real traitor (his own colonel) and is reinstated in the army. He concludes with a long speech in front of his now-proud wife and son. Glad to escape this ordeal, which added nothing to his reputation, Cooper took off with Slim Talbot to hunt grizzly bears on the icy coast of Alaska.

On July 1, 1952 Cooper flew via Hawaii and Fiji to Upolu, the main island of Western Samoa, to make *Return to Paradise*, based on the novel by James Michener. The islands, home of Robert Louis Stevenson in the early 1890s, were once owned by Germany and had been under New Zealand mandate since 1920. Cooper lived on the top floor of a beach house, five minutes from the center of Apia. They shot the film on the other side of the island, about an hour away by car. He woke up at dawn and worked very hard during the hot, humid, tiring days. When he had some free time, he'd read travel magazines, play the bongo drums and go snorkeling.

Cooper's letters to Rocky and Maria, one of them decorated with his drawing of a native hut, describe his initial enthusiasm and prompt disillusionment as well as the difficulties of making a movie so far from Hollywood:

We've been sitting here without stuff to make a picture and no word from the ship yet. . . . You just barely set foot on the ground here and you know why Gauguin stayed. It is more beautiful than you imagine, the villages are like parks. The *fales* (houses) are all high poled thatch roofs open on all sides. They decorate everything with flowers and the shoreline is nearly one solid continuation of villages and the people dress and look exactly as Gauguin painted the Tahitians years ago.

Big disappointment—the swimming!!! All sewage goes into the

water and the water inside this coral reef surrounds the island. . . . I
hear the sharks, barracudas and eels are plentiful. . . .
You wouldn't like it for long!! The food!!! * Phewww!

Shipped in from Australia and New Zealand, the food was badly cooked
in the English way. Cooper, whose ulcers made it difficult for him to eat,
had his meals specially prepared and then whipped in the blender. A ship-
ping strike in San Pedro delayed the movie equipment, which was
transferred to a Panamanian boat and arrived a month late. He wrote
Rocky that "the ship came over the horizon Monday. No word from her
on account of a different wave length and about a mile beyond the reef
we identified her as not a local craft. Everyone's spirits rose, big excitement and much work unloading a hundred and twenty tons of
equipment. The picture is *really* going to start."

Two weeks later Cooper gave a lively account of the magnificent
setting, the unreal yet exhausting life in the tropics, and the problems of
working with the hedonistic and lackadaisical islanders:

Dear sweet girls—Mama and Cakes
    It doesn't seem to make any difference whether you work or don't
work here—the time goes so fast. It's like looking back on having a
fever. You don't know where the devil the time has gone and you can
never do all the things you set out to do on a Sunday off. You don't
write because you know the mail won't go out for another ten days or
so and also I've come home from work several times at 7:30 or 8
o'clock, kicked off my shoes, had some soup and gone off to sleep—
with clothes on and up again before daylight. The parade of bright days
and starry nights flickers by so fast you really wonder if you'll ever get
out of here to see your own world and your own people.
    From where I sit now you can look up on the high jungle-covered
hill that dominates the town and on the top of which Robert Louis
Stevenson is buried. In the day time it is usually backed by a huge white
cumulus cloud, and in the evening flying foxes (an animal like a bat but
a little bigger than "Charley" the crow) fly in from the higher hills to
feed on the fruit trees at night. Will try to get a movie of one before I
go.
    The picture is going pretty well considering the Samoans are a *little*
green, and also that money doesn't mean a damn thing to them. About
the only thing they buy is cloth for their clothes, mostly the *lavalava*

(sarong, to you). Every other darn thing they use, eat or live in comes from the trees and the plants around them. They believe in the long siesta at noon and think we are crazy to work right through the day. They swim and bathe a couple of times a day (but are still a little high!) but so are we I notice after just a few minutes exposure to work. . . .

It would be good to see my two girls about now. I miss you very much and love you very much and I want to come home!!![1]

Interviewed by Hedda Hopper when he returned to California in October (he was allowed thirty days in the United States during his time abroad), Cooper emphasized his spartan living conditions, exhausting work hours and ill health: "Their stores are limited. They buy from New Zealand. Have a few canned goods. Very little variety. There was no hot water. . . . The hotel was equipped to handle twenty people. . . . When we got there there were sixty extra people. They were swamped. They cook on crude stoves. Food wasn't bad, but not too good. . . . We didn't have much time for pleasure. Got up at 6; leave the hotel at 7; drive out to location; get back at 7:30 or 8; finish dinner at 9 or 9:30; then fall in the sack. . . . Too pooped to work on Sunday. I went spear fishing a couple of days—caught small stuff. When I had two days off I had a sore throat and stayed in bed."

Cooper's co-star, Roberta Haynes, had spent a week on location in Sonora for *High Noon*, but her small role as a sensuous Mexican girl had been cut from the film. Born Roberta Schack in Texas, Haynes was raised in Hollywood. After working briefly off Broadway, she returned to California, heard that the producers had been unable to find an island girl and aggressively pursued the role. She had dark hair and eyes, an olive complexion and a sensuous figure, and worked hard to learn how Samoans spoke and moved. To stimulate interest in Roberta, her agent had her photographed in her underwear. The sexy photo appeared in many magazines, the censors were outraged and the publicity worked. She got the part and spent three months isolated on Samoa with Cooper. The medicine he was taking for ulcers diminished his sexual desire. "Otherwise," he rather apologetically told her, "I'd make a pass at you." She was twenty-five, he was fifty-one. She liked younger, healthier, more aggressive men, and to her he seemed much older than his actual age. They did not have an affair, and never even kissed off camera.[2]

Just as Cooper had refused to fight for himself or for Pat Neal when she wanted Bacall's part in *Bright Leaf*, so he also exasperated Haynes by refusing to complain about the primitive housing provided for himself and other actors: "His dressing room was absolutely minuscule. There wasn't even a chair, much less a bed to lie down on. Cooper needed rest more than ever, as his ulcers were bleeding." To ease the pain, he drank "quite a bit," spiking his coconut milk with vodka. He also told Haynes, as he'd told Neal, to deal with awkward dialogue by speaking it so badly that it would have to be edited out of the film. Haynes observed Cooper closely and, like most actors who worked with him, was impressed by his easygoing but thorough professionalism: "He would say he didn't know [his part] very well, but he knew it backwards and forwards. Yet I never saw him pick up his script and study it. I would sometimes look at him on the set, off in a corner, practicing hand movements and gestures. I'd later see him using them. He knew exactly what he was doing. He knew what lens was on the camera. He was a master, a consummate film actor."

Combining the decor of Trader Vic's with the earnest documentary approach of *National Geographic*, *Return to Paradise* has beautiful color and scenery. But the exotic houses, food, dancing and social customs of the island are merely a colorful background to the potboiling story of gentle natives oppressed by a fanatical missionary. Cooper, his hair tinged with gold, looks tanned and fit. Wearing a beachcomber's beltless white trousers and short-sleeved blue shirt, he suddenly turns up to challenge the rigid man of God ("I'm not taking orders from any two-bit Mussolini") and free the good people ("We've been waiting for a man like you"). The docile and devoted native girl (Haynes) moves into his hut, becomes pregnant and dies in childbirth. Cooper then leaves the island, and the movie splits into two loosely related halves.

Sixteen years later, during World War II, he returns to the island, now dressed more respectably with tie, watch chain and sea captain's hat. When told about his teenaged daughter, he looks stern and uneasy, and stares silently at her as she babbles on nervously. He plays the strict father and expresses a sense of remorse for abandoning her. He first finds it difficult to respond to her, but is soon charmed by her winning ways. Remembering and recreating with her the kind of life he'd once led with her mother, he finally decides to remain on the island. Cooper was drawn to this story for personal reasons. Abandoning and then returning to his lost daughter in the film was uncannily like his separation from and eventual return to his real daughter, Maria. When the cast and crew finally returned to Los Angeles, they couldn't land because of heavy fog and flew on to a desert airport. Inside the terminal, Alice Cooper was waiting to greet her son.

A delightfully ambiguous publicity release from Juniper Films, making a movie on the island in 1996, announced that "during the course of filming in Western Samoa, we came across a number of people called Gary Cooper. It is a tribute to the impact Gary Cooper had on that small nation that people were named after him." (The release did not specify how many of these children were his.) Gary Gilmore, the notorious Utah murderer, was also named after Cooper because (his mother said) "he's going to grow up to be handsome, just like the actor." As an adult Gilmore would imitate his namesake and cock his head "in his best Gary Cooper fashion."[3]

Blowing Wild (1953), Cooper's second film made abroad, had a budget of $1 million. The first of three shot in Mexico, it was originally planned for French Morocco. Lauren Bacall had refused the part eventually played by his old friend Barbara Stanwyck. Recently separated from Robert Taylor, Stanwyck was in bad shape and "couldn't even find her mouth to put her drink in." On March 19, 1953, in the midst of making the film, both Cooper and his co-star, Anthony Quinn, won Oscars, for best actor in *High Noon* and best supporting actor in *Viva Zapata*. Quinn wrote that during that memorable evening the two men, with Stanwyck between them, were lying out on the lawn of their hotel in Cuernavaca, gazing up at the stars. Meanwhile, another girl waited in Cooper's hotel room. Noticing that his friend's hand had disappeared, Quinn looked over to see what had happened: "Barbara had her eyes closed and was feigning sleep. Coop was working his hand quite diligently between her thighs and she moved with him. He kept up with his talking, going on and on about women, all the while diddling the famous lady who lay at his side."[4]

In the rather absurd *Blowing Wild* (whose title refers to a Mexican oil well), Cooper plays a wildcatter who's had an affair with Stanwyck, now Quinn's wife, but is currently in love with a younger American girl (Ruth Roman). After Stanwyck murders Quinn to get Cooper, bandits blow up the oil well and kill her. The script by Philip Yordan, who hired black-listed writers and took credit for their work, is a doubly derivative mishmash of familiar episodes. The theme song is belted out behind the titles by Frankie Laine, who'd made a popular record of the ballad from *High Noon*. Cooper, down and out in Mexico, begs money from a prosperous countryman just as Bogart did in *The Treasure of the Sierra Madre*.

To get money, Cooper agrees to drive a truckload of nitroglycerine. When he delivers the goods and asks for payment, the boss, with a boat ticket in his back pocket, says he has to go to the bank (as in *To Have and Have Not*) and is beaten up by the men he tried to cheat (as in *Sierra Madre*). Like Bacall in *To Have and Have Not*, Roman is stranded and alone in a foreign country, but doesn't leave when Cooper (like Bogart in the earlier film) buys her a ticket home. Stanwyck expresses her passion, as Neal did in *The Fountainhead*, by chasing Cooper on horseback. After she's killed, Cooper leaves with his sidekick (Ward Bond) and girlfriend (Roman) just as Bogart did with Walter Brennan and Bacall at the end of *To Have and Have Not*. During the shooting of this misconceived movie, Cooper was hit by fragments of the dynamited oil well and suffered severe bruises and contusions in his stiff right shoulder.

II

Cooper played around with many obscure women between breaking with Neal in December 1951 and meeting the "stunning half-Mexican, half-Swedish model" Lorraine Chanel exactly a year later. Born in Mexico in 1924 and raised (like Lupe Velez) in San Antonio, at the age of seventeen Chanel had been briefly married to a wealthy Cuban. She'd modeled in a San Antonio department store, appeared in many Mexican movies and was trying to graduate from bit parts to more important roles in Hollywood.

Lorraine met Cooper in Mexico City when Bo Roos, the well-known Hollywood business manager, summoned her to his hotel to discuss her film career. Cooper, along with many other movie stars, had been invited to the inauguration of the Mexican president and was staying at the same place. "Blumie" Blumenthal—a dubious character managing the hotel—turned up with Cooper. Lorraine had a bad cold and was not properly made up. Cooper stared at her intently, but said nothing. The next day, December 6, her birthday, Blumenthal called and announced: "Your next husband wants to speak to you."

Cooper wanted to escort Lorraine to the inaugural festivities. He sent her flowers, and they went out every night to places like the Normandie restaurant and the Capri nightclub. Their names appeared as an "item" in Hedda Hopper's column. When Mexicans recognized Cooper and wanted his autograph, they always asked Lorraine's permission to approach him. Impressed by their politeness, Cooper gladly gave his signature. Cooper and Lorraine also took trips to the beach at Acapulco, where he whittled and flew a toy airplane that Rocky had sent him. Lorraine was with him when he ran into John Wayne and asked him to accept the Oscar on his behalf.

Despite his courses at Grinnell, his relationship with Lupe and long stays in Mexico, Cooper never learned much Spanish and depended on Lorraine to see him through. In Mexico City he didn't go to museums or read books, but looked through many screenplays. He rarely used obscene words but, when frustrated by congestion in the streets, would complain about the "traffuck." He loved to tell long, unfunny shaggy dog stories, imitating the different accents. Rocky would tell him to finish the story or to keep quiet, but Lorraine never interrupted him, and he told her: "You're such a good listener." He was also sensitive to her feelings. When she heard her favorite dog had died and started crying, he cried with her.

Cooper told Lorraine that he didn't really want to be an actor and would have preferred to grow corn. When she joked that he'd done this in the movies, he was not amused. He said he'd disliked the hard work on the Montana ranch, but (perhaps remembering Rocky's grandfather) that he'd always wanted to breed horses. But he couldn't ride horses in Mexico; his legs hurt and he was in pain. He was troubled by his hernia, and Lorraine begged him not to smoke so much. Despite health problems, he was well satisfied with his life and told her: "I can't complain, even if I died tomorrow. I've had everything."

One of the few things Cooper didn't have was the French actress Corinne Calvet. In a photo taken while he was dining with Lex Barker, Celeste Holm and Hedda Hopper, he gazed at Calvet's formidable breasts (Lorraine said) "as she was telling us about her nipples and how she started to develop and how hard they got. Why? I have no idea. We were not on that subject at all. We all cringed except Gary. Corinne became quite graphic. French, you know."

One night in a restaurant the waiter, thinking the famous star had given him an enormous tip, kept the change. Cooper then embarrassed Lorraine by calling for the change and leaving the usual amount. Always careful with money, Cooper was not as generous with Chanel as he had been with Neal. He sent her gloves from Paris and gave her a gold ring with small diamonds. He once arrived at her flat with an elaborate jewel case, which seemed to contain an expensive gift. When she opened it, she was greatly disappointed to find two pheasant feathers. One day they went shopping to buy Rocky a ten-piece silver samovar set with a decorated tray. When Cooper asked, "What do *you* like?" she thought he was also going to buy a gift for her. They looked at a teapot, a coffeepot and a tray, all of which had to be brought down from a high shelf and individually priced. Finally, he bought her a ten-dollar sugar bowl and called it the beginning of her silver service. When she asked about his gold tiepin (a present from Neal), he hurt her feelings by saying, "It's none of your business."

Cooper had attracted homosexual men as well as women—the bearded man who kissed him on the mouth when he was a child, his roommate Anderson Lawler, the photographer Cecil Beaton, the actor Charles Laughton—and he was always uneasy about this. He once wanted to wear a brightly colored Mexican shirt and asked Lorraine if he looked feminine in it. Seriously concerned about his appearance and image, he finally rejected it because people "might think he was queer." After breakfast one Sunday at his hotel, an elderly gray-haired "flaming queen" pressed him to come to a party. Unwilling to offend by a direct refusal, Cooper politely muttered, "we'll see," and didn't turn up. The following Sunday the old man, red-faced and furious, confronted Cooper, screamed: "How dare you not come, the party was for you," and made vague but embarrassing threats. Cooper, forced into an awkward situation by an acquaintance who wanted to exploit him, could neither please the man nor avoid him. Such were the penalties of fame.

Cooper thought Gable and Stanwyck the greatest "stars" (as opposed to the greatest actors). His early love affair with Carole Lombard later intensified his rivalry with Gable, who held the same position at MGM as he did at Paramount. "Coop is a right guy," Gable said, "the kind you liked to hunt and fish with and not talk about making movies. I laid it on him one time about his romance with Carole and he got pale as hell. She told me about it during a drunken argument we had. After that, Coop and I didn't hunt together so much and when we did, we kept an eye on each other. She used to throw him up to me in my face and that was hard to take, especially since I didn't know the whole truth until years later. I got to admit I was jealous." Gable was especially wounded when Lombard confronted him with the truth because Cooper was a great lover and, as Lombard crudely confessed, "God knows I love Clark, but he's the worst lay in town."[5] No wonder, then, that Gable's Duesenberg had to be a foot longer than Cooper's. But Cooper was also professionally jealous of Gable and resented it when he was called the King. When Lorraine told Cooper that Gable's head was shaking in one of his late films, they went back to see it together, and he whispered, "tell me when the shaking starts."

After attending the Berlin Film Festival in June 1953, Cooper bought a Mercedes-Benz at the factory in Stuttgart, had it shipped to Veracruz and then driven to Mexico City. As he and Lorraine were driving it north to Los Angeles in February 1954, Cooper said he felt tired and asked her to take over. But after only five minutes he became restless and wanted to drive himself. As they approached the border, he told her: "I bet I won't have to pay customs duty." Sure enough, he flattered and charmed the officials, who let him through free of charge. During that journey Lorraine felt depressed. The affair was clearly coming to an end, and "it was good-bye without *saying* adios." Though a newspaper announced, "Lorraine Chanel says she will marry Gary Cooper," they never spoke of marriage.

During their two years together Lorraine was trying to get ahead with her modeling and film careers. She worked hard, lived in her own apartment and supported herself. She was Cooper's lover, not his kept mistress. He always called her "baby" (never Lorraine), the generic name for all his girls, perhaps to avoid getting them mixed up. He was terribly jealous and possessive, unusual for an Anglo man, and she never saw other men while he was in Mexico. She remembered his clean, fresh smell, like a baby or a little boy, and his conventional sexual behavior. "Well endowed," he made love to her two or three times a night—always in the missionary position. He loved big breasts, slept with her in his arms, and was a considerate and tender but not a romantic or passionate lover. Lorraine, shy in bed, "didn't touch it" or "do *Playboy* things." He was (as Neal had also said) "the love of her life."

Departing from his formulaic "baby," Cooper addressed Lorraine quite imaginatively in the twenty letters he wrote her from Europe and America between 1953 and 1955. At various times he called her darling, sweet, beautiful, *mi vida*, baby sita (sitter), lil Lo, little señorita and little Yo T.Q. y T.A. ("*Ti Quiero*" and "*Ti Amo*": I love you). Writing from the Hôtel Lancaster in Paris in May 1953, just after leaving Mexico, he complained of exhaustion and the incessant demands made upon him. He reported that apart from eating many good meals, he'd "done nothing but damn business, and making contacts with press and movie producers." He also wrote, affectionately and longingly: "I was very sad and missed you so much. You have been so sweet and good to me and *for* me, I don't know how to thank you, beautiful girl. . . . Certainly about the happiest and most wonderful times of my life were in Mexico and due entirely to your sweet and wonderful people, and to a sweet wonderful girl—hmm!! . . . Missing you too more than ever darling. If I haven't already told you, you are the loveliest and the best and the sweetest."[6] Cooper's sense of self-worth partly depended on being attractive to women—an important aspect of his success in films. His relationship with Lorraine showed that he wanted much more than a girl to show off in public or a purely sexual connection. For all his fame, he was lonely and insecure during his years abroad. As with Neal, he bound Lorraine to him with tender and affectionate letters.

III

The actor Robert Stack once called Cooper and said, "Let's go duck hunting," to which he replied: "I'm going to the south of France for young girl hunting." Though a good hunter of girls, he sometimes became their prey. At the bar of the Hôtel Majestic, during the Cannes Film Festival in May 1953 (two months after he'd won his second Oscar), Cooper met the Jacques Fath model and minor film actress Gisèle Pascal. Chanel wrote, with a tinge of bitterness, that "he had me at his beck and call as his interpreter, companion, guide, and when he left Mexico to go to a film festival in Cannes he 'engaged' Gisèle Pascal to pick up where I left off."

Born Gisèle Tallone in Cannes in about 1920, the daughter of a French mother and an Italian father, who was a florist, she was blond and blue-eyed, with "a funny little catch in her voice that turned her laughter into music."[7] Like Cooper, Gisèle was interested in cars, sports and animals. She was divorced, and since 1947 had lived on the French Riviera with Prince Rainier of Monaco. Rainier planned to marry her, despite his family's disapproval, and even had Monaco stamps designed with her portrait.

Instead of marrying Rainier, Gisèle ran off with Cooper. Questioned about their affair, Cooper was all innocence. On May 21 he wrote Lorraine, who'd already heard about them: "She's a nice gal, good company and I'm sure very much in love with the Prince fellow." He was even more disingenuous with a reporter from *Modern Screen*. When asked, "Didn't you know that Mlle. Pascal is almost engaged to the Prince of Monaco?" he replied: "Didn't know a thing about it. . . . Never even heard of the gent." When a journalist from *Paris Match* wouldn't let him get away with such an answer, he played a terribly discreet *père de famille*: "I'm not able to tell you anything. My wife and daughter are coming next week and they wouldn't at all like this kind of interview."[8]

Unwilling to give up his mistresses but still deeply attached to his family, Cooper—with sublime egoism—had it both ways while sustaining the possibility of a reconciliation with his wife. His affair with Gisèle was interrupted when the school year ended in California and Rocky and Maria arrived to accompany him on a three-month tour of Europe. "We were always interrupting his love-life," Maria said. "Our timing was exquisite." Asked what her father liked to do when traveling in Europe, she wittily replied: "You mean with or without his family?" At the end of their affair, Neal had written: "I heard myself asking if he was going back to Rocky, if he was seeing other women." In a similar way Gisèle wrote letters to Gary (Lorraine said) insisting that he "tell her who I was. Was it serious with me? Were we to be married? And on and on—in a jealous vein. He never answered her—but she persisted." Having renounced the throne, as it were, for Gary Cooper, who returned to Mexico and Lorraine in November, Gisèle married the French actor Raymond Pellegrin, had a daughter and resumed her film career. Cooper rather gallantly said their affair had ended "not because of Rainier, but because she fell in love with another actor. Can you beat that?"[9]

In May 1953, shortly before his wife and daughter arrived in Europe, United Artists arranged for Cooper to attend openings of *High Noon* in Brussels, Essen, Frankfurt and Düsseldorf, and to visit U.S. Army hospitals in Germany. Wearied but stimulated by the trip, he wrote Lorraine that "Brussels was very interesting historically and the Bürgermeister presented me with a nice gold movie award. They are sweet people but life looks very dull there, and it was a complete mobbing with those fans. . . . Went all through the Rhine—steel districts, cities—some of the most heavily bombed places, and the rebuilding and recovery of these people must be admired."

Cooper also became involved in European politics that summer. Germany had been divided, Berlin blockaded and a wall built between the east and west sectors of the city. Russia was now the enemy. Cooper was recruited as a spokesman by the American Federation of Labor, which had been anti-Communist since the 1920s and in 1933 had strongly opposed American recognition of the Soviet Union. In May 1953 Cooper told Lorraine that he was "now lining up a lot of stuff through the A.F. of L. head here to fight communism and promote work for our free unions in Europe. The commies are quite strong in France, including a lot of movie actors. It seems to be the element that is holding the country back." In June the three Coopers traveled to West Berlin with Irving Brown of the AFL to meet with fifty-five labor and literary leaders and campaign against Communism. Experiencing for the first time the effect of Cooper's influence abroad, Maria was surprised to see thousands of people turn up at Tempelhof Airport to greet her father. Separated from her parents in the crush, she was terrified of falling down and getting trampled. They attended a big political rally in the West Berlin stadium, one-third empty because East Germans were not allowed to cross into the western sector of the city.

A similar mob scene occurred two years later when Cooper visited Stockholm. Maria's nanny Elvira Borg wrote that the normally sedate "town stopped in its tracks to greet him, streetcars and buses out of schedule and everybody going crazy." The wild Swedes seemed to be reenacting the climactic scene in Nathanael West's Hollywood novel, *The Day of the Locust* (1939), when the deranged Homer provokes a riot by killing the child actor Adore. As women in the milling mob wonder how the chaos began, one tells the other: " 'The first thing I knew . . . there was a rush and I was in the middle.' 'Yeah. Somebody hollered, "Here comes Gary Cooper" and then wham!' "[10]

The rest of the summer was more tranquil. Cooper tried to "give the girls a good time here as I feel I've been a pretty bum father these last couple of years." They drove around the hills above the French Riviera in his new Mercedes and went skin diving at Cap d'Antibes. On the way from Provence to Biarritz the family stopped in a fancy restaurant in the wine country. As the waiters and wine steward deferentially bustled about, Cooper—with straight face and furrowed brow—asked: "Do you have any good Bordeaux?" Though Cooper liked good food, he wasn't fussy and "took the fare that came."

On June 26, 1953 the Coopers had an audience with Pope Pius XII in Rome. Cooper always wore the St. Christopher medal that Rocky had given him, and was buying a lot of rosaries and medals to give to friends when an official with a scepter announced the imminent arrival of the pope. As the room fell silent and Cooper nervously genuflected, the medals fell out of his hand and rolled noisily across the floor. Greatly embarrassed, he knelt down and desperately tried to pick them up. He sent one of the gifts to Lorraine, saying: "This little medal I held while the Pope blessed it. 'Each time you kiss it,' he said, 'is a thousand days of perfect health.' "

Recognized and followed by crowds wherever he went in Italy, Cooper remained calm and never got rattled. He did, however, take an obscure room rather than the doge's suite at the Hotel Daniele in Venice in order to have more privacy. When he and a friend went out for a stroll, an Italian at the back entrance of the hotel offered himself as guide and took the well-dressed men to a local brothel. When the whores heard who'd arrived, they all dropped their clients and ran downstairs—half naked— to see him. Cooper enjoyed his celebrity and sat around chatting with the girls. Rocky did not believe this visit was entirely innocent and became quite furious about this escapade. She tore "everything apart—bed, dresser, closet—and then locked herself in Maria's room.¹¹ Gary clearly enjoyed this episode and seemed to love the fire in Rocky's jealousy." On November 3 Cooper triumphantly concluded his European tour at the other end of the social scale. At the command performance of *High Noon* in the Odeon Theatre in Leicester Square he was presented to the newly crowned Queen Elizabeth.

IV

After greeting the queen, Cooper returned to Mexico to make *Garden of Evil* and *Vera Cruz* (both 1954). Unlike Bogart, who tried to escape from stereotyped criminal roles, Cooper cultivated the Western image that had recently been enhanced by *High Noon*. Six of the ten films he made between *Dallas* and *Vera Cruz* were Westerns. According to Jessamyn West, an assistant "reads scripts for Cooper and keeps track of the number of shots fired. She won't let Cooper appear in a picture in which he fires fewer shots than anyone else."

Garden of Evil was made in Acapulco, Cuernavaca and the rugged country around Uruapan, west of Mexico City, where "the cast was dragged through banana tree jungles, ancient deserted villages, and the black volcanic sands surrounding Paricutín Mountain." Because of regulations about foreigners working in Mexico, no one could leave and reenter the country before the shooting was over in early February 1954. Howard Hughes managed to secure permission for Susan Hayward to get away, but everyone else had to stay there for Christmas, when Rocky and Maria flew down for a visit. Cooper had a brief fling with a local girl during the shooting and earned a comfortable $300,000.

In *Garden of Evil*, directed by Cooper's old favorite Henry Hathaway, three adventurers—Cooper, Richard Widinark and Cameron Mitchell—are marooned in a Mexican village. Susan Hayward, the wife of a prospector who's been half buried in a distant gold mine, asks for their help and leads them through the spectacular coastal and mountain scenery of Apache territory. In the end the comradeship of the men is more important than their desire for girls or gold. The picture ends sententiously as Cooper (sounding like Walter Huston in *Sierra Madre*) declares: "If the earth was made of gold, I guess men would die for a handful of dirt"—and rides off into the sunset with Hayward.

Widmark, fond of Cooper, called him sophisticated, professional and a perfect work mate: "He was one of the *best* movie actors. . . . He was underrated, for like all good actors he made his work look effortless—as if he were doing nothing—you saw no wheels turning—what every artist in any field tries to achieve." Commenting on the film, François Truffaut explained how Cooper used his weariness and awkwardness to express character: "Gary Cooper seems exhausted and tired of an already long career. He does not take off his hat once in the course of the movie, and it is easy to guess why; the wrinkles covering his face do not alter the look in his eyes, which is always marked by an astonishing blueishness. He still makes use of a native clumsiness that became—thanks to Capra—a very effective acting style. Because of his looks, Cooper can kill with a face expressing complete goodness."[12]

Cooper made *Vera Cruz* (1954), another blustering Western, immediately afterward, in the spring of 1954. After seeing Burt Lancaster in *From Here to Eternity* (1953), Gable had advised Cooper to turn down the film and warned: "That young fella will wipe you off the map." Sure enough, Lancaster was a dynamo of energy. A reporter, visiting the location in the desert south of Cuernavaca, contrasted the styles of the two actors: "From sunup to sundown, Lancaster was a one-man tornado, directing camera angles, fussing over details of script, makeup, music, wardrobe. He rested little, ate less. While Burt stewed, Coop snoozed, visited ruins, chatted with anyone who'd talk." The contrast in their characters continued on screen as well as off, and Lancaster was forced to concede the superiority of Cooper's laidback style. As Lancaster practiced twirling his six-shooter, Cooper quietly remarked: "Gettin' pretty fancy, ain't you, Burt?" He then "executed a series of dazzling spins, tossed his weapon into the air, caught it, whirled it back into the holster and walked off the set." Lancaster said: "There I was, acting my ass off. I looked like an idiot and Cooper was absolutely marvelous."[13]

In the movie, which takes place in Mexico just after the American Civil War, there's constant conflict in both love and war between the two uneasy allies. Lancaster is an amoral mercenary, Cooper a fairminded and chivalrous ex-Confederate colonel. As the revolutionary followers of Benito Juárez battle the French-imposed puppet emperor Maximilian, the two soldiers of fortune keep changing sides, constantly stealing and losing the shipment of gold they are taking to Vera Cruz. But in a reversal of roles, the base Lancaster lusts after the fair French countess while the noble Cooper is drawn to the dark Mexican girl.

In the film Lancaster cynically comments on his rival's character by remarking: "Colonel Ben is a real Southern gentleman. He likes people, and you can't count on a man like that." Despite—or perhaps because of—the gnawing conflict between his secret sexual immorality and heroic public image, Cooper prided himself (Lancaster said) "on representing certain values. He was very decent, a man of high morality. He represented the hero—all American. He didn't want his character to be identified with the heavy. If his character appeared to be a man of evil, he would object, and we would have to rewrite the script."

Vera Cruz was a difficult job. Cooper needed time to learn his lines, and was disturbed because the script, according to the director, Robert Aldrich, was "totally improvised." It was "always finished about five minutes before we shot it, and we'd sit right down and work it out and then shoot it as we went along." Lorraine Chanel—who appeared in an evening gown at the emperor's ball, shot at Chapultepec Palace—said Cooper was still troubled by his old injury during the action scenes: "Gary was in pain when I was with him—something about his hip—fall from a horse—his double could not work that day and Gary decided to dare it—and he was sorry because the pain never subsided." The pain was compounded by an accident, a year after the dangerous explosion in *Blowing Wild*, when Burt Lancaster accidentally fired a rifle right next to him. The wadding from the blank shell pierced Cooper's shirt and burned his skin. Finally, according to Lorraine, the fastidious Cooper "couldn't bear to kiss" the twenty-six-year-old Spanish–Arab actress Sarita Montiel: "He came back from location and said he was almost suffering from having to touch her or kiss her. She never shampooed her hair. Her hairdresser told me that she just added olive oil on her hair daily."[14]

The absurd, action-filled picture has lots of low-angle shots and a few good touches. Slim Talbot does an amazing leap over a precipice, and Lancaster is comically crude at the imperial ball. In the final shootout the gentle Cooper gives the wild Lancaster a fair chance to draw ("That old soft spot, eh, Ben?"), kills him and then feels remorse. Truffaut, who had a weakness for inferior Westerns, anatomized the complicated plot and was impressed by "the repetition of themes: two encirclements by the Juaristas; two thefts of the same loot; Cooper saves Lancaster's life and Lancaster Cooper's." The more hard-nosed Bosley Crowther convincingly concluded: "The presence of both Gary Cooper and Burt Lancaster is a waste of potential manpower. Nothing that either is called to do in this big, noisy, badly photographed hodgepodge of outdoor melodrama is worthy of their skill."[15] Despite its obvious defects, *Vera Cruz*, produced by Lancaster's own company, cost $3 million and earned $9 million. If, according to one source, Cooper got a salary of $500,000 plus 10 percent of the gross, he made a cool $1.4 million.

V

In February 1954—after a three-year separation and one and a half years of unsettled existence in Samoa, Mexico and Europe—Cooper drove north with Lorraine. Weary of wandering and longing for a settled existence, he had a reconciliation with Rocky and moved back into their house. His love for Maria, who was sixteen by now, was a crucial factor. Lorraine recalled that when she'd offered to give Maria an embroidered Mexican dress, Cooper emphatically refused, and explained that Rocky still chose all Maria's clothes. This was never a problem for Maria, who shared her mother's tastes. Rocky also took Maria's best friend, the young actress Dolores Hart, in hand when they were visiting Paris. Insisting that Dolores could no longer look like a Marymount girl and mistakenly assuming she'd be reimbursed for her wardrobe by the studio, Rocky spent Dolores' last $800 on clothes and left her with no money. But like the malleable Maria, Dolores was glad to be guided by an experienced woman of the world. Rocky was also a dominant mother, and everyone agreed that Maria was immature for her age, overprotected and too dependent. Cooper undoubtedly felt that she needed a father's guidance.

The Coopers, anxious about giving the beautiful Maria a normal child-hood, never encouraged her to become an actress. It took her a while to discover her true interests. During her last year at Marymount High School she had an anxiety attack and got poor scores on her college apti-tude tests, which made her realize that she did not want a strictly academic education and was happy living at home. After a year at Santa Monica City College, she spent four happy years at the Chouniard Art Institute in Los Angeles. She became an artist and had exhibitions in Los Angeles and New York.

Cooper sometimes arranged dates for Maria with Jody McCrea and other handsome young actors who'd appeared in his films, Anthony Perkins and Tab Hunter. Jody turned up to take out Maria wearing a tuxedo and brown brogues. Appalled by his outfit, she got him a pair of her father's handmade alligator shoes. As they sat around chatting, Cooper stared at the elegant footwear and thought they looked familiar but was too polite to say anything. "Kinda naive about things," he didn't seem to know that Perkins was homosexual. Hunter accepted the pleasant duty, and was insightful about Maria's character and relations with her parents: "When you took Maria out on a date, she was very held back and suppressed. Maria was a very pretty girl. She needed to give vent. She was a late-bloomer. . . . Her mother wanted so much for her, only the best. I don't think she ever allowed Maria her freedom. Maria was always walking on egg shells, afraid to make a mistake. Coop went along with it. I'm sure he felt this was what one should do."[16]

Maria, a conventional girl who adored her father, said Cooper was as patient as Job. Kind, easygoing and with a great sense of humor, he nonetheless had his boiling point, and when he reached it, you'd stay out of his way. Cooper, who adored her, simply said: "I've never known her to do anything that wasn't right. . . . She is my life." He tried hard, through troubled times, to retain Maria's respect and admiration. According to Frances Dee, Maria told Cooper: "If you divorce mother, I'll never forgive you." Roberta Haynes believed that he went back to Rocky "because of his daughter. I don't think it was a happy decision for him. He was . . . not an outgoing man . . . not an aggressive man. . . . He began to look very careworn. I don't think people who get ulcers are terribly happy."[17]

Other close friends saw Cooper's return in more positive terms. Arlene Dahl, who noted that he'd come to Rocky's parties during his time with Neal, thought he came home because with Rocky he had everything:

wealth, style, elegance. Though Rocky was demanding, she was also indispensable. Dolores Hart thought he didn't want to break up the family, valued his old life and—in the end—wanted Rocky more than any other woman. Rocky, with self-effacing dignity, told Louella Parsons: "I think we have both learned a lesson. It was worth waiting to have him come back." Maria observed that the marriage was stronger when he returned and was sustained by abiding companionship, respect and love. As Hemingway wrote in *A Farewell to Arms*, "The world breaks every one and afterward many are strong at the broken places."[18]

Cooper had saved a great deal of money during his tax-free years abroad and decided to start the new phase of their marriage in a "dream" house. The rural atmosphere of their Brentwood neighborhood had changed when a big school and nursing home were built right next to them, and they accepted a good offer for the house from a nearby Catholic church. They also sold the ill-fated Aspen house. In July 1953, while Cooper was abroad, they began to build a lavish, six-thousand-square foot mansion on one and a half acres at 200 North Baroda Drive in Holmby Hills, between Beverly Hills and Bel Air. The modernistic house, completed in the spring of 1954, could have been designed by the architect in *The Fountainhead*. Built on one level, with a wooden roof towering above the entrance, it had lots of glass, redwood and huge Palos Verdes stone walls. "It was so advanced in outline," Cooper said, "that we sometimes wonder if we're in the year 2000." Enhanced by a sculpted garden, it had four bedrooms, a guest and double maids' quarters, an open floor plan and floor-to-ceiling windows. Cooper had a workroom where he cleaned his guns and kept his Indian artifacts and trophies (the FBI had confiscated the eagles he'd illegally shot in Sun Valley). The staff included a live-in cook and butler as well as a chauffeur-gardener—though Cooper liked to do some of the gardening himself.

When Dolores Hart first came to the house, she saw a man in old clothes kneeling on the ground with his back to her. She asked, "Are you the gardener?" and Cooper replied, "Yup, planting potatoes." On later visits he always jumped up to shake her hand and welcome her, and somehow managed to make Hollywood seem familial and normal. Tab Hunter, a frequent visitor to Baroda Drive when dating Maria, recalled that "the house was very chic and modern, with marble floors and Picasso paintings, and Rocky was so pulled together. You'd see Coop sitting there in a robe and slippers. He looked like he didn't belong in those luxurious surroundings."[19]

The new house confirmed their preeminent social position in Hollywood. Rocky, a close friend of the Henry Fords, provided the connection between the Los Angeles elite and millionaire society in New York, Southampton, London, Paris and the French Riviera. Society wanted celebrities, and many celebrities had the money to move in society. In 1931 at the Villa Madama Cooper had socialized with the royalty and nobility of Greece, Italy and England. He now found high society terribly keen to meet *him*. Such people amused him for short periods of time, and he was always relaxed and at ease with them.

Lorraine said that Cooper "was always mentioning 'high' places he had visited and would name-drop nobility, queen of England—the rich and the famous." But he was still a good old Montana boy and, as Kipling wrote in one of Cooper's favorite poems, could "talk with crowds and keep [his] virtue, / Or walk with Kings—nor lose the common touch." On one grand occasion in June 1959, Cooper joined the Churchills and a number of royals when Aristotle Onassis invited them to a supper party at the Hotel Dorchester to celebrate Maria Callas' opening night in *Medea*. Cooper told Hedda Hopper that he "knew King George—he was a very nice regular guy." He also went shooting quail and pheasant with the Duke of Rutland and the Duke of Windsor, who shared his taste for expensive clothes, and impressed the British with his superior marksmanship. At a dinner party with the Windsors in Paris in 1955, Cooper was more elegant than the duke. Famous for being stiff and dull, and for speaking German to people who didn't know the language, the duke angered Rocky ("even if they are royal . . .") by turning up late. He had cut himself shaving and appeared, exquisitely attired, with a piece of toilet paper stuck to his nose. Cooper enjoyed wealth and hobnobbing with the great, but he was usually the main celebrity and attraction. Like Scott Fitzgerald after meeting the Mountbattens and the Marchioness of Milford Haven, he realized the limitations of the rich and titled, and could say he was "very impressed, but not very, as I furnished most of the amusement myself."[20]

18

Love in the Afternoon

1955–1958

I

After Cooper returned to Rocky and moved into the house on Baroda Drive, the family resumed the pattern of summer holidays in Southampton and Europe, and he made two stodgy movies to pay for it all: *The Court-Martial of Billy Mitchell*, a ponderous courtroom drama, and *Friendly Persuasion*, a sanctimonious portrayal of Quakers during the Civil War. Straining under domestic bondage, he regressed to his old habits and had a scandalous affair. He collected modern art, hung out with celebrities and formed an unexpected acquaintance with Picasso. The seven movies since *High Noon*—from *Springfield Rifle* to *Friendly Persuasion*—had all been mediocre, but in the late 1950s he broke out of stereotyped roles and made seven good films in a row. He appeared as an aging rake in *Love in the Afternoon* and a failed politician in *Ten North Frederick*, and in both pictures played a middle-aged man having an affair with a much younger woman. In *Man of the West*, a complex and rather perverse Western, he played an old outlaw drawn back into his evil past.

The history of aviation ran parallel to the history of movies. Cooper's series of flight films—which began with *Wings*, *The Legion of the Condemned*, *Lilac Time* and *Today We Live*—culminated in *The Court-Martial of Billy Mitchell*. The real Billy Mitchell (1879–1936), a brilliant army pilot in World War I, had been rapidly promoted to brigadier general. After the war he'd fought for the creation of an air force. An outspoken critic of the dominant role of the navy, he believed it had a disproportionate share of military resources and that air power would be far more important in future wars. As director of military aviation, he conducted controversial bombing tests in 1921. Branded as a trouble-maker, he was relieved of his post in 1925, reduced to colonel and exiled to a base in Texas. His provocative attacks on the "incompetence and criminal negligence" of the War and Navy departments led to his court-martial in October–December 1925. He used the trial to proclaim his views, emphasizing the importance of submarines in future wars and predicting air attacks like the one that took place on Pearl Harbor. In his final plea the military prosecutor, Major Adam Guillion, eloquently asked for "the dismissal of the accused for the sake of the Army whose disci-pline he has endangered and whose fair name he has attempted to discredit . . . for the sake of those young officers of the Army Air Force whose ideals he has shadowed and whose loyalty he has corrupted. . . . Finally, we ask it in the name of the American people whose fears he has played upon, whose hysteria he has fomented." Found guilty and sentenced to a five-year suspension, Mitchell resigned from the army in February 1926. He continued to propagate his farsighted ideas, which led to the foundation of the air force after World War II and the establish-ment of the Department of Defense in 1947.

Like *Task Force*, which had also argued the importance of aviation and specifically referred to Mitchell, *The Court-Martial of Billy Mitchell* (1955), with Lieutenant General "Hap" Arnold as consultant, was based on massive research. As with the film biography of Lou Gehrig, the researcher warned the producer–screenwriter, Milton Sperling, that altering the facts of the life would spoil the natural impact of the story. The Billy Mitchell script will be difficult to produce, he said, "because you are dealing with factual events and actual people, and also because you have changed those events somewhat and fictionalized the charac-ters. . . . [The story] is best told when the closest possible adherence to facts is maintained. . . . The actual events of Mitchell's life were so dramatic, that it would be difficult indeed to improve on the drama through fictionalization. . . . Although the overall story holds pretty true to the events and meaning of Mitchell's life—the individual elements have been changed so much that the cash customers will recognize this fact and be disappointed."[1]

Otto Preminger, the Viennese-born director, had made several unusual and important films: *Laura, The Moon is Blue, Carmen Jones* and *The Man with the Golden Arm*. He had played the camp commandant in *Stalag 17*, and in 1960 would help break the Hollywood blacklist by hiring Dalton Trumbo to write *Exodus* under his own name. One screen-writer called Preminger "a Nazi on the set and a kind, generous, cultivated man in private life." Like Fritz Lang in *Cloak and Dagger*, the autocratic Preminger clashed with the producer. And like Sam Wood in *Saratoga Trunk*, Milton Sperling exasperated everyone and wasted a lot of money by constantly changing his mind. "Whenever he suggested something," Preminger said, "and we liked it, and incorporated it into the script, he came back the next day and changed it again. This went on until neither [the writer] Ben Hecht nor I had the patience to go through with it. He was the only man I ever saw Gary Cooper get angry at." Preminger also praised Cooper's technique, and contrasted the naive screen image with the sophisticated real man: "The actor Cooper created the film star. The slow, hesitant speech and movement, the downward look, the so-called shit-kicking were invented by him in order to face the camera with a semblance of the complete reality that the medium demands."[2]

Rod Steiger plays the prosecutor, and his cross-examination, punctuated by savage ridicule and irony, is the most powerful part of the movie. Though the vicious lawyer is meant to contrast with the high-minded Mitchell, Cooper's silent presence is quite swamped by Steiger's bravura performance. Cooper plays Mitchell as a worthy but dull hero, a *Sergeant York* or Dr. Wassell, rather than a bitter, caustic and prophetic Howard Roark. As in *Mr. Deeds*, he remains quiet through most of the trial to make his final speech more dramatic. But we know what he'll say (since he's already said it in the course of the film) and that he'll inevitably be found guilty. Though Mitchell has faith in himself and feels justified in speaking out against army policy, he cannot, as Roark does in *The Fountainhead*, persuade the tribunal that he is right. The movie is therefore flat and predictable.

Preminger had noted the contrast between Cooper's on and off screen character, which soon became notorious. Cooper employed a public relations firm, which cost $2,000 a month at the beginning of the decade and rose to $3,000 at the end, to minimize the startling difference between his heroic film roles and his philandering private life. He had always charmed the press, which respected him and didn't pry into his personal affairs. Public relations men like John Springer in New York and Warren Cowan in Los Angeles had fended off all the journalists who wanted to interview him about Pat Neal. They also tried to enhance his image with positive publicity. When one of his new films came out, they would meet with the staff of the studio, go over the ads and plan the publicity campaign. If an event was really important, Cooper would participate. They also arranged major articles in *Life* and *Look*, appearances on the television shows of Edgar Bergen and Ed Sullivan, and the testimonial dinner at the Friars Club in 1961. Cooper desperately needed his PR men for damage control during his scandalous affair with Anita Ekberg.

Since his marriage in 1933 Cooper had slept with Bergman, Neal, Aldon, Kelly, Chanel and Pascal—without counting others in between as well as the anonymous local and "luscious" women during the shooting of *The Plainsman*, *Blowing Wild* and *Garden of Evil*. His mistresses got younger—and less classy—as he grew older. It was a long way from Bergman (his first Swede), who was born in 1915, to Ekberg, born in 1931 and only six years older than Maria. The five-foot, seven-inch Swedish bombshell had a thirty-nine-inch bust and (five years before she became famous in *La Dolce Vita*) satisfied all his fantasies about big breasts. He rapturously told Virgil Sherrill that Ekberg was so good-looking that she could give French models like Pascal a handicap.

In January 1956 *Confidential* magazine quoted the randy and rejuvenated Cooper saying: "I'm a 52-year-old lover and I'm just getting started." He had stolen Ekberg away from Frank Sinatra just as he had snatched Pascal from Prince Rainier, and the competition no doubt intensified the pleasure. In August 1955 the merciless magazine had spotted Cooper in a Los Angeles nightclub, and described him "slowly, scientifically, and with obvious relish, sticking toothpicks—one after another—down the front of Anita's low-necked evening gown. . . . In a matter of minutes, the top of her dress was edged with a miniature but neat picket fence." Later on reporters followed him with a stopwatch as he picked her up at her apartment on Beverly Glen, bought groceries and took her to a friend's house on Pacific Coast Highway. The lights went on, then off, and they spent two nights in the love nest. Though annoyed that Anita had asked him for a fur piece on their first date, he eventually came across with a mink coat and a gold bracelet. Furious, after all they'd been through, that he'd resumed his philandering and become involved in such a humiliating scandal, Rocky exploded with rage and asked: "How could you do such a thing?" Cooper tried to defuse her with a shamefaced one-liner: "It seemed like a good idea at the time."[3]

II

An early title for *Friendly Persuasion* (1956), *Mr. Birdwell Goes to Battle*, echoed *Mr. Deeds Goes to Town* and foreshadowed Cooper's role as a stressed-out idealist. Robert Wilson had written the original screenplay for Frank Capra in 1946, and William Wyler revived the project a decade later. Other writers had revised the script, but the Writers Guild of America, after arbitration, gave sole credit to Wilson. He had won an Oscar for *A Place in the Sun* (1951) and, after refusing to answer questions when summoned by HUAC that year, had been blacklisted. Though Wilson had finished the screenplay long before the blacklist existed, the film producers' association ruled that no blacklisted author could receive screen credit. His name was excised and (most unusually) no one got credit for the screenplay. When Wilson was nominated for an Academy Award, he was again declared ineligible under the academy's bylaws. He subsequently filed a $250,000 lawsuit against Allied Artists and Wyler for conspiring to deny him credit on political grounds, and the suit was eventually settled out of court. While still blacklisted, he was the uncredited co-author of two extremely successful films: *The Bridge on the River Kwai* (with Carl Foreman) and *Lawrence of Arabia*.

Wyler, who had directed Cooper in *The Westerner* (1940), had great difficulty casting the leading lady. He desperately wanted Katharine Hepburn—"no one else would do"—and also considered Jane Russell (not exactly Quaker material); Margaret Sullavan, his former wife; Ingrid Bergman, still risky because of scandal; Maureen O'Hara, too fiery; Mary Martin, too hard to photograph; Vivien Leigh, too English; and Eva Marie Saint, too young, before settling on Dorothy McGuire, a compromise candidate he never really liked.

Cooper, the ideal American, was an obvious choice to play the Quaker paterfamilias. Jessamyn West, who wrote the stories that formed the basis of the movie and was called in to revise the script, was as eager to get him as Ayn Rand had been. "If Gary Cooper had been born a hundred years ago," she said, "a Quaker Hoosier, he would have looked like Jess Birdwell." But Cooper, like Hepburn, had doubts about the part. Though now fifty-five, he didn't want to be an unromantic father with a self-righteous wife and grown children ("I ain't ever played a pappy yet and I ain't aiming to start now"). Well aware of the conflict between the screen persona and the real man, he didn't know if he could play a devout believer. To prepare him for the part and convince him to accept it, West took him to a Quaker meeting so he could worship among the plain people. The studio, with admirable restraint, agreed to let him pray without benefit of camera. Cooper seemed to enjoy the contemplative silence and said: "I liked going to that meeting. . . . They were still and they were quiet. I liked being with them."

After he'd accepted the role of Birdwell, Cooper's doubts remained. West emphasized that Birdwell's difficult decision to stay out of the war, as opposed to his son's decision to fight in it, was a test of individual conscience. Cooper insisted that his fans expected him to do something. After considerable discussion Wyler agreed that Cooper had to be seen as a man of action, and invented a scene in which Cooper (fighting the Civil War for about the seventh time in his career) hitches his horse to a captured Confederate cannon and uses it to destroy the enemy artillery. Wyler had to confess to West that he'd betrayed her conception of Birdwell's character. "And Jess wins the war?" she incredulously asked. Though he assured her that Cooper "doesn't fire a shot," she was devastated. She didn't say anything, afraid she might burst into tears.

Slim Talbot, playing many of the action scenes for Cooper, had spent his whole adult life profitably but resentfully imitating him. West understood the frustrations and disappointments of Slim's professional career. "Cooper's double, Slim, is here," she wrote, "a sad man, more granite-faced than Cooper. Any actor is, in a way, a shadow. He is the image, when he is acting, of someone else. How would it be to have been for twenty-five years, as Slim has, the shadow of a shadow? Cooper spent a large part of his life being some one non-Coop; and Slim spends his life being a non-Slim being a non-Coop."⁴

Friendly Persuasion was filmed mainly at the two-hundred-acre Rowland Lee estate, an hour's drive from Hollywood, in the San Fernando Valley. The place had been transformed—complete with barn, cow shed and cornfields—into an 1862 Indiana farm. The sharp, deep focus of the camera tried to capture the quality of old Dutch masters, and (the cinematographer wrote) "the stylized lighting employed permitted the fine woodwork of the interiors to take on a rich, warm coloring. At the same time, it brought into sharp detail the textures of the woodwork, and of the props and costumes, all of which were so essential in pointing up the atmosphere and mood of the time."

But creating a serene rural atmosphere was not without problems. The generator lights failed, noisy planes flew overhead and McGuire had somehow to walk on straw without making a crackling noise. Animals proved recalcitrant: the horse in the barn missed its cue and failed to look up when Cooper entered, and Richard Eyer, playing Cooper's ten-year-old son, had great difficulty with Samantha, an unpleasant goose that had two stand-ins. Eyer rehearsed for two weeks to get used to them while the handlers tried to teach the geese to "bite his butt" on command. He had leather pads sewn inside his trousers, held a lettuce leaf between his legs when he bent over and got a few nasty pinches in a pointless exercise that didn't work. Finally, the leading goose was attached to a wire pulley which gave it electric shocks. When it got a bit of voltage, it took off on schedule and bit the plucky Eyer as he was drawing water from the well.

Eyer got along much better with Cooper, who'd play around with him (as he'd done with Dickie Moore on *Sergeant York*), lift him up, wrestle a bit and do a ski jump with his finger on Eyer's turned-up nose. Eyer was also amused by Wyler's comical facial expressions as he peered behind the camera. He noticed that there was considerable tension on the set because the picture took so long to complete and was so expensive to make. The producer, Walter Mirisch, said it was impossible to control Wyler, who shot a great deal of extravagant coverage. Though Wyler commiserated with Mirisch about the endless delays, he went "outrageously, 100% over budget."[5] Anthony Perkins, who played the older son, Josh, was fascinated by Cooper's eyes and imitated his looselimbed walk. Eager to learn as much as he could, he'd ask: "Coop, tell us about when you were a young actor." Still sensitive about playing a "pappy," Cooper replied with unusual rudeness: "Cut all this youth shit out."

No one, however, can persuade me to be friendly to this film. The squeaky-clean, picture-postcard, brightly Technicolored farm, which looks like a stockbroker's residence in a prosperous suburb, conveys a nostalgic and sentimental view of rural life. Like *Sergeant York*, which also has corny characters, a thin plot and no real action till the end, *Friendly Persuasion* is filled with pinafores and shawls, bonnets and Bibles, horses and buggies, ceremonies and prayers. It too preaches family values and seemly behavior. A race to the church, an unruly goose, a wholesome teenage courtship and a quarrel about a new organ are not nearly enough to sustain one's interest till Cooper finally rescues the wounded Perkins from war, refuses to harm a Rebel soldier and then returns to his idyllic life. The Quaker atmosphere is mainly conveyed by awkward, sententious and mock-humorous second-person dialogue. As the rigidly orthodox McGuire tells Cooper: "If thee talked as much to the

Almighty as thee dost to thy horse, thee'd have a much better understanding." Stuck with a limited part, Cooper, though rather wooden,
manages to convey a kind of gentle power. He always plays a virtuous
character in movies, but he's unbearably good in this one and has no
witty dialogue or sexual aura to carry him beyond mere goodness.

Friendly Persuasion has the same pacificist theme as *Sergeant York* and
High Noon (in which Grace Kelly is a non-thee-and-thouing Quaker),
and all three films concern the conflict between religious beliefs and civic
duty. But the last movie is tedious as well as hypocritical. McGuire is the
strictest member of the family, Cooper the next and Perkins the least. But
all three bend, then break the traditional rules. As Robert Hatch persuasively wrote in the *Nation*, the Birdwells "race horses on Sunday, admire
themselves in mirrors, secrete a parlor organ in the attic, dance at county
fairs, kiss soldiers in corners, and take up arms to repel the invaders.
They are steadfast only to their conviction about the second person
singular."[6]

The anodyne, "heartwarming" movie did very well. In 1957, in a state
of temporary insanity, the judges at the Cannes Film Festival awarded the
Palme d'Or to *Friendly Persuasion* instead of to Ingmar Bergman's *The
Seventh Seal*. It cost $3 million to make and had earned $8 million by
1960. In May 1988 President Ronald Reagan took a tape of the picture
to Moscow and during a state dinner presented it as a personal gift to the
Soviet premier Mikhail Gorbachev.

III

In *Friendly Persuasion* Cooper played the character he was supposed to
be; in *Love in the Afternoon* (1957), one of his most autobiographical
films, he revealed many aspects of his own character. Wilder originally
wanted Cary Grant or Yul Brynner to play a Continental charmer based
on the wealthy playboy Aly Khan. But he was glad to get Cooper to play
Frank Flannagan, whose character instead was based on Howard Hughes.
The real Cooper was wealthy, sophisticated and cosmopolitan; he knew
all about grand hotels, fine cuisine, vintage wine and pretty women. His
youthful-looking twenty-eight-year-old co-star, Audrey Hepburn, was
about the same age as Grace Kelly and Mari Aldon, and two years older
than Anita Ekberg. Wilder thought the virtuous image of *High Noon*
hovered above Cooper, whom Hepburn's Ariane compares to "a cowboy

or Abraham Lincoln." (Her father, played by Maurice Chevalier, slyly adds that Lincoln was "shot in the middle of a performance.") Fearing that the public wouldn't accept Cooper as the debonair but debauched seducer of an innocent young woman, and wanting to emphasize his romantic qualities, Wilder tried to disguise Cooper's age with gauzy filters and shadowy lighting, a strong contrast to the extreme close-ups that had accentuated his bruised and battered look in *High Noon*.

In *Love in the Afternoon* Wilder returns to the same theme and the same actress as in *Sabrina* (1954). In *Sabrina* the gruff, unfeeling Wall Street businessman (Bogart) gradually falls in love with the charming Hepburn and carries her off to Paris; in the later film the young lady wins the callous middle-aged seducer and runs off with him to Cannes. In both films American tycoons become more warmhearted and sympathetic through the love of a French-bred woman. In both the innocent Hepburn sets out fearlessly to catch her man.

A music student who lives with her father, a private detective, Ariane falls in love with Flannagan's photograph, pores over his file and saves him from being murdered by a jealous husband. Though familiar with his romantic routine, which includes employing a quartet of Gypsy musicians, she seeks sexual tuition at the hands of a master and confesses: "I'm very susceptible, you know." Cooper first takes her gloves, then her fur coat, and the musicians, slipping tactfully out of his suite, signal the start of the seductive sex for which she repeatedly returns. (Before shooting the film, Wilder played the record of "Fascination" for Walter Mirisch and told him: "Wait till you see what I'm going to do with this!") As Hepburn becomes more worldly and self-possessed, she repeats Cooper's own expressions—"relaxez-vous," "domestic [i.e., French] champagne"—in an ironic fashion. By cleverly keeping her life outside the hotel room completely private, Ariane arouses Flannagan's interest. A more complex character than Sabrina, she's both innocent and knowing, beguiled and beguiling, willing to risk all for the sake of experience.

Cooper's first film made in Europe was shot in Paris in the Studios de Boulogne. "We could have made the picture just as well in Hollywood," Wilder remarked. "But why not be in Paris?" After fog, mosquitoes and airplane noise had interfered with the outdoor shots of the picnic-on-the-lake scene, made at the Château de Vitry outside Paris, and had pushed the cost up to $2.1 million, Cooper said: "I never knew a seducer's work could be so hard." Wilder's biographer wrote that the designer, Alexandre Trauner, "had built the most lavish sets ever on a French sound-stage, including a full-scale replica of the second floor of the Ritz Hotel with corridors and working elevators, the entire first floor of the Paris Conservatoire, and a luxury suite. As the cello-playing music student, Audrey Hepburn was required to learn the finger-movements for the cello part of Haydn's Eighty-eighth Symphony. One of the most spectacular scenes took place in the Opéra, where Wilder had 960 extras in evening gowns and white tie and tails fill the orchestra and boxes for a gala performance of *Tristan and Isolde*."[7] The film has beautiful couture clothes and elaborate sets, yet succeeds most of all because it focuses on three well-developed and strongly motivated characters. They are all bound together by the recurrent "Fascination" theme, an intensely romantic melody that is variously comic, seductive, nostalgic and poignant.

Just as *High Noon* had echoed *The Virginian*, so the witty and beautifully constructed *Love in the Afternoon* recalled the French ambience and sophisticated romantic comedy of Lubitsch's *Bluebeard's Eighth Wife*, also written by Wilder. The later film is full of subtle personal allusions. Hepburn, who has no sexual past, plays the cello in the evening and is free only in the afternoon. Cooper, who has a lurid past, rather desperately courts women around the clock. The title, an ironic echo of Hemingway's *Death in the Afternoon* (1934), his meditation on the art of bullfighting and of writing, suggests the art of seduction. The film also exploits other Hemingway connections. Hemingway had "liberated" the Hôtel Ritz after the German occupation of Paris and set up his headquarters in the bar; Cooper now makes that luxurious hotel his love nest. Hemingway had aroused Cooper's interest in bullfighting; Hepburn gives an ecstatic description of the gore wounds of her (imaginary) bullfighter boyfriend in Spain. Hemingway had described his ultimately tragic love affair with Adriana Ivancich in his Venetian novel, *Across the River and into the Trees* (1950); in the film Cooper's cast-off Venetian mistress has tried to kill herself.

Under Wilder's direction Cooper gives his famous two-fingered salute from *Morocco* when he first says good-night to Hepburn, and during their picnic—Wilder's *Déjeuner sur l'herbe*—again alludes to *Morocco* by wearing a carnation behind his ear. The flower, like the "Fascination" music, suggests an important sexual motif in the film. Hepburn takes it home and puts it in the refrigerator, and when Chevalier finds it, he knows she's become romantically involved. The picture, in fact, gives a vivid sense of how Cooper seduced his ladies—with flowers and gifts, champagne and room service (to the sound of muffled drums), music and dancing (he says, "I'm not much of a talker," and "finds the gypsies very helpful"). Wilder's wife Audrey appears as Cooper's companion at the opera. And, in a bold allusion to the mistresses of both Cooper and Wilder (who made love in the afternoon and then went back to their wives), Cooper, departing for New York, orders flowers for "Miss Chanel and Miss O'Neil."

Most delightful of all (and Cooper was a good sport about this), he's spied on by Hepburn's father (wearing a bowler hat and carrying a furled umbrella to make him a more English detective), who establishes a precise timetable of his love life and secretly takes photographs—exactly as *Confidential* magazine had done to Cooper shortly before the movie was made. (Hepburn spies on Cooper at the opera just as Chevalier does in the Place Vendôme.) The scandalous episode of "the twin sisters in Stockholm," which Hepburn discovers in her father's file on Cooper, is an unmistakable allusion to Ekberg's monumental breasts. To drive this point home, Wilder includes a shot of Cooper as the "Man of the Year"— not on the cover of *Time* but of *Confidential*.

As Cooper leaves the Ritz for the last time, Hepburn gives a satiric account of the emotional development of Americans (an elaboration of the shop sign, "American understood," in Lubitsch's film). This speech, expressing a European perspective, seems to distance her from Cooper and finalize their farewell: "They're very odd people. When they're young they have their teeth straightened, their tonsils taken out, and gallons of vitamins pumped into them. Something happens to their insides. They become immunized, mechanized, air-conditioned and hydromatic."

Chevalier, after revealing himself to Cooper and asking him not to treat Hepburn in his customarily heartless way (he didn't object when a jealous husband threatened to kill Cooper), follows them to the railroad station. At the last moment the once-villainous seducer scoops Hepburn onto the moving train like a cowboy pulling a girl onto his horse and does the decent thing by marrying her. Chevalier, who adores Hepburn as much as Cooper adored Maria, reluctantly gives her up—though there's no knowing whether she will be able to reform the libertine.

Like other directors before him, Wilder said he'd originally underesti-mated Cooper's acting: "When I shot a scene with Gary Cooper, it didn't look like anything. But when you saw it on the screen in the rushes, there was an added something going on—some kind of love affair between the performer and the celluloid." Well pleased with a role in which he could play his real self, Cooper commented: "Naturally, the nearer the character you play comes to the character you are, the more authenticity you give it. You are not acting so much as being. The result is realism."[8]

For all its wit and brilliance (Cooper sliding the drinks' cart across the floor to the Gypsies, Chevalier discovering the wilted carnation in the refrigerator and then connecting Hepburn to Cooper through the "Fascination" theme) *Love in the Afternoon* was not a commercial success in the Eisenhower fifties—a square decade. Despite Wilder's chiaroscuro photography, audiences couldn't accept the age difference between Cooper and Hepburn and were repelled by what seemed to be a dirty old man corrupting a virginal woman. Even Cooper, at his best in romantic comedy, was forced to concede: "That was a mistake. Here was an old Joe like me being amorous with a young girl like Audrey Hepburn." But, he explained, he was weary of virtuous parts like the father in *Friendly Persuasion*. In *Love in the Afternoon*, as in all his late films, he was willing to test himself and risk new roles: "Yes, I guess I offend against the Code. First time I've ever done that. I'm quite a guy with women in this film— married ones, too—and I don't come to a sticky finish. How do I square that with my principles? I don't. I'm taking a chance. There comes a time when you gotta do that. I've been virtuous one hell of a long time. Maybe it won't look too wrong because it happens in Paris."[9]

After completing *Love in the Afternoon* in 1956, Cooper met Pablo Picasso, through the American photographer David Douglas Duncan, on the French Riviera. They impressed each other and got "pretty chummy"—Hemingway was a mutual friend—and the artist invited the Coopers to visit him again at La Californie, his vast villa above Cannes. The friendship was not as odd as it seemed. Cooper had hoped to be an artist and, with Rocky's guidance, had built up an impressive collection of modern paintings. They owned works by French masters—Renoir, Gauguin, Bormard and Vuillard—as well as by American artists: George Bellows, Georgia O'Keeffe, Walt Kuhn, Max Weber, Fairfield Porter and Paton Miller. They also acquired Picasso's painting of an artist's studio (an allusion to Velázquez's *Las Meninas*), two of his bullfight scenes painted on ceramic plates, and two photographs of Picasso and the Coopers with his colored decorations on the frames.

Picasso had learned a bit of English from Gertrude Stein, Cooper dredged up some Spanish, and Rocky and Maria interpreted in schoolgirl French. Advised by Duncan about Picasso's taste for exotic gifts, Cooper

brought him the ten-gallon Stetson he'd worn in *Saratoga Trunk* and a
Colt .45 pistol complete with bullets. The artist, who had known
cowboys in the Camargue, was interested in Buffalo Bill and the Wild
West and had once signed a letter to Braque, "your pard, Picasso." So he
welcomed with boyish enthusiasm the gifts of gun and hat from the cinematic embodiment of the American cowboy. Picasso livened things up by
firing shots at the palm trees in his garden. As the pigeons took off from
the balcony, Duncan said, Picasso imitated Gary by standing "flint-eyed
and blowing smoke from the barrel. Cooper could be heard muttering,
'It's a heck of a lot easier in the movies!' "

Picasso invited Cooper to try on the costumes in his studio while he
hung a bull's tail under his Indian headdress. Duncan took photos of
Cooper wearing Picasso's black cape and Cordoba hat, and of Picasso in
Cooper's white Stetson; of Cooper showing Picasso the revolver and
watching him shoot, and presenting the artist's wife with a box of fancy
Viennese chocolates. Picasso told Cooper, "I like Maria's work, and I
understand it," to which he frankly replied: "I like your work, but I *don't*
understand it."[10]

IV

Ten North Frederick (1958), another film with some poignant parallels to
Cooper's own life and character, was an American version of *Love in the
Afternoon*. In both films he falls in love with a young woman (Suzy
Parker, the model turned actress, was four years younger than Hepburn)
and moves from stiff dignity to more spontaneous behavior. The earlier
picture reflected Cooper's relations with his mistresses; the later one
attracted him because it was astonishingly close to his own family life. Off
screen, Parker was a close friend of Cooper's seventy-year-old father-in-
law, Paul Shields, and may even have had an affair with him. Just as
Cooper had said, "the nearer the character you play comes to the character you are, the more authenticity you give it," so, when the
screenwriter-director Philip Dunne asked him why he wanted to play the
part of Joe Chapin, a promising politician whose career is destroyed by
scandal, he spoke metaphorically and explained "it was because at last he
had a chance to wear his own clothes in a picture" (the same was true, of
course, for *Love in the Afternoon*). Dunne added, more incisively: "I
think that he really was saying that in Joe Chapin, a gentleman to his

fingertips, he had found a part completely consonant with his own character in private life." The quintessential westerner, Cooper was also perfect in the role of an upper-class easterner.

After Dunne had quarreled with the head of production at 20th Century-Fox, Buddy Adler, who felt his authority was being challenged, the budget was ruthlessly slashed: "Color was out; a projected location trip to [John] O'Hara's Pennsylvania was cut out; we were forced to use warmed-over sets from other pictures. . . . Even a five-mile location trip to a Santa Monica amusement park was cut out, in order to save a total of, at most, two thousand dollars." The lack of glamour and recycled sets were a devastating blow to a film that portrayed the lives of wealthy people in luxurious surroundings. The producer thought that if the studio "had let us spend another two hundred thousand, we'd have increased their profit by ten million."

Spencer Tracy had originally agreed to play Cooper's role, but refused to act with the inexperienced Suzy Parker. When Cooper saw her screen test, he kindly said: "Well, she's prettier than my horse." Parker had a terrible time with her part, and Cooper, in order to help her, agreed to a grueling series of rehearsals. She remembered that they worked intensely from early in the morning, and when their stomachs started to growl and the microphones picked up the noises, they had to stop for lunch. Ray Stricklyn, who played Cooper's son, wrote that Cooper's generosity paid off. *"Ten North Frederick* was Suzy Parker's best film performance. And I'd say a lot of that was due to Cooper's patience and kindness toward her during filming. They'd spend hours on getting a scene right, shooting it over and over, and not once did he seem to be upset or addled by the delays." Dunne, a kind and overly tolerant man, complicated matters by allowing the drama coach of Diane Varsi (who played Cooper's daughter) to look through the camera, then huddle with her and whisper advice.

Stricklyn, like Anthony Perkins and other young actors, observed Cooper carefully and tried to learn as much as possible from the apparently effortless old pro:

I had only about three scenes with Cooper, but I always hung around and watched him working in other scenes. And when I did my big emotional scene on the staircase when I'm telling off Geraldine Fitzgerald—*he* was watching me. When I finished I was stunned to see Gary leading the crew in applauding my efforts. The next day I was rewarded with my own set chair—with my name on it. A big moment for a young actor. . . .

Cooper was an actor of depth and great subtlety—so subtle, in fact, that in watching him work he seemed to be doing almost nothing. Yet what emerged on film was often magic. . . . One of my final lines in the film seems to be very right to describe Gary Cooper: "He was a gentleman in a world that no longer respects gentlemen."

Ten North Frederick, based on the novel by John O'Hara, opens in April 1945 at Joe Chapin's funeral, where his widow feigns grief, and then flashes back to 1940. At his birthday party and still in the prime of life, he dances with his daughter and smiles when reminded that he's fifty. His decline begins when his friends bribe a political boss to nominate him for lieutenant governor. Meanwhile, his "favorite, special darling, lovely daughter" falls for a lowly Italian trumpeter, gets pregnant and secretly marries him. Under pressure from his ambitious wife, Chapin bribes his unwelcome son-in-law to leave his daughter and then warns him to "get out of here before I kill you." Fearing scandal, Chapin withdraws from the political race. Alienated from both his son and daughter, he has nothing left now but his unhappy marriage. In a powerful scene, his bitchy wife (Geraldine Fitzgerald) admits she's had affairs and bitterly declares that she's wasted her life with him. Chapin begins to drink heavily and confesses that (like Cooper) he "frequently hurts people without meaning to."

In a desperate move to escape from his misery, Chapin begins a secret affair with his daughter's beautiful friend (Suzy Parker). When they are out on a date and he's mistaken for her father, he realizes that their age difference is too great and breaks it off. Later his daughter discovers the affair, and tells the dying Chapin that her friend still loves him. After the funeral his son denounces the phony, self-serving political allies and the scheming wife who have made his life wretched. Parker is too stiff to make their love affair completely convincing, but Cooper persuasively plays a tormented character whose integrity—a key word in many of his films—is under assault. He seems to be acting out his personal history. Though Fitzgerald is a much more negative character than Rocky, the renunciation of Parker is like Cooper's break with Neal, and his relations with Varsi—who looks like Maria and was exactly the same age—are very close to those with his beloved daughter. In the film Varsi discovers his affair and is pleased that he'd finally got some joy out of life. But in *Ten*

North Frederick, as in real life, Cooper renounces his young lover, is reconciled with his family, and returns to his wife and daughter. Unlike Flannagan in *Love in the Afternoon*, a middle-aged man who finds a young woman and a new life, Chapin suffers the loss of family, political ambition and the hope of a better life through rejuvenating love. Cooper brings great conviction and controlled anguish to his performance, which John O'Hara called sensitive, understanding and true.[10] Cooper conveys, with sorrow and dignity, the sense of despair, waning powers and premature old age, because he too, I think, had experienced some loss of confidence and hope for the future when he gave up Patricia Neal.

Love in the Afternoon and *Ten North Frederick* were linked to the themes of young love and reconciliation in *Return to Paradise*. *Man of the West* (1958), Cooper's most pathological Western, was very different. It shows the plight of helpless captives and portrays the themes of impotent rage, murderous impulses and sexual humiliation, of sadism, rape—and redemption. The cast and crew of the movie were snowed in as soon as they arrived in the Sierra Nevada. As they sat in their log cabins—talking, drinking and watching the fire while waiting for the storm to pass—the director, Anthony Mann, had ample opportunity to observe his star. Like Truffaut and Anthony Perkins, Mann was fascinated by Cooper's strangely more than blue eyes: "It's all in the eyes. The heroes, all the stars that the public loves, have very light blue eyes or green eyes. . . . The eyes reflect the inner flame that animates the heroes. The guys with dark eyes play supporting roles or become character actors."

Cooper rides into the frame behind the movie titles, draws on his cigarette and then canters off into the distance. In the opening scene he backs away and seems nervous as the train steams in. A reformed criminal who's now a trusted family man, he's traveling to Fort Worth to hire a schoolteacher for his town. When the train is robbed in a remote spot, he loses the money he's carrying to pay the teacher and is left behind on the tracks with a girl (Julie London). He leads her to his old home, a farm now held by his uncle (Lee J. Cobb) and the men who robbed the train, and pretends to join his former gang in order to protect "his woman." While holding a knife to Cooper's throat, the gang force the girl to strip but don't cause further harm. When she asks, "How could you have been with them? You're not like them at all," he tersely responds: "I was." Cobb overacts in his Lear-like role and makes theatrical speeches instead of actually talking to his men. He'd taught Cooper "killing and stealing," and Cooper had to decide to become either a human being or a rat like the rest of them.

Having regenerated himself in the past, Cooper must now do so once again. He beats one of the gang in a brutal fight and strips him, as the villain had stripped the woman, but can't bring himself to kill him. The grateful Julie London falls in love with him, but Cooper, with no gun till the very end, wants to survive, get back the money and return to his family. After an aborted bank robbery, the gang comes after him. During the gunfight they turn him back into a murderer. "I want to kill all the Tobins," he says, "and that makes me just like they are." Cobb rapes the woman, and Cooper takes revenge by killing him and the other four men in the gang.

Carl Foreman hated *Man of the West*: "I thought it was appalling—one of the sickest films I've ever seen. This was obviously a psychological Western, with pretensions at being an adult Western, and actually it was only an exercise in pure sadism." Cooper, aware of the problem, agreed that "kids get too steady a diet of violence today," but felt such films were justified "only if the good guy overcomes tremendous odds to lick the bad guy."[12] The film, which shows the redeemed hero fighting his violent instincts as well as the pathological killers, does have a crude power. Torn by moral conflicts in his own life, Cooper understood the anguish of a character striving to retain his integrity. He brought authentic feeling to the role of a tempted and tormented, yet essentially decent man.

19

The Long Day Wanes

1958–1959

I

In the 1950s the accidents and illnesses that had plagued Cooper since his teens in Montana and years as a stuntman caught up with him and finally undermined his remarkably tough constitution. After several operations for ulcers and hernias, his health broke down and he began to look older than his years. Though he had a stiff shoulder and bad back, and was often in great pain, he continued to work in action films. He formed his own company, Baroda Productions, and with it made three unusual films in 1959: *The Hanging Tree, They Came to Cordura* and *The Wreck of the Mary Deare.* In April of that year he followed his wife and daughter into the Catholic Church. In November, after meeting Nikita Khrushchev in Hollywood, he went on a government-sponsored trip to the Soviet Union. The following spring he had, within six weeks, two major operations for cancer. Though gravely ill, in the fall of that year he made his last picture, *The Naked Edge.*

Before forming Baroda Productions, Cooper replaced his longtime lawyer-agent, I.H. Prinzmetal (Maria once heard them having a terrible quarrel) and divided up his duties. Deane Johnson—senior partner of a prestigious Los Angeles firm that specialized in entertainment and later married to Rocky's friend the former Anne McConnell Ford—became his lawyer. Charles Feldman—a handsome, cultivated, genial host and very successful lawyer, agent, producer and entrepreneur—became his agent. After his birthday party in May 1957 Cooper, who was fond of Feldman, wrote: "It ain't showing the right appreciation inflicting my handwriting on anyone, but just the same I think it was swell of you to come and thank you for the loot."

Cooper sometimes used euphemisms to disguise his more unseemly illnesses. In January 1945 he became ill from hemorrhoids—which he called amoebic dysentery and had supposedly contracted on his South Pacific tour of 1942—and entered the hospital for treatment that May. Writing to his nephew, then serving in the Pacific war, Cooper joked about his painful condition: "I feel tops now after having my tail operated on a short while ago. Was only in the hospital seven days. The first craparoo was like giving birth to some broken beer bottles." Other health problems came from making movies. His hearing, affected by a gun blast in Africa in 1931, was further impaired by the dynamite explosion in *Blowing Wild*. His skin was burned by a blank shell in *Vera Cruz*, and he also had tapeworm from eating bad beef when shooting in Mexico in 1953.

Between 1951 and 1953, while separated from Rocky, Cooper had six operations. In 1951 and again the following year he twice had surgery for duodenal ulcers, brought on by the crisis and break with Pat Neal. He first got a hernia in the 1940s from using an enormous bow with a ninety-pound pull, and aggravated this condition by repeatedly lifting Grace Kelly in *High Noon* and by picking up a heavy teakwood bench in Samoa. These exertions cost him dearly and required four more surgical procedures between August 1951 and August 1953. Cooper's doctor flew to Paris and Biarritz, so that Cooper could remain outside the United States for tax reasons, for follow-up surgery in the spring and summer of 1953. In August of that year he wrote Lorraine Chanel: "I got sewed up for the fourth time. It was a double hernia on my left side; Dr. Ochsner was good to come over and fix me up. Now I am pretty sewed up in front, both sides." During these ordeals Cooper's weight dropped from 206 to 180 pounds, and in his later films he was often in pain.

Billy Wilder felt he had to disguise Cooper's age in *Love in the Afternoon*, but in that film a cyst on his right jaw was still visible. On April 16, 1958, a year after the film's release, Cooper entered the Manhattan Eye, Ear and Throat Hospital for a face-lift and other cosmetic surgery by Dr. John Converse, one of the leading plastic surgeons in America. Newspaper articles commenting on the effects of the operation said his face now looked quite different and the procedure had not been successful. In 1959 a friend told Pat Neal that Cooper had fallen down while leaving mass. "He got up quickly, but she sensed that something was very wrong."[1]

Cooper had never been an observant Christian, though many friends believed he had a deeply spiritual side. Now, his deteriorating health and the ever-present danger of death during surgery, as well as regrets about his personal behavior, led this solitary, reserved and reflective man to think seriously about religion. In Hollywood great stars rarely concerned themselves with spiritual matters, but Cooper, a modern Don Juan, repented his sins and mended his ways. Maria said that her father rarely discussed his conversion with his family and that she and Rocky never put any pressure on him to join the church for their sake. He had never gone to church with them, apart from mass at Christmas and Easter, and always looked on religion as their affair. But one Sunday, instead of reading the newspapers in bed, he suddenly said, "Hey, girls, wait for me," and began attending church regularly. Maria later said: "I guess that maybe on some of his many drives or walks or times alone in the mountains he began to feel there was something that the Catholic religion had to offer that he wanted. He didn't talk about it very much to us. Again, he was a very private man and it was his private affair, but I know he did get a lot of strength and comfort from it."

Maria may not have known that the original impetus had come from Rocky, who "never let up until he finally became a Catholic." Father Harold Ford was assigned to the posh Beverly Hills Church of the Good Shepherd (locally known as Our Lady of the Cadillacs) as a young priest in 1954. He scarcely knew the Coopers, who were traveling a good deal of the time. One Sunday Rocky came up to him and said, in her direct manner: "I want to make my husband a Catholic. What can we do about bringing him into the church?" Ford replied: "That depends on him. I'll talk to him." During Cooper's period of instruction Ford, whom Cooper called "Father tough stuff," became a family friend. He sometimes stayed to dinner and liked to talk about guns. Ford learned to scuba dive in their pool, and when he became proficient the whole family chartered a boat and took him to Catalina Island for a weekend of diving.

Cooper asked Ford, "What do I have to do to become a Catholic?" and the priest brought him the basic texts of the faith to study. Cooper had been taught Christian beliefs in Dunstable and been baptized in the Church of England when he was ten years old. Rocky and Maria had already paved the way for him, and he was knowledgeable about the basic Catholic doctrines: the Trinity, Creed and Confession. Ford came by once a week to talk to him individually. He'd ask Cooper about the texts he'd been reading, discuss his questions and provide explanations. He prayed with Cooper and asked him if he knew what he wanted to do. After several months of study and discussion, Cooper had the necessary desire, knowledge and acceptance, and seemed ready to make an affirmation of faith. He asked, "Where do we go from here?" and Ford told him that he was satisfied with his progress. Though there was no way that Ford could know Cooper's (or anyone's) real intentions, he seemed to be sincere. He said he was ready and was baptized as a Catholic on April 9, 1959.[2]

When asked about his conversion, Cooper replied, in his homespun fashion, that religion provided a standard of behavior which helped improve the quality of his moral life, and added that it bound the family more closely together:

> Last winter, when I began trying to find out how to be less of a bum, I saw that religion is a sort of check up on yourself, a kind of patterned way of behaving. As I saw it, if a fellow goes to church, any church, and tries to straighten out his mind, it sure helps. After I digested that idea, I began thinking how our family has always done everything together. . . . Therefore, I figured if I was trying to change from the careless sloppy sort of guy I am, it seemed silly to go to a different church from the one my girls attend.

In a second, more probing analysis, he observed that Catholicism was a way to transcend egoism and selfishness, to acknowledge that a higher power had given him an extraordinarily happy and successful life:

> I'd spent all my waking hours, year after year, doing almost exactly what I, personally, wanted to do and what I wanted to do wasn't always the most polite thing either. . . . This past winter I began to dwell a little more on what's been in my mind for a long time. I began thinking, "Coop, old boy, you owe somebody something for all your good fortune." I guess that's what started me thinking seriously about my religion. I'll never be anything like a saint, I know. I just haven't got that kind of fortitude. The only thing I can say for me is that I'm trying to be a little better. Maybe I'll succeed.[3]

The eighty-six-year-old Alice Cooper disliked his conversion and frankly said: "I wish he hadn't done that, but I hope he's happy now."

She also maintained that "Gary will always be a Protestant, no matter what other religious influences enter in his life." Ivan Moffat believed Cooper was doing what he considered to be the right and proper thing, and called his conversion "a matter of formal courtesy." Watson Webb, a neighbor and friend, thought Cooper felt guilty about his sexual immorality and found religion a helpful "padlock" to ensure correct behavior. Dolores Hart, who had become a nun, was convinced that his conversion was deeply felt and absolutely sincere. Wanting to please Rocky and Maria, who "was like a mommy to her parents," he gradually came under their influence and wished to bond with them in their faith. Though it brought him personal solace, his conversion was also Cooper's way of bringing his family together and healing the wounds of their traumatic separation.[4]

II

In an article published a few months before his death, Cooper took an unduly harsh view of his achievement since *High Noon*: "Nothing I've done lately, the past eight years or so, has been especially worthwhile. I've been coasting along. Some of the pictures I've made recently I'm genuinely sorry about. Either I did a sloppy job in them, or the story wasn't right." But there was a great difference between the cowboy movies he made in Mexico, the earnestly dull *Billy Mitchell* and *Friendly Persuasion*, and the more subtle and penetrating Westerns of 1958–59. Cooper felt he had disappointed his audience, but in his last films he extended the range of his acting and tried roles that questioned and transcended his traditional image.

The Hanging Tree, Cooper's finest Western after *High Noon*, portrays a man trying to break away from a troubled past and an interesting, unconventional heroine who's subjected to the pathological impulses of the villain. The film was shot near Yakima, in south-central Washington, from mid-June to mid-August 1958, on a budget of $1.35 million. The director, Delmer Daves, got $100,000 and Cooper earned $275,000. Though Slim Talbot took his rough scenes, Cooper, leaning to the left of his saddle, suffered great pain whenever he had to ride a horse. Karl Malden, who played the villain, recalled that Daves "got sick and had to be hospitalized [for ulcers]. The producers and Cooper, who was backing the film, got together and decided to ask me to direct. There was quite a bit left to do. I told them I wasn't prepared, but Cooper encouraged me."

The Hanging Tree takes place in the Montana gold country in 1873. Cooper plays a doctor and (as in previous films) rides into town in the opening scene. Staring at the ominous and frequently used Hanging Tree, he reflectively inhales and purses his lips. He treats the gunshot wounds of a young robber and befriends him, sets up a medical practice and works a gold claim. His name, Joseph Frail, "suits a man with frail hope."

When a stagecoach is robbed and overturned, the strong yet gentle doctor helps rescue a young Swiss woman, played by Maria Schell. Her father has been killed in the holdup, and she's been "blinded and burnt bad by the sun." As in Gide's *Symphony Pastorale*, a powerful bond—mixing gratitude and love—develops between them as he nurses her back to health and helps her to recover her sight. Karl Malden, a local brute lusting after the helpless woman, sneaks into her darkened room but is stopped just in time by Cooper, who (Malden says) "is gonna keep the lady all to himself." When her bandages are removed, she senses his need for absolute control and asks: "Are you afraid of me because I'm well now?" Cooper is a man with a past. Hurt by his wife, who's betrayed him with his own brother, he remains wounded and embittered. Unable to relate to the newly awakened and now-threatening woman, he tells her to leave.

Schell grubstakes Malden to a failing gold mine which Cooper—seeking power over her and "thinking he can play with people's lives" secretly supports. When a tree uprooted by a storm reveals the hidden gold, Malden throws a wild party. He gets drunk, nearly destroys the town when his huge bonfire blows out of control and once again tries to rape Schell. Cooper kills Malden and kicks his body over a cliff. As the mob tries to lynch Cooper, Schell offers her gold mine to save him. The townsfolk accept, and the empty noose swings on the Hanging Tree as Cooper and Schell embrace. "Foreign, blind and burnt bad," Schell has a richly developed role that transcends the whore-schoolmarm stereotypes of the conventional Western. Cooper is powerful and persuasive as the emotionally scarred man who eradicates evil and, through the sacrifice of a woman, moves from the need to dominate to the desire for love.

They Came to Cordura, though not as good as *Man of the West* and *The Hanging Tree*, is a serious and ambitious film. The screenwriter, Ivan Moffat, confessed that the premise was "fairly unlikely." But he defended the offbeat, cross-grained story that shows how courage and cowardice are tested. As in the previous two Westerns, Cooper plays a man with a dark, oppressive past. Branded as a coward for hiding in a ditch while fighting the Mexicans and called "yellow guts," he is made an "awards officer," as an ironic and humiliating punishment, by a government eager to supply heroes for its recruits in World War I. During the 1916 expedition against the Mexican revolutionary Pancho Villa, Cooper "gallops around the country, looking for heroes," and questions brave men about their motives and feelings. He finds five soldiers who have survived a virtually suicidal cavalry charge and selects them for the Congressional Medal of Honor. As he brings them safely back to their base, they become the means of repairing his damaged pride.

Baroda paid $250,000 for the screen rights to the novel and shot the $4 million film at St. George, in southwest Utah. The producer was Cooper's old friend and partner William Goetz, a witty, charming and greatly loved man. He had a marvelous house, entertained everyone and was at the center of Hollywood society. During a discussion with Goetz in his office at Columbia Pictures, Moffat earnestly explained that in the novel Cooper's character is myopic and wears glasses, and that it was very important for Cooper to wear glasses in the film. Goetz responded by telling Moffat: "Do you see that painting on the wall? It's a Picasso. I'd very much like to keep it. That's why Cooper won't wear glasses in the picture."

In the film Cooper has a chance to put his hand "on the bare heart of heroism." He leads the five men—along with the cheeky, arrogant Rita Hayworth, who's accused of treason for giving sanctuary to the Mexican rebels—back to Cordura (not a real place on the map, but a refuge that means "sanity" in Spanish). During the arduous expedition the soldiers (for various reasons) reject the medals and, mocking their awards, reveal their true natures. One of the "heroes" tries to rape Hayworth (an act now *de rigueur* in Cooper's Westerns), who expresses her disdain by declaring: "I wouldn't give them my sweat if they were dying of thirst." As the men become increasingly vicious, Cooper reveals the exemplary aspect of his character and becomes (in Hayworth's words) "the bravest man I've ever known."

In an extraordinary scene that taxed Cooper's powers of physical endurance, he places the long handle of a railroad cart on his shoulder and drags it along the track like Christ bearing the cross on the Via Dolorosa. Reaching Cordura, he finally achieves redemption and no longer has to atone for his own (and others') sins. Refusing to condemn his vicious followers, he quotes Matthew 7:1—"Judge not, that ye be not judged"—and leads his men over the last hill to their salvation.

The director, Robert Rossen, described an effect that he hoped for but couldn't actually achieve: "I had recourse to a device for the ending: when they climb the hill and look at Cordura, on their faces appears the moment when individually they become heroes, in short, their first acts of courage. Each of them remembers in an instant that great, unique moment." The film, in fact, is more about the effects of cowardice than the triumphs of courage. In his introduction to *Men at War*, Hemingway connected a soldier's cowardice to a hyperactive imagination that made many intelligent men—like Cooper's character at the beginning of Cordura—foresee and dwell on danger. He believed that the best soldiers concentrated on the immediate moment: "Cowardice ... is always simply a lack of ability to suspend the functioning of the imagination. Learning to suspend your imagination and live completely in the very second of the present minute with no before and no after is the greatest gift a soldier can acquire."[5]

In the late 1950s Cooper made several guest appearances on television to publicize his recent Westerns and keep his image vivid in that medium. He turned up with Lena Horne on the *Perry Como Show*, endured some terrible jokes (by his short host) about his height, and was given a lame speech that strained for laughs and never got them. On the fatuous panel game *What's My Line?* he had trouble hearing and seemed nervous. He put his fist over his mouth, mumbled a bit and tried to disguise his voice. But the panel almost instantly guessed who he was, and he apologized for not being able to fool them. When the host mentioned his great new film, Cooper became embarrassed by the hype and said: "I can't sit here and plug the picture."

Cooper had better material when he appeared with his old friend on the *Jack Benny Show*. In the first sketch he wears a western tie, blows his lines and gets a laugh. He then wows the audience by playing the guitar, imitating Elvis Presley's gyrations and singing "He's a Bird Dog" with an Ozark accent. In the second, surprisingly funny sketch, he wears an absurdly piebald Holstein-cowskin vest. Benny, sporting tiltingly high elevated boots to match Cooper's height and imitating his western speech, auditions for the part of Cooper's twin brother in a cowboy movie. After watching the other candidates get badly beaten up during the rough tryouts, the cowardly Benny withdraws from the competition.

Cooper loved scuba diving, and in a letter to Maria from the Bahamas, he described the beauty of the underwater seascape and the startling discovery he made there: "We made a dive today just a mile east from here—over the coral that grows to about fifteen to three feet from the surface and it started on a pure white sand at three feet. Visibility only fair for here because it blew yesterday. . . . We dropped anchor right over the edge of the dark water showing the coral and the aquamarine water, which means a sandy bottom. We all plopped into it for a picture from under, then we swam down to the white sand bottom to look. What do we see but a wire cage some fish collector had lost with a five foot moray eel in it."

Cooper's skill as a diver was a great help during the shipwreck and diving scenes of his next film, *The Wreck of the Mary Deare*, shot in London and the English Channel as well as in Long Beach and the huge tank in the MGM studio between April and July 1959. For the scene in which Charlton Heston boards Cooper's derelict tramp steamer, the technicians created the violent storm with hoses and a wind machine, and "built the starboard side of the ship and all of the bow, full-scale on rockers to make it roll realistically in the storm they created." Heston, twenty-three years younger and in much better shape than Cooper, felt the undersea action made great demands on the actors: "The picture was rather difficult physically, as you know, particularly the diving. It was not at all easy for me. I had to learn to dive to do it. Cooper already knew how to dive, and as I know now, it's not easy when you're past forty. He kept himself in fine shape, did all the dives he was supposed to. He worked all day and it was terribly exhausting. He'd come out debilitated from the big water-filled tank at Metro where we had the full-scale mock-up of a section of the freighter. In every shot we had to get wet and dirty and remain under an awful physical pressure."[6]

Cooper used the same line to deflate hecklers when dining in London with Heston as he had when dining in Paris with Rocky, Maria and Dolores Hart a few years earlier. When a cheeky Parisian loudly asked, "I wonder which one is his wife?" or a London punk sneered, "Oh there goes the big cowboy star," Cooper, borrowing his famous line from *The Virginian*, disarmed them with, "When you say that, smile."

The director, Michael Anderson, had a great success with *Around the World in 80 Days* (1956). He made the scene in which Cooper comes to London to see Virginia McKenna more realistic by having him board the train at Clapham and, unrecognized, arrive at Waterloo Station with the rest of the commuter crowd. Anderson said that Cooper was always well prepared and always went flat out. As soon as Anderson gave his direction, Cooper would say, "Gotcha," respond immediately and incorporate the suggestion into his role. Heston added that Cooper, who liked "to seek out some interesting physical accent for a scene," projected "more than any other actor that's ever lived . . . the kind of man Americans would like to be."

Mary Deare, a good action film with a suspense-filled plot, is partly based on the legend of a spectral, ill-fated ship, the *Flying Dutchman*. The story begins as Heston's tugboat is nearly rammed by a huge, empty freighter. When he boards it for salvage, he's stopped by Cooper, the madman captain alone on the ship. Disturbed by the spooky atmosphere and the corpse floating in the hold, Heston attempts to leave by using ropes, but is again stopped by heavy seas and pulled back to safety by Cooper. Heston learns that the captain put out a fire after his crew had abandoned ship. Wounded in the head, Cooper looks rugged but exhausted. He radiates nervous tension, entering the room uneasily, gritting his teeth during the ordeal and barking out commands to Heston. Hiding his motives and his past, he deliberately steers the ship onto the rocks. He leaves with Heston on a lifeboat, and asks for his help on the court of inquiry that will investigate Cooper's role in the disaster.

During the inquiry Cooper claims that the crew had offloaded the cargo of aircraft engines in Rangoon, then tried to sink the ship and collect the insurance money for engines that were no longer on board. The captain, however, has a dark past. He's lost his last ship and has been jailed for fighting, and the court doesn't believe him. With Heston's help he dives into the hold of the foundered ship and finds that rocks have replaced the engines in the crates. Richard Harris, the caricatured villain responsible for the fraud, harpoons Heston, who then hooks Harris and pulls him into a watery death. Cooper, finally vindicated, declares: "The ship—that's all I want. I guess that's all I ever wanted." *The Wreck of the Mary Deare*, like *They Came to Cordura*, explores the same themes as Conrad's *Lord Jim*: the acute consciousness of lost honor, the desire for self-knowledge, the quest for absolution and redemption, and "those struggles," as Conrad wrote, "of an individual trying to save from the fire his idea of what his moral identity should be."[7]

III

Nikita Khrushchev arrived in Washington the day after Russia became the first country to land a rocket on the moon. Henry Cabot Lodge accompanied him, on his tour across the country, to defend the American way of life. Angered by a hostile audience in Los Angeles, he told Lodge, with a sneer at Americans, "every snipe praises his own bog." Before his tour ended at Camp David for two days of talks with President Eisenhower, the Soviet premier visited Hollywood.

On September 19, 1959, two months after completing *Mary Deare*, at a luncheon organized by Charles Feldman at 20th Century-Fox, Cooper met Khrushchev. The other guests at Cooper's table included William Goetz, Jack Benny, the producer Pandro Berman and the wife of the Soviet foreign minister, Andrei Gromyko. Cooper and Khrushchev said hello, had a friendly chat and told each other: "You have strong worker's hands." When Khrushchev said, "you're a very fine actor," Cooper replied, "and so are you"—and they both broke out laughing. Robert Frost, who met Khrushchev face-to-face in Russia three years later, described him as "very good-natured, hearty, jolly, rough in a way, you'd call it: coarse . . . probably a good deal deeper than I fathomed. . . . We were both so affable that we may both have been self-deceived." But outside his own turf and hot for Mickey Mouse, the premier was (Cooper said) much more cantankerous: "Khrushchev went on and on about his not being able to see Disneyland when it was the one thing he wanted to see. What kind of country is this, he asked, are there gangsters or something there? Actually, it was his own security men who didn't want him to go." Ideologically hostile to Khrushchev and not influenced, as Frost was, by prolonged contact with the affable villain, Cooper declared: "It's impossible to forget the history of what has happened in Russia, and how much he is responsible for some of the things we don't like, in the free world."

Khrushchev redeemed himself, however, by personally inviting Cooper (accompanied by Rocky, Maria and Paul Shields) on a six-day, United States Information Agency-sponsored trip to Moscow and Leningrad. (When Hemingway heard they were going, he vainly asked Cooper if he could get his frozen rubles out of the country.) This rare cultural exchange also publicized the suitably proletarian *Marty* (1957), the first American film to be shown there in many years, which prompted the Russians to send *The Cranes Are Flying* (1957) to the United States. While making *Mary Deare*, Cooper, as conservative as ever, warned an English reporter, "Here in Europe you're moving closer every day to Communism and Socialism."[8] On *What's My Line?* he proudly said that he'd "sprung the first leak in the Iron Curtain."

Maria Cooper, then twenty-two years old, remembered many strange
and vivid incidents on their trip. On the plane to Russia they had to fill
in a long form listing all the jewelry they were taking into the country.
Rocky, annoyed by the tedious paperwork, was amazed to see a customs
official throw away the forms as soon as they arrived. The Harlem
Globetrotters basketball team were also on tour and, for once, towered
over Cooper in the hotel lobby. During dinner at the American Embassy
on their first night the diplomats referred to the embalmed corpses of
Lenin and Stalin, on display in Red Square, as "cold cuts." They also
joked about hidden microphones until someone found a cunningly
disguised bug inside a shield bearing an American eagle. Whenever they
encountered such irritations Cooper became impatient, but Shields "went
ballistic." Because of the lack of cultural contact during the Cold War,
many young Russians had never heard of Cooper, but they always gathered round to stare at the gleaming western car provided by the embassy.
To prove Americans were tough, Cooper refused to wear an overcoat and
caught a nasty cold for his bravado.

During a private tour of the Kremlin, Cooper was shown an emerald
set in a harness under a horse's tail. After seeing such opulence, he said:
"Now I understand why there was a revolution." On the overnight train
to Leningrad their escort, Pavel, a police spy out of central casting,
followed them everywhere. After a few congenial vodkas he complained
to Rocky that he was a henpecked husband and had trouble sleeping at
night. She gave him two Seconals, which knocked him out so thoroughly
that he nearly missed Leningrad and went on to the Finland Station.

Delbert Mann, a courtly southerner who'd won an Academy Award
and the Palme d'Or at Cannes for directing *Marty*, wrote an illuminating
account of the guests, itinerary, art museums, cultural events, royal treatment and oppressive ambience as well as Cooper's response to the tour:

The United Artists party was made up of Harold Hecht, producer,
Arnold Picker of UA, [Edward G.] and Jane Robinson, and Coop,
Rocky and Maria, and, of course, Paddy Chayevsky. . . . Our first lay-
over was in Copenhagen where we went sightseeing and to the [Ny
Carlsberg Glyptotek] art museum where they treated Eddie with much
deference, being the art collector that he was. We went to the
[Carlsberg] brewery to sample the wares.

Then on to Moscow. We stayed at the Metropole Hotel near the
Bolshoi Theatre. We were really treated royally during the few days we

were there, going to the Bolshoi, the Moscow Art Theatre, staying for only part of the performance at each but being seated in the grand boxes. We were given private, rather behind-the-scenes tours of the Kremlin, the royal jewelry and carriages collections, the churches turned into museums, some private quarters and offices. We met with a high minister of Culture. We were wined and dined often with many toasts in vodka.

We were taken to the head of a long line of people waiting in the cold to view the bodies of Lenin and Stalin. It was truly eerie to see the two preserved bodies close to each other.

We attended the screening of MARTY which was a great success, with laughter coming at all the right places. The audience applauded at the end, unusual we were told. We visited the Mosfilm studios and met with many people there. And, of course, toured the city. [At the Pushkin] art museum in Moscow we were again shown many things which are normally held in quiet—wonderful Impressionists bought by the nobility when they were new.

Then by overnight train to Leningrad. I being single and the Coopers a party of three, Rocky and Maria had a stateroom together while Coop bunked in with me. I, of course, insisted on taking the top berth. Coop was very sweet and very taciturn. Not much in the way of conversation all the way to Leningrad! . . .

In Leningrad we visited the Marinsky Theatre, elegant in blue and silver as the Bolshoi had been in eye-catching red and gold. We, of course, visited the Hermitage and were shown many special paintings because of Eddie. We stayed at the Astoria Hotel and again toured the city, the Leninfilm studios, met with a large group of film workers and directors.

Coop and family participated in all the activities and seemed to be having a good time. My memory is of courtesy and pleasantness, so often with that shy little grin on his face, amiable and rather quiet. He seemed to be very interested in all the sights.

Heavy snow was predicted when we finally departed, all going in different directions. It was very gray, gloomy and cold when we finally got on the rickety old Russian prop plane. Awfully glad to have been there, awfully glad to get out and get free again!⁹

The journey to Russia inspired a rare eruption of anger. Back in Hollywood Cooper invited some Soviet visitors to dinner at his house.

When Hedda Hopper heard about it and publicly announced that he was "soft on Commies," he became livid and told her off on the phone.

On April 14, 1960, five months after returning from Russia, Cooper had surgery in Massachusetts General Hospital for prostate cancer. To the press he denied there had been a malignancy and claimed he'd been "living with uremic poisoning for two years." He remained in the Boston Hospital for ten days and was thought to be cured. On May 31, only five weeks later, his bowel became obstructed. He entered Cedars of Lebanon Hospital in Los Angeles and had a malignant tumor removed from his large intestine. Still trying to protect his privacy, he told reporters: "I know some people don't get embarrassed about these things, but I get embarrassed." The surgeons again thought they had excised the malignancy, but the cancer began to spread through his body.[10]

IV

Cooper left the hospital on June 9 and recuperated over the summer. In England in the fall of 1960 he made his last film, *The Naked Edge*. Charles Feldman assured the producer, Walter Seltzer, that Cooper would pass the physical examination required by the insurance company and he did so on August 15. But the work was intense and exhausting, and his health remained precarious. After his intestinal operation he had to make frequent trips to the bathroom, but he didn't give in to illness or miss a day of work. Pete Martin, a Hollywood reporter who saw Cooper when the picture was completed, gave a harsh description of the aging actor's hair and face: "The seams were gone. Somebody—perhaps a plastic surgeon, although he denied it—had ironed them out. And his hair was a kind of orangey light brown. It wasn't a good dye job."

Deborah Kerr, his wife in the film, noted that Cooper had changed mentally as well as physically. He was "a darling man, extremely thoughtful to work with, but he must have already been a very sick man. Sometimes he seemed withdrawn and remote, as though he were no longer with us." Kerr's husband, Peter Viertel, also on the scene, added that "between takes he kept to himself as he was suffering with the disease that finally took his life. He was already in pain."[11]

When Cooper met Joseph Stefano to talk about the movie, the screenwriter explained how he had changed the character from the novel to the film. Cooper, who had a strong supporting cast and didn't want to stand back from the story and do big star turns, told him: "Just don't leave me alone on that screen." The director, Michael Anderson, recalled that Cooper had become faltering and self-conscious about things he'd always taken for granted. When his concentration and coordination failed to come together in one scene, the old pro asked: "What do I do with my hands?" Cooper cost the production time and money by faltering over his lines, and Anderson wanted to cut down the dialogue. At a dinner party given by the Coopers, Rocky stunned the guests by suddenly asking Anderson: "I hear you've been complaining about Gary." Instead of being hurt by this, Anderson was grateful for her honesty and frankness, which brought the problem into the open and enabled them to solve it. Cooper, recalling his difficulties with the dialogue in *Cloak and Dagger* and supporting Anderson, said: "Mike's absolutely right about the need to cut the long lines. You can't blame him—or me."

The Naked Edge, Cooper's only thriller, was shot in London and in Eastbourne on the Channel coast. Cooper stayed at the Hotel Savoy on the Strand and often ate at the Guinea, in Bruton Place off Berkeley Square, which was famous for American steaks. Pete Martin, emphasizing Cooper's negative, even despairing mood, quoted him saying: "I don't know why I'm here. Nobody wants to read about me." But after a huge formal dinner, with Prince Philip as guest of honor and many glasses of good wine, Cooper reminisced with Seltzer about how much England meant to him. He liked the people, the pace of life, even the weather and said: "Let's do more pictures here."[12]

The most recurrent plot in Cooper's films is a false accusation, often ending in a trial, during which he remains silent for a long time and then dramatically vindicates himself. He's wrongly accused of stealing a horse in *The Westerner*, of abandoning his followers in *Meet John Doe* and of being a spy in *Springfield Rifle*. He's tried for insanity in *Mr. Deeds*, for multiple homicide in *Souls at Sea*, for insubordination in *Billy Mitchell* and for wrecking a ship in *Mary Deare*. *The Naked Edge*, varying this formula, begins rather than ends with a trial in which Cooper accuses another man. But (as in Hitchcock's *Suspicion*) the rest of the film casts suspicion on *him*. As Diane Cilento, playing the wife of a wrongly convicted prisoner, tells Deborah Kerr: "Let *him* kill the truth for you . . . the way he killed Jason Roote . . . and my Donald . . . and . . . maybe some day he'll kill you . . . too."

The film begins as Cooper, an American businessman in London, testifies at the Old Bailey against a man in his office, who's found guilty of theft and murder. Cooper suddenly obtains a lot of cash (which he claims has come from a lucky stock market gamble), forms a partnership with Michael Wilding, becomes very rich and lives in a Regent's Park mansion. Six years later his wife confronts him with a long-missing and highly suspicious letter that accuses him of murder. At the end Eric Portman, the real killer, tries to blackmail Cooper. In a scary reprise of the shower scene in *Psycho* (Stefano's previous film) Portman creeps through the shadows and into their house, sharpens a straight razor, gags Kerr (while Cooper is in the next room) and prepares to drown her in the bathtub. Cooper rescues her and exposes the real criminal, who dies after falling down a steep staircase. Cooper says, "I condemned the wrong man," and Kerr replies, "So did I."

Though it's clear from the start that Cooper is not—and could not be—the murderer, the suspense is intensified by throbbing music, shadowy lighting, low camera angles, sudden close-ups and direct cuts (rather than dissolves or fade-outs). Wearing a smart double-breasted suit and meant to be a rather dashing character, Cooper tells Kerr, "I've always had more than my share of . . . male hormones," to which she suggestively responds, "I've noticed that about you—often." But he also looks tense and haggard, and shifts his eyes nervously. His voice seems weaker, his eyes are pouchy, his hair is lifeless. There are deep furrows along his cheeks, mottled skin on his chin and a slight indentation on his right jaw where the cyst had been removed. Cooper's physical decline reinforced his haunted character and made him more convincing as a possible murderer.

The Naked Edge was released in June 1961, and United Artists had to find a way to sell a movie whose star had just died. Instead of mentioning that it was Cooper's last picture, they emphasized the suspense and the connection to *Psycho*, and used a familiar but still-successful strategy. Installing a red light in theater lobbies, they turned it on for the last fifteen minutes of the movie and warned that no one would be admitted during that time.[13]

20

Death of a Hero

1960–1961

I

Rocky learned that Cooper's cancer was fatal on December 27, 1960 but did not tell him about it until the end of February. In those days families tended to protect patients from depressing news in order to make their last months easier to bear. Though he suffered greatly in the terminal phase of the disease, he remained active, and the last months of his life were surprisingly full. In December 1960 he worked on the NBC television documentary *The Real West*, which was broadcast in March. He kept in close touch with Hemingway and, during his annual hunting trip to Sun Valley in January, saw his friend for the last time. In early March he went to Palm Beach for skin diving, and in Miami Beach saw Floyd Patterson knock out Ingemar Johansson in their heavyweight championship fight. He also received several valedictory honors: an evening at the Friars Club in January, his third Oscar in April and the French Order of Arts and Letters, awarded by André Malraux and accepted for him by Fred Zinnemann in Paris on May 6. In May, shortly after his sixtieth birthday, he died.

Toward the end of 1960 news of Cooper's illness began to circulate in the film community, and many friends and admirers rallied to honor him. On January 9, 1961 the Friars, a popular actors' club, gave a dinner to celebrate his career. The $200-a-plate event for 850 club members and friends took place at the Beverly Hilton Hotel and raised $85,000 for charity. Frank Sinatra and Dean Martin were co-chairmen, George Jessel was master of ceremonies and the guests included Governor Edmund Brown, Henry Ford II, Sam Goldwyn, Jack Warner, Greer Garson, George Burns, Tony Curtis and the composer Dmitri Tiomkin. During the traditional "roast," the comedians told good-natured jokes about Cooper's foibles and weaknesses, and expressed their affectionate regard for him. Jack Benny remarked that "Coop was in talkies for five years before anyone realized it" and added: "He skis, skin-dives, hunts . . . and he's seriously thinking of taking up acting." Milton Berle said, "he's about as romantic as Oscar Levant on a desert island with Elsa Maxwell," and then, rather more sharply, called Cooper "Randolph Scott with novocaine lips, the grandpa Moses of the prairie. Shy? This man got green stamps from Polly Adler"—a notorious madam.

Audrey Hepburn made a big hit, reading her own greeting card poem, "What is a Gary Cooper?":

> A male over six feet in length, lanky and bright-eyed . . .
> The tallest, thinnest, kindest man. . . .
> A Gary Cooper is rare, and there is only one,
> And there will never be another under the sun.

The aged poet Carl Sandburg, who had corresponded with Judge Cooper and worked on the screenplay of *The Greatest Story Ever Told* (1960), rather awkwardly called Cooper "a tradition while he's living, something of a clean sport, the lack of a phony." Sandburg then paid him a dubious compliment by declaring: "He is one of the most beloved illiterates this country has ever known."

Billy Wilder helped write Cooper's short response, and the actor was deeply moved as he delivered it. He began by reversing Winston Churchill's homage in Parliament to the wartime RAF and ended by alluding to Lou Gehrig's farewell speech, when he too had a fatal disease: "Never have so many made so much fuss over so little. . . . A great many honors have come to me in those years—my footprints are in the forecourt of Grauman's Chinese, my name is on the sidewalk in front of the Pig 'n' Whistle—and David Susskind called me a personality. . . . The only achievement I'm proud of is the friends I've made in this community. Just looking around this room makes me feel that my life has not been wasted. And if anybody asks me am I the luckiest guy in the world, my answer is—Yup!"[1]

Like the Academy Awards ceremony, this was the kind of occasion with its stand-up comic speeches—beloved of Hollywood. Like all popularity contests, it needed a certain amount of lobbying from Cooper's public relations firm to secure the engagement. The evening itself was a mixture of sweet and sour, with colleagues expressing not only sincere admiration, but also a thinly veiled envy of his athletic ability and success with women. Cooper's speech, borrowing high-flown words from a historical oration, showed an awareness of the essential falseness of the movie world. But there was also an underlying seriousness that stirred the emotions. Though Cooper did not know yet that he was terminally ill, he seemed to sense his fate in the attitudes of the speakers and audience. Instead of sending him off to a happy old age laden with honors, many people there felt he would not live much longer.

Cooper's last work was the narration for *The Real West*, first conceived in early 1960. Jerry Wald had praised the television shows of a talented young producer, Donald Hyatt. Cooper, tired of what was being offered in Hollywood, liked Hyatt's idea of a serious program that would describe the history of the west from the gold rush in 1849 to Little Bighorn in 1876. Hyatt wrote that Cooper "wanted very much to have it accurately and truthfully portrayed on television, and he was completely committed to being part of the effort to do it. 'A lot of what they call Westerns,' he told me scornfully, 'really aren't Westerns at all. They're Eastern gangster stories done in cowboy hats—and not the right hats, even.' "[2]

In 1960 the leading movie stars usually competed with television instead of appearing on it. But Cooper, having heard about the program, called Hyatt directly instead of using an agent and asked: "I wonder if I might drop by sometime?" When they got word that Cooper was coming up to the twenty-eighth floor of the NBC Building, the sophisticated staff acted like starstruck children and gathered in the elevator lobby to await his appearance. On the floor of his office Hyatt spread out the photos he'd accumulated. Cooper, knowledgeable about the Indians, knelt down and spent two hours identifying a great many of them. Hyatt didn't ask, "Will you do it?" but somehow felt he would. Soon afterward Cooper's lawyer, Deane Johnson, called to confirm that Cooper would indeed narrate the program, which cost $200,000 to make. Cooper waived his $7,500 fee, and asked instead for a color television set, which was hard to get in those days.

Concerned about Cooper's worsening illness, Rocky called Hyatt toward the end of 1960 and asked about the progress of the show. Hyatt

flew to Las Vegas to show them all the photos and the outline of the
script. He knocked on the Coopers' hotel room door, and was surprised
to find the unpretentious actor washing out his laundry ("simpler this
way") in the sink. Hyatt spread the photos on the bed; the Coopers
studied them, seemed satisfied and made no suggestions about the script.
At lunch they talked about fast cars and ski runs, Aspen and Sun Valley.
Rocky hinted that "time was running out."

The program was shot in December 1960 on an old MGM set. The
whole studio crew came out to greet Cooper as if he were the King of
England. Obviously fond and proud of him, they were on a first-name
basis and acted as if it were a family reunion. Hyatt knew it was difficult
to play the role of narrator without relating to other actors. Cooper told
him: "I want you to let me know what you like and dislike and tell me
what to do." His narration, flat and undramatic on the first reel, got
better on the second and third, so he gladly did the first part over again.
He spent only an hour and a half on camera, was very easy to work with,
and walked off the screen slowly and naturally at the end of the program.
Three months later, in March 1961, Cooper flew from Florida to New
York to record the off-camera narration. Hyatt particularly remembered
his simplicity and lack of "big star" pretensions. At the sound studio there
was no room for his coat on the rack. As Hyatt started to clear a space,
Cooper told him: "Don't take another coat off. Just throw mine
anywhere."

Cooper's long years of dealing with the industry's insurance companies, as well as his innate sense of privacy and dignity, led him to
minimize his ailments. He never mentioned his real illness, claimed he
had "acute arthritis of the neck" and worked in "constant and excruciating pain." He had to return to his hotel room at noon to lie down and
take oxygen, and came back to the studio in Paul Shields' Bentley. When
the recording was over, he said "it would really be something" to do
another program with Hyatt. The show was broadcast on March 26, only
six weeks before his death, and received high ratings.

Cooper appears at the beginning and the end of the program and at
intervals throughout. He wears a cowboy hat, open shirt and wool jacket,
jeans and boots, and bends a supple stick as he speaks in a still-strong and
vigorous voice. For emphasis he uses many familiar gestures: he shifts his
eyes, pauses, chuckles and presses his lips together. He takes—has to
take!—a deep breath for every new sentence and sometimes slightly slurs
his words. But the imperfections make his speech seem more natural and

real. In this program, where Cooper appears as himself as well as in character as a man of the west, he seems to represent the type that Emerson
described in his essay on "Manners": "Once or twice in a lifetime we are
permitted to enjoy the charm of noble manners, in the presence of a man
or woman who have no bar in their nature, but whose character emanates
freely in their word and gesture."

The documentary, an evocative distillation of western history, focuses
objectively and compassionately on the hardships of the people. It
describes the pioneers' transcontinental trek, mining, cattlemen, gunmen,
women, railroaders, homesteaders, towns, Indians, cavalry and war. It
emphasizes, with several shots of hangings, that life was cheap, and also
includes many moving firsthand accounts. Cooper reads from a pioneer
woman's stoic diary: "Rose about five. . . . Got my housework done. . . .
Baked six more loaves of bread. . . . Made a kettle of mush. . . . Put my
clothes away and set my house in order. . . . Nine P.M.: Was delivered of
another son." The script also includes the last speech of Joseph,
vanquished chief of the Nez Percés, who starkly declared: "Hear me, my
warriors! I am tired. My heart is sad and sick. From where the sun now
stands, I will fight no more . . . forever."[3] The authentic *Real West*,
Cooper's "Apology to the Iroquois," compensated for all the absurdities
in the Westerns he'd made with De Mille.

II

Though Cooper had had two operations for cancer in 1960, the doctors
believed they had excised the malignant tumors. He had the best
surgeons, saw doctors frequently and took medical examinations to
satisfy the insurers before making each film. But the spreading cancer was
not found earlier, Dr. Rexford Kennamer said, because "they did not have
routine checks for the disease in those days and weren't looking for it."
Charles Feldman discussed a three-picture deal for Cooper only eleven
days before Rocky learned that his disease was terminal.

In November 1960, during the shooting of *The Naked Edge* in
London, Dr. Kennamer had dinner with Cooper, who complained of
aches and pains in his neck. They agreed to have a checkup in Los
Angeles at the end of the year. By then the carcinoma, detected by x-rays
on December 23, 1960, had metastasized to his lungs and (most
painfully) to his bones. Once the cancer had spread to this extent, there

was no way to treat it. Even today there's no cure for this kind of disease. Dr. Kennamer waited until after Christmas and then told Rocky. Devastated and in tears, she was still quite controlled. She wanted to have a six-week holiday with Cooper in Sun Valley and decided not to tell him right away. Like Lou Gehrig's wife in *The Pride of the Yankees*, she disguised the illness, and also called it "arthritis of the neck."

Guessing what was wrong in Sun Valley, Cooper asked, "Really, Rocky, is there anything the matter with me that I should know about?" and she did her best to deflect his questions. Deane Johnson couldn't draw up the new contract they had discussed with Feldman, so he stalled for time and told him they were still negotiating. Concerned that the papers might publish the story before Cooper himself knew that he was dying, Johnson called Cooper's public relations man, Warren Cowan, and asked if he could keep the news out of the press. Cowan made a deal with the wire services, the syndicates and the major New York and Los Angeles newspapers. They agreed to keep quiet, and he promised to notify all of them at the same time when Cooper died.[4]

When they returned home in mid-February, Cooper kept asking Rocky, "Baby, what do I really have?" and finally had to be told. Rocky had been under great strain, trying to keep the secret, which, as his disease inexorably progressed, could not be kept much longer. He wasn't taking proper care of himself. He worked on his cars, even washed them in his bathing suit, and she was afraid he'd get pneumonia. He also had to know the truth, she felt, in order to prepare himself spiritually for death. On February 27, 1961 they went to the doctor's office for what Dr. Kennamer called "the most dramatic moment of my life." When Cooper asked if he could sign up for *The Sundowners*, a film about sheepherders to be shot in Australia by Fred Zinnemann, Kennamer said no. This answer made it clear that he was dying. When his wife broke into tears, Cooper said, "Please Rocky, no blubbering." Embarrassed by Kennamer's distress, the next day he called the doctor and sympathetically said, "What an ordeal it must have been for you!" When William Holden, who had heard he was dying, met him at a party, Cooper said there were three more things he still wanted to do: visit Paris, which he adored, go pheasant hunting with Hemingway and say good-bye to his friends.

During his final months Rocky always dressed perfectly in order to please him, and when he could, Gary gardened, read, talked, sunbathed and watched television. One afternoon in Cooper's garden the

Hollywood reporter Joe Hyams organized a spectacular demonstration by five karate experts. Old friends—James and Gloria Stewart, Audrey Hepburn and Mel Ferrer, Sam and Frances Goldwyn, Jack Benny, Danny Kaye, Bill Goetz and Jerry Wald—came by to visit, distract and try to cheer him up. Robert Stack noticed that Cooper wore velvet slippers with a gold insignia. Billy Wilder recalled that he was dressed in stylish pajamas and robe and seemed more composed than his guests. There was also (Maria remembered) a ghoulish celebrity death watch. Larry Schiller, the Paris Match photographer, crept up to the bedroom window with a telephoto lens. Instead of calling the police, Cooper turned the sprinklers on him and made a joke of it.[5]

In March Cooper began to feel exhausted and very ill. He was full of aches and suffered intense pain, his breathing was short and rasping, and he had to take oxygen. Telling Maria, "It's sure easy to get hooked on painkillers," he refused them till the very end. He also rejected cobalt treatments, which would only prolong his life and his misery. After writhing on the floor in agony, he said: "I know what it's like to want to die." But he never asked, "Why me?" and never complained. Rocky read him spiritual books: Bishop Fulton Sheen's *Peace of Soul* (1949), the Trappist monk Thomas Merton's *Seeds of Contemplation* (1949) and *No Man is an Island* (1955). She also prayed "for the alleviation of Gary's excruciating suffering."

Early each morning, in the last month, Dr. Kennamer passed through the press out front and paid a fifteen-minute visit to the miniature hospital room set up in Cooper's house. He checked his patient, made sure the male and female nurses had followed his orders, and asked if there was anything he could do. Cooper went rapidly downhill and did not question him closely about the course of his disease. He suffered severe, gnawing pain from the destruction of his cells and bones, and had to be given increasingly heavy doses of narcotics.[6]

On April 17, watching the Academy Awards ceremony on television, Cooper saw James Stewart—who'd presented Cooper's first award for *Sergeant York* in 1942—accept his third Oscar. This honorary award was for lifetime achievement and for the international recognition he had brought to the movie industry. Calling Cooper "the kind of American who's loved in all four corners of the earth," Stewart said: "I am very honored to accept this award tonight for Gary Cooper. I'm sorry he's not here to accept it, but I know he's sitting by the television set tonight, and, Coop, I want you to know I'll get it to you right away. With it goes all the friendship and affection and the admiration and deep respect of all of us. We're very, very proud of you, Coop. All of us are tremendously proud." As he made this emotional and revealing speech, Stewart broke down and wept. The following day newspapers around the world carried the front-page headline: "Gary Cooper Has Cancer."

Strangely withdrawn into himself, Cooper didn't show any reaction to Stewart's speech. Rocky, always proselytizing, later told Hedda Hopper: "It didn't bother him at all. He thought it very beautiful. He'd been perfectly wonderful throughout the entire illness. What helped him most was his religion." As promised, Stewart brought the Oscar over to Cooper's house that night. The Coopers, though constantly bothered by the press, felt it was better to have his secret out in the open. "He has been wonderfully cheered and heartened," Rocky said, "by all the letters from friends, and strangers."[7]

III

Cooper always kept in touch with Hemingway and saw him as often as possible. Their careers had continued to run parallel and their friendship remained strong throughout Cooper's last decade. *High Noon*, Cooper's greatest film, had opened in New York in July 1952; *The Old Man and the Sea*, Hemingway's most popular novel, had been serialized in *Life* that September. Both actor and artist, two of the preeminent image makers of the twentieth century, had forged a modern masculine style. Kenneth Lynn noted the similarities between the heroic characters that Cooper played and Hemingway created: "Just as Will Kane has to do, Santiago sets out alone to do battle, against an adversary that turns out to be the most formidable of his career. And once again like Kane, he both wins and loses, for the flesh of his record-breaking marlin is totally devoured by sharks." Their long and close comradeship, founded in mutual trust and strengthened by enjoyment of the outdoors, now came to a tragic conclusion.

Eager to play the embittered hero of Hemingway's first postwar novel, *Across the River and into the Trees*, Cooper, as early as May 1945, had urged Hemingway to join him in producing the picture, controlling the artistic quality and reaping most of the profits. "I am sure," he wrote, "that if any important yarn of yours is done on the screen the next time it would be a great advantage all around if you were here on the spot to be part of the company which creates it. . . . I would like nothing better than to produce a picture with you which both of us would make and share in the results. . . . I've had various reports on your activities from time to time and all sound very interesting and weird. I'm sure you're coming out with a hot one about the thing in Europe." Hemingway had just returned to Cuba from reporting the European war and was planning to marry his fourth wife. He had not even started the novel, and did not respond to this proposal.

Besides filmmaking they had many other interests in common. Cooper shared Hemingway's enthusiasm for bullfighting, which they had often discussed and Hemingway had described in his classic *Death in the Afternoon*. Lorraine Chanel wrote that in Mexico City in 1953 "we went to a bullfight and a crowd gathered around him—wanting to shake his hand—all young men. When we were seated he felt in his coat pocket and found that his wallet was missing."[8] The same thing happened to Hemingway in Pamplona later that year.

In July 1953 Cooper wrote Lorraine that "we drove to Toledo to a bull-raising ranch and played with the cape with some very snotty little heifers and had some fun. Also met Sr. Dominguín and had good iced wine and got back to the hotel smelling like *goats*." A few days later, at the opening of the Castellana Hilton in Madrid, Cooper, coached by Hemingway's bullfighter friend Luis Miguel Dominguín, did some cape work with potentially dangerous young bulls at a *tienta*. He later called it "the scariest moment of my life" and described how he felt in the ring: "I've been around dangerous livestock all my life, cattle, broncs, brahma bulls, but I've never known such pure fear as I felt in that arena, walking out with nothing but a cape toward that horned animal. A few moments before in the corral, it had looked so small and tubercular and now looked like a Greyhound bus. I took an awful beating, but I also managed to do a couple of adequate passes and got some *olés*, and that was better than any Hollywood applause I ever received."

When interviewed on British television in 1959, Cooper—influenced by Hemingway—showed he was aware of the ritualistic meaning of the bullfight. "I've seen about thirty or thirty-five bullfights," he said. "I hated the first two or three I saw, then I began to see the interesting part of it. The human psychology part of the bull fight is the crowd in Mexico. You're sitting in the arena with 60,000 people who know every bit about bullfighting, every nuance, every movement, what it means, what the animal does, what kind of animal he is. They can sense, as fast as the matadors, that the whole thing, besides being very spectacular, the costumes and everything, is a sort of study in mass psychology, and this thing we're talking about, bravery or cowardice."⁹

Shortly after meeting Hemingway in 1956 at the Ritz in Paris, where Cooper was filming *Love in the Afternoon*, the actor again tried to draw him into the movie business. This time the hot property was *The Leopard Woman*, and the attraction was not only money but also his companionship on another African safari:

> Would you be interested in doing it with me on a participation set-up, tossing in your ideas and some writing and perhaps, if you feel up to it, going to Africa when it is made and getting some good plinking [pistol shooting] and bird shooting at the same time?
>
> The condition of the picture business makes it possible to come off with some real money if you have got a movie a real cut above the average. . . . Ever since *For Whom the Bell Tolls* I have felt that you have never gotten your share of what you have contributed to stories of yours that have been made into pictures. . . . If you think you want to yak a bit about the African picture, I am always ready to jump aboard and come down to see you [in Cuba].

Hemingway felt morally superior by remaining aloof from Hollywood and had condemned Faulkner for taking money to work on the screenplay of *To Have and Have Not*. He had been seriously injured and reported dead after two plane crashes during his second trip to Africa in January 1954, and was about to leave on a futile journey to Peru in search of huge jumping marlin for the film version of *The Old Man and the Sea*. As soon as he received the letter, he wrote that he would have nothing more to do with the disgusting producers who made movies: "Coops the picture business is not for me and no matter how much dough we could make, how would we spend it if we were dead from dealing with the characters we would have to deal with. After *The Old Man and the Sea* is finished I will not ever have anything to do with pictures again so Help Me God. God is capitalized."

In Hemingway's view, Cooper's craving for wealth was a major defect in his character. Pat Neal agreed that Cooper "adored people with money. That was what had happened with the Countess di Frasso. When he met Rocky, he knew her step-father was rich, rich, rich and he wanted to marry her and, in fact, they were very happy. When you met him, he pretended not to care about money, but he loved it. He loved to live well, and he did live well: fabulous suits, ties, shirts and shoes which he had made for himself. He was the best dresser I've ever known."

Hemingway, who disliked Gatsby-like attire and dominating women, resented Rocky, who would sometimes jerk the chain, cut short an all-male hunting trip and force Gary to return for a social event in Sun Valley. She in turn disliked Cooper's stories about the novelist's real, imagined and often drunken exploits. Hemingway tried to support Cooper when they discussed his intention to convert to Catholicism. But he disapproved of Rocky's influence on his friend's religion and sardonically remarked that by entering the Church Coop could have "all that money *and* God."[10] Hemingway told another friend that Cooper now loved money more than most people love God. He believed Cooper had converted to please his wife and felt rather bitter about it because he had done precisely the same thing when he married Pauline Pfeiffer in 1927.

Despite Hemingway's forceful rejection of both *The Leopard Woman* and Hollywood, Cooper revived his old plan to make a film based on *Across the River and into the Trees*, which had been published in 1950. He discussed the idea with Hemingway during their annual hunt in the fall of 1958 and the project made some progress. By September 1960 Cooper was actively trying to acquire the screen rights to the novel and Hemingway was calling him in London to find out about the deal. In October Hemingway's emissary, after meeting Cooper in London, announced that the contracts would soon be drawn up in Hollywood. On October 21, referring to Hemingway's *Islands in the Stream* (posthumously published in 1970), Rocky wrote to Charles Feldman: "I keep thinking of the big, big story that must be nearly finished. How great to do it really independently cutting Ernest in. It seems Gary is the only guy he really trusts in Hollywood."

Later that year this film project was finally canceled. On May 2, 1960, while recuperating from his first cancer surgery, Cooper tried in a letter to Hemingway to make light of his condition: "I was hooked up to a P[iss] bottle with a tube coming out of 'you know what' and I looked like some sort of 'still' making a low-grade grape juice." As one man became physically sick, the other was prey to mental illness. In the summer and fall of 1960, while Cooper was recovering, Hemingway began to suffer from obsessions, delusions, paranoid fears of poverty and persecution, inability to work, severe depression and suicidal impulses. In late November 1960 he entered the Mayo Clinic and had a series of shock treatments, which obliterated his memory and intensified his depression. In late December, while Hemingway endured purgatory in the Mayo, Rocky Cooper was told that Gary's cancer was fatal.

In January 1961, after the testimonial dinner at the Friars Club, Hemingway printed out a strained message in childish capital letters: "DEAR COOPS. MARY AND EYE COULDNT BE PROUDER OR HAPPIER AND ITS WONDERFUL TO HAVE THE FIRST GUY HONORED. DESERVE IT COMPLETELY AS MAN AND SO MUCH FINER ACTOR THAN ANYBODY KNOWS INCLUDING YOU. LOVE FROM US BOTH AND SEE YOU AND ROCK SOON AT THE VALLEY. PAPA."[11] In late January, after Hemingway was released from the clinic, the two doomed friends had a poignant reunion in Sun Valley and tried to sustain each other as they hiked and talked for the last time.

On April 18 Hemingway, watching television at his home near Sun Valley, saw James Stewart accept Cooper's Oscar. When Stewart revealed that Cooper was dying, Hemingway was visibly shocked. Lloyd Arnold recalled: "There was a noticeable wincing in Papa, a squirming—in his chair at the moment—an odd little utterance, like an 'mmmph!' But it was not particularly alarming, even when he got up, paced about, joining the normal comments about Coop. . . . Mary [Hemingway] suggested a call be put through to Coop—congratulate him, cheer him up. . . . Papa resisted strongly." When Mary called anyway, talked to both Rocky and Cooper, then handed the phone to Hemingway, "it was torture to poor Papa. . . . 'What will I say to Coop, what can I say?' " Obsessed by the illness of the always strong Cooper—who was close to death and had grimly predicted, "I bet I make it to the barn before you"—Hemingway, taking up the gambling metaphor, exclaimed that his friend "had been dealt the Big C but would go fifteen rounds with it."

A week later Hemingway reentered the Mayo for the second and even more disastrous series of shock treatments. Now it was Cooper's turn to offer condolences. On April 29 the Coopers sent a sympathetic telegram: "DEAR PAPA. WHAT'S THERE TO SAY EXCEPT THAT YOU HAVE OUR LOVE. GARY AND ROCKY." Sustained by religion as he was devoured by cancer, Cooper provided a terrifying warning to Hemingway. He kept his word and died before his friend. Hemingway was too ill to attend Cooper's funeral and, less than two months later, shot himself. It was left to Rocky to say: "I know there was no person that Gary held in greater regard."[12]

IV

In November 1959, before he became seriously ill, Cooper told an interviewer: "I'd say, yeah, I'm afraid of death. I don't want to kick the bucket yet. I got a lot of things to do." But when cancer took hold of his body and brought him close to death, he found comfort in religion, accepted his condition and was not afraid of the future. After great pain, a formal feeling came. "I'd like it to be different," he said, "but if that's God's will, that's the way it's meant to be."

When Hemingway's emissary met Cooper to discuss their plans for the future, Cooper told him: "The medics have given me the word on that operation I had—it was cancer. They say I'm not gonna hang around too long. I hope to Christ they are right." A month later Cooper was "a wasted figure, lying immobile in a darkened room. . . . He was hit by a big pain and his face contorted as he fought it off; sweat instantly covered his face. When the pain had passed, Cooper reached his hand over to the bed table and picked up a crucifix, which he put on the pillow beside his head. 'Please give Papa a message. It's important and you mustn't forget because I'll not be talking to him again. Tell him . . . that time I wondered if I made the right decision'—he moved the crucifix a little closer so that it touched his cheek—'tell him it was the best thing I ever did.' "[13]

During the last week of his life Cooper was fed intravenously and remained under heavy sedation. Rocky and Maria could talk to him until the last two days, when he was thoroughly dosed with morphine and drifted in and out of consciousness. Father Ford had moved to another parish; Monsignor Daniel Sullivan, who visited him every day for the last two weeks, administered the last rites the day before his death. Following Bogart in 1957, Flynn in 1959 and Gable in 1960—all of whom died prematurely—Cooper passed away, at home with his family, on Saturday, May 13, 1961 at 12:47 P.M.

Several months earlier Cooper, Rocky and Maria had picked out his burial plot, between pine and fig trees, with an ocean view, in the St. Anne Grotto of Holy Cross Cemetery in Culver City. Cooper had cracked jokes about it, and only the undertaker was squeamish and sweaty. Cooper wanted a private burial, but before the police could put up a cordon, a photographer sneaked in, climbed a tree and then fell to the ground. The local newspaper reported that the Beverly Hills police chief, though pleading for decent and restrained behavior at the funeral, correctly predicted: " 'Private or not, nobody is going to bury a star like

Cooper quietly.' There will be 70 policemen at the Roman Catholic Church of the Good Shepherd where the Mass will be held. Hundreds more will line the route to Cooper's home. . . . The sight of star mourners . . . may turn the occasion into a 'premiere spectacle.' " In addition to Cooper's mother, brother, wife and daughter, a great number of celebrities turned out. There were old friends: Buddy Rogers, Joel McCrea, James Stewart and Cesar Romero; colleagues who had worked with him: Joan Crawford, Audrey Hepburn, Burt Lancaster, Karl Malden, Dorothy McGuire and Dmitri Tiomkin; social companions: Merle Oberon, Peter and Pat Lawford; and others who came to pay their respects or to be seen paying their respects: Jack Warner, George Cukor, John Ford, John Wayne, Edward G. Robinson, Frank Sinatra, Dean Martin, Randolph Scott, Bob Hope, Jimmy Durante, Norma Shearer, Fred Astaire, Walter Pidgeon, James Mason, Alec Guinness, Tony Curtis and Janet Leigh. Some stars protested about where they were seated in the church and, when not moved to a better place, went off in a huff. Marlene Dietrich, thinking of their distant love affair, "was photographed looking 'stricken.' "[14]

The pallbearers included Henry Hathaway and James Stewart (but not Cooper's brother, Arthur) as well as four Jewish friends: Jack Benny, Bill Goetz, Jerry Wald and Charles Feldman. Benny and Goetz, puzzled by the Catholic service, asked: "What's the priest doing with the incense?" Timothy Manning, auxiliary archbishop of Los Angeles, tactfully ignoring Cooper's infidelities, delivered the eulogy: "His family life and home were sacred to him. . . . He was the husband of one wife, the faithful image of a father. . . . He was immune from the corrupting influences of the publicity and praise which he merited above his fellows. He was unparalleled in the perfection of his art." Throughout the world Cooper was mourned as a symbolic figure. In Stockholm the *Svenska Dagbladet* described him as "the incarnation of the honorable American"; in Naples the actor-director Vittorio de Sica called Cooper "the greatest actor the screen ever had."

Cooper's will, filed on February 27, 1961 (the day Rocky told him about his illness), left more than $3.5 million. He left half to Rocky and half in trust to his mother and Maria, and made several bequests: $1,000 to Thomas Merton's Our Lady of Gethsemane Abbey in Kentucky; $5,000 each to Arthur, Georgia and Howard Cooper; and $10,000 to the Motion Picture Relief Fund. If Maria had no heirs, the estate would be divided in equal thirds and given to the American Cancer Society, the

American Heart Fund and the Roman Catholic bishop of Los Angeles. Rocky gave Cooper's own hat, chaps, holster and saddle to the Museum of the West in Oklahoma, and donated other Stetsons, guns and saddles from his movies to the Museum of Memorabilia in Hollywood.

Heeding the advice of the agent Swifty Lazar, who told her, "You don't live in Hershey, Pennsylvania, if you're not in chocolate," Rocky decided to leave Hollywood.[15] She sold the Baroda Drive house and moved with Maria to New York. Cooper had always loved the ocean and Long Island. In May 1974 his body was removed from Holy Cross Cemetery and reburied, under a three-ton boulder from a Montauk quarry, in the Sacred Heart Cemetery in Southampton and near his family on the East Coast.

V

Cooper's death marked the end of an era, but his image continued to have a significant impact on literature, politics and the movies. In 1961 the *Corriere della Sera* had declared: "With him there is ended a certain America, that of the frontier and of innocence, which had or was believed to have had an exact sense of the dividing line between good and evil." The French novelist Romain Gary, who had met Cooper when he was French consul in Los Angeles in 1959–60, took up this idea in his novel *Adieu, Gary Cooper* (1969). In a crucial scene the hero, lamenting the death of the actor, associates him with vanished certainties, now swept away by the political and social revolutions of 1968: "It's finished, Gary Cooper. Finished forever. Finished, the quiet American, sure of himself and of his rightness, who fights the bad guys, is always for the good cause, makes justice triumph and always wins in the end. Goodbye American certitudes. Now, it's Vietnam, the exploding universities, the black ghettoes. *Ciao*, Gary Cooper."

The image of Cooper's rock-like honesty reappeared in moments of national crisis. During the Suez showdown of November 1956 a British cartoonist portrayed Prime Minister Harold Macmillan, as Sheriff Cooper, confronting Nasser and Co. in front of the Suez saloon. During the Watergate scandal that led to Richard Nixon's resignation, Cooper, the man who could sort out and deal with the bad guys, appeared on the cover of *New York* magazine of August 13, 1973 with the caption "Where Are You, Gary Cooper, Now That We Need You?" In the historic Polish elections in June 1989 the Solidarity union used Cooper's powerful image to emphasize the need to stand together against the Communist government. The movement "unveiled as its final campaign poster the image of Gary Cooper, as a grimly resolute sheriff, 'striding toward the viewer, the union's red logo emblazoned on the horizon behind him, a simple caption underneath—*High Noon!*' "[16]

In the parodic and bitter *Midnight Cowboy* (1969) Jon Voight, a Texan hustling in New York ("To tell you the truth, I ain't a real cowboy. But I'm one helluva stud!"), is impressed by a woman on a radio program who thinks Cooper is the ideal man. In *Dirty Harry* (1972) Clint Eastwood plays a vigilante cop who identifies with Cooper and fights criminals on his own. Contemptuous of the legal system, he takes private revenge, then imitates Cooper's final gesture in *High Noon* by throwing his police badge into the water where the killer's corpse is floating.

The most durable of all Hollywood heroes, Cooper began his career in silent films, became a major star in the golden age of the great studios and remained prominent by founding his own companies during the era of independent production. He quickly became a star and—despite troughs in the mid-1930s, late 1940s and early 1950s—remained at the peak of his profession. The emotional upheavals of middle age strengthened his acting, and he finished strongly with a series of impressive films. His career, one of the longest in movie history, lasted from 1925 to 1961, and he was one of the leading moneymakers for sixteen years. He headed the popularity polls in the 1940s and appeared in the *Motion Picture Herald*'s Top Ten film personalities from 1936 to 1958.

Rugged in his twenties, romantic in his thirties, distinguished in his forties and poignant in his fifties, Cooper will always be remembered for his greatest scenes: flying to his death in *Wings*, confronting Walter Huston in *The Virginian*, gazing languidly at Marlene Dietrich in *Morocco*, staring upward while wheeled into the operating room in *A Farewell to Arms*, sliding down the banister in *Mr. Deeds Goes to Town*, defending the desert fort in *Beau Geste*, massacring the "krauts" in *Sergeant York*, saying farewell in *The Pride of the Yankees*, romancing Ingrid Bergman in *For Whom the Bell Tolls*, rock drilling in *The Fountainhead*, defeating the villains in *High Noon* and sweeping Audrey Hepburn off her feet in *Love in the Afternoon*.

Cooper's purity of style and controlling intelligence seemed larger than life. He could touch and move an audience, who always admired and identified with him. Nunnally Johnson observed that "he was a success for so long partly because he was beautiful, partly because he has one of the most winning personalities that ever came in front of a camera." In his films, as in his life, Cooper emphasized action over intellect, and combined the heroic qualities of the romantic lover, exotic adventurer, tough fighter and ordinary man. Instead of transforming himself into the character he was playing, the strong, silent, charming Cooper gave each part the imprint of his own character. An Everyman in extraordinary situations, he could do in movies what others only dreamed of and became what everyone wanted to be.

The great theme of his films was the conflict between action and reflection. They expressed essential American values: connection with nature, scepticism about experts, distrust of government, independent endeavor, modesty about one's achievements. In close-ups his face—like Jefferson's and Lincoln's—symbolized the inner qualities of the national hero whom the poet Rupert Brooke had described in 1916: "the tall, thin type of American, with pale blue eyes of an idealistic, disappointed expression." John Updike, defining the spiritual grace and power that the camera captured on film, observed that Cooper's "leathery face, with its baleful Nordic eyes and slightly frozen mouth, so inert-seeming in the cluttered glare of the sound stage, possessed a steady inner life."[17]

Notes

Chapter One: Montana

1. Gary Cooper, "When I Was a Boy," *St. Nicholas Magazine*, 63 (November 1935), 21; Gary Cooper, as told to George Scullin, "Well, It Was This Way," *Saturday Evening Post*, February 25, 1956, p. 78; Michael Malone, Richard Roeder and William Lang, *Montana: A History of Two Centuries*, revised edition (Seattle, 1991), pp. 67, 108.
2. Federal Writers Project, "Helena," *Montana: A State Guide Book* (New York, 1939), p. 164; Malone, *Montana*, p. 194; Letter from Charles Cooper to Hedda Hopper, November 14, 1945, Margaret Herrick Library, Academy of Motion Picture Arts and Sciences, Beverly Hills, California.
3. Cooper, "Well, It Was This Way," February 25, 1956, p. 80; Dudley Nichols, screenplay of *For Whom the Bell Tolls* (Hollywood: Script City, 1942), p. 80.
4. Interview with Charles' granddaughter Georgia Cooper Burton, Huron, Ohio, August 31, 1996; Interview with Charles' grandson, Howard Cooper, Peoria, Arizona, October 20, 1996; Jane Ellen Wayne, *Cooper's Women* (1988; London, 1989), p. 27.
5. Gary Cooper, "The Hollywood Greats," pp. 1–2, BBC interview, November 30, 1959, courtesy of Maria Cooper Janis.

    As Charles' law career prospered, the family moved off a main thoroughfare to three other houses, near each other and in a better part of town: a large three-story, stucco, turreted duplex at the corner of Fifth and Beattie; a shuttered two-story, wood frame house, with a railed front porch, up a steep hill at 15 Shiland; and a brick dwelling, with a big front window and arched entrance leading to the front porch, across the street at 712 Fifth Avenue.
6. Patsy DuBuis, "Gary," *Screen Play*, June 1933, pp. 34-35; Alice Cooper, *Women in Their Lives*, filmed interview with mothers of the stars, UCLA Film Archives; Gary Cooper, "Their First Jobs," *New Movie Magazine*, 1930.

7. James Kotsilibas and Myrna Loy, *Myrna Loy: Being and Becoming* (New York, 1987), pp. 7-8, 14; George Carpozi, Jr., *The Gary Cooper Story* (New Rochelle, N.Y., 1970), p. 18; Cooper, "When I Was a Boy," p. 21; Interview with Lorraine Chanel, San Antonio, Texas, November 3, 1996.

8. The ranch site can still be seen today. Drive north on I-15, take exit 244 and go back toward Helena for two miles on the frontage road. At milepost 242, on the west side of the highway, there's the white-painted 7 Bar 9 sign above the gatepost and the abutment of the old footbridge.

9. "Gary Cooper's Real Romance," Philipsburg *Mail* (Montana), April 27, 1928; Larry Swindell, *The Last Hero: A Biography of Gary Cooper* (Garden City, N.Y., 1980), p. 11; Cooper, "The Hollywood Greats," p. 3.

10. Alice Cooper, *Women in Their Lives*; Cooper, "Well, It Was This Way," March 3, 1956, p. 56; Vivian Paladin and Joan Bancus, *Helena: An Illustrated History* (Norfolk, Va.: Donning, 1983), p. 188; Cooper, "When I Was a Boy," p. 21.

Chapter Two: Dunstable and Grinnell

1. Cooper, "Well, It Was This Way," February 25, 1956, p. 81; F.M. Bancroft, *A Short History of Dunstable School, 1888–1963* (Dunstable, England: Parsons, 1963), pp. 5–6; William Plomer, in *The Old School*, ed. Graham Greene (1934; Oxford, 1984), p. 115; Bancroft, *Short History of Dunstable School*, p. 7; Cooper, "Well, It Was This Way," February 25, 1956, p. 82.

2. Gary Cooper, "I Remember Pinewood and the Days of Celluloid City," *News of the World* (London), October 24, 1937, p. 5; "Gary Cooper on His Dunstable Schooldays," Dunstable *Gazette*, October 25, 1937; Letter from Charles Cooper to Gary Cooper, May 13, 1909, Doheny Library, University of Southern California; "Secrets of Gary Cooper's Boyhood in Britain," *Film Pictorial*, August 15, 1936, p. 8. I owe this and other valuable information to Colin Bourne of Dunstable.

3. John Buckledee, "Boyhood Chums Recall Hollywood Hero," Dunstable *News-Gazette*, July 31, 1986, p. 14; Cooper, "Well, It Was This Way," February 25, 1956, p. 82; Gary Cooper, as told to Dorothy Spensley, "The Big Boy Tells His Story," *Photoplay*, 35 (April 1929), 134; Harold Nicolson, in *The Old School*, p. 91.

4. "Gary Cooper on His Dunstable Schooldays," Dunstable *Gazette*, October 25, 1937; Cooper, "Well, It Was This Way," February 25,

1956, p. 81; Ted Bonnet, "Home Town Tales of Gary Cooper: Limburgered the School and Greased the Rails," Helena, November 21, no citation, USC.

5. Letter from Gary Cooper to Wellington Rankin, October 9, 1946, Montana Historical Society, Helena; Letter from Alice Cooper to Wellington Rankin [December 1961], Montana Historical Society; Peter Hassrick, *Charles M. Russell* (New York, 1989), p. 17; Gary Cooper, "Shooting Clichés on the Western Range," *Hollywood Reporter*, November 24, 1958; Frederic Renner, *Charles M. Russell* (New York, 1967), pp. 12–13.

6. Cooper, "I Remember Pinewood," p. 5; Cooper, "Well, It Was This Way," February 19, 1956, p. 110 and Gary Cooper, "The Big Boy Tells His Story," *Photoplay*, 35 (May 1929), 71; Interviews with Maria Cooper Janis, New York and Bethlehem, Connecticut, November 16–27, 1996.

7. Malone, *Montana*, p. 252; Pete Martin, "Tall in the Saddle," *Pete Martin Calls On* (New York, 1962), p. 364; Gary Cooper, as told to Leonard Slater, "I Took a Good Look at Myself, and This Is What I Saw," *McCall's*, January 1961, p. 140.

8. *Reports of Cases Argued and Determined in the Supreme Court of the State of Montana*, volume 60: 1921 (San Francisco: Bancroft-Whitney, 1922), p. 109; *Reports*, volume 63: 1922 (San Francisco, 1923), p. 221; *Reports*, volume 58: 1920 (San Francisco, 1921), p. 401; *Reports*, volume 66: 1923 (San Francisco, 1924), pp.193–194.

9. Quoted in Perry Tschida, "Charles Henry Cooper," term paper for a History of Law class at the University of Montana School of Law in Missoula, Montana Historical Society. This paper has been a valuable guide through Charles' legal career; Letter from Charles Cooper to Hedda Hopper, November 14,1945, Herrick; Interview with Howard Cooper; Carpozi, *The Gary Cooper Story*, p. 192.
   Rankin retired from the bench in 1925 and was appointed U.S. district attorney for Montana.

10. Bonnet, "Home Town Tales of Gary Cooper"; Swindell, *The Last Hero*, p. 33; Gladys Hall, "In His Own Quiet Way," October 1940, p. 9; Herrick; Interview with Cooper's high school classmate Mac Walton Lessley, Bozeman, Montana, October 19, 1996.

11. Letter from Montana State University, Bozeman, to Jeffrey Meyers, October 16, 1996; Graduation Book of Gallatin County High School, courtesy of Maria Cooper Janis; Willie Scobee, "Gary Cooper's First Appearance," *Modern Screen*, November 1931, p. 55; "Gary Cooper's Last Trip Home," *Look*, July 18, 1961, p. 54, with a photo of Ida Davis.

12. Ruth Suckow, "Grinnell," *College Humor*, May 1930, p. 98; William

Deminoff, "Gary Cooper Was a Three-Time Loser at Grinnell," Cedar Rapids *Gazette*, May 11, 1986; Interview with Richard Seeland, Grinnell, Iowa, March 16, 1997; William Crouch, "Through College with Gary Cooper," p. 106, no citation, USC.

13. In 1922–23 he took World History, English Archeology, Greek, Spanish, Speech, Physical Training and Hygiene; in 1923–24, English Literature, English Composition, Economics, Business Administration 101 and 314, Zoology and Physical Training.

14. Letters from Gary Cooper to Lorraine Chanel, May 26, 1953 and August 5, 1953, courtesy of Lorraine Chanel; Interview with Fay Wray, Los Angeles, December 7, 1996; Stuart Kaminsky, *Coop: The Life and Legend of Gary Cooper* (New York, 1980), p. 18.

15. Deminoff, "Gary Cooper Was a Three-Time Loser at Grinnell"; Suckow, "Grinnell," pp. 100–101; "Cooper," *Grinnell Scarlet and Black*, October 19, 1929, p. 1; Carpozi, *The Gary Cooper Story*, p. 36.

Chapter Three: Stuntman to Star

1. Carpozi, *The Gary Cooper Story*, p. 33; Cooper, "Well, It Was This Way," February 25, 1956, p. 78 and March 3, 1956, p. 52; Cooper, "The Big Boy Tells His Story," May 1929, p. 84; Slim Talbot, as told to Bruce Lee, "I Was Gary Cooper for 35 Years," *Climax: Exciting Stories for Men*, June 1962, p. 91; Hall, "In His Own Quiet Way," pp. 1–2; Letter from Gary Cooper to a fan, *Screen Play*, c. 1930, USC.

2. Carpozi, *The Gary Cooper Story*, p. 42; Stan Opotowski, "The Gary Cooper Story," New York *Post Daily Magazine*, April 24, 1961, p. 25; Interview with Howard Cooper; DuBuis, "Gary," p. 67.

3. Kaminsky, *Coop*, p. 24; Fay Wray, *On the Other Hand* (New York, 1989), pp. 55–56; Cooper, "Well, It Was This Way," March 10, 1956, p. 92.

4. Kevin Brownlow, *The Parade's Gone By* (Berkeley, 1968), pp. 115–116; Cooper, "I Took a Good Look at Myself," p. 141; R. Dixon Smith, *Ronald Colman: Gentleman of the Cinema* (Jefferson, N.C., 1991), p. 74; Jesse Lasky, with Don Weldon, *I Blow My Own Horn* (Garden City, N.Y., 1957), p. 211.

5. Patsy DuBuis, "After a Year of Fame," *Picture Play*, September 1929, p. 28; Kotsilibas and Loy, *Myrna Loy*, p. 56; Interviews with Howard Cooper and Georgia Cooper Burton; "At the Foot of the Class," [1931], no citation, New York Public Library.

6. Molly Haskell, *From Reverence to Rape* (New York, 1974), p. 359;

John Kobal, *People Will Talk* (New York, 1986), p. 290; Boze Hadleigh, *Conversations with My Elders* (Boston, 1978), p. 84.

7. Cooper, "Well, It Was This Way," March 17, 1956, p. 108; Interview with Angela Allen (speaking about a friend), London, July 23, 1996; Interview with Luise Rainer, London, July 26, 1996; Budd Schulberg, *Moving Pictures: Memories of a Hollywood Prince* (New York, 1981), p. 266; Wayne, *Cooper's Women*, p. 77.

8. Barry Norman, "Gary Cooper," *The Hollywood Greats* (New York, 1980), p. 100; Hector Arce, *Gary Cooper: An Intimate Biography* (1979; New York, 1980), p. 55; Interview with Arlene Dahl, New York, November 21, 1996.

9. F. Scott Fitzgerald, "Flappers Are Just Girls with a Splendid Talent for Life," *F. Scott Fitzgerald: In His Own Time*, ed. Matthew Bruccoli and Jackson Bryer (1971; New York, 1974), p. 280; F. Scott Fitzgerald, "A Patriotic Short" (1940), *The Pat Hobby Stories* (1962; New York, 1988), pp. 119–120.

10. Cooper, "The Big Boy Tells His Story," p. 110; David Stenn, *Clara Bow: Runnin' Wild* (1988; New York, 1990), pp. 95; 100; 94; 102; Arce, *Gary Cooper*, p. 35; Wayne, *Cooper's Women*, p. 124.

11. Brownlow, *The Parade's Gone By*, p. 168; Richard Schickel, *The Men Who Made the Movies* (New York, 1975), pp. 205–206; Kaminsky, *Coop*, p. 35; Scott Eyman, *Mary Pickford: America's Sweetheart* (New York, 1990), p. 187; Errol Flynn, *From a Life of Adventure* (Secaucus, N.J., 1980), p. 173.

12. Patrick McGilligan, *George Cukor: A Double Life* (New York, 1991), p. 50; Capozi, *The Gary Cooper Story*, pp. 87; 83; Arce, *Gary Cooper*, p. 33; Esther Ralston, *Some Day We'll Laugh* (Metuchen, N.J., 1985), p. 103; Sam Jaffe, oral history, p. 114, Herrick.

13. Margaret Chute, "The Saga of a Happy Warrior—Gary Cooper," [1935], no citation, courtesy of Colin Bourne; Stenn, *Clara Bow*, pp. 121; 101; 98; 306.

Chapter Four: Lupe Velez and The Virginian

1. Kobal, *People Will Talk*, p. 114; Floyd Conner, *Lupe Velez and Her Lovers* (New York, 1993), p. 81; Cooper, "The Big Boy Tells His Story," May 1929, p. 110; Conner, *Lupe Velez and Her Lovers*, p. 79.

2. Kobal, *People Will Talk*, p. 106; Interview with Fay Wray; Arce, *Gary Cooper*, p. 47.

3. Arthur Pettit, *Images of the Mexican-American in Fiction and Film* (College Station, Texas, 1980), p. 141; Katherine Albert, "Roping Gary," c. 1938, no citation, New York Public Library; Conner, *Lupe*

Velez and Her Lovers, p. 89; Jan Herman, *A Talent for Trouble: The Life of Hollywood's Most Acclaimed Director, William Wyler* (New York, 1995), p. 95.

4. Interview with Howard Cooper; Adela Rogers St. Johns, "Gary Cooper's Love Story in Three Acts," *Love, Laughter and Tears: My Hollywood Story* (1978; New York, 1979), p. 246; Sheilah Graham, *The Garden of Allah* (New York, 1970), p. 80.

   Graham, unreliable as always, claimed she was with Fitzgerald at the time of the incident in 1936–37. But Cooper had broken with Lupe long before then. The event must have occurred during Fitzgerald's earlier trip to Hollywood in 1931—five years before he met Sheilah.

5. Jim Tully, "The Man from Montana," *New Movie Magazine*, August 1931, p. 61; Edward Churchill, "Gary Cooper Faces Thirty," *Silver Screen*, 1931, p. 74; Cooper, "Well, It Was This Way," March 24, 1956, p. 139.

6. Conner, *Lupe Velez and Her Lovers*, p. 53; Norman, *The Hollywood Greats*, pp. 100–101.

7. Schickel, *The Men Who Made the Movies*, p. 166; Jeff Corey, "Gary Cooper: Natural Talent," *Close-Ups: The Movie Star Book*, ed. Danny Peary (1978; New York, 1988), p. 501; Jeffrey Brown, 'Putting on the Ritz: Masculinity and the Young Gary Cooper," *Screen*, 36 (Autumn 1995), 193.

8. Walter Wagner, ed. *You Must Remember This: Oral Reminiscences* (New York, 1975), p. 136 and Wayne, *Cooper's Women*, p. 33; Pauline Kael, *For Keeps* (New York, 1994), p. 125; Robert Warshow, *The Immediate Experience* (1962; New York, 1970), pp.142–143.

Chapter Five: The Man in Morocco

1. Sheilah Graham, "Coop," *Confessions of a Hollywood Columnist* (1969; New York, 1970), pp. 290–291; Hall, "In His Own Quiet Way," p. 6; Walter Brennan, as told to James Reid, "My Pal, Gary Cooper," July 1941, pp. 85–86, no citation.

2. Interview with Maria Cooper Janis; Interview with Sidney Wood, Southampton, New York, November 16, 1996; Talbot, "I Was Gary Cooper for 35 Years," p. 90.

3. Joe Hyams, "Hollywood's Ageless Stars," New York *Herald Tribune*, April 10, 1957; Kobal, *People Will Talk*, p. 299; Wayne, *Cooper's Women*, p. 143; Jessamyn West, *To See the Dream* (New York, 1957), p. 100.

4. Interview with Annabella Power, Paris, France, June 18, 1996;

Interview with Maria Cooper Janis; Richard Schickel, "Gary Cooper: An American Abroad," *Schickel on Film* (New York, 1989), p. 187; Kaminsky, *Coop*, p. 189.

5. Kaminsky, *Coop*, p. 19; Rex Lease and Kenneth Harlan, eds., *What Actors Eat—When They Eat* (Los Angeles: Lyman House, 1939), p. 57; Interview with Douglas Fairbanks, Jr., New York, November 25, 1996; Hugo Vickers, *Cecil Beaton* (Boston, 1985), p. 127.

6. Tully, "The Man from Montana," p. 61; Interview with Georgia Cooper Burton; "Coop Reared in Helena," *Independent-Record* (Helena), January 6, 1976, p. A-12; Heritage Plantation, *The Automobile Collection* (Sandwich, Mass., 1986), pp. 36, 38; Clifford Odets, *Golden Boy* (New York, 1937), p. 78.

7. Hall, "In His Own Quiet Way"; Letter from Gary Cooper to Ruth Wood, a fan, July 2, 1930, USC; Interview with André De Toth, Burbank, California, December 8, 1996; Interview with Evie Johnson, Palm Beach, Florida, December 14, 1996; Carpozi, *The Gary Cooper Story*, pp. 204; 212.

8. Gary Cooper, "Murder in the Midst of Make-Believe," *News of the World* (London), November 14, 1937, p. 5; Maria Riva, *Marlene Dietrich* (1992; New York, 1994), p. 91; Steven Bach, *Marlene Dietrich: Life and Legend* (New York, 1992), p. 134; Donald Spoto, *Blue Angel: The Life of Marlene Dietrich* (New York, 1992), p. 71; Riva, *Marlene Dietrich*, p. 97.

9. Peter Bogdanovich, *Pieces of Time* (New York, 1973), p. 121; Gary Cooper, "Foreword" to Josef von Sternberg, *Fun in a Chinese Laundry* (1965; San Francisco: Mercury House, 1988); Swindell, *The Last Hero*, p. 122; Cooper, "Foreword"; von Stemberg, *Fun in a Chinese Laundry*, pp, 247–248.

10. [Jules Furthman], "*Morocco*" and "*Shanghai Express*" (New York, 1973), p. 13; Letter from the Breen Office to B.P. Schulberg, April 15, 1930, Herrick; [Furthman], *Morocco*, pp. 23; 26; 31.

11. Raymond Durgnat, "Six Films of Josef von Sternberg," *Movies and Methods*, ed. Bill Nichols (Berkeley, 1976), 1: 265; Riva, *Marlene Dietrich*, p. 101; Homer Dickens, *The Films of Gary Cooper* (Secaucus, N.J., 1970), p. 87.

12. Cooper, "Well, It Was This Way," March 24, 1956, p. 142; Tom Milne, "*City Streets*," *Rouben Mamoulian* (Bloomington, Ind., 1969), p. 31; Evan William Cameron, ed., *Sound and the Cinema: The Coming of Sound to American Film* (New York, 1980), p. 94.

13. Wayne, *Cooper's Women*, p. 67; Larry Swindell, *Screwball: The Life of Carole Lombard* (New York, 1957), p. 146.

Chapter Six: Breakdown and the Countess di Frasso

1. Wayne, *Cooper's Women*, p. xv; Conner, *Lupe Velez and Her Lovers*, p. 91; Cooper, "Well, It Was This Way," March 24, 1956, p. 140.

2. Wayne, *Cooper's Women*, p. 31; Marion Leslie, "I'm Through Being Bossed," *Photoplay*, 42 (October 1932), 99; Arce, Gary Cooper, p. 73.

3. Alice Cooper, as told to Dorothy Spensley, "Gary's Mother Speaks at Last," *Modern Screen*, [1931], pp. 52–53; Conner, *Lupe Velez and Her Lovers*, pp. 227, 229.

4. Swindell, *The Last Hero*, p. 30; Carpozi, *The Gary Cooper Story*, p. 109; Interview with Howard Cooper; Alice Cooper, "Gary's Mother Speaks at Last," p. 93.

5. "At the Foot of the Class," [1931], no citation, New York Public Library; Leslie, "I'm Through Being Bossed," pp. 98; 34; Churchill, "Gary Cooper Faces Thirty," p. 59 and Gary Cooper, "The First 10 Years," Rochester *Democrat and Chronicle*, July 19, 1936.

6. Cooper, "Well, It Was This Way," April 7, 1956, p. 120 and March 24, 1956, p. 142; "The King of Heroes," [1931], p. 56, no citation, USC.

7. Carpozi, *The Gary Cooper Story*, p. 111; Interview with Douglas Fairbanks, Jr.; Interview with Mary Taylor Zimbalist, Ojai, California, December 15, 1996.

8. W.E. Greenwood, *The Villa Madama: A Reconstruction* (London: J. Tiranti, 1928), p, 2. See also Georgina Masson, *The Companion Guide to Rome*, revised edition (London, 1972), pp. 512, 544; David Heymann, *Poor Little Rich Girl: The Life and Legend of Barbara Hutton* (London, 1985), p. 68; Cooper, "The First Ten Years."

9. Ernest Hemingway, *Green Hills of Africa* (New York, 1935), pp. 217, 40; Laura Benham, "Gary's Back," *Picture Play*, July 1932, p. 72; George Freer, "Can It Be? Star That Exults That He Has No Stars," New York *Herald Tribune*, no citation, New York Public Library.

10. Cooper, "Well, It Was This Way," March 31, 1956, p. 129; Interview with Suzy Parker, Santa Barbara, California, December 12, 1996; Wayne, *Cooper's Women*, p. 143.

11. Clare Boothe, *The Women* (New York, 1937), pp. 137; 150; 140; Humphrey Bogart, "Why Hollywood Hates Me," *Screen World*, 22 (January 1940), 68; Norman, *The Hollywood Greats*, p. 104; Joel McCrea, "My Friend Coop!" *Photoplay*, October 1939, p. 21.

Chapter Seven: Paramount Star

1. "Paramount: Oscar for Profits," *Fortune*, 35 (June 1947), 219–220; Sylvia Shorris and Marion Bundy, eds., *Talking Pictures: With the People Who Made Them* (New York, 1994), p. 35; Dennis Schaefer and Larry Salvato, eds., *Masters of Light: Conversations with Contemporary Cinematographers* (Berkeley, 1984), p. 12.
2. Doug McClelland, ed., *Hollywood on Hollywood—Tinsel Town Talks* (Boston, 1985), p. 196; Cooper, "Well, It Was This Way," March 24, 1956, p. 139; April 7, 1956, p. 120.
3. Simon Callow, *Charles Laughton: A Difficult Actor* (1987; London, 1988), p. 44; Walter Brennan, oral history, p. 25, Columbia University.
4. For photos of this house, see Scott Berg, "Gary Cooper: Bachelor Living for Best Actor in *Sergeant York* and *High Noon*," *Architectural Digest*, 47 (April 1990), 176–179. Cooper, of course, lived in this house long before he won his Oscars.
5. Arce, *Gary Cooper*, pp. 84, 86; Callow, *Charles Laughton*, pp. 98; 50; Swindell, *The Last Hero*, p. 144 and Callow, *Charles Laughton*, p. 51; Norman, *The Hollywood Greats*, p. 99.
6. René Jordan, *Gary Cooper* (New York, 1974), p. 56; Norman, *The Hollywood Greats*, p. 103; Carpozi, *The Gary Cooper Story*, p. 129.
7. Frank Laurence, *Hemingway and the Movies* (New York, 1981), p. 54; Mike Cormack, *Ideology and Cinematography in Hollywood, 1930–1939* (New York, 1994), p. 118; Laurence, *Hemingway and the Movies*, pp. 44–45.

   The flat, baldly repetitive and fatuously optimistic dialogue of the screen version is a great deal weaker than Hemingway's. In the novel, as Frederic tries to comfort the doomed Catherine, their conversation has ironic and tragic overtones:

   > "I'm not brave any more, darling. I'm all broken. They've broken me. I know it now."
   > "Everybody is that way."
   > "But it's awful. They just keep it up till they break you."
   > "In an hour it will be over."
   > "Isn't that lovely? Darling, I won't die, will I?"
   > "No. I promise you won't."
   > "Because I don't want to die and leave you, but I get so tired of it and I feel I'm going to die."

   Ernest Hemingway, *A Farewell to Arms* (1929; New York, 1969), p. 323.

8. William Wellman, Jr., "Howard Hawks: The Distance Runner," *Focus on Howard Hawks*, ed. Joseph McBride (Englewood Cliffs, N.J., 1972), p. 8; Niven Busch, in *Backstory: Interviews with Screenwriters of Hollywood's Golden Age*, ed. Pat McGilligan (Berkeley, 1986), p. 94; Joseph McBride, *Hawks on Hawks* (Berkeley, 1982), p. 57; William Faulkner, "Today We Live," *Faulkner's MGM Screenplays*, ed. Bruce Kawin (Knoxville, Tenn., 1982), pp. 255; 114; 110.

9. Marion Davies, *The Times We Had* (1975; New York, 1977), p. 249; Charlton Heston, *In the Arena* (New York, 1995), p. 212; Doug Fetherling, *The Five Lives of Ben Hecht* (New York, 1977), p. 114.

10. David Thomson, *A Biographical Dictionary of Film*, 3rd edition (New York, 1994), p. 456; Cooper, "Well, It Was This Way," March 31, 1956, p. 130; James Robert Parish, *The Paramount Pretties* (New Rochelle, N.Y., 1972), p. 235.

11. Haskell, *From Reverence to Rape*, p. 101; Letter from Joseph Breen to Paramount, August 2, 1940, Motion Picture Association of America files, Herrick; Kaminsky, *Coop*, p. 68; Scott Eyman, *Ernst Lubitsch: Laughter in Paradise* (New York, 1993), p. 209; Courtesy of Maria Cooper Janis.

Chapter Eight: Marriage to Rocky

1. Interview with Rocky's first cousin Harry Balfe, New York, November 21, 1996; Interview with Evie Johnson; *Time*, May 23, 1938, p. 51.

2. Townsend Hoopes and David Brinkley, *Driven Patriot: The Life and Times of James Forrestal* (New York, 1992), p. 108; Truman Capote, "A Beautiful Child," *Music for Chameleons* (New York, 1980), p. 237; Interview with Suzy Parker (on Vreeland); F. Scott Fitzgerald, *The Great Gatsby* (1925; New York, 1953), p. 6.

3. Michael Webb, "Cedric Gibbons and the MGM Style," *Architectural Digest*, 47 (April 1990), 112; Wray, *On the Other Hand*, p. 135; Interview with Fay Wray; Richard Gehman, "In an Exclusive Interview Mrs. Gary Cooper Tells the Moving Story of Her Husband's Last Days," *American Magazine*, August 13, 1961, p. 5; Louella Parsons, "Personal Memories of Gary Cooper," *Modern Screen*, August 1961, p. 55.

4. Confidential interviews (on Rocky); Wayne, *Cooper's Women*, p. 63; Interview with Connie Wald, Beverly Hills, California, December 6, 1996; Interview with Ivan Moffat, Los Angeles, California, December 7, 1996.

I met Rocky in November 1996, when she was old and ill, though still attractive and living in a luxurious and immaculate apartment. I was surprised by her personal warmth and responsiveness, and touched when she held my hand between hers when we were introduced and kissed me good-bye when I left.

5. Jack Hemingway, *Misadventures of a Fly Fisherman* (Dallas: Taylor, 1986). p. 78; Elza Schallert, "Gary's Lily-White Bride," *Picture Play*, June 1933, p. 63.
6. Interview with Robert Stack, Los Angeles, December 4, 1996; Swindell, *The Last Hero*, p. 182; Wayne, *Cooper's Women*, p. 14.
  The struggle over his animal trophies continued into the 1950s. When Cooper told Hedda Hopper he'd shot a bear, she challenged him with "I bet Rocky won't let you have the hide in the house" and he proudly replied: "It's in the house"—or at least in his separate gun room, workshop and den (Hedda Hopper, interview with Gary Cooper, October 1952, p. 4, Herrick).
7. Liza, "Easy Does It!" p. 72, no citation, New York Public Library and Swindell, *The Last Hero*, p. 181; Cooper, "Well, It Was This Way," March 31, 1956, p. 132. For photographs of the house, see "The New Brentwood Heights Home of Mr. and Mrs. Gary Cooper," *California Arts and Architecture*, August 1936, pp. 17–19.
8. Hall, "In His Own Quiet Way," p. 7; Frances Marion, *Off with Their Heads!* (New York, 1972), p. 137; Otto Preminger, *Preminger: An Autobiography* (1977; New York, 1978), p. 97.
9. Carpozi, *The Gary Cooper Story*, p. 141; Interview with Lorraine Chanel (on Cesar Romero); Interview with Maria Cooper Janis.
10. Wayne, *Cooper's Women*, p. 69; Interview with Richard Widmark, Santa Barbara, California, December 1, 1996; Henry Hathaway, oral history, p. 29, Columbia University; Interview with Shirley Temple Black, Woodside, California, September 15, 1996.
11. F. Scott Fitzgerald, *The Last Tycoon*, ed. Edmund Wilson (1941; New York, 1986), p. 124; Philip Dunne, oral history, p. 187, American Film Institute, Los Angeles; Talbot, "I Was Gary Cooper for 35 Years," p. 89.
12. Interview with Alice Fleming, Newport Beach, California, December 2, 1996; Interview with Walter Seltzer, Sherman Oaks, California, December 8, 1996; Cooper's will, February 1936, legal files, USC.

Chapter Nine: American Apollo

1. Otis Ferguson, *Film Criticism*, ed. Robert Wilson (Philadelphia, 1971), p. 69; Ralph Bellamy, *When the Smoke Hit the Fan* (Garden

City, N.Y., 1979), p. 185; A. Scott Berg, *Goldwyn: A Biography* (1989; New York, 1990), p. 243.

2. Letter from the Catholic Lending Library to Joseph Breen, [1936], Herrick; Letter from the Breen Office to Paramount, February 18, 1936, Herrick.

3. Graham Greene, *The Pleasure Dome: The Collected Film Criticism, 1935–1940*, ed. John Russell Taylor (London, 1972), p. 64; David Shipman, *Movie Talk* (New York, 1988), p. 41; Alistair Cooke, ed., *Garbo and the Night Watchman* (London, 1937), p. 86; *Schickel on Film*, p. 179.

4. Frank Capra, *The Name Above the Title* (1971; New York, 1972), p. 202; Schickel, *The Men Who Made the Movies*, pp. 73–74; Capra, *The Name Above the Title*, p. 204 and Schickel, *The Men Who Made the Movies*, p. 76.

5. Joseph McBride, *Frank Capra: The Catastrophe of Success* (New York, 1992), p. 345; Robert Riskin, *Mr. Deeds Goes to Town*, 1935, unpublished screenplay, pp. 3; 13; 24; 67; 73; Gerald Weales, *Canned Goods as Caviar: American Film Comedies of the 1930s* (Chicago, 1985), p. 172.

6. Capra, *The Name Above the Title*, pp. 204–205; Riskin, *Mr. Deeds Goes to Town*, p. 106; Glenn Phelps, "The 'Populist' Films of Frank Capra," *Journal of American Studies*, 13 (December 1979), 381.

7. Riskin, *Mr. Deeds Goes to Town*, pp. 179–180, 196; John Stuart Mill, "A Treatise on Flemish Husbandry," *Principles of Political Economy* (Boston, 1848), 1.321; Riskin, *Mr. Deeds Goes to Town*, p. 199.

8. Raymond Carney, *American Vision: The Films of Frank Capra* (Cambridge, England, 1986), p. 289; Donald Spoto, *Camerado: Hollywood and the American Man* (New York, 1978), p. 7; McBride, *Frank Capra*, p. 345.

9. Swindell, *The Last Hero*, p. 300; Gladys Hall, "If I Hadn't Been an Actor," July 10, 1936, p. 5, Herrick; Riskin, *Mr. Deeds Goes to Town*, p. 32.

10. Capra, *The Name Above the Title*, p. 206; *The New York Times Film Reviews*, ed. George Amberg (New York, 1971), p. 162; Greene, *The Pleasure Dome*, pp. 96–97.

11. Paul O'Neil, "Hollywood Mourns a Good Man," *Life*, May 26, 1961, p. 30; Margaret Brenman-Gibson, *Clifford Odets: American Playwright. The Years from 1906 to 1940* (New York, 1981), pp. 408; 407; Cooper, "Well, It Was This Way," April 7, 1956, p. 121.

12. Greene, *The Pleasure Dome*, p. 112; Gerald Weales, *Clifford Odets: Playwright* (Indianapolis, 1971), p. 111; Brenman-Gibson, *Clifford Odets*, p. 408; Weales, *Clifford Odets*, pp.112–113.

13. Anthony Quinn, *The Original Sin: A Self-Portrait* (1972; New York, 1974), pp. 289–291; Iron Eyes Cody, as told to Collin Perry, *Iron Eyes: My Life as a Hollywood Indian* (New York, 1982), p. 200; "Mourning Universal," *Independent-Record*, May 14, 1961; Jon Tuska, *The Filming of the West* (Garden City, N.Y., 1976), p. 353.

14. Arthur Marx, *Goldwyn* (New York, 1976), p. 199; "Paramount," *Fortune*, 15 (March 1937), 204; Swindell, *The Last Hero*, pp. 205–206; Shipman, *Movie Talk*, p. 169.

15. Wray, *On the Other Hand*, p. 176; Liza, "Easy Does It!" p. 73; Capra, *The Name Above the Title*, p. 245.

16. Undated letter from Cooper to Maria; Letter from Maria to Cooper, summer 1942, both courtesy of Maria Cooper Janis; Interview with Maria Cooper Janis.

Chapter Ten: "Keep Shooting"

1. Arce, *Gary Cooper*, p. 134; *Sunday Graphic* (London), September 16, 1956; Letter from S.V. Stewart to "Jack," July 24, 1937, Montana Historical Society.

2. Lana Turner, *Lana: The Lady, the Legend, the Truth* (New York, 1982), p. 32; Christopher Finch and Linda Rosenkrantz, *Gone Hollywood* (Garden City, N.Y., 1979), p. 343; David Niven, *The Moon's a Balloon* (1972; New York, 1973), p. 201.

3. Finch and Rosenkrantz, *Gone Hollywood*, p. 261; Jordan, *Gary Cooper*, p. 84; Charles Higham and Roy Moseley, *Princess Merle: The Romantic Life of Merle Oberon* (New York, 1983), p. 103; Capra, *The Name Above the Title*, p. 335; Swindell, *The Last Hero*, p. 210.

4. David Shipman, *The Great Movie Stars: The Golden Years* (1970; Boston, 1995), p. 123; Schickel, *The Men Who Made the Movies*, p. 220; Memo from Tony Luraschi to Robert Carson, [1937], Herrick.

5. Karl Shapiro, *The Younger Son* (Chapel Hill, N.C., 1988), p. 196. In 1990 the U.S. Postal Service issued a commemorative 25¢ *Beau Geste* stamp.

6. Frederick Low, "The Real Glory," *Photoplay Studies*, 5 (1939), 5; Kaminsky, *Coop*, p. 103; Greene, *The Pleasure Dome*, p. 262.

7. Cooper, "Well, It Was This Way," March 31, 1956, p. 132; Berg, *Goldwyn*, p. 347; Herman, *A Talent for Trouble*, p. 206.

8. Niven Busch, in *Backstory*, p. 98; Berg, *Goldwyn*, pp. 347–348; Sheilah Graham, *The Real F. Scott Fitzgerald* (New York, 1976), p. 211.

9. *The Harper Encyclopedia of Military History*, ed. R. Ernest Dupuy

and Trevor Dupuy, 4th ed. (New York, 1993), p. 996; *The Fifty Worst Films of All Time*, ed. Harry Medved and Randy Dreyfuss (New York, 1978), p. 168; Julie Gilbert, *Opposite Attraction: The Lives of Erich Maria Remarque and Paulette Goddard* (New York, 1995), p. 272.

10. *The Fifty Worst Films of All Time*, p. 167; Ferguson, *Film Criticism*, p. 331.
11. Carney, *American Vision*, p. 352; Capra, *The Name Above the Title*, pp. 334–335; *Pete Martin Calls On*, p. 362; Ferguson, *Film Criticism*, p. 351.
12. [Robert Riskin], *Meet John Doe*, ed. Charles Wolfe (New Brunswick, N.J., 1989), pp. 115–116; Jordan, *Gary Cooper*, p. 90; [Riskin], *Meet John Doe*, pp. 100; 168; Richard Pells, *Radical Visions and American Dreams* (1973; Middletown, Conn., 1984), p. 278.
13. Gladys Hall, "I Just Try to Keep in Touch with the Guy I Was," 1941, p. 75, Herrick; Schickel, *The Men Who Made the Movies*, p. 78; Capra, *The Name Above the Title*, p. 336; Eric Smoodin, " 'The Business of America': Fan Mail, Film Reception and *Meet John Doe*," *Screen*, 37 (Summer 1996), 121.

Chapter Eleven: Homespun Killer

1. See George Pattullo, "The Second Elder [in the Church of Christ] Gives Battle," *Saturday Evening Post*, 191 (April 26, 1919), 3–4; 71; 73–74; *Sergeant York: His Own Life Story and War Diary*, ed. T.J. Skeyhill (Garden City, N.Y., 1928); and T.J. Skeyhill, *Sergeant York, The Last of the Long Hunters* (New York, 1930). York also inspired two characters in the novels of Robert Penn Warren: Private Porsum in *At Heaven's Gate* (1943) and Jake Herrick in *The Cave* (1959).
2. Pattullo, "The Second Elder Gives Battle," p. 3.
3. David Lee, *Sergeant York: An American Hero* (Lexington, Ky., 1985), p. 35.
4. Kobal, *People Will Talk*, p. 500; Memo from Hal Wallis to Howard Hawks, January 10, 1941, USC; Interview with Joan Leslie, Los Angeles, December 15, 1996; Kobal, *People Will Talk*, p. 498.
5. Interview with Richard Moore, Los Angeles, December 15, 1996; Dick Moore, *Twinkle, Twinkle, Little Star: But Don't Have Sex or Take the Car* (New York, 1984), p. 148; Leonard Maltin, ed., "Dickie Moore," *Hollywood Kids* (New York, 1978), p. 87; Pattullo, "The Second Elder Gives Battle," p. 3.
6. Howard Koch, "Sergeant York," *As Time Goes By* (New York, 1979), p. 74; Arce, *Gary Cooper*, p. 155; Gary Cooper, "The Role I Liked

Best," *Saturday Evening Post*, May 6, 1950, p. 216; Hall, "I Just Try to Keep in Touch with the Guy I Was," p. 74.

7. Koch, *As Time Goes By*, p. 74; Norman, *The Hollywood Greats*, pp. 99–100; Memos from Eric Stacey to T.C. Wright, February 4; April 7; February 21; April 5; March 20; April 1; April 30, 1941, USC.

8. Ezra Goodman, *The Fifty Year Decline and Fall of Hollywood* (1961; New York, 1962), p. 292; Cooper, "The Role I Liked Best," p. 216.

9. Cooper, "I Took a Good Look at Myself," p. 142; Hall, "In His Own Quiet Way," p. 9; Robert Sklar, *City Boys: Cagney, Bogart, Garfield* (Princeton, 1992), p. 206.

10. David Thomson, *America in the Dark* (New York, 1977), pp. 72, 78; François Truffaut, *The Films in My Life*, trans. Leonard Mayhew (New York, 1978), p. 104; Mason Wiley and Damien Bona, *Inside Oscar* (New York, 1978), p. 120.

Chapter Twelve: New Guinea

1. Gladys Hall, "So You Want to Be Happy?" *Movie Show*, October 1947, p. 43; Hedda Hopper, Los Angeles *Times*, May 19, 1950.

2. Gehman, "Mrs. Gary Cooper Tells the Moving Story of Her Husband's Last Days," p. 4; Cooper, "The Hollywood Greats," p. 10.

   Cooper also appeared on Edgar Bergen's show on December 14, 1947 and April 18, 1948, on Louella Parsons' show on September 5, 1948, and on the television programs of Bergen, Jack Benny and Ed Sullivan. Like many leading actors, he also appeared in ten adaptations, mostly of his own films, on the Lux Radio Theater between 1935 and 1945.

3. Maurice Zolotow, *Billy Wilder in Hollywood* (New York, 1977), p. 94; William Shakespeare, *Richard III* (1.2.204–209); Robert Creamer, *Babe: The Legend Comes to Life* (New York, 1974), p. 216.

4. Carol Easton, *The Search for Sam Goldwyn* (New York, 1976), p. 207; Frank Nugent, "The All-American Man," *New York Times Magazine*, July 5, 1942, p. 27; Cooper, "Well, It Was This Way," April 7, 1956, p. 120.

5. Arce, *Gary Cooper*, p. 165; Swindell, *The Last Hero*, p. 241; George Custen, *Bio/Pics: How Hollywood Constructed Public History* (New Brunswick, N.J., 1992), pp. 162–163.

6. Jordan, *Gary Cooper*, p. 99; Carpozi, *The Gary Cooper Story*, p. 162; Berg, *Goldwyn*, p. 373.

7. Military Orders to Cooper, October 26, 1943, National Archives; Phyllis Brooks, as told to Mary Jane Manners, "My South Sea Island

Flight with Gary Cooper," *Silver Screen*, 14 (May 1944), 60; Neil McDonald, *War Cameraman: The Story of Damien Parer* (Melbourne: Lothian Press, 1994), p. 219.

8. Brooks, "My South Sea Island Flight," pp. 60; 62; Letter from Gary Cooper to Howard Cooper, June 14, 1945, courtesy of Howard Cooper, "Gary Cooper Moved Greatly on Pacific Tour," Los Angeles *Times*, [early 1944].

9. Gary Cooper, USO tour speech, courtesy of Maria Cooper Janis; Kaminsky, *Coop*, p. 130.

Chapter Thirteen: Hemingway and *For Whom the Bell Tolls*

1. Laurence, *Hemingway and the Movies*, p. 60; Interview with Bud and Ruth Purdy, Picabo, Idaho, December 14–15, 1996; Ernest Hemingway, "The Snows of Kilimanjaro," *Short Stories* (New York, 1953), p. 71.

2. Interview with Patrick Hemingway, Bozeman, Montana, September 14, 1996; Ernest Hemingway, *Selected Letters, 1917–1961*, ed. Carlos Baker (New York, 1981), p. 518; Swindell, *The Last Hero*, p. 285.

3. Hemingway, *Selected Letters*, p. 519; Lloyd Arnold, *High on the Wild with Hemingway* (Caldwell, Idaho, 1968), p. 127; Wayne, *Cooper's Women*, p. 132; Cooper, "Well, It Was This Way," March 31, 1956, p. 132.

4. McCrea, "My Friend Coop!" p. 85; Jeffrey Meyers, *Hemingway: A Biography* (New York, 1985), p. 425; Laurence Leamer, *As Time Goes By: The Life of Ingrid Bergman* (1986; London, 1987), p. 163.

5. Swindell, *The Last Hero*, p. 284; Hemingway, *Selected Letters*, p. 529; Swindell, *The Last Hero*, p. 243; Gregory Hemingway, *Papa* (Boston, 1976), p. 44; A.E. Hotchner, *Papa Hemingway* (New York, 1966), p. 202.

6. Ernest Hemingway, *For Whom the Bell Tolls* (New York, 1940), p. 3; *Conversations with Ernest Hemingway*, ed. Matthew Bruccoli (Jackson, Miss., 1986), p. 24; Ingrid Bergman and Alan Burgess, *Ingrid Bergman: My Story* (New York, 1980), p. 96; Gregory Hemingway, *Papa*, p. 46.

7. Letters from Gary Cooper to Rocky Cooper, July 14 and July 30, 1942, courtesy of Maria Cooper Janis; *Memo from David O. Selznick*, ed. Rudy Behlmer (1972; New York, 1973), p. 377; Letters from Rocky to Gary, August 29, 1942 and [August] 1942, courtesy of Maria Cooper Janis.

8. Paul Henreid, with Julius Fast, *Ladies Man: An Autobiography* (New York, 1984), p. 131; Bergman, *My Story*, p. 114; Leamer, *As Time Goes By*, p. 92; Bergman, *My Story*, pp. 113; 116.

9. Howard Koch, *Casablanca: Script and Legend* (Woodstock, N.Y., 1973), pp. 155–156; Nichols, *For Whom the Bell Tolls*, pp. 199–200; James Agee, *On Film: Reviews and Comments* (1958; Boston, 1964), p. 49; Nichols, *For Whom the Bell Tolls*, pp. 116; 79–80.

10. Carlos Baker, *Ernest Hemingway: A Life Story* (New York, 1969), p. 371; Bernard Dick, *The Star-Spangled Screen: The American World War II Film* (Lexington, Ky., 1985), p. 30; Gene Phillips, *Hemingway and Film* (New York, 1980), p. 42; Agee, *On Film*, pp. 47–48; Hotchner, *Papa Hemingway*, pp. 31–32.

11. Leamer, *As Time Goes By*, p. 130; Rudy Behlmer, *Inside Warner Bros.*, 1935–1951 (New York, 1985), pp. 226; 225; James Agate, *Around Cinemas,* Second Series (London, 1948), p. 266.

12. Interview with Virgil and Betty Sherrill, New York, November 25, 1996; James Robert Parish and Don Stanke, "Gary Cooper," *The All-Americans* (New Rochelle, N.Y., 1977), p. 44; Carpozi, *The Gary Cooper Story*, pp. 181; 183.

13. Interviews with Watson Webb, Los Angeles, December 21, 1996; Howard Cooper; Moe Rothman, New York, September 28, 1996; and Connie Wald.

14. Interviews with Mignon Winans, Beverly Hills, September 14, 1996; Maria Cooper Janis; Patrick Hemingway; Suzy Parker; Rod Steiger, Malibu, November 9, 1996; and Evie Johnson.

15. Interview with Arlene Dahl.
    Cooper never treated Rocky brutally, as Hemingway did his fourth wife, Mary. But she had the same tolerance and endurance as Mary, who forgave Hemingway's excesses and told him: "I'm going to stay here and run your house and your Finca until . . . you tell me truthfully and straight that you want me to leave" (Meyers, *Hemingway*, p. 448).

16. Interviews with Virgil and Betty Sherrill; Suzy Parker; Ivan Moffat; and Walter Seltzer.

Chapter Fourteen: Hollywood Politics

1. Cecil B. De Mille's statement, *Dr. Wassell* file, Herrick; Doug McClelland, ed., *Forties Film Talk: Oral Histories of Hollywood* (Jefferson, N.C., 1992), p. 410; Interview with Dorris Johnson, Beverly Hills, December 3, 1996.

2. Interview with Teresa Wright, Norwalk, Connecticut, June 14, 1997; Tom Stempel, *Screenwriter: The Life and Times of Nunnally Johnson* (San Diego, 1980), pp. 114–115; Interview with Dorris Johnson; Nunnally Johnson, "Along Came Cooper," *Photoplay*, 27 (August 1945), 96.

3. Nunnally Johnson, oral history, pp. 244; 239–240, Herrick; Nunnally Johnson, *Letters*, ed. Dorris Johnson and Ellen Leventhal (New York, 1981), p. 42; James Bacon, "Gary Cooper, Now in the 35th Year in Movie Business, Is Still Shy and Likeable," *Independent-Record* (Helena), June 22, 1958, p. 12.

4. Cooper, "I Took a Good Look at Myself," p. 140 and Cooper, "Well, It Was This Way," April 7, 1956, p. 36; Johnson, *Letters*, p. 24.

5. Charles Higham and Joel Greenberg, *The Celluloid Muse: Hollywood Directors Speak* (New York, 1972), p. 117; Interview with Ring Lardner, Jr., Westport, Connecticut, October 30, 1996.

   Jesper's first name, Alvah, gave him a Left-wing tinge by alluding to Alvah Bessie, a militant Communist who had fought in the Abraham Lincoln Battalion during the Spanish Civil War. In 1947, along with Lardner and Maltz, he became one of the Hollywood Ten, who were persecuted and jailed by the House Un-American Activities Committee. In 1953, seven years after *Cloak and Dagger* and during the McCarthy witch-hunts, Oppenheimer's security clearance was withdrawn. He had opposed development of the hydrogen bomb and superiors doubted his loyalty.

6. Stephen Jenkins, ed., *Fritz Lang: The Image and the Look* (London, 1981), p. 162; Jordan, *Gary Cooper*, p. 108; Interview with Ring Lardner, Jr.; Publicity notes, *Cloak and Dagger* file, USC; "Gary Cooper Catching Up at Night School," April 27, 1946, no citation, USC.

7. Richard Corliss, ed., *Hollywood Screenwriters* (New York, 1990), p. 140; Memo from Frank Mattison to T.C. Wright, June 20, 1946, USC; Lilli Palmer, *Change Lobsters and Dance* (1975; New York, 1976) p. 163; Peter Bogdanovich, "*Cloak and Dagger*," *Fritz Lang in America* (New York, 1967), p. 73.

8. Memo from Mattison to Wright, March 21, 1946, USC and Dick, *The Star-Spangled War*, p. 122; Memos from Mattison to Wright, June 6 and May 6, 1946, USC; Bogdanovich, *Fritz Lang in America*, p. 71.

9. Palmer, *Change Lobsters and Dance*, pp. 165–166; Dick, *The Star-Spangled War*, p. 122; Lotte Eisner, "*Cloak and Dagger*," *Fritz Lang* (1976; New York, 1986), p. 267.

10. Interview with Howard Cooper; Letter from Gary Cooper to Wellington Rankin, October 9, 1946, Montana Historical Society;

Letter from S.V. Stewart to "Jack," July 24, 1937, Montana Historical Society; Letters from Alice Cooper to Hedda Hopper, October 1, 1946 and [1952], Herrick.

11. Thomson, *Biographical Dictionary of Film*, p. 182; John Brosnan, *Movie Magic: The Story of Special Effects* (New York, 1974), p. 61; Brownlow, *The Parade's Gone By*, p. 187.

12. Serge Daney and Jean-Louis Noames, "Entretien avec Leo McCarey," *Cahiers du Cinéma*, 163 (February 1965), 20 (my translation); Arce, *Gary Cooper*, p. 188; Contract, October 22, 1947, Warners legal files, USC; Cooper, "I Took a Good Look at Myself," p. 142.

13. Carey McWilliams, "Hollywood Plays with Fascism," *Nation*, 140 (May 29, 1935), 623–624; Larry Ceplair and Steven Englund, *The Inquisition in Hollywood: Politics in the Film Community, 1920–1960* (Garden City, N.Y., 1980), p. 97; Nancy Schwartz, *The Hollywood Writers' Wars* (New York, 1982), p. 205.

14. Anthony Slide, "Hollywood's Fascist Follies," *Film Comment*, 27 (July–August 1991), 63; Garry Wills, *John Wayne's America* (New York, 1997), p. 247.

15. Charles Higham, *Merchant of Dreams: Louis B. Mayer, MGM, and the Secret Hollywood* (New York, 1993), pp. 270, 300; David Irving, *The War Path: Hitler's Germany, 1933–1939* (New York, 1978), p. 81 (on Saxe-Coburg).

According to Higham, Flynn was a Nazi spy, Grant a secret agent and Cooper a crypto-Fascist. In a typically vicious, sensational and inaccurate book, *Errol Flynn: The Untold Story* (1980), he falsely accused Flynn of being a Nazi agent. Flynn's FBI file does not substantiate Higham's claim, which was thoroughly refuted by Tony Thomas, *Errol Flynn: The Spy Who Never Was* (New York, 1990).

16. Charles Higham and Roy Moseley, *Cary Grant: The Lonely Heart* (New York, 1989), p. 87; Slide, "Hollywood's Fascist Follies," p. 62; Higham, *Merchant of Dreams*, p. 287.

17. David Irving, *Göring: A Biography* (New York, 1989), pp. 26, 452; Swindell, *The Last Hero*, p. 216; William Safire, 'Libeling the Dead," *New York Times*, April 13, 1989, p. A-27.

18. Schwartz, *The Hollywood Writers' Wars*, p. 206; Randy Roberts and James Olson, *John Wayne: American* (New York, 1995), p. 333; Carpozi, *The Gary Cooper Story*, pp. 167–168.

19. Schwartz, *The Hollywood Writers' Wars*, p. 209; Ceplair and Englund, *The Inquisition in Hollywood*, p. 281; Peter Roffman and Jim Purdy, *The Hollywood Social Problem Film: Despair and Politics from the Depression to the Fifties* (Bloomington, Ind., 1981), p. 285.

20. "Philadelphia Story," *Newsweek*, 30 (August 18, 1947), 21;

Interview with Ring Lardner, Jr.; United States Congress, House of Representatives, Committee on Un-American Activities, 80th Congress, 1st Session, October [23,] 1947, *Hearings Regarding the Communist Infiltration of the Motion Picture Industry* (Washington, D.C.: U.S. Government Printing Office, 1947), pp. 221–222; 219–220; K. Ross Toole, *Twentieth Century Montana: A State of Extremes* (Norman, Okla., 1972), p. 152.

21. Cooper, HUAC testimony, pp. 220; 220–221; 224; Ceplair and Englund, *The Inquisition in Hollywood*, p. 281.

22. Wayne, *Cooper's Women*, p. 111; Walter Goodman, *The Committee* (1968; Baltimore, 1969), p. 209; Interview with Ring Lardner, Jr.; Kaminsky, *Coop*, p. 151.

   Wood, whom the mention of Communism turned into a "snarling, unreasoning brute," specified in his will that "no prospective heir, with the exception of his widow, could inherit unless that person filed, with the clerk of the probate court, an affidavit swearing that they 'are not now, nor have they ever been, Communists' " (Ceplair and Englund, *The Inquisition in Hollywood*, p. 209).

23. Robert Carr, "The Hollywood Hearings," *The House Committee on Un-American Activities, 1945–1950* (Ithaca, N.Y., 1952), pp. 60; 55; "Gary Cooper and the Star System," *New Knowledge*, 3 (1965), 449; Hall, "So You Want to Be Happy?" p. 43; Cooper, "Shooting Clichés on the Western Range," n.p.

Chapter Fifteen: The Fountainhead and Patricia Neal

1. Louella Parsons, Los Angeles *Times*, May 23, 1950, USC; Gary Cooper, "The Place I Like Best," no citation, courtesy of Maria Cooper Janis; Ayn Rand, *The Fountainhead* (Indianapolis, 1968), p. 207.

2. John Walker, *"The Fountainhead,"* *Art and Artists on the Screen* (Manchester, England, 1993), p. 99; Barbara Branden, *The Passion of Ayn Rand* (Garden City, N.Y., 1986), p. 209; Robert Twombly, *Frank Lloyd Wright: His Life and Architecture* (New York, 1979), p. 384; Aline Mosley, "Frank Lloyd Wright Pans Stars' Homes," *Citizen–News* (Hollywood), January 24, 1950.

3. Branden, *Passion of Ayn Rand*, p. 211; Ayn Rand, *Letters*, ed. Michael Berliner (New York, 1975), pp. 197, 456; King Vidor, *A Tree Is a Tree* (New York, 1952), p. 207.

4. Memos from Eric Stacey to T. C. Wright, August 26 and August 7, 1948, USC (a contractor's sign on one of Roark's early buildings reads "Stacey and Blanke," an allusion to the unit manager and the

producer); Letter from Stephen Jackson, censor of the Motion Picture Association of America, to Jack Warner, June 24, 1948, USC.

5. Stephen Gardiner, *Epstein* (London, 1992), pp. 128, 131; Humphrey Carpenter, *A Serious Character: The Life of Ezra Pound* (Boston, 1988), p. 813. Gardiner's illustration 13 reproduces the *Rock-Drill*. See also Ulku Tamer, *Ezra ile Gary: Ezra Pound ve Gary Cooper icin siirler* [Ezra with Gary: Poems for Ezra Pound and Gary Cooper], (Istanbul, 1962).

6. Kevin McGann, "Ayn Rand in the Stockyard of the Spirit," *The Modern American Novel and the Movies*, ed. Gerald Peary and Roger Shatzkin (New York, 1978), p. 327; Ayn Rand, *The Fountainhead*, unpublished screenplay, p. 130, USC; Higham and Greenberg, *The Celluloid Muse*, p. 240; Herb Lightman, "*The Fountainhead,*" *American Cinematographer*, 30 (June 1949), 221 and 225.

7. Interview with Patricia Neal, New York, November 27, 1996; Howard Barnes, New York *Herald Tribune*, no citation, USC; John McCarten, "Down with Beaux-Arts," *New Yorker*, 25 (July 16, 1949), 47.

8. Bosley Crowther, *New York Times*, July 9, 1949; "Architecture and Love in Mix-up," *Cue*, July 9, 1949.

9. Lightman, "*The Fountainhead,*" p. 200; George Nelson, "Mr. Roark Goes to Hollywood," *Interiors*, 108 (April 1949), 111; Andrew Saint, *The Image of the Architect* (New Haven, 1983), p. 163.

10. Behlmer, *Inside Warner Bros.*, p. 3 10; Charles Silver, Notes on King Vidor, Museum of Modern Art, September 1972, Pacific Film Archive, Berkeley.

11. McCrea, "My Friend Coop!" p. 85; Kaminsky, *Coop*, pp. 166–167; Interview with Patricia Neal.

12. Wray, *On the Other Hand*, p. 133; Sidney Skolsky's column, no citation, USC; Kaminsky, *Coop*, p. 161; Interview with Suzy Parker.

13. Wanda Hale, New York *Daily News*, no citation, USC; Dickens, *The Films of Cary Cooper*, p. 224.

14. Graham, *Confessions of a Hollywood Columnist*, p. 292; Wayne, *Cooper's Women*, pp. 134; 65; Patricia Neal, *As I Am* (New York, 1988), p. 104 and *Schickel on Film*, p. 193.

15. Neal, *As I Am*, pp. 97; 100–101; Interview with Patricia Neal (on car crash); Neal, *As I Am*, p. 112.

16. Interview with Patricia Neal (on Aspen trip); Neal, *As I Am*, pp. 124; 127; 131; Maria Cooper Janis, "My Poppa, Gary Cooper," *Parade*, November 19, 1989, p. 11; Maria Cooper Janis, in *The Life and Times of Gary Cooper*, Nashville Network, TNN, October 31, 1995; Confidential interviews (about the effect on Maria).

17. Neal, *As I Am*, pp. 133–134; McCrea, "My Friend Coop!" p. 86; Interview with Patricia Neal; Neal, *As I Am*, pp. 130–131.

Though Neal describes the visit to Hemingway before the abortion, the abortion took place in October 1950, after she made *Operation Pacific* with John Wayne, and the visit to Hemingway at Christmas that year.

18. Interview with Maria Cooper Janis; Carpozi, *The Gary Cooper Story*, p. 187; Arce, *Gary Cooper*, p. 202.
19. Transcript of phone conversation between Cooper and Hedda Hopper, May 1951, Herrick; Neal, *As I Am*, p. 129; Kendis Rochlin, "Candid Kendis," Los Angeles *Mirror*, November 30, 1953; Interview with Barnaby Conrad, Santa Barbara, California, December 11, 1996.
20. Neal, *As I Am*, p. 140; Interview with Lorraine Chanel; Arce, *Gary Cooper*, p. 198.
21. Interview with Patricia Neal; Interview with Evie Johnson; Interview with Dorris Johnson; Neal, *As I Am*, pp. 117; 116; 141–142; 145.
22. Carpozi, *The Gary Cooper Story*, p. 188; Radie Harris, *Radie's World* (New York, 1975), p. 99; Interview with Patricia Neal.
23. Neal, *As I Am*, p. 193; Interview with Maria Cooper Janis; Neal, *As I Am*, p. 150; Interview with Howard Cooper; Carpozi, *The Gary Cooper Story*, p. 194.

Chapter Sixteen: High Noon

1. Memos from Eric Stacey to T.C. Wright, December 8, 20 and 15, 1948, USC; Interview with Jane Wyatt, Los Angeles, December 7, 1996 (on Cooper's acting).
2. *Variety*, November 4, 1949.
3. Talbot, "I Was Gary Cooper for 35 Years," p. 90; Raoul Walsh, *Each Man in His Time* (New York, 1974), p. 357; Letter from Gary Cooper to Hedda Hopper, May 10, 1951, Herrick.
4. Interview with Mari Aldon, Los Angeles *Times*, June 3, 1951; Edith Roosevelt's article, January 28, 1954, no citation, USC.
5. Interview with Fred Zinnemann, London, July 12, 1996; Wagner, *You Must Remember This*, p. 294; Cooper, "Well, It Was This Way," April 7, 1956, p. 121; Carpozi, *The Gary Cooper Story*, p. 192.
6. Floyd Crosby, oral history, pp. 518–519, 271, American Film Institute, Los Angeles; John Howard Reid, "A Man for All Movies," *Films and Filming*, 13 (May–June 1967), 8; Behlmer, *Behind the Scenes*, p. 278.
7. Hedda Hopper, interview with Cooper, October 1952, p. 17, Herrick; Interview with Fred Zinnemann; "Gary Cooper and the Star System," *New Knowledge*, p. 449.

8. Sarah Bradford, *Princess Grace* (New York, 1984), p. 63; James
   Spada, *Grace* (Garden City, N.Y., 1987), p. 59; Bradford, *Princess
   Grace*, p. 62; Spada, *Grace*, pp. 32; 58.
9. Interview with Patricia Neal; Letter from Lorraine Chanel to Jeffrey
   Meyers, November 30, 1996; Arce, *Gary Cooper*, p. 210.
10. Carl Foreman, "*High Noon*," *Three Major Screenplays*, ed. Malvin
    Wald and Michael Werner (New York: Globe, 1972), pp. 168; 173;
    Behlmer, *Behind the Scenes*, p. 281; Foreman, "*High Noon*," pp.
    212; 243.
11. Louis Gianetti, "Fred Zinnemann's *High Noon*," *Film Criticism*, 1
    (Winter 1976–77), 5; Faulkner, "Today We Live," p. 115n7.
    One of N.C. Wyeth's pupils said of the artist: "You'd never want
    to bump up against him. It was just like *High Noon*" (Richard
    Meryman, *Andrew Wyeth: A Secret Life*, New York, 1996, p. 26).
12. "Dialogue on Film: Carl Foreman," *American Film*, 4 (April 1979),
    36; Peter Brown and Jim Pinkston, *Oscar Dearest: Scandal, Politics
    and Greed Behind Hollywood's Academy Awards, 1927–1986* (New
    York, 1987), p. 243 and Gianetti, "Fred Zinnemann's *High Noon*,"
    p. 4.
13. Victor Navasky, *Naming Names* (1980; New York, 1981), p. 158;
    Foreman, "*High Noon*," p. 220; Interview with Ring Lardner, Jr. (on
    Foreman and Cooper); Interview with Patricia Neal.
14. Carl Foreman, "I Prayed for Coop," *Daily Herald* (London), May
    15, 1961, reprinted as "Coop—Honest, Gentle and Simple, The
    World's Best Film Actor," *Screen*, May 26, 1961; Brown and
    Pinkston, *Oscar Dearest*, p. 244; Interview with Warren Cowan, Los
    Angeles, December 5, 1996 ("use my name"); Kaminsky, *Coop*, p.
    175; Brown and Pinkston, *Oscar Dearest*, p. 245; Letter from Carl
    Foreman to Gary Cooper, June 17, 1957, courtesy of Maria Cooper
    Janis.
15. Ronald Davis, *The Glamour Factory: Inside Hollywood's Big Studio
    System* (Dallas, 1993), p. 282; Donald Spoto, *Stanley Kramer, Film
    Maker* (1978; Hollywood, 1990), p. 103.
16. Nora Sayre, *Running Time* (New York, 1978), p. 176; Hollis Alpert,
    "Happenings in Hadleyville," *Saturday Review*, July 5, 1952, p. 29;
    "*High Noon*," *Time*, July 14, 1952, pp. 94, 92.
17. These figures may be unreliable. The $3.75 million comes from
    Tuska, *The Filming of the West*, p. 542, $18 million from James
    Spada, *Grace*, p. 60, $600,000 from Goodman, *The Fifty Year
    Decline and Fall of Hollywood*, p. 420; Kaminsky, *Coop*, p. 172.
18. Cooper, "Hollywood Greats," p. 14; Veronica Cooper, as told to
    George Christy, "How I Faced Tomorrow," *Good Housekeeping*,
    September 1963, p. 160.

19. Penelope Gilliatt, "Gary Cooper Was Like His Heroes," *Observer*, May 14, 1961; James Harvey, *Romantic Comedy in Hollywood from Lubitsch to Sturges* (New York, 1987), pp. 156–157; Richard Brooks, in *Backstory Two: Interviews with Screenwriters of the 1940s and 1950s*, ed. Pat McGilligan (Berkeley, 1991), p. 68.
20. Navasky, *Naming Names*, p. 210; Roberts and Olson, *John Wayne: American*, p. 349; Schickel, *The Men Who Made the Movies*, p. 121; Gianetti, "Fred Zinnemann's *High Noon*," p. 4.
21. Roberts and Olson, *John Wayne: American*, p. 439; Andrew Sarris, "The World of Howard Hawks," *Focus on Howard Hawks*, p. 57. The absurd and otiose *High Noon, Part II: The Return of Will Kane* came out in 1987.

Chapter Seventeen: The Wandering Years

1. Interview with André De Toth; Letters from Gary Cooper to Rocky and Maria Cooper, July 24, August I and August 14, 1952, courtesy of Maria Cooper Janis.
2. Hedda Hopper, interview with Gary Cooper, pp. 1–2; Interview with Roberta Haynes, Beverly Hills, California, May 9, 1997.
3. Arce, *Gary Cooper*, pp. 218; 219; Publicity release, Juniper Films, October 1, 1996, courtesy of Maria Cooper Janis; Mikal Gilmore, *Shot in the Heart: One Family's History in Murder* (London, 1994), pp. 85, 306.
4. Interview with Lorraine Chanel; Anthony Quinn, with Daniel Paisner, *One Man Tango* (New York, 1995), p. 225.
5. Barnaby Conrad, *Name Dropping: Tales from My Barbary Coast Saloon* (New York, 1994), p. 133; Wayne, *Cooper's Women*, p. 55.
6. Interview with and letters from Lorraine Chanel; Letters from Gary Cooper to Lorraine Chanel, May 14, 4 and 21, 1953.
7. Interview with Robert Stack; Letter from Lorraine Chanel to Jeffrey Meyers, November 30, 1996; Anne Edwards, *The Grimaldis of Monaco* (New York, 1992), p. 209.
8. Letter from Gary Cooper to Lorraine Chanel, May 21, 1953; Alice Hoffman, "The Shy Mr. Cooper," *Modern Screen*, August 1953, p. 79; Quoted in "Le Cow-Boy Etait un Casanova," *Paris Match*, octobre 24, 1980, p. 23 (my translation).
9. Interview with Maria Cooper Janis; Neal, *As I Am*, p. 145; Letter from Lorraine Chanel to Jeffrey Meyers, January 5, 1997; Edwards, *The Grimaldis of Monaco*, p. 233.
10. Letters from Gary Cooper to Lorraine Chanel, May 14 and 21, 1953; Interview with Maria Cooper Janis; Letter from Elvira Borg

to Maria Cooper, July 4, 1955, courtesy of Maria Cooper Janis; Nathanael West, *The Day of the Locust* (1939; New York, 1950), p. 183.

11. Interview with Maria Cooper Janis; Letter from Gary Cooper to Lorraine Chanel, [May 1953]; Letter from Gary Cooper to Lorraine Chanel, July 2, 1953; Interview with Virgil and Betty Sherrill; Neal, *As I Am*, p. 106.

12. West, *To See the Dream*, p. 195; Beverly Linet, *Susan Hayward: Portrait of a Survivor* (New York, 1980), p. 156; Arce, *Gary Cooper*, p. 223; Kaminsky, *Coop*, p. 183; François Truffaut, *Early Film Criticism*, ed. Wheeler Dixon, trans. Ruth Hoffman (Bloomington, Ind., 1994), pp. 150–151.

13. Gary Fishgall, *Against Type: The Biography of Burt Lancaster* (New York, 1995), p. 124; Evelyn Harvey, "Cooper Gets Girl, Burt Gets Bullet," *Collier's*, 134 (August 6, 1954), 73; Fishgall, *Against Type*, p. 126.

14. Edwin Arnold and Eugene Miller, "Vera Cruz," *The Films of Robert Aldrich* (Knoxville, Tenn., 1986), pp. 34; 31; Letters from Lorraine Chanel to Jeffrey Meyers, December 7, 1996 and November 30, 1996.

15. Truffaut, *The Films in My Life*, p. 97; Fishgall, *Against Type*, p. 135.

16. Interview with Lorraine Chanel; Interview with Maria Cooper Janis; Interview with Mother Dolores Hart, Bethlehem, Connecticut, November 23, 1996; Interview with Frances Dee, Camarillo, California, May 24, 1997 (on Jody McCrea); Interview with Suzy Parker (on Maria's dates); Arce, *Gary Cooper*, p. 239.

17. Maria Cooper Janis, in *Gary Cooper: American Life, American Legend*, TNT, October 27, 1989; Parsons, Personal Memories of Gary Cooper," p. 54 and Carpozi, *The Gary Cooper Story*, p. 186; Interview with Frances Dee; Arce, *Gary Cooper*, p. 221.

18. Interviews with Arlene Dahl and Mother Dolores Hart; Louella Parsons, "A Lesson in Love," *Pictorial Review*, November 21, 1954; Interview with Maria Cooper Janis; Hemingway, *A Farewell to Arms*, p. 249.

19. Cooper, "Well, It Was This Way," March 31, 1956, p. 132; Interview with Mother Dolores Hart; Arce, *Gary Cooper*, p. 231.

For a photo of the Coopers in the Baroda Drive house, see Dickens, *The Films of Gary Cooper*, pp. 20–21. Paintings by Bonnard and Vuillard are hanging above Maria's head, and a Renoir is behind Rocky. In 1993 the house was sold by its then owners for $3 million.

Bogart also seemed out of place in his luxurious Holmby Hills house, which was also bought (in 1952) to please his luxury loving wife. I could put a down payment on an entire foreign country for the dough this joint set me back," Bogart said. "When Betty [Bacall] showed me through the place she pointed out the suites for herself, the babies, the butler and the maid; then she showed me an oversized closet and said, 'That's your room' " (Jeffrey Meyers, *Bogart: A Life in Hollywood*, Boston, 1997, p. 261).

20. Letter from Lorraine Chanel to Jeffrey Meyers, November 30, 1996; Hopper, interview with Cooper, p. 13; Interview with Stephan and Lillian Groueff, Southampton, New York, November 16, 1996; Jeffrey Meyers, *Scott Fiegerald: A Biography* (New York, 1994), p. 158.

Chapter Eighteen: Love in the Afternoon

1. Burke Davis, *The Billy Mitchell Affair* (New York, 1967), p. 324. For Mitchell's views, see his book *Winged Defense: The Development of Modern Air Power—Economic and Military* (New York, 1925); Custen, Bio/Pics, pp. 116–118.
2. Walter Bernstein, *Inside Out: A Memoir of the Blacklist* (New York, 1996), p. 259; Gerald Pratley, *The Cinema of Otto Preminger* (New York, 1971), p. 116; Preminger, *An Autobiography*, pp.174–175.
3. Interview with John Springer, New York, November 19, 1996; Horton Streete, "Gary Cooper's Lost Week-End with Anita Ekberg," *Confidential*, January 1956, pp. 20–21 (courtesy of Fred Crawford); Interview with Virgil Sherrill.
4. West, *To See the Dream*, pp. 93; 194; 236; 268–269.
5. Ellsworth Fredricks, "Photographing *Friendly Persuasion*," *American Cinematographer*, 37 (April 1956), 250; Interview with Richard Eyer, Bishop, California, December 14, 1996; Interview with Walter Mirisch, Los Angeles, December 6, 1996.
6. Charles Winecoff, *Split Image: The Life of Anthony Perkins* (New York, 1996), p. 101; Robert Hatch, "Films," *Nation*, 183 (November 24, 1956), 467.
7. Interview with Billy Wilder, Beverly Hills, California, December 5, 1996; Interview with Walter Mirisch; Kevin Lally, *Wilder Times* (New York, 1996), p. 260; Axel Madsen, *Billy Wilder* (Bloomington, Ind., 1969), p. 110.
8. Interview with Lorraine Chanel; Lally, *Wilder Times*, pp. 262; 263; Hall, "If I Hadn't Been an Actor," p. 6.
9. Anthony Carthew, "The Aging Romeos," *Daily Herald* (London), November 14, 1959; Thomas Wiseman, "Cowboy Cooper Trades His Horse for a Sofa," *Evening Standard* (London), July 27, 1956.

The ironic tone of Cooper's last sentence recalls Jake Barnes' comment in another luxurious Paris hotel: "I sat down and wrote some letters. They were not very good letters but I hoped their being on Crillon stationery would help them" (Ernest Hemingway, *The Sun Also Rises*, 1926; New York, 1954, p. 41).

10. David Douglas Duncan, *The Private World of Pablo Picasso* (New York, 1958), p. 122; Swindell, *The Last Hero*, p. 300.

11. Philip Dunne, *Take Two: A Life in Movies and Politics* (1980; New York, 1992), pp. 287; 286; 291; Interview with Suzy Parker; Letter from Ray Stricklyn to Jeffrey Meyers, November 8, 1996; Letter from John O'Hara to Gary Cooper, April 25, 1958, courtesy of Maria Cooper Janis.

12. Jordan, *Gary Cooper*, p. 132; Carl Foreman, oral history, p. 6, Columbia University; Carpozi, *The Gary Cooper Story*, p. 8.

Chapter Nineteen: The Long Day Wanes

1. Letter from Gary Cooper to Charles Feldman, May 9, 1957, American Film Institute; Letter from Gary Cooper to Howard Cooper, June 14, 1945, courtesy of Howard Cooper (during the war Papa sometimes referred to himself as "Ernie Hemorrhoid, the poor man's Ernie Pyle"); Letter from Gary Cooper to Lorraine Chanel, Paris, [August 1953]; Neal, *As I Am*, p. 222.

2. Interview with Maria Cooper Janis; Norman, *The Hollywood Greats*, p. 111; Interview with Frances Dee (on Rocky and conversion); Interview with Father Harold Ford, Long Beach, California, December 5, 1996.

3. Ruth Waterbury, "The Real Reason Gary Cooper Became a Catholic," *Motion Picture*, 1959, p. 88; Norman, *The Hollywood Greats*, p. 111.

4. Arce, *Gary Cooper*, p. 239; Interviews with Ivan Moffat; Watson Webb; Mother Dolores Hart; Howard Cooper; Moe Rothman; Mignon Winans (on Maria as mommy); Lorraine Chanel; Patricia Neal.

5. Cooper, "I Took a Good Look at Myself," p. 62; Kaminsky, *Coop*, p. 200; Interview with Ivan Moffat; Alan Casty, *The Films of Robert Rossen* (New York, 1969), p. 37; Ernest Hemingway, *Men at War* (New York, 1942), p. xxvii.

6. Letter from Gary Cooper to Maria Cooper, March 6, 1960, courtesy of Maria Cooper Janis; Heston, *In the Arena*, p. 211; Kaminsky, *Coop*, p. 205.

7. Interview with Mother Dolores Hart; Heston, *In the Arena*, p. 213;

Interview with Michael Anderson, Gibsons, British Columbia, January 4, 1997; Kaminsky, *Coop*, p. 206; Joseph Conrad, *Lord Jim* (1901; New York, 1931), p. 81.

8. Mark Frankland, *Khrushchev* (London, 1966), p. 165; Jeffrey Meyers, *Robert Frost: A Biography* (Boston, 1996), pp. 339–340; Gary Cooper, "The Hollywood Greats," pp. 7–8; Lewis Mallory, "How Gary Cooper Finally Disillusioned Me," *News Chronicle* (London), June 11, 1959.

9. Interview with Maria Cooper Janis; Letter from Delbert Mann to Jeffrey Meyers, October 23, 1996.

10. "Actor Gary Cooper Is Dead of Cancer," Bozeman *Daily Chronicle* (Montana), May 14, 1961; Swindell, *The Last Hero*, p. 302; Interview with Cooper's physician, Dr. Rexford Kennamer, Beverly Hills, California, December 4, 1996.

11. Interview with Walter Seltzer; *Pete Martin Calls On*, p. 359; Eric Braun, *Deborah Kerr* (New York, 1978), p. 182; Letter from Peter Viertel to Jeffrey Meyers, September 27, 1996.

12. Interview with Joseph Stefano, Beverly Hills, California, December 4, 1996; Interview with Michael Anderson; *Pete Martin Calls On*, p. 359; Interview with Walter Seltzer.

13. Joseph Stefano, *The Naked Edge*, unpublished screenplay, pp. 85; 126; 53, courtesy of Joseph Stefano; Interview with Joseph Stefano; Interview with Walter Seltzer.

Chapter Twenty: Death of a Hero

1. Army Archerd, *Variety*, January 10, 1961; Friars Club file, courtesy of Maria Cooper Janis; Swindell, *The Last Hero*, p. 302; Dickens, *The Films of Gary Cooper*, p. 281; Friars Club file.

    In 1961 the Friars Club commissioned a bust of Cooper by the Beverly Hills sculptor Voris Marker. It didn't look much like Cooper and was rather unattractive.

2. Donald Hyatt, "Gary Cooper," McCall's, March 1963, p. 152.

    In a rare attack, the usually circumspect Cooper also criticized the selfishness and ugliness of the new generation of Method actors:

    > It is hard to dig them because they are like hermit crabs—they have to have a shell to crawl into and they don't want anyone to get to know them. . . . They are offbeat and strange and always thinking about themselves. They are always asking themselves, "Where do I fit in; what's in it for me?"
    > These youngsters are doing it the hard way. They make a

thorough study of being natural and of being unnatural. The girls go around looking like they're made up for a death scene in a hospital room. I don't know why if a girl goes out in public she wants to make herself look ugly instead of a little bit attractive [Joe Hyams, "Cooper Chides New Crop," New York *Herald Tribune*, October 8, 1958].

3. Interview with Donald Hyatt, Woodbury, Connecticut, November 23, 1996; Ralph Waldo Emerson, "Manners," *Essays*, introduction by Irwin Edman (New York, 1951), pp. 367–368; Hyatt, "Gary Cooper," pp. 152–153.
4. Interview with Dr. Rexford Kennamer; Veronica Cooper, "How I Faced Tomorrow," p. 166; Interview with Deane Johnson; Interview with Warren Cowan.
5. Interview with Dr. Rexford Kennamer; Interview with Billy Wilder; Interview with Maria Cooper Janis.
6. Interview with Maria Cooper Janis; Veronica Cooper, "How I Faced Tomorrow," p. 166; Interview with Dr. Rexford Kennamer.
7. Anthony Holden, *Behind the Oscar: The Secret History of the Academy Awards* (New York, 1993), p. 239; Kaminsky, *Coop*, p. 213; Hedda Hopper, interview with Rocky Cooper, May 1961, Herrick; Parsons, "Personal Memories of Gary Cooper," p. 55.
8. Kenneth Lynn, *Hemingway* (New York, 1987), p. 569; Letter from Gary Cooper to Ernest Hemingway, May 1, 1945, Hemingway Archive, John F. Kennedy Library, Boston, Massachusetts; Letter from Lorraine Chanel to Jeffrey Meyers, November 30, 1996.
9. Letter from Gary Cooper to Lorraine Chanel, July 16, 1953; Interview with Barnaby Conrad; Conrad, *Name Dropping*, p. 134; Cooper, "The Hollywood Greats," p. 12. For photos of Cooper playing the bulls, see *Life*, August 3, 1953, p. 97.
10. Letter from Cooper to Hemingway, March 5, 1956, Hemingway Archive; Hemingway, *Selected Letters*, p. 855; Kaminsky, *Coop*, p. 167; Interview with Patrick Hemingway; Peter Viertel, *Dangerous Friends* (New York, 1992), p. 10.
11. Letter from Rocky Cooper to Charles Feldman, October 21, 1960, American Film Institute; Letter from Cooper to Hemingway, May 2, 1960, Hemingway Archive; Message from Hemingway to Cooper, [January 9, 1961], Hemingway Archive.
12. Arnold, *High on the Wild*, p. 332; Interview with Valerie Hemingway, Bozeman, Montana, September 7, 1996; Telegram from Cooper to Hemingway, April 29, 1961, Hemingway Archive; "Novelist Mourned by Cooper's Widow," Los Angeles *Mirror*, July 3, 1961.

13. Cooper, "The Hollywood Greats," p. 10; Norman, *The Hollywood Greats*, p. 112; Hotchner, *Papa Hemingway*, pp. 279; 289–290.

    Hotchner, whom Hemingway called "a sharp customer," is notoriously unreliable. He did visit the dying Cooper (partly to gather material for his future book), but Cooper did not (as Hotchner claims) know he was dying in January 1961 and did not discuss plans for a film with Hemingway after he knew he was doomed. Hotchner claimed to have seen him in May, but Cooper was in no condition to talk to anyone that month. To make his account more dramatic, Hotchner may have taken what Cooper said from other sources or even invented the conventional and rather sentimental scene ("he moved the crucifix . . . so that it touched his cheek").

14. Interview with Maria Cooper Janis; Peter Evans, "Police Stand by for Gary Cooper Funeral," *Daily Express* (London), May 15, 1961; Riva, *Marlene Dietrich*, p. 692.

15. Peter Evans, "In His Art He Was a Perfectionist," *Daily Express* (London), May 17, 1961; Hyatt, "Gary Cooper," p. 153; O'Neil, "Hollywood Mourns a Good Man," p. 26; "Industry Mourns Cooper," Los Angeles *Examiner*, May 14, 1961; Interview with Maria Cooper Janis.

16. O'Neil, "Hollywood Mourns a Good Man," p. 26; Romain Gary, *Adieu, Gary Cooper* (Paris, 1969), p. 23, my translation; Ronald Brownstein, *The Power and the Glitter: Hollywood and the Washington Connection* (New York, 1990), p. 14. The cartoon and poster are reproduced in Zinnemann, *A Life in the Movies*, p. 110.

17. Nunnally Johnson, oral history, p. 25, Columbia University; Rupert Brooke, *Letters from America* (1916; Gloucester, England, 1984), p. 9; John Updike, *In the Beauty of the Lilies* (New York, 1996), p. 319.

    Alice Cooper died in a Palm Desert convalescent home, at the age of ninety-four, in October 1967. Arthur Cooper died at the age of eighty-seven in May 1982. In 1964 Rocky married the plastic surgeon Dr. John Converse, who had treated Cooper. Widowed in 1981, she now lives in New York. In 1966 Maria married the concert pianist Byron Janis. In Vanity Fair (November 1996) she appeared in a stunning Coach ad, looking twenty years younger than her real age.

Cooper's Films

I. Best Films

Morocco (1930), *Desire* (1936), *Mr. Deeds Goes to Town* (1936), *Meet John Doe* (1940), *High Noon* (1952), *Love in the Afternoon* (1957).

II. Important Films

Wings (1927), *The Virginian* (1929), *A Farewell to Arms* (1932), *The Lives of a Bengal Lancer* (1935), *The General Died at Dawn* (1936), *Bluebeard's Eighth Wife* (1938), *Beau Geste* (1939), *Sergeant York* (1941), *Ball of Fire* (1941), *The Pride of the Yankees* (1942), *For Whom the Bell Tolls* (1943), *Ten North Frederick* (1958), *Man of the West* (1958), *The Hanging Tree* (1959), *The Wreck of the Mary Deare* (1959), *The Naked Edge* (1961).

III. Seeable Films

The Winning of Barbara Worth (1926), *It* (1927), *Lilac Time* (1928), *Fighting Caravans* (1931), *City Streets* (1931), *The Devil and the Deep* (1932), *Design for Living* (1933), *Now and Forever* (1934), *The Wedding Night* (1935), *The Cowboy and the Lady* (1938), *The Real Glory* (1939), *The Westerner* (1940), *The Story of Dr. Wassell* (1944), *Along Came Jones* (1945), *Cloak and Dagger* (1946), *The Fountainhead* (1948), *Return to Paradise* (1953), *Blowing Wild* (1953), *Garden of Evil* (1954), *Vera Cruz* (1954), *Friendly Persuasion* (1956), *They Came to Cordura* (1959).

IV. Poor Films

Children of Divorce (1927), *Arizona Bound* (1927), *Nevada* (1927), *The Last Outlaw* (1927), *Beau Sabreur* (1928), *The Legion of the Condemned* (1928), *Doomsday* (1928), *Half a Bride* (1928), *The First Kiss* (1928), *The*

Shopworn Angel (1928), *Wolf Song* (1929), *Betrayal* (1929), *Only the Brave* (1930), *The Texan* (1930), *Seven Days Leave* (1930), *A Man from Wyoming* (1930), *The Spoilers* (1930), *I Take This Woman* (1931), *His Woman* (1931), *If I Had a Million* (1932), *Today We Live* (1932), *One Sunday Afternoon* (1933), *Operator 13* (1933), *Peter Ibbetson* (1935), *The Plainsman* (1936), *Souls at Sea* (1937), *The Adventures of Marco Polo* (1938), *North West Mounted Police* (1940), *Casanova Brown* (1944), *Saratoga Trunk* (1945), *Unconquered* (1947), *Good Sam* (1948), *Task Force* (1949), *Bright Leaf* (1950), *Dallas* (1950), *You're in the Navy Now* (1951), *It's a Big Country* (1951), *Distant Drums* (1951), *Springfield Rifle* (1952), *The Court-Martial of Billy Mitchell* (1955).

Bibliography

1. By Gary Cooper (or published under his name)

"I Walked Up Hollywood's Stairs: Gary Cooper's Own Life Story," North American Newspaper Alliance, August 28, no year.

As told to Dorothy Spensley, "The Big Boy Tells His Story," *Photoplay*, 35 (April 1929), 64–65, 133–135.

——"The Big Boy Tells His Story," *Photoplay*, 35 (May 1929), 70–71, 84, 110.

"Their First Job," *New Movie Magazine*, 1930.

"A College I Love," *College Humor*, May 1930, pp. 56, 109.

"When I Was a Boy," *St. Nicholas Magazine*, 63 (November 1935), 21.

"The First 10 Years," *Rochester Democrat and Chronicle*, July 19, 1936.

"I Remember Pinewood and the Days of Celluloid City," *News of the World* (London), October 24, 1937, p. 5.

"I Remember the Days of the Last Coal," *News of the World*, October 31, 1937, p. 5.

"Work and Play on a Desert Location," *News of the World*, November 7, 1937, p. 5.

"Murder in the Midst of Make-Believe," *News of the World*, November 14, 1937, p. 5.

"What I Think of Everybody's Darling, Shirley Temple," *News of the World*, November 21, 1937, p. 5.

"Leading Ladies I've Known," *Motion Picture*, c. 1948–49, pp. 29, 60.

"The Role I Liked Best," *Saturday Evening Post*, May 6, 1950, p. 216.

As told to George Scullin, "Well, It Was This Way," *Saturday Evening Post*, February 18 and 25, March 3, 10, 17, 24 and 31, April 7, 1956. Serialized in *Reader's Digest*, July and August 1956, pp. 69–78, 144–154. This series of eight long articles is Cooper's most complete, though selective and unreliable, account of his life.

"Shooting Clichés on the Western Range," Hollywood Reporter, November 24, 1958.

As told to Leonard Slater, "I Took a Good Look at Myself, and This Is What I Saw," *McCall's*, January 1961, pp. 62, 138–142.

"Foreword" to Josef von Sternberg. *Fun in a Chinese Laundry*. 1965; San Francisco: Mercury House, 1988, pp. [i–ii]. Concocted after Cooper's death from fan magazines, it offers a misleadingly favorable view of von Sternberg.

II. On Cooper

Arce, Hector. *Gary Cooper: An Intimate Biography*. 1979; New York: Bantam, 1980.

Brooks, Phyllis, as told to Mary Jane Manners, "My South Sea Island Flight with Gary Cooper," *Silver Screen*, May 1944, pp. 22–23, 60–63.

Carpozi, George, Jr. *The Gary Cooper Story*. New Rochelle, N.Y.: Arlington House, 1970.

Cooper, Alice, as told to Dorothy Spensley, "Gary's Mother Speaks at Last," *Modern Screen*, [1931], pp. 52–53, 93, 95.

Cooper, Veronica, as told to George Christy, "How I Faced Tomorrow," *Good Housekeeping*, September 1963, pp. 81–83, 160–168.

Corey, Jeff. "Gary Cooper: Natural Talent." *Close-Ups: The Movie Star Book*. Ed. Danny Peary. 1978; New York: Simon and Schuster, 1988, pp. 498–501.

Foreman, Carl, "Dialogue on Film," *American Film*, 4 (April 1979), 35–46.

Gehman, Richard, "In an Exclusive Interview, Mrs. Gary Cooper Tells the Moving Story of Her Husband's Last Days," *American Weekly*, August 13, 1961, pp. 4–5, 7.

Hemingway, Ernest. *Selected Letters, 1917–1961*. Ed. Carlos Baker. New York: Scribners, 1981, pp. 518–519, 526, 529, 543, 855–857, 908.

Heston, Charlton. *In the Arena*. New York: Simon and Schuster, 1995, pp. 211–215.

Hyatt, Donald, "Gary Cooper," *McCall's*, March 1963, pp. 152–153.

Janis, Maria Cooper, "My Poppa, Gary Cooper," *Parade*, November 19, 1989, pp. 8–9, 11.

Johnson, Nunnally, "Along Came Cooper," *Photoplay*, 27 (August 1945), 38–39, 96.

Kaminsky, Stuart. *Coop: The Life and Legend of Gary Cooper*. New York: St. Martin's, 1980.

Kobal, John, ed. *Legends: Gary Cooper*. Photographs from the Kobal Collection. Boston: Little Brown, 1985.

Martin, Pete. "Tall in the Saddle." *Pete Martin Calls On*. New York: Simon and Schuster, 1962, pp. 359–370.

McCrea, Joel, "My Friend Coop!" *Photoplay*, October 1939, pp. 20–21, 85–86.

Morgan, Thomas. "Gary Cooper." *Self-Creations: 13 Impersonalities*. New York: Holt, Rinehart and Winston, 1965, pp. 22–37.

Neal, Patricia. *As I Am*. New York: Simon and Schuster, 1988, pp. 94–142.

Norman, Barry. "Gary Cooper." *The Hollywood Greats*. New York: Franklin Watts, 1980, pp. 91–113.

Parsons, Louella, "Personal Memories of Gary Cooper," *Modern Screen*, August 1961, pp. 54–56.

St. Johns, Adela Rogers. "Gary Cooper's Love Story in Three Acts." *Love, Laughter and Tears: My Hollywood Story*. 1978; New York: Signet, 1979, pp. 240–257.

Swindell, Larry. *The Last Hero: A Biography of Gary Cooper*. Garden City, N.Y.: Doubleday, 1980.

Wayne, Jane Ellen. *Cooper's Women*. 1988; London: Hale, 1989.

III. Screenplays

Faulkner, William. *"Today We Live."* Faulkner's MGM Screenplays. Ed. Bruce Kawin. Knoxville: University of Tennessee Press, 1982, pp. 100–255.

Foreman, Carl. *"High Noon."* *Three Major Screenplays*. Ed. Malvin Wald and Michael Lerner. New York: Globe, 1972, pp. 145–266.

[Furthman, Jules]. *"Morocco" and "Shanghai Express."* New York: Simon and Schuster, 1972.

Nichols, Dudley. *For Whom the Bell Tolls*. Hollywood: Script City, 1942.

Rand, Ayn. *The Fountainhead*. Unpublished screenplay, 1948.

[Riskin, Robert]. *Meet John Doe*. Ed. Charles Wolfe. New Brunswick, N.J.: Rutgers University Press, 1989.

——*Mr. Deeds Goes to Town*. Unpublished screenplay, 1935.

Stefano, Joseph. *The Naked Edge*. Unpublished screenplay, 1960, courtesy of Joseph Stefano.

IV. On the Films

Behlmer, Rudy. *"High Noon."* *Behind the Scenes*, 1982; Hollywood: Samuel French, 1990, pp. 269–288.

Dickens, Homer. *The Films of Gary Cooper*. Secaucus, N.J.: Citadel, 1970.

Jordan, René. *Gary Cooper*. New York: Pyramid, 1974.

Koch, Howard. "*Sergeant York.*" *As Time Goes By*. New York: Harcourt, Brace, Jovanovich, 1979, pp. 71–75.

Lee, David. "Appalachia on Film: The Making of *Sergeant York.*" *The South and Film*. Ed. Warren French. Jackson: University Press of Mississippi, 1981, pp. 207–221.

Parish, James Robert, and Donald Stanke. *All Americans*. New Rochelle, N.Y.: Arlington House, 1977, pp. 10–77.

Schickel, Richard. "Gary Cooper: An American Abroad." *Schickel on Film*. New York: Morrow, 1989, pp. 177–197.

Slotkin, Richard. *Gunfighter Nation: The Myth of the Frontier in Twentieth Century America*. New York: Atheneum, 1992, pp. 391–396, 433–440.

Truffaut, François. *Early Film Criticism*. Ed. Wheeler Dixon. Trans. Ruth Hoffman. Bloomington, Ind.: Indiana University Press, 1994, pp. 148–151.

——*The Films in My Life*. Trans. Leonard Mayhew. New York: Simon and Schuster, 1978, pp. 95–98.

Walker, John A. "*The Fountainhead.*" *Art and Artists on Screen*. Manchester, England: Manchester University Press, 1993, pp. 95–105.

Weales, Gerald. "*Mr. Deeds Goes to Town.*" *Canned Goods and Caviar: American Film Comedies of the 1930s*. Chicago: University of Chicago Press. 1985, pp. 160–187.

West, Jessamyn. *To See the Dream*. New York: Harcourt, Brace, 1957.

V. Political Background

Carr, Robert. "The Hollywood Hearings." *The House Committee on Un-American Activities, 1945–1950*. Ithaca, N.Y.: Cornell University Press, 1952, pp. 55–78.

Caute, David, "Hollywood." *The Great Fear: The Anti-Communist Purge Under Truman and Eisenhower*. New York: Simon and Schuster, 1978, pp. 487–520.

Ceplair, Larry, and Steven England. "The Congressional Hearings of October 1947." *The Inquisition in Hollywood: Politics in the Film Community, 1920–1960*. Garden City, N.Y.: Doubleday, 1980, pp. 254–298.

McWilliams, Carey, "Hollywood Plays with Fascism," *Nation*, 140 (May 29, 1935), 623–624.

Navasky, Victor. *Naming Names*. 1980; New York: Penguin, 1981, pp. 156–158.

Slide, Anthony, "Hollywood's Fascist Follies," *Film Comment*, 27 (July–August 1991), 62–67.

United States Congress, House of Representatives, Committee on Un-American Activities, 80th Congress, 1st session, October [23] 1947. Hearings Regarding the Communist Infiltration of the Motion Picture Industry. Washington, D.C.: U.S. Government Printing Office, 1947, pp. 219–224.

VI. Television Documentaries

The Tall American: Gary Cooper. NBC-Project 20. March 26, 1963. Produced and directed by Donald Hyatt. Written by Richard Hauser. Narrated by Walter Brennan. 50 minutes.

Gary Cooper: American Life, American Legend. TNT. October 27, 1989. Written, produced and directed by Richard Schickel. Narrated by Clint Eastwood. 50 minutes.

The Life and Times of Gary Cooper. Nashville Network, TNN. October 31, 1995. 40 minutes.

Index

Compiled by Valerie Meyers